Press comments on
THE ROUGH GUIDE TO THE INTERNET

"Brilliant ... MUST HAVE ... provides refreshingly blunt
advice on the Net ... brilliant hints and tips ... the
unmatched leader in its field"
Sunday Times, London

"Well researched, well sourced and well written ...
highly recommended"
What PC

"Über-hip. Smarter than *Dummies*. Now even idiots can
become Internet savants"
Newsweek

"Anyone who isn't ordering and selling this by the lorry-
load shouldn't be running a bookshop"
The Bookseller

"A seriously good book. The best, in fact"
Sun Herald, Sydney

"If knowledge is power, this is a pocket-sized
battering ram"
Kansas Morning Star

The Rough Guide to

The Internet

There are more than two hundred Rough Guide
travel, phrasebook and music titles, covering
destinations from Amsterdam to Zimbabwe,
languages from Czech to Vietnamese, and musics
from World to Opera and Jazz

To find out more about Rough Guides,
and to check out our coverage of more than
10,000 destinations, get connected to the Internet with
this guide and find us on the Web at:

www.roughguides.com

Acknowledgements

Angus would like to thank his agent Lesley Shaw and everyone
at the Rough Guides and Penguin, especially Mark Ellingham,
Jonathan Buckley, Richard Trillo and Niki Smith. Duncan and
Peter thank Andy for editing, Katie for typesetting and
Jonathan for keeping the dream alive.

The Rough Guide to

The Internet

by Angus J. Kennedy

with contributions from
Peter Buckley and Duncan Clark

ROUGH
GUIDES

Rough Guide Credits

Text editor: Andrew Dickson
Series editor: Mark Ellingham
Production: Julia Bovis, Michelle Draycott, Katie Pringle
Design: Helen Prior
Proofreading: Nikky Twyman

Publishing Information

This eighth edition published October 2002 by
Rough Guides Ltd, 80 Strand, London WC2R 0RL,
375 Hudson Street, New York 10014
Email: *mail@roughguides.co.uk*

Distributed by the Penguin Group

Penguin Books Ltd, 80 Strand, London WC2R 0RL
Penguin Putnam USA Inc., 375 Hudson Street, New York
10014, Penguin Books Canada Ltd, 10 Alcorn Avenue, Toronto,
Ontario MV4 1E4, Penguin Books Australia Ltd,
PO Box 257, Ringwood, Victoria 3134,
Penguin Books (NZ) Ltd, 182–190 Wairau Road, Auckland 10

Printed in the United Kingdom by Omnia Books Ltd

Image on p.1 courtesy of size-isnt everything.co.uk

A catalogue record for this book is available
from the British Library
ISBN 1-85828-908-4

Contents

contents

Part two: The guide

Part three: Contexts

Read me

Hooking up to the Internet isn't such a big deal these days. So why do you need a book to get online? Or more to the point, why do you need one if you're already there?

You don't, of course. In fact, most people just install some Internet software, start clicking and worry about the consequences later. That's why they **catch viruses** (p.158), **get scammed** (p.194), **unwittingly install "spyware"** (p.278) and **wonder why their computers keep crashing** (p.112 and p.355). It's why so few know how to **get the best from a search engine** (p.172), **take part in online discussions** (p.214), **collect their email on the road** (p.150), **set up a second account** (p.127), **maintain their privacy** (p.107 and p.154) or **avoid junk email** (p.147). And why most people's time is spent sifting through rubbish websites instead of going **straight to the best** (p.331). You can do it the hard way too – if you don't mind wasting half your life.

Or you can do it the smart way and leave the hard work to us. We've spent years test-driving software, sorting through sites, torturing search engines and figuring out what works best. You'll find the latest results distilled into this small book, plus tips on how to do everything from scoring a free email address (p.120) to building an online photo gallery (p.314).

If you only read one chapter, make it "Find it" (p.167). Know it back-to-front and you'll have the Net around your little finger. You'll be surprised at how quickly you become an expert.

The fact that we find ourselves flipping through this book from time to time suggests that it's as much a desktop reference for old-timers as a beginner's guide. So we hope you'll keep a dog-eared copy by your computer for many years to come. That said, things change, so keep your eyes peeled for each new edition.

Best wishes and bon voyage!

> **Got a favourite site or activity on the Net?**
> **Then let us know by email at:**
>
> angus@easynet.co.uk

51 things to do with this book

There's more stuff on the Internet than you could explore in a lifetime. So where do you start? Here, in no particular order, are 51 ways to idle away your hours online.

1. Look yourself up on the Web

2. Re-ignite an old flame

3. Deactivate an alien implant

4. Get fresh with the US President

5. Go undercover

51 things to do

Part one

Basics

Basics

1

FAQs

Frequently asked questions

Before we get into the nitty-gritty of what you can do on the Internet – and what it can do for you – let's answer a few of the most Frequently Asked Questions, or **FAQs** as they're called online. You'll find more detail on these subjects throughout the book.

The big picture

OK, what's this Internet thing good for?

The Internet, or the **Net** as it's more often called, is a real bag of tricks. You can send documents worldwide in a flash, find an answer to any question, shop the globe, hear new music, dabble in the stock market, visit art galleries, read books, play games, chat, catch up on your latest hometown news, make new friends with similar interests, grab free software, manage your bank account or just fritter away your spare time surfing the Web.

That's not to say the Internet is merely something to play on when you get home from work. Far from it. It's firmly entrenched in the workplace. Millions of companies already use it to promote their products, take orders and support their customers. More communication is done by email than the phone, fax and printed letter combined.

Sounds like fun, but what is it exactly?

Strictly speaking, the Internet is an **international network of computers** linked up to exchange information. The word "Internet" is a contraction of "**inter**national" and "**net**work".

The core of this international network consists of computers permanently joined through high-speed connections. To get on the Net, you simply connect your computer to any of these networked computers via an **Internet Service Provider (ISP)**. Once you're **online** (connected to the Net) your computer can talk to any other computer on the Internet, whether it's next door or in Antarctica.

That's plain enough, but if you want a more picky definition you have to consider what it's used for as well. Two things dominate most people's experience of the Net: the transfer of **electronic mail (email)**, and browsing pages on the **World Wide Web**. So when people say they found something on the "Internet", they didn't find it by randomly zipping around the wires hooking up the computers – they either retrieved it from where it was stored on a computer connected to this international network, or someone sent it to them by electronic mail.

Most importantly, the Net is not about computers or the fancy phone lines that string them together. **It's about people, communication and sharing knowledge**. And that's why you want it.

The Internet and the Web are the same thing, right?

No, but don't be embarrassed. Not too many journalists seem to know the difference either. The **World Wide Web** (or Web) is the popular face of the Internet. It provides a simple way to navigate the vast troves of information stored online. In practice, it works a bit like flicking through a huge magazine by clicking on links with your mouse. But the Internet is much more than just the Web. See p.83.

What's email?

 Electronic mail, or **email**, is a way of sending messages from one computer to another. Messages are composed in special email programs or websites, and can be used to send images and files too. An electronic letter can cross the world in under a second. See p.117.

Is my email private?

Unless you go to the somewhat tedious effort of **encrypting your messages** (p.155), they could potentially be read at a multitude of points along the way. For example, whoever administers your mailserver could quite easily open your mail without you ever knowing. So in effect your messages are like postcards, at the mercy of whoever is delivering them. Whether or not it's deemed acceptable or even illegal makes little difference. If someone has a reason to look, they probably will, especially at your workplace. For more on protecting your privacy, and covering your tracks, see pp.107 and 154.

What are newsgroups, mailing lists and chat?

Usenet – the Net's prime discussion area – comprises around

100,000 **newsgroups**. Each one is a forum dedicated to a specific topic, a bit like an online notice board. So if you have a question, this is the place to raise it. Usenet messages are stored online for a matter of days or weeks.

Mailing lists perform a similar function, but the messages aren't stored online. The discussions are carried out by email. Each list has a central email address. Everything sent to that address goes to everyone on the list.

Chat, on the other hand, is instant – a conversation that you conduct with online pals using your keyboard. It's typically more of a social medium.

For more on discussions, see p.214.

And what about messaging?

Messaging is another way to communicate instantly. You type messages into a special program and send them to friends who are also online using the same program. See p.254.

What's the difference between the Internet, AOL and CompuServe?

CompuServe and AOL are classed as **Online Services**. They plug in to the Internet, and thus form part of it, but each also has exclusive services and content available only to their members and not to the general Internet public. See p.39.

How many people are online and who are they?

Surveys estimate that almost one in ten people worldwide regularly access the Net. That's about 400 million people, with more than a third of them living in the USA. For in-depth demographics, market research, and statistics, see the following websites:

CyberAtlas http://www.cyberatlas.internet.com
InternetStats http://www.internetstats.com
NUA Internet Surveys http://www.nua.org/surveys/
Research Buzz http://www.researchbuzz.com
Web Characterization Project http://wcp.oclc.org

Which is better: the Net or an encyclopedia?

They don't really compare. You can look something up in an encyclopedia and get a concise answer instantly. Encyclopedias are generally well-researched and reliable, and the answer is probably correct. They're also expensive, bulky, parochial, conservative, date quickly and might not provide enough (or any) information.

The Net, on the other hand, isn't edited by a single publisher. So you can find a diverse range of facts and opinions on even the most obscure subjects. That means you're more likely to get a rounded view, but the process might take longer. And the Net has the best of both worlds – most of the major encyclopedias have their very latest editions online. What's more, they're mostly free! See p.442.

Can I shop online?

Of course – that's why we've dedicated a whole chapter to it (see p.193).

Is there a lot of really weird stuff?

Yes, lots. Just like in real life, except it's easier to find. See p.484.

So is it basically a geek hangout?

It's about as geeky as you want it to be – which can vary between twin hip-slung logic probes with matching pocket protector, to not in the slightest. They say if you're bored with the Net, you're bored with life itself.

But isn't it yet another male-dominated bastion?

No, those days are well behind us. In the USA, **women actually outnumber men online**. And the rest of the world isn't far behind.

Will I make friends on the Internet?

It's easy to meet people with common interests by joining in **Usenet (newsgroup) or mailing list discussions**. And being able to discuss sensitive issues with strangers while retaining a comfortable degree of anonymity often makes for startlingly intimate communication.

However, translating online friendships – or even romance (see p.447) – into the real world is another matter.

So who's in charge?

No one actually "runs" the entire Internet but there are several major players who exert a great deal of influence. To illustrate how it works in practice, let's separate it into levels.

There are various bodies involved in the **theoretical and administrative levels**: these include **ICANN**, which coordinates domain names; the **Internet Society** which, amongst other things, acts as a clearing house for technical standards; and the World Wide Web Consortium (**W3C**), which mulls over the Web's future. You're unlikely to encounter any of these groups directly.

At the **practical level**, such aspects as software, network routing and wiring are controlled by corporations such as Microsoft, Cisco, AOL and the world's cable providers. Each element is an independent product. So if you have a problem with a program, for example, you'd have to complain to the shop that sold it to you or the software developers. Or if you had connection problems, you'd need to call your ISP. **There is no official body responsible for tying it all together**.

The **legal level** is governed by local authorities. What's OK in one territory may be an offence in another. That means if you break a local law, you're liable to prosecution – irrespective of whether you're accessing something that's legal, or overlooked, at the source. So just because you can download a pirated copy of Photoshop from a Russian Web server doesn't make you immune to copyright laws at home. And, conversely, while you might have the freedom to express your views about a foreign government, nationals of that state may not be so free to read it.

But isn't it run by the Pentagon?

When the Internet was first conceived thirty-odd years ago, as a network for the American Defense Department, its purpose was to act as a nuclear-attack-resistant method of exchanging scientific information and intelligence. But that was then. In the 1970s and 1980s several other networks, such as the **National Science Foundation Network** (NSFNET), jumped on board, linking the Internet to research agencies and universities. It was probably no coincidence that as the Cold War petered out, the Internet became more publicly accessible. These days, **Intelligence agencies** have the same access to the Internet as everyone else. The extent to which they use it to monitor insurgence and crime is simply a matter for speculation.

Can I make money out of it?

Possibly, but perhaps it's better to ask: "Can I continue to make money without the Internet?" A few years back there was a gold rush in the computer hardware, software, training and publishing industries. Some who got in early made a killing getting businesses on the Web – the Net's "commercial zone". But around 2000 the bubble burst and a lot of people lost a lot of money: hundreds of so-called "**dotcom**" companies vanished almost as quickly as they had emerged. Today it's settled down somewhat, and investors are no longer prepared to back any old scheme just because it has the word "Internet" attached. Programming talent, which used to be in incredibly short sup-

ply, has stabilized too – web-page designers are now commonplace, and can no longer charge extortionate rates unless they're tied in with a major agency.

If you're wondering whether to throw a website into your existing **marketing mix** to help boost sales, the answer's probably yes. But rather than use it to try to attract customers, it's better to think of the Net as a place to post in-depth product literature, provide customer support and canvass feedback. Not too many firms make big money from **direct sales** – though that's improving, particularly for hard-to-get products or deep-catalogue items such as CDs, books and computer parts.

Another way to profit is to charge others to **advertise on your webpage**. You'll either need to run a very popular site or attract a certain type of customer, and you're usually paid according to the number of times visitors pursue links from your site to your sponsor's. Alternatively, if your site generates heavy traffic and looks promising, someone may want to buy you outright.

Can I make money by bulk emailing?

Advertising on the World Wide Web is perfectly acceptable but emailing protocols are more delicate. **Never, ever, ever, send bulk email** other than to people you know or who've requested information. And never post an advertisement in Usenet or to a mailing list. **Junk email is called "spam", and those who send it (spammers) are universally detested.** Try it and you'll be flooded with hate mail, and possibly kicked offline by your ISP.

On the other hand, if you use it properly, email is by far the most efficient direct-response device you'll find. For instance, you could set up an **autoresponder** to send out product details upon receipt of a blank message. No dictating over the phone, no data entry from a coupon. It's instant and informal. Plus you'll have their email address on record to follow up later. So next time you place an advertisement or *Yellow Pages* listing, add your email address too, and compare response rates.

What is "new media"?

Advertising suits and recruitment agencies use the term **new media** mainly to differentiate between the old media world of print, radio and television, and the new media world of audio, video, print and software publishing on the Internet and other digital formats such as CD-ROM.

Getting online

How hard can it be?

The short answer is "not very". The technology is becoming more intuitive by the day. It really can be as simple as popping to a store, buying a computer, plugging it in to a phone socket and clicking a couple of icons. Conversely, it can be as painful as having teeth extracted, so read on and arm yourself.

What do I need to get started?

Although you can access the Net through all kinds of gadgets from mobile phones to televisions, to get the full Internet experience you'll need a **personal computer** (either a PC or a Mac), equipped with the appropriate **network device** for the type of access you're seeking. Unless you're willing to pay extra for high-speed (**broadband**) access, you'll most likely be connecting via a **modem** hooked into your normal **telephone line**. Almost all new computers come with a modem – nearly everyone wants to get online – so the only other thing you'll need to get rolling is an **Internet access account**, and possibly some **extra software**. For more details see p.27.

What's an Internet access account?

You can access the Internet through any **Internet Service Provider (ISP)**, a company that acts as a gateway between your computer and the rest of the Net. They normally offer a range of accounts, which may include standard **modem dial-up**, **ISDN**, **ADSL** and **cable.** There might also be a selection of pricing plans and added extras. Regardless of the type of Internet access you choose, you should able to do the same things, though perhaps at different speeds. For help choosing an ISP, see p.42.

What about free Internet access – is it really free?

Of course not. Internet access is a costly business to run, so revenue has to come from somewhere. In the UK, where free ISPs have flourished to the point of becoming the norm, they survive by pocketing a slice of your phone bill, both while you're online and through premium-rate support lines. This scam only exists due to the UK's extortionate timed local call charges.

In other parts of the world, where local calls are unmetered or free, such deals must be subsidized by bombarding customers with advertising, tracking their movements or by locking them within their sponsor's sites. As yet, these aren't wildly successful or attractive.

Where do I get an email address?

You should get at least one **email address** thrown in by your ISP with your access account. Many providers supply five or more addresses – enough for the whole family. The only problem with these addresses is that they tie you to that provider. If you want to switch providers, you'll either have to negotiate a mail-only account or obtain an address you can take on the road with you (see p.120). It's a hassle either way, so choose your provider carefully.

If you already have an email address, say at work or college, but want something **more personal or funky**, you can ask any ISP for a POP3 mail-only account, try a mail specialist such as Net Identity (http://www.netidentity.com) or sign up with a webmail or redirection service. That way you can choose an address and use it over any connection. To score a free email address, see p.123.

Is Hotmail the same as email?

No, Hotmail (see p.121) is one of the more popular webmail services. But there are loads of different services out there (see p.122).

How can I find someone's email address?

The best way is to ask them. See p.140.

Who pays for the international calls?

The Internet is barely affected by political boundaries and distance. For example, suppose you're in Boston and you want to buzz someone in Bangkok. Provided you both have Net access, it's as quick, easy and cheap as sending a message across the street. You compose your message, connect to your local ISP, upload your mail and then, if you're finished, disconnect.

Your **mail server** examines the message's address to determine where it has to go, and then passes it on to its appropriate neighbour, which will do the same. This usually entails routing it toward the **backbone** – the chain of high-speed links that carries the bulk of the Net's long-haul traffic. Each subsequent link will ensure that the message heads towards Bangkok rather than Bogotá or Brisbane. The whole process should take no more than a few seconds.

Apart from your Internet access subscription, **you pay only for the local phone call**. Your data will scuttle through many different networks, each with its own methods of recouping the communication costs – but adding to your phone bill isn't one of them.

Then how does the pricing model work?

Once you're on the Net, most of what's there is free. But unless you have free access through work or study, you'll probably need to pay for the privilege of being connected. That means paying an **ISP** to allow you to hook into its network. Depending on where you live, that could be a set price per month or year, an hourly rate or a tariff based on how much you download. Then on top of that you might have some sort of **telephone, ISDN or cable charge**. It's possible – indeed probable – that none of this money will ever go to the people who supply the content you'll be viewing. It simply goes toward maintaining the network. This imbalance is unlikely to continue: in the future many people expect certain publications (or sites) to charge a subscription. As yet that's still rare, other than for technical and financial publications – so enjoy it while it lasts.

What's bandwidth and broadband?

Bandwidth describes Internet connection capacity. It measures the speed at which you can download material from the Net, described in bits per second (bps). Modems are only capable of achieving a relatively **low bandwidth** connection. **Cable**, **satellite** and **ADSL** fall into the so-called **broadband** category, meaning that they're much **faster than modems**. Strictly speaking, though, the bits and bytes don't move any faster (they're limited by the speed of light). A faster connection simply means you can move more of those bits and bytes across the wires at a time.

Bits? Bits of what?

A **bit** is the smallest unit of data that computers recognize, representing either a 0 or a 1. And the Internet is all about lugging these bits from A to B. You might hear people talking about "56K" modems, for example. What they're actually referring to is 56Kbps, a device capable of shifting 56,000 bits of data each second.

What if?

What if I want to cancel an email I've sent?

You can't. So you'd better think before you click "send".

What if my email doesn't arrive?

In general Internet **email** is considerably more reliable than the postal service. If a message doesn't get through immediately, it should bounce back to you telling you what went wrong. The recipient's mail server might be overloaded or down for maintenance, for example, in which case your mail might be delayed for minutes, hours, or even a weekend. Although it's highly unlikely, it's not impossible for an email to go astray – so if someone says they didn't receive your mail, you'll have to give them the benefit of the doubt. If you don't get a reply within a few days, you could send your message again. At worst, it will act as a reminder. If you find your mail regularly takes more than a few minutes to arrive, consider switching providers.

What if I get loads of junk email?

Unfortunately, once the serious junk starts to arrive you can't do much about it – someone has got your address and it'll be difficult to persuade them not to use it. So you might have to change your address and keep it a bit more private this time. See p.147.

What if I'm harassed online?

It's not easy to harass someone seriously via the Net and get away with it. After all, it generates evidence in writing and there have already been convictions for relatively mild threats posted to Usenet newsgroups. Apart from the nature of the harassment, whether you have a case for action will depend on where you're both based. Across US state lines, it becomes an FBI matter, while internationally you might have no recourse other than to appeal to their ISP.

If you're being harassed by email, in a newsgroup, mailing list or chat channel, or on a webpage, you needn't put up with it. Though to start with maybe you should – if you simply ignore them, they'll probably go away. And if you're being harassed unfairly in a public forum, others will usually come to your aid. But if it persists, or the harassment becomes serious, you may have to react.

Your first action should be to contact them personally and politely ask them to desist. If that doesn't work, you'll have to decide whether reporting them to their ISP, and getting them booted offline will start an ongoing vendetta. Whether you have their email address or not, you can find out their ISP by tracing their IP address. This is where a TraceRoute/WHOIS tool such as **NeoTrace** (http://www.neoworks.com) comes in handy. Even if they've forged their email address, you should be able to figure out where it's come from by picking through the headers for the originating IP address. Once you have the domain responsible, try an email to: **abuse@thatdomain**. If this sounds too technical, call your ISP support for help, or turn the matter entirely over to them. For more, see: **http://www.cyberangels.org** and **http://www.getnetwise.org**

What if my children discover pornography or drugs?

If you're at all prudish, you'll get a nasty shock when you hit the Web. You only need type **the merest hint of innuendo** into a search engine to come face to face with a porno advert. In fact, what once wasn't much more than schoolboys trading *Big & Busty* scans has become the Net's prime cash cow. Most perfectly normal kids will search on a swear word the first chance they get – after all, children are pretty childish. So if they're the slightest bit curious about sex, it won't be long before they encounter a porno merchant. That's the truth, if you can handle it.

To be blunt, the Net isn't meant for kids; furthermore, it's not a babysitter. If your children are at a sensitive age and you leave them online unsupervised, you are a bad parent. While there are plenty of online activities that are perfectly suitable for all ages, risky material is never more than a few clicks away.

What can you do about it? Well, that depends whether you'd rather shield or prepare them. There are **censoring programs** that attempt to filter out questionable material, either by letting only known sites through, banning certain sites or withholding pages containing shady words. Internet Explorer and Netscape, for example, can restrict access according to a rating system (see p.106). But bear in mind that a smart kid – and no doubt that's what you're trying to raise – will find a way to veto these filters. Whatever the case, if you're worried about your kids, the Net and sex, then talk to them about it.

As for **drugs**, there's no way to get them from the Net. In fact, they're likely to find out the dangers of abusing them – so when they come across them in real life they'll be informed. And that can't be such a bad thing.

If you'd like to spy on their online activities, simply click on their browser's "History" button (see p.94). Should they be smart enough to work out how to cover their tracks, they're probably smart enough to know how to handle what they find.

What about bomb plans?

While the thought of your teenage son locked in his bedroom stacking his hard drive with porn might make you feel a bit uneasy, at least you know it won't kill him. Unfortunately, the same can't be said of the advice contained in the **Anarchist's Cookbook** and its ilk. Again, like porn, it's mostly a boy thing, and you'll have to assume he'll find it. Not that you can get mad at him for being interested: things that go bang have been the focus of teenage fascination long before the Internet arrived.

As fun as these websites might make it all sound, it's vital for him to know he can't trust their recipes. These guides are ill-researched, entirely irresponsible and downright dangerous. And, of course, about as against the law as it gets. The sooner you discuss the subject, the better.

Will being on the Internet put me at risk?

Unless you go out of your way to invite trouble, the Internet should impose no added risk on your **personal safety**. However, you should still take a few precautions.

Don't put your home address or phone number in: your email or Usenet signature; your mail program's address book; an online email address register; or your chat profile. And, it goes without saying, bring a friend along if you decide to meet up with someone from a chat room.

On the other hand, **going online suddenly exposes your computer to all sorts of new risks**, particularly if you're using the Windows operating system. To protect your computer against viruses and hackers, turn to p.157.

Couldn't someone steal my credit card number?

Believe it or not, your credit details are actually safer online than when you pass your card over in a shop. Even so, you could still be ripped off. Before entering into any online transaction, read the advice on p.178.

Should I forward virus warnings?

Except for the odd petition, any email that insists you **forward it on to everyone you know** is almost certainly a **hoax**, or at best a **chain letter**. While the hysterical virus warnings might seem vaguely credible, there is absolutely no excuse to fall for any email that suggests you might be **rewarded in some way**

for forwarding it. If you get such a message, don't forward it to everyone you know. Instead, flaunt your superiority by directing the peabrain who *did* forward it to:

http://urbanlegends.about.com
http://www.breakthechain.org
http://www.chainletters.org/gallery.shtml
http://www.cs.rutgers.edu/~watrous/chain-letters.html
http://www.vmyths.com

Getting technical

What's the difference between a homepage and a website?

On the World Wide Web, **homepage** has two meanings. One refers to the page that appears when you start your browser and acts as your home base for exploring the Web. Whenever you get lost or want to return to somewhere familiar, just click on your "Home" button and back you go.

The other usage describes the front door to a set of documents that represents someone or something on the Web. This set of interconnected documents is called a **website**. For instance, Rough Guides' "**official**" homepage – which is found at http://www.roughguides.com – acts as the publishing company's site index. You can access every page in the Rough Guides site by following links from the homepage. Play your cards right and you'll end up at this book's homepage.

If a site hasn't been endorsed by whom it represents, it's called an "**unofficial**" homepage. This is typical of the celebrity worship sites erected by doting fans. Some film and pop stars have so many they're linked into "webrings" (http://www.webring.org).

What are hosts, servers and clients?

In Net-speak, any computer that's open to external online access is known as a **server** or **host**. The software you use to perform online operations such as transfer files, read mail, surf the Web or post articles to Usenet is called a **client**. A **Web server** is a machine where webpages are stored and made available for outside access.

I have a fast connection – so why are some sites still slow?

The speed at which you connect to your ISP can make a huge difference to the speed at which you can cruise the Web, listen to audio and download files, but it's not the final word. Once you start accessing material stored **outside your ISP's server** – often everything except your mail – you're at the mercy of the bandwidth of all the links between you and the external server. It's not unlike driving across town. At peak hours, when there are lots of other cars on the road, it's going to take longer. So if a site is painfully slow, try again later and hopefully the traffic will have subsided.

How do I read an email address?

Internet email addresses might look odd at first glance but they're really quite logical. They all take the form **someone@somewhere**. As soon as you read that aloud, it should begin to make sense. For example, take the email address **angus@roughguides.com** – the **@** sign says it's an email address and means "at", so the address reads "Angus at Rough Guides dot com". From that alone you could deduce that the sender's name is "Angus" and he's somehow associated with "Rough Guides", which is a company of some kind. It's not always that obvious, but the format never changes.

The **somewhere** part is the **domain name** of the Internet **host** that handles **someone**'s mail – often their Internet Service Provider or workplace. Anyone who uses **someone**'s provider or works with them could also share the same **domain name** in their email address, but then they wouldn't be called **someone**, of course. That's because the **someone** part identifies who, or what, they are at that host address – usually a name or nickname they choose themselves, or (with companies), a function like "help" or "info".

What's a domain name?

A **domain name** identifies and locates a host computer or service on the Internet. It often relates to the name of a business, organization or service and must be registered in much the same way as a company name. It breaks down further into the subdomain, domain type and country code. With **sophie @thehub.com.au**, the subdomain is **thehub** (an Internet Service Provider), its domain type **com** suggests it's a company or commercial site, and the country code **au** indicates it's in Australia.

Every country has its own distinct code, even if it's not always used. These include:

au	Australia
ca	Canada
cc	Cocos Islands
de	Germany
es	Spain
fr	France
jp	Japan
nl	Netherlands
no	Norway
uk	United Kingdom

If an address doesn't specify a country code, it's more than likely, but not necessarily, in the USA. At present, domain types are usually one of the following:

ac	Academic (UK)
com	Company or commercial organization
co	Company or commercial organization (UK, NZ)
edu	Educational institution
gov	Government
mil	Military
net	Internet gateway or administrative host*
org	Non-profit organization

However, **ICANN** – the Internet Corporation for Assigned Names and Numbers – are in the process of introducing seven new offical top-level domains including **.info** and **.biz** (see **www.icann.org**). For more on the way domains work, see: **http://www.internic.net/faq.html**

---

* Because of the domain name shortage, it's now become acceptable for commercial sites to use **.net** as well.

What's an IP address?

Every computer on the Net has its unique numerical **IP (Internet Protocol) address**, which represents its official location on the Internet. A typical address comprises four numbers separated by dots, such as **149.174.211.5**, and your computer will be assigned an IP address when you log on. (If your computer's IP address is **dynamically**, or **server**, **allocated**, the last few digits could vary each time you connect.)

Thankfully, you don't have to use these numbers when accessing other computers. A table is used to translate numbers into names – so **204.52.130.112**, for instance, becomes **roughguides**.

Not all IP addresses have attached domain names, but a domain name will not become active until it's matched to an IP address. The table is coordinated across a network of **Domain Name Servers** (DNS). Before you can send a message to **someone@somewhere.com**, your mail program has to ask your Domain Name Server to convert **somewhere.com** into an IP address. This process is called a **DNS lookup**.

How can I get my own webpage?

Putting a page on the Web is a two-step process. First you have to prepare it in **HTML**, the Web's mark-up language, so that other people's browsers can understand it. Even a word processor can do a basic job by saving a document as HTML. To prepare something more elaborate, you need to use a dedicated HTML editing tool, or to learn HTML code – which, for a computer language, isn't too hard. Once you have an HTML document ready to go, you need to transfer it to your own special reserved **Web space**. For more on this, flip to p.320.

What's a portal?

The tools for searching the Net have improved exponentially over the last few years, but the methodologies have barely changed. Despite that, they now cluster under a variety of new names courtesy of those very smart people with MBAs. And you can bet those names will continue morphing into even more marketing-friendly nonsense.

You'll almost certainly come across the term **portal**. A site can be classed as a portal if you go there to be directed elsewhere. All search engines and directories (see p.168) are portals. If it concentrates on a specific subject, it's classed as a **vortal** (vertical portal). A site is a **hub** if you would go there regularly for news or information contained within the site. But if they make a concerted effort to attract repeat visitors by setting up bulletin boards, discussion lists, chat forums or free Web space for members, they might prefer to call themselves a **community**.

What's an Intranet?

The mechanism that passes information between computers on the Internet can be used in exactly the same way over a local network such as in an office. When this isn't publicly accessible, it's called an **Intranet**. Many companies use Intranets to distribute internal documents – in effect publishing webpages for their own private use.

How does the data know where to go?

For a surprisingly entertaining explanation of how networks, routers, switches and firewalls shunt data in the right direction, download this movie: **http://www.warriorsofthe.net**

2

Get online

Or get left behind

By now you should've seen the Internet in action. After all, it's infiltrated almost every office, every school and even every shopping centre. No matter where you live, there's bound to be somewhere nearby where you can rent time online. Or if you'd like to set it up at home, you needn't wait. It's possible to get everything you need to be up and running in a day or two. The good news is it's not unreasonably expensive or complicated, and it's becoming cheaper and easier all the time.

You don't need to be a computer geek

Perhaps you're not already hooked up because you find the whole computing world a bit off-putting. Well, this is the perfect opportunity to get over it. The rewards of being online far outweigh the effort involved in learning to use a computer.

Although there's ample information in this guide to get you started on the Net, if you're entirely new to computers ask someone computer-literate to babysit you through a session or two. If you don't know anyone suitable, drop into a **cybercafé** or **Internet centre** (p.28) and ask an attendant to kickstart you onto the World Wide Web. Helping out newbies is a big part of their business, so don't be afraid to admit you're green. Getting started is surprisingly simple. You should be able to figure out how to surf the Web within a matter of minutes. Finding your way around is another matter, but you're at an advantage – you have this book.

If you do strike problems, remember that the **online community** – other folks on the Net – is always on tap for help as long as you direct your queries to the right area. Just wait and see; before long you'll be sharing your new-found expertise with others.

Public Internet access

Even if you don't own a computer or use one at work, you can still get online through a range of **public Internet facilities**. These can also be handy if you're away from home and need to **collect your mail**, say, or tap the Web for some last-minute **shopping research** (see p.193). Public access most commonly comes in the form of so-called **cybercafés**, which are basically coffee shops or bars with a few Net-connected terminals for public use.

Lately, though, the concept of mixing cakes, coffee and computers is giving way to **communication centres** complete with faxes, discount phones, printing and network ports to plug in your laptop computer. On top of these, you'll also come across isolated access points in the form of Net-enabled public telephones and coin-operated Netbooths in places like airports, major hotels or shopping malls. Singapore's Changi Airport, for example, boasts free access via video public phones and infrared docking ports. The biggest drawback of all these options, however, is that **they can be very slow**, especially when busy. It's not unknown to be unable to log into Hotmail (p.121) without timing out.

Whatever the case, all these places should allow you to buy **blocks of Net time** at a reasonable price. If you hunt around you might even find free access offered somewhere, such as your local public library.

Finding public access

You shouldn't have any trouble finding a cybercafé. There's sure to be at least one close

to the main street or tourist district in any town. If not, try asking at a hotel, backpackers' guesthouse, post office, public library or computer store. Failing that, consult Yahoo! (http://www.yahoo.com) or the following directories:

Cybercafé Guide http://www.netcafes.com

Cybercafé Search Engine http://www.cybercaptive.com

Cybercafés of Europe http://www.kiosek.com/eurocybercafes/

easyInternetCafé http://www.easyinternetcafe.com

Internet Café Guide http://www.netcafeguide.com

Collect your mail from any computer

You can send and receive your mail from any computer connected to the Internet. That means if you can get to a cybercafé or Net terminal, you can stay in touch, no matter where you are in the world. To find out how, see p.150.

Your own machine

Public-access points are fine for light duties like collecting your mail or playing networked computer games (see p.300), but nothing beats having your own computer. Sure, they're expensive, confusing and sometimes troublesome, but it's the only way to experience everything the Net has to offer.

Getting connected at home is very easy. You'll need just three things: a **computer** with enough grunt to drive a **Web browser** (p.68); a modem or similar piece of hardware to connect the computer to the Internet (p.34); and an account with an **Internet Service Provider** (p.38).

Buying a new computer

Practically any new computer will be more than powerful enough to get you online and will come with a modem built in, so you'll basically be ready to go. **Don't feel obliged to invest in the most powerful machine available**, especially if you only plan to use it for Web-surfing and email. On the other hand, if you're planning on getting into video phone calls, Web design or other advanced tasks, the more powerful the machine, the smoother your experience will be. And bear in mind that you may end up using the computer for far more that you initially think.

One decision you'll have to make is whether to go for a **PC** (generally running Microsoft's Windows operating system) or a **Mac**, short for **Macintosh** (running the Mac operating system). Macs are a range of personal computers produced by a company called Apple – in recent years they've been recognizable by their slick design and colourful shells.

They have traditionally been favoured by the design and publishing industries, but have disadvantages for the Web user. Although nowadays you can do almost anything online with a Mac, the Internet is still more PC-friendly. If you drop by any software archive, for example, and compare the offerings for Mac and Windows, you'll find that there's far less available for Macs – reflecting the fact that the vast majority of people use PCs. Also, a tiny percentage of sites simply won't work on a Mac (though this is increasingly rare). All this means that you should think carefully before locking yourself in the Apple closet.

For more on choosing and using a new computer, see *The Rough Guide to Personal Computers*.

Older machines

It's possible to access the Net with almost any contraption you could call a computer, so if you already have a machine you may find that it's perfectly capable of becoming your Internet station. However, if you can't run your Web browsing and mail software together without a lot of pauses and chugging noises coming from your hard drive, you'll probably get frustrated pretty soon.

Sure, you can squeeze online with an old **486 IBM-compatible PC** or **Macintosh 68030** series by sticking to old software, but it won't be much fun. Things don't get bearable until you hit the **Pentium II 200 MHz** or **Apple G3** mark, and they'll behave better with 64 megabytes of RAM or more. Ideally, though, you'll want something much faster.

Your mouse matters

A sure-fire way to boost your computing efficiency – especially online, where pointing and clicking are your modes of transport – is to equip yourself with a **sturdy wheel mouse**. If your computer is equipped with a no-name mouse that doesn't feel right,

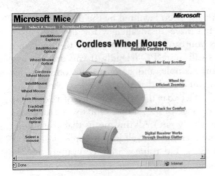

or anything with fewer than two buttons and a wheel, it's time to upgrade. Once you've used a wheel to scroll pages, and adjusted to context-sensitive right-click menus (little menus that differ according to what your click), you'll feel trapped by anything less. Macs with a single-button mouse, especially, will benefit from the upgrade. Anything from Logitech or Microsoft will be top-quality.

A new mouse may also be **optical**, meaning that it recognizes movement with a light beam instead of a rubber ball. Older rubber-ball models have to be cleaned out regularly or they soon get sluggish and unresponsive.

Laptops

Anyone serious about work mobility has a **laptop** (or **notebook**) computer, often instead of a desktop machine. After all, almost anything you can do on a desktop you can do on a portable – albeit on a smaller screen and at a much higher price. If you plan to travel a lot with your laptop, be sure to go for a thin, light model, and ensure that it has long battery life, supports dual voltage (100–240V and 50/60Hz) and comes with a healthy **international warranty** – having a notebook break down with all your mail and data on board is one of life's least rewarding experiences.

Almost all new laptops come with a **built-in modem**, but

Connecting on the move

With a laptop or other portable device and a suitable cellular phone it's possible to get online anywhere you can get reception and dial your ISP (see p.38). Though connection speeds aren't great and it can work out pretty pricey, this can come in very handy for people who are on the move a lot. The basic requirements are a data-compatible phone – ask in any phone shop to find out which models fit the bill – and a way to connect it to the computer. Most people do this with cable running from the phone to a PCMCIA modem, or from the phone to the computer's serial port (the latter usually combined with a software modem). A slicker but more expensive option is to connect to the phone wirelessly, either using infrared (which is notoriously problematic) or something better like Bluetooth. Perhaps the neatest option of all is to get a PCMCIA card with a data-compatible phone built into it, such as such Nokia's Card Phone 2.0 (see **http://www.nokia.com/phones /cardphone2_0/**). Similar high-speed cards are also available, which allow you to connect to specific wireless ISPs (see p.41).

PCMCIA and USB models are also available (see p.35); they sometimes have better specs, and you can swap them between machines.

Modems are convenient for home and personal use, but a **Network card** (NIC) or **USB to Ethernet** adapter will allow you to plug into an office network – great for when you're at work or travelling on business. This way you'll probably get a faster connection and you won't have to pay for call charges. Ask the office IT manager about hooking your laptop into the network.

Pocket gadgets

You can go even smaller and lighter by moving towards **sub-notebooks**, though you'll pay a premium for miniaturization.

If features aren't a priority, for a lot less money you could get a **handheld** or **palm-top**. Many provide Net connectivity along with the ability to run cut-down Windows programs and the abilty to connect to your main machine.

While many of these **PDAs** and **Pocket PCs** are capable of connecting to the Net, don't expect to browse the Web on a match-box-sized screen. Nothing small enough to fit in your pocket, or lacking a decent keyboard, can ever compare to a real computer. They can prove useful, though, if used in conjunction with a proper PC, or for simple tasks when you're away from your desk. For example, you could: download an online newspaper with your desktop computer using AvantGo (http://www.avantgo.com), transfer it to your Pocket PC and read it on the train; send a short email from your phone; check your stock prices under the boardroom table; or, more likely, pull it out in a bar to impress your friends.

WAP phones feed close to the bottom of the Internet gadget pool. If you're patient and dexterous, you can tap into the Net to collect and send email, and browse online information in a very limited way from certain sites. Keep your expectations low, though, or you'll be disappointed. **3G** (Third Generation) mobile phones and devices promise much more, but it will be some time before they're widely available and affordable. For the latest news, see: http://www.3gnewsroom.com

Modems and more

To get online, you'll need a piece of hardware to connect your computer to the Internet. What you'll use depends on the type of connection you opt for.

Unless you're hooked up through a network or a high-speed broadband service (see p.50), you'll need a device called a **modem** to connect your computer to the telephone line. It works by converting the telephone line's analogue data into digital data that your computer can grapple with, and vice versa. Most home users connect in this way, through the standard telephone system. This is called a "**dial-up connection**".

If you bought your computer within the last few years, odds are it'll have a modem built in – practically all do, these days – and you'll be ready to "dial up." Otherwise, you'll need to hit the shops.

Buying a dial-up modem

Modems come in three flavours: internal, external and PCM-CIA. Here's the lowdown on each:

➡ **Internal modems** are the cheapest and most common. They plug into a slot inside your computer called a "bus". Installation isn't difficult, but you do have to open your machine and follow the instructions carefully (or have a computer store do it). Because they're hidden inside, internal modems don't take up desk space, clutter the back of your machine with extra cables or require an external power source. On the downside, they lack the little lights to tell you how your call is going, require an empty slot and can't be swapped between computers without removing the case. Avoid **Soft Modems** (such as Winmodems)– these cut costs by using your PC's processor to do some of their work. If your PC is not up to it, you can experience all sorts of problems, such as frequent dropped connections. Best to spend a little more to be safe.

➡ An **external modem** is easier to install. Depending on the model, it will simply plug straight into your computer's serial or USB port, making it easy to swap between machines (and simple to upgrade). USB is preferable, if your computer supports it (check first!), as they usually don't require an external power supply. All serial (RS232) modems, however, will.

➡ Notebook users with a computer that lacks an internal modem can choose either an external modem, as described above, or a credit-card-sized **PCMCIA modem**. These fit into the PC card slots common in most modern notebooks and remove easily, to free the slot for something else. Being small makes them portable, which is important when you're travelling. They don't require an external power source, but they are expensive and you can't use them with a desktop computer. You can also connect via an appropriate cellular phone and modem (or an integrated phone/modem), so you can surf on the move (see p.33).

Something most travellers don't consider is whether their modem is **approved internationally**. Technically, you could be breaking the law if you're caught using a non-approved modem. If you're trotting the globe, check out 3Com's Global Modem PC cards. They have built-in digital line guards, tax impulse filtering, widespread approval and software to tweak your modem to the tastes of almost every country's telephone network. See http://www.3com.com

All the way with 56K

Whichever type of modem you choose, the major issue is speed, which is measured in **bps** (see box). The current modem standard is **56K** (**V.90**), which allows you to download at up to 56 Kbps and upload at up to 33.6 Kbps. Unfortunately, because of phone line dynamics, **you will never actually connect at 56K** – but you should still be able to get well above 33.6 Kbps, the previous speed barrier. **Don't waste your money on anything less**.

Data transfer speed

Data transfer speed is measured in **bps**, meaning bits (not to be confused with bytes) per second. As with metres and other measurements, a "K" before the figure simply means "times one thousand", and a "M" means "times one million". So:

1 Kbps = 1000 bps
1 Mbps = 1000 Kbps

It can take up to ten bits to transfer a single character of text, so a modem operating at 2.4 Kbps would transfer roughly 240 characters per second. That's about a page of text every eight seconds. At 28.8 Kbps, you could send the same page of text in two-thirds of a second.

If you already have an older modem – such as a 14.4 Kbps (V.32) – seriously consider upgrading, as for a very small amount of cash you can vastly improve your online experience. And if you're paying by the minute for access, you'll probably save yourself a reasonable sum of money in the long run. Even if you have an **X2** or **K56flex** modem, it's worth upgrading to V.90 if possible. For more info, see: **http://www.56k.com**

An emerging and slightly faster standard, **V.92**, is also being tested but isn't supported by many ISPs yet. It may never really take off, but if you have the option, you might as well favour a new modem that sup- ports – or can be upgraded to – V.92. See: http://www.v92.com

Finally, whichever modem you buy, **make sure it will work with your computer**. Modems usually pose few problems in this respect, but it's always worth making sure. If you need help, try one of these sites:

http://808hi.com/56k/
http://www.modemhelp.com
http://www.modemhelp.org
http://www.modemhelp.net

Computer, check. Modem, check. Now what?

To connect to the Internet, you'll need someone to allow you to connect into their computer, which in turn is connected to another computer, which in turn ... That's how the Internet works. Enter the **Internet Service Provider**.

Internet Service Providers (ISPs)

Companies in the business of providing Internet access are known as **ISPs (Internet Service Providers)**. The industry has matured steadily over the last few years to the point that most established ISPs deliver reasonable performance and service. However, all providers aren't equal, and it's difficult to tell a good one from a bad one, until you've used them over time. Try a few before settling – poor access will jade your online experience. Some, for example, try to squeeze too many people onto their connection, resulting in frequent busy tones when you dial and slow transfer rates once you're online. To help you find the most suitable ISP, we've provided a list of questions to ask ISPs (see p.38) – some of which will be important to you, others not. First, though, let's look at a few different categories of ISP.

"Free" ISPs

No one gives away free Internet accounts without a catch. **In the UK**, it's quite simple – "free" ISPs take a cut of your phone bill, so the longer you stay online, the more you pay. This situation can only exist because of the UK's archaic metered local call system. On top of this, the ISPs normally fleece you by the minute for phone support.

This is fine if you're a light user, but otherwise you'd do better going for an **unmetered (freecall) account**, where you pay a fixed monthly fee for both Internet and phone charges. Unfortunately, as the metered call system remains in place, there are still usually **strings attached**. For instance, you can't use the account from another phone line. You can read all about them here:

http://www.net4nowt.com

http://www.ispreview.co.uk

Where local phone calls are unmetered or free such as in the **US**, **Canada** and **Australia**, the only way to turn a profit is to charge, or take commissions from, advertisers and market data hounds. To exchange your privacy for Internet access, scan the lists at:

http://www.emailaddresses.com/email_internet.htm

Online Services

CompuServe and its new parent, **AOL**, are the last major players standing in the special class known as Online Services. What sets them apart from normal ISPs is that they value their exclusive online offerings more than their Internet access. They are, to a certain extent, relics of the past. The Internet now offers far more than any Online Service could ever hope to produce in-house. Indeed, much of their content either comes from the Net or directs you to material located there.

chapter 2

AOL is a family-orientated service with the emphasis squarely on entertainment, whereas **CompuServe** fancies itself as a content provider for young professionals without kids. The one thing they have in common is that their access software (which they make or encourage you to use instead of a standard Web browser and email program) is very much **dumbed down** for the new user. While you might find this an appealing prospect, it will soon become a shackle that will hinder your progress online.

But if you regularly travel abroad, a CompuServe account can get you connected in some 150 countries – the only catch being that it will attract a premium charge on top of your regular access bill. Call for rates and access details before you set off; otherwise you could be up for a nasty credit card shock on your return.

If you feel like giving the Online Services a whirl, you'll find their disks on the cover of nearly every computer magazine, and probably in your mailbox once in a while. By all means try the free trials, but if you're not absolutely delighted, be sure to cancel your account. Otherwise you'll be billed a minimum monthly charge whether or not you use the service. And be sure to **completely uninstall their software once you've finished with them**, as it's known to cause problems.

Before committing yourself to either CompuServe or AOL, compare their network speed, software standards (particularly email), pricing, line availability and telephone support with those of a regular ISP.

Connecting away from home

If you often travel with a portable computer, you'll soon appreciate an account that offers instant local call access in the cities you visit. As mentioned, the Online Services are one option, but you might find better value if you shop around. For a range of choices, see Global Roaming (p.48).

Wireless ISPs and WAP

Going cordless seems the way of the future, but right now the offerings aren't ideal for everyday use. You can get online with your laptop via a suitable cellular phone (see p.33), but it's quite slow and often prohibitively expensive. Another option is to connect your portable to a dedicated wireless ISP such as **GoAmerica** (http://www.goamerica.net) or **AirWave** (http://www.airwave.com) using one of the new high-speed wireless PC card standards. Rates and services vary, but it's not hard to find unlimited access for an affordable monthly charge – at least in the USA. The rest of the world hasn't quite caught on yet. For more on wireless connectivity, see:

Yahoo! http://mobile.yahoo.com

Wireless.com http://www.wireless.com

Wireless Advisor http://www.wirelessadvisor.com

WAP, on the other hand, is almost everywhere, accompanied by hearty hype but few applications and limited content. Drop into any phone sales shop to hear the spiel. For more on WAP, see: http://wap.wapaw. com and http://www.thefeature.com

Another type of cordless connection is a community wireless LAN (Local Area Network), many of which have been set up by hobby groups, allowing members to share their bandwidth and eschew traditional ISPs. This is still very much a fringe interest, though it's starting to gain ground. To find out about the wireless networks in your area, visit: http://www.wirelessanarchy.com

Choosing an ISP

It's important to pick the right ISP. You want a **reliable**, **fast connection**, good **customer support** and a company who'll stay in the game, so you won't need to change account or (worse) email address. We've listed a few of the most popular providers from p.49, but it's definitely worth doing your own research.

The best approach is to **ask around, read magazine reviews and see what others recommend**. If someone swears by an ISP, and they seem to know what they're talking about, give it a go. That's just about the best research you can do. However, there's lots of infomation available on the Web – so sign up temporarily, get online and consult one of these directories:

http://www.thelist.com
http://www.cynosure.com.au/isp/ (AUS)
http://www.internet-magazine.com/isp/ (UK)
http://www.net4nowt.com (UK)
http://www.ispcheck.com (USA)
http://www.ispreview.co.uk (UK)

Some of these sites offer **reviews and advice**, though unfortunately their lists aren't comprehensive. Also check out your local computer/Internet publications; in the UK, for example, *Internet* magazine runs monthly performance charts.

Local call access

Your first priority is to find a provider with **local call access**, preferably without paying a higher tariff for the convenience. And if you often travel with a portable computer, you'll soon appreciate an account that offers instant local call access in the cities you visit. As mentioned, the Online Services are one option, but you might find better value if you shop around. For a range of choices, see Roaming (p.48).

Do your homework

If you know someone who's hooked up to an ISP you're interested in, **ask them these questions**: Is it fast and reliable? Does it ever get so slow you feel like giving up? Is it ever difficult collecting or sending mail? Do you often strike a busy tone when dialling in? What's support like? Have you ever been overcharged?

If you have to do your own research, **interrogate potential ISPs**. Over the next few pages we've listed the questions you should ask. Some will not apply, of course – but it's worth scanning the lot just to make sure. Then use a few of the Freecall numbers listed in the following section (p.48) and compare information packs and access software. It might seem laborious, but it's not as painful as being stuck with poor access.

What's it cost?

For details on how much you should expect to pay, turn to p.56. For now, consider the folloing:

Can you access for the price of a local call?

Remember while you're online with a modem that you're also on the phone.

Is there a free trial?

If you can try out a service without having to install any special software, you've little to lose (except the email address) if you decide not to proceed.

Is there a minimum subscription period or a startup/installation cost?

These shouldn't necessarily put you off, though it will be money down the drain if the provider turns out to be a chocolate kettle.

Do they offer unlimited access for a fixed fee? If not, what's the price structure?

A no-limitations, all-you-can-eat account is preferable for moderate to high users. That way you'll know your bill in advance and won't have to keep watching the clock. Otherwise you could be up for all sorts of permutations, often based around a monthly minimum, followed by usage charges.

Is there a download limit?

Some, mainly broadband (see p.50), ISPs charge a flat fee but impose a megabyte transfer restriction. Once you hit the ceiling, you're billed extra per megabyte. Avoid this plan like the plague.

Does it have or offer national or global roaming, and how is it charged?

If you travel a lot it's handy to know that you can get connected wherever you are, though if it comes at a high price it may not be worth it.

What about the basics?

Does it offer free phone support? What are the hours?

Free phone support until the mid-evenings is standard fare. But a few ISPs, most notably the free UK outfits, charge by the minute. Free or not, if you do run into trouble you won't want to wait until Monday morning to get an answer.

Will you get one or more POP3 email addresses?

A recent trend amongst cheapskate providers is to issue a webmail account in lieu of a proper POP3 address. This is rarely a satisfactory alternative. Sure, you can collect webmail from any computer, but you can do the same with POP3 through free services like **Mail2Web** (http://www.mail2web.com). You'd even be better off with a free third-party webmail account (p.105), as you won't lose it if you switch providers. But ultimately, you should get a POP3 account – or even better, multiple POP3 addresses. Then you can keep separate addresses for different types of mail, and dish out an address or two to family and friends.

Is your name available?

You always have the option to choose the first part of your email address. You might like to use your first name or nickname. This will then be attached to the provider's host name. Check if your name's available and what the host name would be. The trouble with bigger providers is that most common names will already be taken. You really don't want an address like: John3434@aol.com

Does it run a Usenet server? If so, how many groups?

Usenet has around 100,000 groups and it's still growing. That's 95 percent more than you'll ever want to look at in your lifetime. Most providers carry only a portion, but it's still usually over 15,000. The first ones to be axed are often foreign language, country-specific, provider-specific and the adult (alt.sex and alt.binaries) series. If you particularly want certain groups, your provider can usually add them, but it may have a policy against certain material. If it says no to Usenet, keep shopping.

And what about a games server?

A games server (see p.302) will hugely decrease lag time.

Does it throw in some free Web space?

Most ISPs include a few megabytes of storage free so you can publish your own website. In general, if you go over that megabyte limit there'll be an excess charge. Again, like webmail, you might be better off with one of the free Web space providers (p.320) so you don't lose your homepage if you switch. That said, if the ISP offers a page free of pop-up banners or adverts with an attractive address, it might be worth considering. Don't make it a decider, though.

Does it go on about its content?
Your priority is to get fast, reliable Internet access. Forget about local content such as news and chat rooms. There's more than enough on the greater Net.

What else does it offer?
While your first priority should be the quality of your Internet access, see what else you can get with the deal – either as part of the bundle or as an added extra.

Is it fast and reliable?

What's its background?
Big names may offer certain advantages such as national and even global dial-up points, security, guaranteed access, stability and close proximity to the high-speed backbone. However, they can be slow to upgrade because of high overheads, and may have dim support staff. Small, younger providers can be more flexible, have newer equipment, more in-tune staff, cheaper rates and faster access, but conversely may lack the capital to make future critical upgrades. There aren't any rules; it's a new industry and all a bit of a long-term gamble.

Which backbones does it connect to, and at what speed?
Backbones are the high-speed long-haul connections that carry Internet traffic between ISPs and around the globe. A good ISP should tell you which backbone it uses and how big its connections are – or even provide a map of its backbone links around the world. Be suspicious of any ISP that can't answer this question. Better ISPs connect to more than one ISP – a practice called **multi-homing**. This means they're not bound

to one route and can thus choose the fastest connection per request.

For more about backbones – including the current state of traffic – see:

http://www.cybergeography.org and http://www.mids.org/weather/

What is its maximum user-to-modem ratio?

The lower this ratio, the less chance you'll strike a busy tone when you call. As a yardstick, anything over 10:1 should start sounding warning bells that they're underequipped.

How do I get started?

Can they supply you with a sheet of clear setup instructions?

If you're running any version of Windows since 98 or NT, an iMac or any other Mac with OS 8.5 or later, you already have the software – you only need the configuration settings and a little guidance filling them out. **Unless you're running an older system or hooking up broadband, avoid any provider that insists you have to install their special connection software.** Nothing will muck up your system faster than meddlesome ISP-ware. Assure them that as soon as you get online you intend to download the latest version of Internet Explorer. If they have a problem with that, take a hike.

Some popular ISPs

The following list contains some of the major Internet Service Providers (ISPs) in Britain, North America, Australia and New

Roaming

If you travel with a notebook, look for an account with instant local call access in your destination cities. **Nationally** this isn't hard to find. Most of the larger ISPs – all those we've listed, for example – offer local dial-up access across the country, or at least in the major cities. All the same, you should double-check first, as there might be restrictions.

Internationally is another story. While a handful of Online Services and ISPs have a genuinely international presence, the convenience often attracts steep premiums away from home, depending on the countries concerned. So before you sign up and head off, check the fine print first. Compare the rates at:

AOL http://www.aol.com

AT&T http://www.attbusiness.net

CompuServe http://www.csi.com

Inter.net http://www.inter.net

UUdial http://www.uu.net/products/uudial/

Alternatively, you could join an ISP that belongs to a **global roaming** group, such as:

GRIC http://www.gric.com

iPass http://www.ipass.com

This means you can dial into any ISP in the group. Again, you'll be handsomely charged by the minute for the convenience – not too bad for email, but if you plan to spend long hours on the Web it might be worth signing up with a local provider.

Be sure to test the foreign numbers before you leave – better to risk the expense of an international call than wait until you have to wrestle with the hotel's phone system and a directory enquiries that can't understand your accent .

Zealand. It's by no means complete and **inclusion shouldn't be taken as an endorsement**. We've selected the larger, established providers with multiple dial-in access points, as these are the most versatile. If you only access from home, it's possible you might get a better deal from a smaller, local operator.

Australia and New Zealand

Clear Net (NZ)	0508 888 800	http://www.clear.net.nz
Dodo	1300 666 330	http://www.dodo.com.au
Dot	02 9281 1111	http://www.dot.net.au
Internode	1800 685 999	http://www.on.net
Netspace	1300 360 025	http://www.netspace.net.au
Optus Internet	13 33 45	http://www.optusnet.com.au
Ozemail	13 28 84	http://www.ozemail.com.au
Telecom XTRA (NZ)	0800 22 55 98	http://www.xtra.co.nz
Telstra Big Pond	13 12 82	http://www.bigpond.com.au

North America

AT&T Canada (CA)	1 888 655 7671	http://www.attcanada.ca
AT&T WorldNet (US)	1 800 967 5363	http://www.att.net
EarthLink (US, CA)	1 800 395 8425	http://www.earthlink.com
Inter.net (US)	1 866 468 3736	http://www.us.inter.net
Inter.net (CA)	1 800 920 SURF	http://www.ca.inter.net
MSN (US)	1 800 FREE MSN	http://free.msn.com
NetZero (Free) (US)	1 800 333 3633	http://www.netzero.com
Prodigy (US)	1 800 213 0992	http://www.prodigy.com
Verizon	1 800 422 3555	http://www.verizon.com
XO (US)	1 888 699 6398	http://www.xo.net

UK

BT Openworld	0800 800 001	http://www.btopenworld.com
Claranet	0800 358 2828	http://www.clara.net
Demon	020 8371 1234	http://www.demon.net
Easynet Dial	0800 053 0551	http://www.easynetdial.co.uk
Freeserve	0800 970 8890	http://www.freeserve.com
Madasafish	See website	http://www.madasafish.co.uk
Netcom	08705 668 060	http://www.netcom.net.uk
NTL Internet	0800 183 1234	http://www.ntl.com
Pipex	0845 600 4454	http://www.pipex.net
Tiscali	0845 660 1001	http://www.tiscali.com
Virgin.net	0500 558 800	http://www.virgin.net

Broadband – high-speed access

What's good about modems is that they are the right-here, right-now standard worldwide and work over the regular telephone system without any excess charges. But once you try the Net at full speed over a **broadband** connection, you'll find it hard to go back. If you're fortunate enough to live somewhere where broadband is available and affordable, it might be worth checking out. However, if you already have a modem and you're new to the Net, stick to dial-up access until you know your demands. Most importantly, don't put money down on a year's subscription if you don't know what you're getting into. **One thing is certain over the next few years: speeds will go up and prices will come down.**

Doubling-up modems

One little-known way to achieve a faster connection is to connect via two or more phone lines simultaneously, each with its own modem. This should give you a bandwidth equal to the sum of the individual connections, and it often works out cheaper than ISDN. It's simple to set up in Windows 98 or later versions: just right-click on your provider's Dial-up Networking entry, choose "Properties" and add another device under "Multilink". In Windows XP, select the modems you want to use in the dropdown menu under the General tab, and then check the settings under the Options tab.

The hardest part is finding an ISP that supports Multilink.

ISDN

We should've all been using ISDN's superior line handling and speed for the best part of the last decade, but overpricing put it **out of most home users' reach**. And now, with much faster alternatives available, it's not so appealing. It provides three channels (1x16 Kbps and 2x64 Kbps) that can be used and billed in various ways. ISDN Internet accounts don't necessarily cost more but, depending on where you live, the line connection, rental and calls can cost anywhere from slightly to outrageously more than standard telephone charges. One bonus is that instantaneous connection mean you'll only be charged while you're transferring data.

Cable

If you can get cable TV, chances are you can get cable Internet too. Cable access offers mega-speed rates (potentially up to 10 Mbps, though more likely considerably less than 1 Mbps) without call charges. So, if you have cable in your street, make some calls. For rates, availability and local operators, try:

Australia

Optus@home **http://www.optushome.com.au**

Telstra **http://www.bigpond.com/broadband/**

North America

AT&T **http://www.attbroadband.com**

Charter Communications **http://www.chartercom.com**

Road Runner **http://www.rr.com**

UK

NTL **http://www.askntl.com/broadband/**

Telewest **http://www.blueyonder.co.uk**

DSL

If you haven't already heard of **DSL**, or its most common form **ADSL** (Asymmetric Digital Subscriber Line), you soon will. Although it's been commercially available across much of the USA for quite a few years, the rest of the world has been slow to catch on. ADSL is potentially capable of download speeds up to 6 Mbps and uploads up to 640 Kbps, all via the normal telephone system. And it doesn't interfere with your voice service, meaning that you can surf the Net and talk on the phone at the same time over one line (for a more in-depth explanation, see: **http://www.howstuffworks.com/dsl.htm**). But, like cable, **it's rarely offered at its full potential**. In the UK, for instance, consumer access goes out at a mere 512 Kbps downstream and 128 Kbps upstream. Because the technology uses the phone system and requires upgraded exchanges, the main providers of ADSL are the phone companies and their resellers. To see if it's available and affordable, make your first enquiry to your local phone companies, and then try the larger ISPs in your area, such as:

get online

Australia
iPrimus http://www.iprimus.com.au
Telstra http://www.bigpond.com.au/broadband/

North America
AT&T http://www.att.com/dsl/
Bellsouth http://www.fastaccess.com
Earthlink http://www.earthlink.com
Qwest http://www.qwest.com/dsl/

UK
BT Openworld http://www.btopenworld.com
Claranet http://www.clara.net
Demon http://www.demon.net
Freeserve http://www.freeserve.com

Cable or DSL – which one to go for?

Until you've tried both in your own home there's no way to tell which is better. Although the technologies have their own distinct advantages, in practice the speed and reliability differs between installations. Theoretically DSL should be superior because you get your own dedicated line; with cable, you have to share your bandwidth with your neighbours, so if everyone on your street is downloading MP3s at once, you'd expect it to slow down. On the other hand, DSL degrades as you move further from the exchange. If it stretches to more than 3.5km (2.2 miles), you may find yourself disadvantaged. That's if you can get it at all. And the situation is further complicated by other factors such as the individual provider's equipment and the number of existing subscribers. The best you can do is ask around your local area for advice. Be prepared for some horror stories.

Read the fine print

Although broadband deals are typically "**always on**" or "**unlimited access**", they're not always "**all you can eat**" – there may be **caps** on the amount of stuff you can download. Check the fine print carefully: if you're charged by the megabyte, once you go over your limit you could get a nasty shock on your first bill. Unless you're a light user, if it's not "all you can eat", it's probably worth avoiding. And if it mentions something about an "**acceptable use policy**", find out exactly what that means before proceeding.

Can't get DSL or cable?

The catch with cable and DSL is that you need the right wire coming into your house. As DSL is only good for a couple of miles, if you live outside a metro area you have Buckley's chance of seeing it in a hurry – if ever. Your best chance of getting broadband will probably be from the air: via satellite, microwave cable or some other form of wireless link. Although there's talk of rolling broadband out along rural power lines, it hasn't yet seen commercial fruition.

Satellite access is typically capped at around 400 Kbps downstream, but it's capable of being much faster. The upstream speed depends on whether it's a one-way or two-way system. In a one-way system, you have to connect to a regular ISP to complete the return leg, thus restricting the upstream speed to that of a modem (33.6 Kbps). Up to 256 Kbps is possible through the two-way system. While that's fast in theory, it suffers from fairly savage latency, making it useless for online gaming (p.300). Because the downstream leg is shorter, microwave cable and other tower-based wireless systems have lower latency. However, any one-way system will introduce an undesirable lag. **Don't sign up until you've seen it in action**. For availability and pricing of satellite access, check out:

Chello (INT) http://www.chello.com

DirecPC (INT) http://www.direcpc.com

Starband (US) http://www.starband.com

Telstra (AUS) http://www.bigpond.com/broadband/

Powerline Internet

Another possible framework for creating high-speed computer networks is the powerline system. Powerline Internet isn't something that's really taken off as yet, but some see it as an important develpoment. For more information, see **http://www.homeplug.com**

High-speed wireless access

There's little doubt the future of broadband Internet access is **wireless**. We already have the technology, but as yet it's only sparsely available. Though mark our words, it's on its way…

Installation

Cable, ADSL and satellite (downfeed) services are "always on" – you won't have to dial, but you'll still need a special modem-like device to connect between your computer and the line. Depending on the service provider this might work like a cable TV contract, where they rent you the box and charge you some kind of one-off installation fee. As these speeds are in excess of serial card capacity, you'll either need to hook in through a network card, USB port or their own special card. Whichever way, it shouldn't be a drama if you have a newish PC. Mac support is relatively thin on the ground.

Tweaking it

Broadband is pitched at the power user and enthusiast, so a little research mightn't hurt. You'll almost certainly get better results if you tweak your **MTU settings**. See the following sites for tips, reviews and news:

http://www.adsl.com

http://www.broadband-help.com

http://www.dansdata.com/sbs33.htm

http://www.dsllife.com

http://www.cable-modem.net

http://www.cablemodemhelp.com

http://www.cable-modems.org

http://www.cable-modem-internet-access.com

http://www.speedguide.net

http://www.tweak3d.net/tweak/cable/

http://www.whirlpool.net.au

What's it cost?

Ever shopped for a mobile phone? Well, that was easy compared to trying to get the best deal on Internet access. And the range of pricing plans and varieties will get even more confusing as broadband goes mainstream.

Dial-up plans

The simplest and most ideal access plan is an "all-you-can-eat" account that allows you to stay online for as long as you like for a set fee per month.

In the **US,** this commonly goes for around $20 per month with no hidden charges. As local calls are usually free there, that's all you should have to pay. To shop for the cheapest deal across the USA, try: **http://www.getconnected.com**

Most **Australian** ISPs offer an assortment of plans, though few offer unlimited hours or unlimited downloads on their fastest network. Expect to pay around $25 per month, or between $1 and $2 per hour. To see what's available look up: **http://www.cynosure.com.au/isp/**

The **UK** remains a more bewildering market, thanks to the fact that local phone calls are timed and charged. For light users – who spend less than a couple of hours per week online – the cheapest option is to sign up with one of the numerous **"free" ISPs**. This way you only pay for your calls, charged by the minute at local rate (the ISPs survive by taking a cut of these charges). Heavier users, though, will save money by opting for a **flat-rate plan**, which will allow "all-you-can-eat" access for around £15 per month, or unlimited off-peak access for around £10 per month (with peak-time access charged by the minute). For a list of plans in the UK, see: **http://ispreview.co.uk**

Broadband plans

Broadband access is usually considerably more expensive, but that's not always the case. **Cable**, for example, can work out just as cheap if you subtract the price of phone line rental. For example, AT&T offer unlimited cable access for around $40 flat per month in the US. In the UK, NTL charges in the region of £25 per month, and offers packages combining Internet with phone and digital TV. **DSL** (**ADSL**) is generally tiered into speed levels, and offered around the same price as cable. Earthlink (**http://www.earthlink.com**), for example, charges about $50 a month for unlimited access across the USA, while a similar plan in the UK costs around £25. Compare UK prices and services at: **http://www.adslguide.org.uk**

In Australia, broadband is widely available but excess megabyte charges make it impractically expensive for all but very light users. It's also notoriously unreliable. Shop around at: http://www.broadbandchoice.com.au

Installation fee

Some ISPs also charge a **one-off setup fee**. This might include a startup software kit, but if you have Windows 98, Mac OS 8.0 or later, you're much better off asking for instructions to set it up manually (see p.64). Broadband setup fees are usually much higher, as they often include hardware rental or purchase and a physical installation, as with cable TV (though some DSL providers give you a reduction for doing the installation yourself).

Other providers, especially the Online Services, might offer a free trial period, but if you check their pricing for an average year it might not work out cheaper overall.

Watch your phone bill

If you intend to connect through a telephone line, ensure your ISP has a **local dial-up number**. And, if you travel, favour one with national access numbers, otherwise you might run up some serious phone bills.

These dial-up numbers are called **Points Of Presence (POPs)**. In the US, if you need to call your provider from interstate, it may offer a free 1-800 number that could carry a surcharge of up to $10 per hour. If you have free local call access, make sure your provider has a POP in your local zone.

Local calls in Australia are flat-rate, which means it's cheaper to stay online all day than to dial up for a few minutes each hour to pick up mail. Check if you'd save money by switching to a telco with cheaper local calls.

While local calls remain metered in the UK, monthly plans

that include both access and phone charges are the wisest option for all but light users. Be wary, however, of ISPs that offer support through an expensive premium-rate number – after all, you're likely to call support at some point.

Some telcos offer a discount to your choice of frequently called "**Friends and Family**" numbers. Put your provider on this list, as it's sure to become your most-called number. Also ask about the possibility of capped monthly charges to certain numbers. This is sometimes offered with timed ISDN.

More than one computer

If you have more than one computer, you may want to network them together so that you can share an single Internet connection. This isn't too difficult – for instruction, visit:
http://www.practicallynetworked.com/sharing/sharing.htm

3

Let's connect

Get ready to dial

Before you can dial into your newly acquired Internet account, you'll need to fill in a few blanks. Unless you're running a very old operating system (Windows 3.1 or pre-System 8.0 Mac), you already have all the software you need to get started. The aim of this section is to **get you online for the first time**.

Which operating system?

The process involved in connecting to the Internet has become progressively easier over the last few years with each new release of Windows and Mac OS. Of course, this also means the steps involved differ slightly between, say, Windows 95, Me and XP. So, before you call your ISP for setup instructions, you'll need to know which system you're running.

If that turns out to be Windows 3.1, 95a or a pre-System 8.0 Mac, you'll need to either upgrade your operating system or

install some extra connection software. Ask your ISP to send you an installation disk for your system, along with the necessary instructions. If they can't help, keep trying ISPs until you find one that's more receptive. Bear in mind you won't be able to run the latest Internet software (or newer operating systems) on an old computer.

Preparing Windows

Modern versions of Windows come ready to connect, but if your computer isn't stright out of the box, you may want to check that you machine has what it takes (the appropriate **protocols**) to establish a dial-up connection. In Windows Me and earlier, right-click on "Network Neighborhood" or "My Network Places" (on your Desktop) and select "Properties" from the menu; check

you have Client for Microsoft Networks, TCP/IP protocol and Dial-up Adapter installed. If not, click "Add" and install each in turn – Microsoft is the manufacturer in all cases. Then choose "Client for Microsoft Networks" or "Microsoft Family Logon" as your Primary Network Logon. Do not enable File or Printer sharing unless you want to let outsiders from the Net into your computer. If the network icon isn't on your

Desktop, open the Control Panel, go to "Windows Setup" in "Add/Remove Programs" and add "Dial-up Networking" under "Communications". In Windows XP, these settings can be found and checked in the Network Connection window's "Advanced" menu under "Advanced Settings", though you're unlikely to need them.

Ask your ISP

Setting up isn't difficult, but it can be confusing for newcomers. That's why we suggest asking your ISP for guidance on your first time. After all, it's in their best interest to assist – the sooner you get online, the sooner they see your money. Most ISPs provide a setup disk that installs their own custom software and automates the signup process. If possible, rather than install from a disk, ask for step-by-step instructions to configure it yourself, or have them walk you through it over the phone. Try to avoid dial-up ISPs that insist you need to use their software in order to connect. The less you let them meddle with your system, the better it will run – especially if you switch ISPs later on.

If you'd like to know how to set it up yourself or install a second connection, read on. Otherwise, just follow your ISP's instructions, skip over the next few pages and prepare to arm yourself with the latest Web browser (p.68).

Set it up yourself

You can set up as many ISP connections as you like under Windows or Mac OS 8+, and as many email and Usenet accounts as you like in any version of Outlook Express. Although the various **Internet Connection Wizards** can set them up in one go, connecting to the Internet and collecting your mail are completely independent processes. That means if

you're doing it manually, you'll need to set them up in two stages. First, set up your connection (TCP/IP and dialling), and then your mail and news. Before you can start, however, you'll need all the details from your ISP. Once you have all the numbers and addresses, enter them into the Internet Connection Wizard, or follow the instructions under **Setting it up manually** – preferably the latter, as it will give you a better understanding of your system. Either way, it should take no more than a few minutes.

Connection Wizards

When you install or upgrade Windows (98 onwards) or Internet Explorer, it will place a shortcut (icon) on your Desktop called "**Connect to the Internet**". Clicking on this icon will start the **New Connection Wizard** in XP or the **Internet Connection Wizard** in older versions. This tool will guide you through the process of setting up an Internet connection, followed by your mail and news accounts. It can even find you an ISP if you don't already have one. If the icon isn't on the Desktop, you'll find the Wizard in the Start menu, usually under "Communications" or "Internet Tools". Alternatively, opening Internet Explorer for the first time (click on the big "e" on the Desktop) will also usually start the Wizard. As long as you follow the instructions, it's hard to go wrong. All the same, it's simple to rework the settings manually, or repeat the exercise if it doesn't work. You'll find the entry it created in the "Network

chapter 3

Connections" folder in Windows XP or in "Dial-up Networking" in older versions.

The Mac (OS 8.0 and later) has a similar wizard called the **Internet Setup Assistant**, under "Assistants" in the hard drive. Just follow the prompts. The iMac's Setup Assistant can also guide you through the process painlessly.

Setting it up manually

Setting up your connection manually is a little more involved, but gives you greater control over the configuration. In Windows ME and earlier, open the "Dial-up Networking" folder from My Computer or Control Panel and click on "Make new connection". Name the connection (after your ISP perhaps) and select your modem from the dropdown menu. Ignore the "Configure" button for now – you can also alter your modem settings later if necessary. Click on "Next", enter your ISP's phone number and then select "Finish". Your new connection should now appear in the Dial-up Networking folder. In Windows XP, open "Network Connections" and click "Create a new

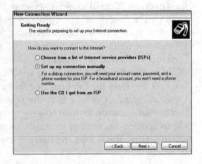

connection". Choose "Connect to the Internet" and then "Set up my connection manually". When you're done, the new connection will appear in the Network Connections folder.

If your ISP has given you an **IP address** or any **name server (DNS) addresses**, you'll now need to configure the **TCP/IP**. Right-click on your new connection's icon and choose "Properties". You'll find everything you'll need to configure your connection under the tabs and buttons before you. Add your IP and/or name server addresses within TCP/IP under the Network tab. Go through the tabs and make sure the only protocols allowed are TCP/IP (not Netbui or IPX) and that "Log onto network" is unchecked. Enabling any of these options will delay your logon. Unless instructed otherwise, leave the type of Dial-up Server set to "PPP", enable software compression and uncheck "encrypted password".

Once that's complete, all you'll need to add is your **user name** and **password**. Fill these in when you first connect (p.74). To connect, just double-click on the new connection.

The process is much the same on a **Mac**. Just open "Remote Access" from under the Control Panel, click on "Setup" then "Options", and fill in your details.

Setting up mail and news

You'll be prompted to enter your email and Usenet account details the first time you open Outlook Express. So if you already have them, just click on the Outlook Express icon on your Desktop, on your Quick Launch bar or under the Programs menu. Once that's done, you can fine-tune and change them, or add more addresses under "Accounts" in the Tools menu in Outlook Express. For more on setting up Outlook Express, see p.124.

To set up the Mac version of Outlook Express, add the same details under "Internet" in the Control Panel, or under "Accounts" in the Tools menu.

chapter 3

What you'll need from your ISP

The minimum information you'll need to log onto your dial-up ISP is your:

User name Your account name with the ISP.

Dial-up password Your secret access code.

Dial-up access number The number your modem dials to access the ISP.

Some ISPs also require you to configure these TCP/IP parameters:

IP address Your location on the Internet. Most ISPs allocate a new one each time you log in. If so, you won't be given a numerical address, you'll be told to choose "server assigned" or "dynamically allocated". In which case you can forget about it, as this is the default setting.

Two name server (DNS) addresses These servers convert friendly domain names into numerical Internet addresses. Again, the trend is to allocate the addresses dynamically, so you mightn't have to touch anything. If not, they'll be numerical, in the form: 123.345.123.12

Script It's rare to need extra commands to log in. If the occasion arises, your ISP will need to instruct you how to set it up as a script.

If you're being supplied with a **POP3 email address** (p.122), you'll need the following to set up your email program:

Adding another ISP account

Once your dial-up connection is set, you should be able to forget about it unless you have to **dial a different provider**. You can add as many ISP accounts as you wish, in the same way as the first. However, if you want one to be your main (default) account, you'll need to specify in Internet Options (see p.102).

Email address: The address where you'll receive your mail. Will be in the form **someone@somewhere** where the **somewhere** part is a domain name.

Mail login The name you choose as the someone part of your email address.

Mail password The secret code used to pick up your mail.

Outgoing mail server (SMTP) The server that will handle all mail you send. It will be a domain name, eg **mail.somewhere.com**

Incoming mail server (POP/IMAP) Where your mail is stored. Also a domain name.

In order to access **Usenet newsgroups**, you'll need to know the:

News server address (NNTP) Most ISPs maintain a Usenet server. Enter its domain name into your newsreader, such as Outlook Express (see p.124.

And finally, you might be given an optional, or compulsory, address:

Proxy server Some ISPs use a proxy server to manage traffic flow and possibly speed up your connection. If so, you'll need to enter this address into your browser's options (p.102) as instructed by your ISP. It might also affect other programs, so be sure to ask. Proxies sometimes play up. Try surfing with and without, and see which you prefer.

The same goes for Macs. Open "Configurations" under the File menu in "Remote Access", duplicate your connection and then edit the details. Or, in **FreePPP**, **MacPPP** and **OT-PPP**, just look for the option "New" to start a new account.

The Web browser

Almost everything you do on the Internet will rotate around one program. It will provide the buttons, bars and menus to help you navigate through the billions of pages stored online. It will act as the window through which you view the World Wide Web, look after your downloads and shuttle off activities to other programs such as media players. This program is called a **Web browser**.

Choosing a Web browser

A few years back, choosing a Web browser was something of an issue. First **Mosaic**, then **Netscape**, dominated the browsing software market. Today, whether you like it or not, the choice has pretty much been made for you. Although Netscape and several other companies still make browsers, Microsoft's **Internet Explorer** commands more than ninety percent of the market share, and there's little incentive for you to buck the trend. Though many praise the considerable features of alternatives such as **Opera** (see p.70), Internet Explorer is not only fast, sturdy and functional, it's free – and you probably already have it.

Internet Explorer (IE)

Internet Explorer comes in various flavours, catering for Windows XP, Windows 95/98/ME, Windows NT/2000, Windows 3.1, Windows CE, Power Mac, Mac 68k, Mac OS X and Unix. On top of that, each version has several releases (see box).

If you're running **Windows 98, 2000 or later**, you won't need to

Microsoft**Internet Explorer**

Playing by numbers

You can judge how up-to-date a program is by its number. Taking Internet Explorer as an example, you might come across IE4.01, IE5.0 and IE5.01, among others. The number before the decimal point tells you the **series**, in this case 4 or 5. As you'd expect, the higher the number, the more recent the release. The number after the decimal point tells you if it is the original release (.0) or an **interim upgrade** (0.1, 0.01, 0.2, etc) within the series. The various versions of the same series are often collectively referred to with an "x". So, "IE5.x" refers to any series 5 release.

Interim upgrades generally fix problems and add on a few minor features. In doing so they render the previous release in that series obsolete. A new series (which in the case of IE is released roughly once a year) usually heralds major changes, new features and bug fixes, but also often adds extra system demands. Thus, if your computer resources are low, you may find an earlier series more suitable.

To make matters a bit more confusing, developers sometimes release a new build of the same program. So you and a friend may both have IE5.5 – but if you downloaded it later, you might have a later build that's fixed a few minor bugs. To see a program's build number, choose "About" from the Help menu.

download Internet Explorer (also called **IE**) – it's built into the operating system. However, you will need to update it (p.71). Microsoft's policy has been to integrate the browsing experience into the Desktop, so **Windows Explorer and IE share the same interface**, meaning that, whether you're surfing the Web or ferreting through your hard drive, things will look and feel similar. Installing Internet Explorer on Windows 95 achieves almost the same effect.

Internet Explorer is also on the Desktop of every iMac, and any Apple running Mac OS 8.5 and later. If it's not on the Desktop, you'll find it in the system installation CD. Internet

Explorer's **Macintosh versions** are written entirely afresh for the Mac OS, so expect quite a few differences – some good, some bad – if you move between the two platforms.

Netscape

Netscape is in such a mess it's very hard to recommend even trying the browser, let alone basing your Internet existence around it. Its 4.7 series is slower, less stable and technologically behind IE5 and IE6 on both the PC and Mac. Although the 6 series (forget about 5.0), has been dramatically revamped by the general programming public at Mozilla.org and  embellished by parent company AOL, it's still too slow, chronically buggy and cluttered. That's if you can get it to load at all. Despite Netscape's shortcomings, some people still prefer its way of doing things – most notably the Linux community, who as a rule oppose anything made by Microsoft. Of course, Microsoft does have a case to answer (literally, in the US at the moment) and Internet Explorer is a long way from perfect. If you're curious to see whether Netscape plays more to your tune, and are prepared to risk the aftereffects, you can download it from:

Netscape **http://browsers.netscape.com**

Opera

Opera is fast and well-featured browser that is particularly popular with the Linux community. It's flexible and powerful and does various amazing things such as loading pages in the

Simply the Best Internet Experience
BeOS | Linux/Solaris | Mac | OS/2 | QNX | Symbian OS | Windows
OPERA software
search:

background, creating bookmarks that open more than one page and remembering all the sites you're looking at when you close the program so that next time you run it they'll pop up automatically. The only problem is that the free version includes an advertisement bar. For more info, see:

Opera http://www.opera.com

Want more information?

For the latest on browsers, reviews, tests, comparisons, tips and downloads for a wide range of brands and platforms, see:

Browsers.com http://www.browsers.com

Browser News http://www.upsdell.com/BrowserNews/

For discussion of the latest betas (test versions – see p.262), see:

BetaNews http://www.betanews.com

For help with Internet Explorer problems:

IE Info Site http://www.ieinfosite.co.uk

Important – get the latest version

It's very **important to keep your browser up-to-date**, not so much to gain new features, but to **fix bugs** and protect you against **security threats**. However, always check the minimum requirements (see p.73) before downloading a new version, as old systems will struggle or be unable to run the newest series.

Updating IE

As Internet Explorer is part of Windows 98 and later, you can update it to the latest version through **Windows Update**. Once you're online, you can reach Windows Update through several channels. You'll find an entry under the Windows Start menu; the Tools menu in IE5 (and later); under "Product Updates" in

chapter 3

the Help menu in IE3 or IE4; or by entering this address in your browser:

Windows Update **http://www.windowsupdate.com**

Once the page has loaded, click on "**Product Updates**". The server will automatically interrogate your system to determine which components you need to bring yourself up-to-date. Then it's just a matter of picking what you want. It should be obvious what's important. If you want to use email, you should download Outlook Express. You can safely avoid MSN Messenger (p.256) for the time being.

If Windows Update won't work, drop into Internet Explorer's home, download the latest setup file, and then call back into Windows Update to top up with critical updates:

Microsoft IE Home **http://www.microsoft.com/ie/**

To update the **Mac versions** of Internet Explorer and Outlook Express, download the separate installation files from:

Mactopia **http://www.mactopia.com/ie/**

Before you start downloading, beware that it could **take an hour or more** – depending on which options you pick, how busy the sites are and at what speed you connect. If conditions are normal, you should be able to download well over 10 MB per hour with a 56Kbps modem. It's preferable to download it from the Net rather than install it from a magazine CD or an

ISP installation disk. That way you can be sure it's the latest version and free from unwelcome branding. If you'd like **remove the branding**, such as your ISP's logo, see p.103.

System requirements

If you're running Windows 98/ME/NT/2000/XP then you already have IE, and should be fine installing the most recent version. But frankly, if you're running IE5 or later on anything **less than a Pentium 200 with 64 MB of RAM, it's going to hurt.** If you're a Windows 98 user with only 16 MB of RAM or a Windows ME/NT/2000 user with only 32 MB, you'll certainly benefit from some extra memory, especially if you're struggling to run IE and other programs simultaneously.

As for Macs, all versions of Internet Explorer for the Mac since IE4.5 require at least a **PowerPC processor** with 12 MB of RAM, and **Mac OS 7.5.3 or later**. Again, these are the official specs, but realistically you'll be happier with a faster machine and more RAM. If you have an earlier **iMac with only 32 MB of RAM**, you should chock it up to at least 64 MB, so you can browse and read mail with a modicum of dignity.

Humble computers

If your computer doesn't have the operating system or specs to run the most recent version of IE, you'll need to get hold of an earlier realease. The best choice for older PCs running **Windows 3.1** is **Internet Explorer 3.03**. It can get by (just about) on 4 MB of RAM and as little as 7 MB of disk space for a browser-only installation, plus it also includes the TCP/IP dialling software that Windows 3.1 omits. Windows 95 users should be able to cope with anything up to IE5.x, depending on hardware specs.

If disk space is your main concern, consider not installing all the brower's components – some IE versions require more than

80MB for a full installation, but you can cut this down to about 27MB by only installing the browser. Furthermore, new releases normally write over the old files, so upgrades don't require too much extra space.

Mac 68K machines can run IE4, though IE3 requires less RAM and disk space, so it might be preferable. If it's still too heavy, **Netscape 2.0x** is better than no browser at all. Whatever the machine, browser or version number, Macs work best with Virtual Memory switched on.

Alternatively, investigate **Opera** (see p.70), some versions of which pack a browser, mail sender and newsreader into only a couple of MB.

If you're after an old version of a browser, you won't find it on the manufacturer's website. Not to worry, though – you'll find just about every browser ever released across all systems (including **Amiga, OS/2**) and **BeOS**, for free download at: http://browsers.evolt.org

Your first time

Once you've configured your dial-up networking and mail software to your ISP's specifications, you should be ready to hit the Net. Ideally you're already armed with a Web browser, so the perfect exercise for your very first connection would be to get straight onto the World Wide Web. If not, install any version of any browser you can find – you can always get a new one once you're online.

Connecting...

Plug your modem into the phone line and **click on the icon that connects you to the Net**. Which icon? Well that depends on the way you've set it up. Most ISP installations place

a short cut on your Desktop or under the Windows Start menu. If it's not obvious, ask your ISP.

Irrespective of how you've set it up, there will always be a few ways to kickstart your dialler. The best option, especially if you've set it up yourself, is to go straight to the connection entries in "**Connect To**" in Windows XP (on the Start menu) or "**Dial-up Networking**" in earlier versions (either in My Computer or the Control Panel). Rather than open this folder every time you want to connect, drag a shortcut from the individual connection onto your Desktop or Quick Launch Toolbar (just to the right of the Start button). That way it's easy to get to in future.

The process is similar on the **Mac** but differs between system versions. It won't take you long to work it out. In OS 8.0x and later, the dial-up networking aspect is called "**Remote Access**". Again, like Windows, you can approach it from several angles, depending on the system. You'll find it under the Apple Menu, in the Control Panel and along the Control Strip. To dial, click on "Remote Access" and then the "**Connect**" Button.

Negotiating

If your modem speaker volume is turned up (look under your modem properties), it will make all kinds of mating noises while connecting, like a fax machine. These sounds will cease once the connection's negotiated. At this point your provider's server will need to identify you as a customer, so if you haven't already

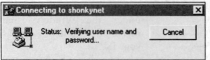

entered your **user name and password**, you'll have to do so now. Once that's done, **click the box that says "Save Password"**; otherwise you'll have to enter it every time you log in. Make sure you keep this password private – anyone could use it to rack up your bill or, perhaps worse, read your mail (although you should be issued with a separate password to retrieve mail). If you fail to connect, try again. If it keeps failing, you'll need to work out what's going wrong – see p.77.

Online

Once you're in, Windows should display a large intrusive box telling you you're connected. You won't need it again, so choose to **"never see this box again"**. You'll then see a smaller box which will tell you your connection speed, how long you've been connected and how many bytes you've sent and received. Click on "OK" to dismiss it. To bring it back, double-click on the twin computers icon in the System tray (left bottom corner, next to the clock). If you're charged by the minute or megabyte to be connected, you might find this information handy. It works similarly in Apple's Remote Access.

Testing, testing

Congratulations – you're online! Now **start your Web browser** and enter a few of the addresses from our Web guide (p.331). You'll find instructions on how to browse the Web starting on p.83. If you can access the Web, it's close to plain sailing from now on. If not, you'll need to find out what's wrong. See p.77.

Disconnecting...

To finish your session, either right-click on the twin computers icon in the System tray and choose "**disconnect**", or double-click on it and click on the "disconnect" button. On the Mac, re-enter Remote Access and click on "disconnect".

Troubleshooting

Rest assured, you'll eventually have problems with your connection, and it won't necessarily be your fault. It happens to everyone. But before you bellow down the phone line at your ISP's support staff, make sure it's not something obvious you can fix yourself.

Getting to the settings

To access all the connection settings in Windows (modem, scripting, TCP/IP, phone and dialler), open "**Network Connections**" in Windows XP (on the Start menu) or "**Dial-up Networking**" in earlier versions (in My Computer or the Control Panel). Right-click on the troublesome connection and choose "Properties". To change the log-in settings, simply double-click as if dialling.

If you are using a **Mac with Free PPP** (or equivalent), you can access the settings by opening the **Free PPP** window and clicking on "General", "Accounts" or "Locations". You may also need to adjust the settings in your **TCP/IP file**, which you access through the Control Panel under the Apple symbol (top left-hand corner of the screen). **In later Macs**, look under **Remote Access**, **TCP/IP** and **Modem** under the Apple menu Control Panel folder.

If you didn't get through

If you **didn't succeed in connecting to your provider**, there's probably something wrong with your Dial-up Networking or modem configuration. The most common errors are:

➡ **No modem detected:** Is your modem installed, plugged into the right port and switched on? To install or diagnose a modem in Windows, click on the "Modem" applet in the Control Panel.

➡ **Dial tone not detected:** Is your phone line plugged in? If this isn't the problem, try disabling "Dial Tone Detect" or "Wait for Dial Tone" under the modem settings in the Control Panel. If the option greyed out in Windows, you'll either need to re-install the modem with its correct driver (preferable) or manually enter the initialization string X1 into the modem's Advanced Connection Settings (in pre-XP Windows, do this via the properties of the specific Dial-up connection, not through Control Panel, as this only affects new connections).

➡ **No answer:** Do you have the right phone number? You can verify that your modem's working by dialling a friend. If their phone rings you'll know your Dial-up Networking is talking to your modem.

➡ **Busy/engaged:** Access providers' lines sometimes fill up at peak hours such as the end of the working day. Keep trying until you get in: even though you dial a single number, there are several modems at the other end. If it happens often, complain, or get a new provider with a **lower user-to-modem ratio**.

You got through but were refused entry

If you **succeeded in connecting** but were **refused entry**, check your user name, password and script (if used). If it **failed to negotiate network protocols**, verify your TCP/IP settings. You might need your ISP's help on this one. Keep the settings on-screen and phone them.

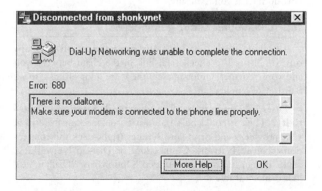

You're online but not on the Web

If you've **managed to stay connected but can't access any websites**, either your DNS settings are incorrect, you've failed to establish an IP connection, you haven't specified your ISP's proxy properly or there's a temporary outage. Log off, verify your TCP/IP and proxy settings, and try again. DNS servers go down occasionally, so (unless yours are server-assigned) make sure you specify more than one. Again, call your ISP and ask if there are network problems.

You can't access one or more websites

For details on how to locate errant Web addresses, see p.187.

You're on the Web but another program won't work

If your browser's working, but your chat, search agent, newsreader or FTP client won't connect to any sites, check the individual program's proxy settings. Ask your ISP for the address and port number if you're unsure.

Your connection keeps going down

If everything works fine but **your connection often drops out**, you'll need to check each link in the chain between you and your provider. Unfortunately there are a lot of links, so it's a matter of elimination.

➡ **Does it happen only after an extended period of inactivity?** Then it could be an automatic defence mechanism at your provider's end or in your settings (right-click the connection's icon in Network Connections or Dial-up Networking, click "Properties" and look under "Options" or "Dialling" for "Disconnect if idle for…").

➡ **Do you have telephone Call Waiting?** If it's enabled and you're called while online, those little beeps will knock out your connection.

➡ **Pick up your phone. Does it sound clear?** Crackling sounds indicate a poor connection somewhere. Modems like a nice clean line.

➡ **Do you share a line or have more than one handset?** Picking up an extension will drop your connection.

➡ **Do you have the latest modem driver and firmware revision?** Check your modem manufacturer's homepage.

As a **last resort**, try a different ISP, phone line and modem. For more troubleshooting advice, contact your ISP or see: http://php.iupui.edu/~aamjohns/

OK, it works – but it's very slow

When the **Net gets overloaded**, transfer rates slow down: it can happen to the whole Internet backbone at peak hours, particularly with transoceanic routes. If transfers are slow from everywhere, however, it usually means the problem lies closer to home. It could be that your **provider or office network** has too many users competing online, or too much traffic accessing its Web area from outside. In this case your provider or office needs to increase its bandwidth to the Net.

ISPs tend to go through cycles of difficult traffic periods. If they have the resources and the foresight to cope with demand, you won't notice. But as it's such a low-margin business, they're more likely to stretch things. Always call or email your provider when you have complaints with its service. If you're not treated with respect, no matter how trivial your inquiry, take your money elsewhere.

To test and compare your connection speed, check out http://www.tcpiq.com/tcpiq/linespeed/

chapter 3

Finding the bottleneck

If you'd really like to know what's slowing things down, arm yourself with some network diagnostic tools. The staples are: **Ping**, which works like a radar to measure how long it takes a data packet to reach a server and return; and **TraceRoute**, which pings each router along the path to see which one's causing the holdup.

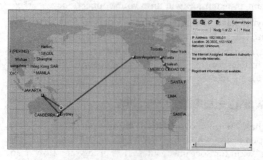

Windows users have plenty of choices for obtaining these programs. **NetScanTools** (http://www.nwpsw.com) has Ping, TraceRoute and loads more. **MyVitalAgent** (http://www.myvitalagent.com) can tell you exactly where it's breaking down, whether your provider is falling short, monitor trends and send off a complaint report. Programs like **Visual Route** (http://www.visualware.com) and **VisualTrace** (http://www.neoworx.com) add another level to TraceRoute by identifying who owns the routers, and then maps it all out in Hollywood style. The latter is preferable, but it no longer offers a free demo.

For Macs, try **WhatRoute** (http://crash.ihug.co.nz/~bryanc/) for tracing routers and **CyberGauge** (http://www.neon.com) to monitor bandwidth.

4

Surf the Web
The world at your fingertips

When you see something like
www.come.and.get.me on an ad, business card
or news story, you're being invited to visit
an address on the World Wide Web (the Web), the
biggest breakthrough in communications since
TV. You'll have no trouble finding such addresses
online – all you have to do is type them into your
Web browser.

In fact, you'll find all sorts of interesting stuff once you get started. The Web is so cheap and easy to use that it has sparked off more
publishing, both professional and DIY, than at any time in history.

Although getting about the Web is undeniably simple, you'll
still need a little help to get off the ground. As preparation, we've
dedicated this section to explaining **how to set up your Web
browser** and point it in the right direction. There's another section on **how to find things** once you're there (see p.167); and
most of the back half of this book (see p.331) consists of reviews
of **interesting and useful sites**.

chapter 4

What to expect

The Web is the Internet's glossy, glamorous, point-and-click front door: a colourful assault of shopping, investment services, music, magazines, art, books, museums, travel, games, job agencies, movie previews, radio broadcasts, self-promotion and much, much more. It has information on more than twenty million companies and is accessed by more than four hundred million users in every corner of the globe from Antarctica to Iceland. It will bring the world to your computer. It's better than the best encyclopedia, and for the most part it's free. **There's no doubt: if you're not on the World Wide Web, you're missing out**.

How to read a Web address (URL)

In tech-speak **a Web address is also called a URL** (Uniform Resource Locator). Every Web page has a unique URL that can be broken into three parts. Reading from left to right, they are: the **protocol** (such as **http://** **ftp://** or **news:**); the **host name (domain)** (everything before the first single forward slash); and the **file path** (everything after and including the first single forward slash). Consider the address: **http://www.star.com.hk /~ Chow/Yun/fat.html** The **http://** tells us it's a HyperText file located on the World Wide Web, the domain **www.star.com.hk** tells us it's in Hong Kong, and the file path indicates that the file **fat.html** is located in the folder (directory) **/~Chow/Yun/**

Anyone who's serious about their presence on the Web has their own domain name. Typically, a company will choose an address that relates to its business name or activity. It's also common, but **certainly not a rule**, for such addresses to start with **http://www.** For example, you'll find: Apple computers at **http://www.apple.com**; the BBC at **http://www.bbc.co.uk**; and lots of non-leather footwear at: **http://www.vegetarian-shoes.co.uk**

So what do you do with the address? Enter it into your browser, of course. Read on to find out how...

Starting out

When you enter a **Web address** into your browser, it will retrieve the corresponding page from wherever it's stored on the Internet and display it on your screen. The page is likely to contain a mixture of text and images, laid out rather like a magazine. But what makes a Web page special is that it can contain **links** (also called hyperlinks). When you **click on a link, something happens**. Generally, it brings up another page, but it might do something else like launch a Net radio broadcast or start a file download.

How to start Internet Explorer

The most convenient way to open Internet Explorer is to click on the short cut in the Windows Quick Launch toolbar (beside the Start button). The icon looks like a big blue letter "e". You'll also find one on the Desktop, as well as in the Start menu under "Programs". If you're not already connected to the Net when you click it, you'll be prompted either to connect or work offline (see p.95).

How to enter an address

To visit a website, you have to submit its address to your browser, either by keying it in or clicking on a link. However, you'll need to be connected to the Internet for it to work, so go online before trying out an address.

Once you're online, open Internet Explorer. It will probably try to access a start (home) page. Let it go about its course and ignore whatever comes up. See the bar running horizontally

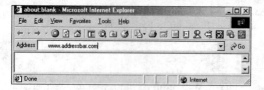

above the browser pane that says "Address" on the left-hand side? That's the **Address bar**. Click inside it, type **www.yahoo.com** and hit Enter – or click on the Go button at the far right of the bar.

Your browser will examine the address and work out what to do next. If you've submitted a legitimate Web address, it will contact your DNS server to convert the host name into an IP address. You'll see this process happening in the lower left corner of your screen. Once it's converted, the browser will contact the website's server and request the page.

It rarely takes more than a minute or two to locate and load Web pages. With a 56K modem, the average time is around thirty seconds, but if you've a broadband connection it can be almost instantaneous. If all works well, your browser will retrieve the page and display it on your screen. In this case, you'll arrive at **Yahoo**, a giant site offering a massive directory and lots of other services (see p.177).

If you receive an error message, try again. If that fails, see p.177 and p.187 for help troubleshooting.

Other ways to enter an address

There are dozens of less convenient ways to enter a Web address, especially in Windows. For example, through "Open" under the File menu in Internet Explorer; in "Run" under the Start menu; or directly into the address bar in Windows Explorer (click on My Computer). In all cases, you simply need to type in the address and click on OK or hit your Enter key.

What about the http:// bit of the address?

Although the formal way to write a Web address is to start it with **http://** (for example, **http://www.yahoo.com**) **you don't need to enter the http:// part** into your browser. For that reason, you'll often see Web addresses expressed without it – for example: **www.yahoo.com**

It won't make any difference which way you enter the address, as your browser will automatically add it on if you omit it. This will only cause problems if the address isn't a Web address; that is, it starts with something other than: **http://**

Other addresses (non-http)

You can also access **FTP** (see p.268), **Telnet** and **Usenet** (see p.229) from the helm of your Web browser.

To **use FTP**, you just add **ftp://** to the file's location. So, to retrieve **duck.txt** located in the directory **/yellow/fluffy** from the anonymous FTP site **ftp.quack.com** you should enter: **ftp://ftp.quack.com/yellow/fluffy/duck.txt** (In fact, with recent browsers you can omit the **ftp://** part as they know that any domain starting with **ftp.** is an FTP site.)

Telnet – an ageing system that's still used by some institutions for email (see p.153) and library catalogues, among other things – works in exactly the same way. So does **Usenet**, except that it omits the // part. Thus, to access the newsgroup **alt.ducks**, key in: **news: alt.ducks**

Addresses starting with **file:///** are located on your own hard drive. You can browse your own computer by entering a drive letter followed by a colon (eg **c:**).

Important – take care with capitals

Note that Web address path names are **case-sensitive**. So, key them carefully, taking note of capitals as well as their bizarre punctuation. Host names are almost always written in lower case, but are actually case insensitive. In other words, entering **www.BigStick.com** is the same as **www.bigstick.com**, but **www.bigstick.com/Bigstick/** isn't the same as **www.bigstick.com/bigstick/**.

Address guessing – helpful

Once you've been online for a short time you'll notice Internet Explorer will start trying to guess the address you're entering. It will present a dropdown list of all the sites it knows that so far match your keystrokes. You can either complete the address or click on one of the selections. These are supplied by your **History** (p.94).

Address guessing – not so helpful

If you enter a word or phrase rather than a properly formed address, your browser will also try to guess or search for the site. If that sounds like it might save you time, just try it – you probably won't bother again, as it's really not very useful. The various options can be set in the "Search in Address bar" section of the Advanced tab in Internet Options (p.102). If you acually want to search for something, you'd be better off using a search engine (p.168).

Clicking on links

You rarely have to enter addresses to get around the Web, because most of the time you'll simply be **clicking on links**. Web pages are written in **HTML** (HyperText Markup Language), which lets documents **link** to other documents. Clicking on such a link effectively turns the page. This creates a sort of third dimension.

Unless you've changed the settings (see p.94), **text that contains links** to other documents (or another part of the same document) will usually be highlighted in blue and underlined. As well as text, images and movies can also contain links – and not just one, either. Pictures might contain links that relate to what's in the picture. For example, clicking on a town's name on a map might send you to a site about that town. In Webspeak, this type of picture is called an "**image map**".

When you pass over a link **your mouse cursor will change from an arrow to a pointing hand** and the target address should appear in a bar at the bottom of your browser. It's easy for site programmers to override this and **place alternative text in the bottom bar**, or **make your mouse do funny things like leave trails**, so don't be alarmed if it doesn't always work in the same way.

To pursue the link, simply **click on the relevant text or image**. A link is only a **one-way connection**, like a signpost. So when you get to the new page, there won't necessarily be a link back, but that's no problem as you can simply use your browser's **back button**...

Surf the Web

All the main **navigation buttons** are located on the toolbar above the main browser window. Displaying them is optional, but they're hard to live without.

You'll use the **Back** and **Forward** buttons most. To **go back to a page** you previously visited, click the Back button until you find it. To **return to where you were**, keep pressing Forward. And to go back to your home page (see p.102) hit **Home**.

You can go back and forward through pages pretty much instantly once you've visited them during a session, as your computer stores the documents in memory. How much material you can click through in this fashion, however, depends on the amount of storage space allocated to **Temporary Internet Files** in your settings. For more, see "Browse Offline" (p.95).

Two other important buttons are **Stop** and **Refresh**. To **cancel a page request** – because it's taking too long to load a site or you've made a mistake – just hit the Stop button. Occasionally, you might have to hit Stop before Back will work. Alternatively, if a page doesn't load properly, you can hit **Refresh** to load it again. You'd also do this if a page changes regularly, and you want to load a new version rather than one that's stored in your Temporary Internet Files, or on your ISP's proxy server (see p.104).

The **Mac versions are laid out slightly differently** with a tabbed toolbar running vertically down the left-hand side. At its top there's a little arrow that gives you the option of putting the main navigation toolbar on the left.

Change the buttons

You can customize the way the buttons and bars appear, which is handy because in the default state they take up too much screen room. So once you're familiar with the buttons, choose to display them **small and without text**. To access the settings, right-click on the toolbar and choose "**Customize**", or look under "Toolbars" in the View menu.

Move the bars

You can also move the bars around to your liking, by dragging and dropping them using their left-hand edges. If you're running IE6.0 or later, you'll need to right-click on the toolbar and unlock the bars first.

Use your mouse

The next most important navigation controls are accessed with the **right mouse button**, which will yield a little menu of options when clicked. The menu will change depending upon what you click. For instance, if you click on a link, you'll have the option of opening the target page in a new window. Click on an image and you'll see the option to save it to disk. You'll also find Back, Forward, Refresh and Print in there.

Although it's **preferable to upgrade your Apple mouse** (see p.31) to get the wheel and extra buttons, you can access the same "right button" menus by **holding down the Control key** as you click. The Mac versions don't have as many options under the mouse menus, but what's there is still useful.

Find a page later – save it to Favorites

Whenever you find a page that's worth another visit, file it into your "**Favorites**" for later reference. Favorites are often also referred to as "**Bookmarks**", which is what they're called in Netscape and some other browsers. **Internet Explorer** stores each Favorite as an individual "**Internet Shortcut**" in the same way it makes shortcuts to programs in Windows. To **arrange your Favorites** into logical folders, choose "**Organize Favorites**" from the Favorites menu. To move them, click on the entries and drag and drop them into place. Alternatively, right-click on the tree and choose "explore". Then you can delete or move the shortcuts around like any other Windows file.

When you add an address to your Favorites, it will ask if you'd like to **make it available offline**. If you agree, it will check the page at whatever intervals you specify to see if it's changed. At the same time it can also download the page, and others linked to it, so that you can later browse the site offline (see "Browse Offline" – p.95).

You can also **save an address as a shortcut or alias** on your Desktop (or anywhere else you fancy). Either drag and drop the page icon to the left of the address in the browser, or choose "**Send Shortcut to Desktop**" from under the File menu.

The links bar – add your favourite sites

You're sure to visit certain sites quite frequently, such as your favourite newspaper and search engine. Rather than type in the address every time or click through your Favorites, you'll find it's quicker to put a link to them in your **Links bar**. The Links toolbar is usually located below the Address bar – or wherever you choose to put it. If it's not there, right-click on the top toolbar in IE and put a tick beside "Links".

While it might look like any old toolbar, the Links bar is actually a special folder within your Favorites. That means you can add to it, or organize it just like any other Favorites folder. You can also drag and drop links directly from the Address bar onto the Links bar. But before you put it to use, clear out all the junk supplied by Microsoft, Apple or whoever provided the browser. Rather than stack your Links bar with individual links, try creating a few folders on it using "Organize" in the Favorites menu.

Make the most of your session

Nothing happens instantly on the Net, so **make sure you're always doing at least three things at once**. You might as well download news, mail and the latest software releases while you browse several sites at once. If you're reading with nothing happening in the background, you're wasting time online.

It's simple to open multiple sites. While you wait for one page to load, open a **New Window** or **New Browser**, and look elsewhere while you wait. For instance, when reading an online newspaper, scan for interesting stories, and then quickly fire them all open in separate windows. Just click each link in turn while **holding down the Shift key** (the Apple key on the Mac) or by selecting "**Open in a New Window**" from your **right-click menu**. Then you can read it all instantly, perhaps even offline.

Bear in mind, however, that each process is competing for **computer resources** and bandwidth, so the more you attempt, the higher the likelihood that each will take longer – and that your machine might crash. Mac users might need to allocate extra memory to the browser, otherwise it won't be able to open more than three or four windows. To do this, select the program icon (not a shortcut), press the Apple and "I" keys, select "memory" from the dropdown, and increase the "Preferred Size".

Opera (see p.70) is a browser specifically designed to encourage this practice. It can easily open forty or more site windows within the main window, at a fraction of the resources needed in IE or Netscape.

chapter 4

Retrace your steps

During a session browsing the Web, you can **return to recently visited sites** through the dropdown menus found by either
holding down the Back and Forward buttons or clicking on the
adjacent down arrows. And you can return to the sites you visit
most by scrolling through the dropdown menu where you enter
addresses. These, however, only keep track of the current session
in that window. If you want to retrace through previous sessions,
go straight to your **History**.

Find it again – through your History

Whenever you visit a site, its name and address go into your
History. Clicking on the History button will toggle a panel on
the left-hand side of the window. You can sort the sites by date,
name, order of visits or number of visits. To revisit a site, either
click through the links or search through the contents. We'll discuss the latter in **Browse offline** (see opposite).

How to tell where you've been

An **unvisited link** is like a signpost to a new page. You click on
the link to go there. It's then called a **visited link**.

You can customize links by displaying them as **underlined**
and/or in a **special colour**. The setting is in Internet Options
(p.102) under Colors in the General tab. The default is usually
underlined blue for unvisited links and either black, purple or
red for visited links. However, individual sites can override these
settings and display their own customized colors.

See how this works for yourself. Look at any page. Links you
haven't followed should appear blue and underlined. Now click
one and load the page. Next, click "Back" and return to the previous page. The link will have changed colour.

What's more, **visited links will appear in the new colour wherever they crop up**, even on a completely different page that you are visiting for the first time. This can be useful if you're viewing directories and lists, as you can instantly note what you've seen before.

Visited links eventually expire and revert to their old colour. You can set the **expiration** period under Internet Options. It's wise to keep the expiry time short (no more than twenty days). A big **History** can dramatically slow things down, especially if you surf a lot. After a month or so, click on "**Clear History**" under the General tab in Internet Options and see if it speeds things up. If it does, reduce your expiry period.

Browse offline

If you're subject to timed charges, consider **gathering pages** rather than reading. Any pages you load go onto your hard drive, and are available for reading offline later. That means you can run back through your session after you hang up. You can prevent Internet Explorer from trying to go online by choosing "Work Offline" from the File menu.

Once in this mode, you can **call up sites** by typing in their addresses, following links as if you were online or by clicking on their entries in your History. The contents of the pages are stored temporarily in a folder called **Temporary Internet Files**. Their primary purpose, however, is to speed up browsing. When you return to a page, your browser will check this folder first rather than download its components again from the Net.

Clear your Temporary Internet Files

The Temporary Internet Files settings are under the General tab in **Internet Options** (see p.102). You can change their location, how much disk space to allocate and when to check for newer versions. This is also the proper place to delete all the stored pages. **If you try to do it manually, it will cause problems.**

It's best to select the option to **check for newer versions** every time you start Internet Explorer. Then, if you suspect the document's changed during a session revisit, just hit Refresh. Unless you plan to read offline, it's wise to **delete these files every week or two** as, like the History folder, if it gets too big, it can slow things right down – especially if you have an elderly machine.

If your **browser is playing up** and not loading pages properly, try clearing these temporary files out. It's often an instant fix.

Search your History

As mentioned earlier, the History folder makes it very easy to backtrack your session. But, even better, you can **search the contents of the pages stored in your Temporary Internet Files**. It's just like having your own search engine.

Mind you, these pages won't sit on your hard drive forever – they're governed by your Temporary Internet Files settings and will be overwritten next time you visit that same address. If you wish to archive a page permanently, save it.

Save a page

To save a page, choose "**Save as**" from under the File menu. You can choose between saving in text or HTML. If you **Save as HTML**, you'll only be able to view it in programs that understand HTML such as Web browsers. Save it as text and you can read or edit it in any text viewer or word processor.

The problem with this method is that you'll save the text, but not the images. If you want the images as well, you'll need to save as a **complete webpage** or **Web archive**. The first option automatically saves the images into a separate folder. The latter combines all the elements into a single, transportable file that can only be viewed in IE5 or later.

Save an image, movie or sound file

Webpages often display reduced images. In Web art galleries especially, such images often have links to another with higher resolution. To save an image, right-click on it and choose **Save as** or **Save Image as** from the menu. You can also save images as **Desktop wallpaper**. To save a movie or sound clip, click on the link to it and choose **Save Target as** from the mouse menu.

Mass Downloader (http://www.metaproducts.com) integrates into your browser's mouse menu, giving you the option of sending files its way instead. This is ideal for large files as it's faster and can resume broken downloads. It can also scan a page and download all links of your chosen type – handy if you come across a movie archive.

Print a page

To print a page, simply choose "**Print**" from under the File menu. Note the various layout selections on the pop-up print window. To alter the margins, headers and footers, and other details, select **Page Setup**. To view how it will look on a page, select **Print Preview**.

Download entire sites while you sleep

If you'd like to read an online newspaper offline – for example on the train to work – you can set up Internet Explorer to go online while you sleep and download as much of the site as you want (handy if your access or phone charges are less late at night and you'd like to browse a large site during working hours). Just save the site to **Favorites**, choose "**make available offline**", and then click on "Customize" to set how many pages to download and when to grab them. To edit or delete your deliveries, choose "**Synchronize**" from under the Tools menu. The process is called "**Subscribe**" in earlier versions of IE and IE5+ on the Mac.

But if you're serious about ripping the contents from a site, look no further than **Offline Explorer** (http://www.metaproducts.com). You can set it up to extract only certain types and sizes of files, and configure all manner of keyword restrictions in the server and directory names. For example, you could visit a music site before you retire, right-click on the page, choose "download page with offline explorer", set the parameters and wake up to a folder full of MP3s.

Know your browser

Rummage through the far reaches of your menus, buttons and options, and you might think you have a long way to go before you can understand your browser. Well, thankfully, that's not true. Most of the obscure settings can – and should – be left in the default state, and few of the auxiliary features will change your life for the better. Still, it won't do you any harm to gradually investigate the extra powers of your browser, even if only to find out its limitations.

Find something on a page

To search for a word or phrase within a webpage, choose "Find" under the Edit menu, or use the shortcut **Ctrl+F**.

AutoComplete

Apart from suggesting addresses from your History, Internet Explorer can also **suggest form entries** (such as search engine terms, user names and passwords) if you choose to enable **AutoComplete**. You'll find various settings, and the option to delete the current data, by clicking the "AutoComplete" button under the Content tab in Options. To remove an individual entry, select it and hit the Delete key.

Change the text size

To change the size of the text on a webpage, take your pick under "Text Size" in the View menu. Alternatively, try holding down **Ctrl** as you roll the mouse wheel.

Copy and paste

To copy text from webpages, highlight the section, choose "**Copy**" from the Edit or right-click mouse menu (or use the usual shortcut keys), then switch to your word processor, text editor or mail program and select "**Paste**".

chapter 4

Send addresses to a friend

One of the first things you'll want to do online is **share your discoveries** with friends. The simplest way is to copy the site's address into a mail message, along with a note or perhaps a section copied and pasted from the page as described above. Alternatively, you can send a link or **whole page** by choosing "**Send**" from under the **File** menu in Internet Explorer. However, if you send a whole page to someone who uses a mail system that doesn't understand HTML mail (eg Lotus Notes), it will come through as mumbo jumbo.

That's straightforward enough, but what if you want to **send a whole list**? This is one area where Internet Explorer and Netscape differ markedly. Both browsers file addresses into folders for later retrieval, but approach the task from very different angles. Netscape stores them in an HTML file – it's actually a webpage in itself which means you can **put it on the Web**, specify it as your homepage or **attach it to mail** as a single file. Internet Explorer saves each address individually as a shortcut, which makes them less convenient to transfer. To send in bulk, **export** a single folder or the whole list as an HTML file with the **Import/Export Wizard** under the File menu in IE. Then drag and drop the result into an email message like any other attachment (see p.142), and the recipient can either **view it like a webpage** or **import** it into their Favorites.

Send email from a webpage

You'll often come across an invitation to **email someone from a webpage**. It mightn't look like an email address – it might be just a name that contains a link. Whatever, it will be obvious from the context that if you want to contact that person you should click on the link. If you pass your mouse over this link it will read something like: **mailto: someone@somewhere.com**. And then when you click on it, it will call up your mail program, addressing a new message to **someone@somewhere.com**. Just type your message and send it. Any replies will arrive through the normal channels.

If it doesn't work, your **browser/mail combination** isn't set up properly. Before you can send email, you have to complete your email details. You can use any mail program with Internet Explorer. Just choose it from the list under "Programs" in Internet Options. For instructions on setting up mail, see p.126.

Join a newsgroup from the Web

A webpage might **refer you to a newsgroup** for more information. When you click on the link, your newsreader should open in a separate window. You can continue browsing as you wait for the newsgroup subjects to arrive; again you'll need to be set up for Usenet. With Internet Explorer, if you're using any Usenet program other than Outlook Express or Internet Mail and News, you'll have to specify it in Internet Explorer under "Programs". For more on newsgroups, see p.229.

Download files

Most, if not all, your future **file downloads** and **software upgrades** will be initiated by a link from a webpage. Whether the object is stored on a Web or FTP server makes little difference. The file transfer operation can be handled entirely by your Web browser. For more on file transfer, see p.260.

Uncover the source

The smartest way to **learn Web design** is to peek at the raw HTML coding on pages you like. Choose "**Source**" from View or the right-click mouse menu. For more on webpage design, see p.307.

What's related

If you're bored, Internet Explorer can offer you a list of related sites courtesy of **Alexa** (http://www.alexa.com). Click on "**Show Related Links**" under the Tools menu. It looks impressive at first, but power users will get better value by going straight to the search engines and directories (see p.168).

Internet Options

Internet Explorer's main settings lurk under a selection of tabs and buttons in **Internet Options**. You'll find it under the Tools menu in Internet Explorer; by clicking on Internet Options or "Internet" in the Windows Control Panel; or by right-clicking the desktop Internet icon (the big "e") and selecting "Properties". Again, the settings are **laid out differently on the Mac**, but the functions are much the same. Look under "Preferences" in the Edit menu. Before you set about changing everything you can find, beware that the default settings are preferable in most cases. Having said that, there is one thing you'll probably need to change, and that's your **home page**.

Lose the home page

Tired of waiting for a useless page to load every time your open your browser or a browser window? Annoyed that whenever you open Internet Explorer it tries to go online and retrieve this page? If your answer's yes, it's time to get rid of the **home** (start) **page**. Don't worry, you don't need it now, and you won't need it ever again.

You'll find the solution under the General tab in Internet Options. You can change the homepage to any address you like, even one located on your own hard drive. However, **it's better**

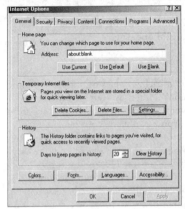

to start with a blank page. That way you don't have to wait for anything to load before you start a Web session, and it won't cause problems when you open your browser while you're offline.

Remove the branding

If your browser came from anywhere but Windows, Apple or Microsoft's website, it's highly probable that the middle party will have added their own touches. Apart from bludgeoning you with their own homepage, Links (p.92) and Favorites (p.92), they might also have **plastered their name and logo** in various places. Don't worry – it's easy to restore IE and Outlook Express (p.124) to their virgin states. Close all programs and at the "Run" command in the Start menu, type this line and click "OK":

rundll32.exe iedkcs32.dll,Clear

If you'd like to slap your very own brand on either program, try the **Internet Appearance Wizards** on X-Setup:

http://www.xteq. com

Stop it trying to connect all the time

If you find your machine trying to connect at inopportune moments, such as when you're reading your mail offline, go to the Connections tab in Internet Options and choose "**Never**

chapter 4

dial a connection". Repairing or reinstalling Internet Explorer (p.114) can sometimes reset this and other options, so be prepared to change it again one day.

Proxy settings

Many ISPs run a server that caches copies of popular websites. If you specify this machine's address as your **proxy server**, it might make browsing faster – because you're downloading from closer to you. The real purpose is not for your benefit, however; it's to reduce traffic across your ISP's links to the Net. But because you're downloading a copy of the site and not the original, it might not be the latest version. Hitting the Refresh button, however, should bring down the page from the source.

Some ISPs won't let you access the Net directly, so specifying the proxy address is compulsory – if you don't enter it, you won't be able to browse at all. If this is the case, ask your ISP for the address and enter it under the **Connection tab** in Internet Options. Select the connection and click on the "Settings" button. If you have a choice, experiment with or without the proxy to see which is faster and more reliable. Proxies tend to get in the way more than they help.

Cookies

A **cookie** is a small file placed on your computer by a Web server as a sort of ID card. This means that next time you drop by, it will know you. Actually, it doesn't quite know it's "you", it only recognizes your individual browser. If you were to visit on another machine or with a different browser on the same machine, it would see you as a different visitor. Or, conversely, if someone else were to use your browser, it couldn't tell the difference.

Most websites routinely **log your visit**. They can tell a few harmless things like which browser you're using, which pages you've requested and the last site you've seen. This is recorded against your IP address. However, because most dial-up users are issued a different IP address each time they log on, this information isn't useful for building individual profiles. If analysts can log this data against a cookie ID instead, they have a better chance of recognizing repeat visitors. Amongst other things, this makes their lives easier when it comes to looking for sponsorship – which means the site has a better chance of staying afloat.

On the next level, if you **voluntarily submit further details**, they can store it in a database against your cookie and use it to do things like tailor the site to your preferences, or save you entering the same data each time you check in. This won't be stored on your computer, so other sites can't access it. And, most importantly, they won't know anything personal about you – not even your email address – unless you tell them.

In IE5 you can choose to block, or be warned before accepting, cookies. Look under the Security tab in Internet Options. You'll need a good reason, though, as it will end up driving you nuts if you're prompted each time someone wants to use a cookie. IE6 has introduced more control over cookies through the **Privacy tab** in Internet Options, which is usually best left

Kill the ads

There are various techniques for avoiding pop-up ads, which admittedly can get very annoying, especially at certain types of sites. One approach is to use cookies to opt out of various major ad networks (http://technoerotica.net/mylog/optouts.html). Another option is to use your Hosts file (http://ssmedia.com /utilities/hosts/), though bear in mind this may slow down your lookup. If you're really angry with the ad people, you may want to invest in a serious plug-in like Pop-up Ad Filter (http://www.meaya.com).

in the default (medium) state. It also lets you delete them under the General tab. For more on cookies, see:

Cookie Central http://www.cookiecentral.com

Censor Web material from kids

It's possible to **bar access to certain sites** that might be on the wrong side of educational. Internet Explorer employs the **PICS** (Platform for Internet Content Selection) system. You can set ratings for language, nudity, sex and violence. Look under the **Content Advisor** settings within the Content tab in Internet Options. If you **forget your password**, you'll need to delete a reg-

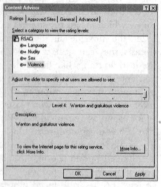

istry key to restore full use of the browser. For instructions, see:

http://www.ieinfosite.co.uk/tip_view.asp?id=16

There are several third-party programs such as Surf-Watch, ImageCensor, Cybersitter and NetNanny, which can impose all sorts of restrictions. None, however, is foolproof or particularly satisfactory. See:

http://www.peacefire.org

http://www.censorware.net

http://www.rsac.org

If you're really concerned about what your children are viewing on the Web, you might do better to spend a few hours each week surfing the Web with them. After all, banning something will only make them want it more.

Hide your tracks

Because your browser records all your online activities, it's easy for someone to find out where you've been spending your time. If you'd like to keep that area of your life private, then, you'd better find out how to hide your tracks. Traces of your online activities are stored in five areas: your **History**; **Address bar**; **Temporary Internet Files**; cookies; and **AutoComplete** entries. Let's examine how to clear them out.

As you know, every site you visit is stored in your **History**. So if you open your History folder you'll instantly see where you've been. More evidence is stored under the **Address bar**. Just click the down arrow on the right-hand side of the bar to reveal a list of recent sites. The contents of those pages are stored in the **Temporary Internet Files**, and it's very likely the sites deposited their own telltale **cookies** in the special cookie folder. Finally, if you've entered anything into a form such as a search engine, double-clicking in that form will reveal a list of previous entries courtesy of **AutoComplete**. So, how do you cover your tracks? You must either delete all these files and records, or ensure they're not recorded in the first place.

You can **delete your Temporary Internet Files, History and Cookies (IE6 only)** under the General tab in Internet Options. Deleting History will also clear the entries from your **Address bar**.

To **clear the Address bar but leave your History intact**, right-click on a blank section of the taskbar at the bottom of your screen and choose "Properties". In Windows ME, go to the Advanced tab and click the "Clear" button. In Windows 98, the Clear button is in the "Documents" menu section. If you'd prefer your browser didn't prompt you with addresses from the History, enforce your preference by clicking the "**AutoComplete**" button under the Content tab in Internet

Options. While you're there, you can clear or disable your **AutoComplete** entries.

To **delete individual sites from your History**, click on the History button, right-click on the entry and choose "delete" from the pop-up menu. To **disable History**, set the "**number of days to keep pages in History**" to zero.

Rather than **disable the saving of Temporary Internet Files**, it's wiser to check the box to "**Empty Temporary Internet Files folder when browser is closed**" under the Advanced tab. Bear in mind this will prevent you from browsing offline, or searching through the contents of your past sessions.

Turn off your multimedia

The drawback of the Web's sights and sounds is the time it takes to download them. If your connection is very slow, there is an option of **not showing images and other multimedia**. Look under the Advanced tab in Internet Options.

While declining images might load pages faster, some pages contain nothing but images with links behind them. If you come across such a page, select the broken image and choose "**Show Image**" from your mouse menu on Explorer, or change your settings and refresh the page.

Installing IE's **Web Accessories pack** will lob an **image toggle switch** on your toolbar. Clicking it will turn images on or off.

ActiveX, Java and plug-ins

Although your browser can recognize a mind-boggling array of multimedia and other file formats, you'll occasionally come across something it can't deal with. Generally, there'll be an icon nearby suggesting you grab a **plug-in** or an **ActiveX control.** If not, you'll see a broken image which, when clicked on, will tell you what you need and where to get it.

A **plug-in** is an auxiliary program that works alongside your browser. You download this program, install it, and your browser will call on it when need be. **ActiveX controls** work similarly, but their scope is far greater. When you arrive at a site that relies on an ActiveX control, it checks to see if you already have it, and (if not) installs it automatically after you approve the publisher's certificate. As a rule, **don't accept certificates unless you're satisfied the publisher is reputable**. ActiveX currently only works in Internet Explorer for Windows. While you can change all manner of permissions under the Security tab in Internet Options, they're best left set to "medium".

Java and JavaScript

When **Java** – Sun Microsystems' vision of a platform-independent programming language – arrived, it was instantly pounced upon by the Web community. What was once a static environment quickly sprang to life with all sorts of "animated" applications thanks to its simple HTML adjunct, **JavaScript**. Java involves downloading and running a small program (called an applet) whereas JavaScript is interpreted by your browser.

Designers can create some cool effects using Java and JavaScript, but if they're not implemented properly they might work inconsistently or even crash your browser. Scripts only tested on Netscape might cause Internet Explorer to crash, and vice versa. It's worse with earlier versions. If scripts frequently cause problems, you probably need to update or repair your browser (see p.114). Alternatively, you could experiment with the settings. Click on the "Custom" button under the Security tab in Internet Options. To revert to the default settings, reset it to "medium".

chapter 4

Shockwave and RealMedia

There are two plug-in/ActiveX controls you'll definitely need: **RealOne Player** (which includes **RealAudio** and **RealVideo**) for online Internet music and video, and **Macromedia's Shockwave and Flash players** for multimedia effects. Whether or not they came with your browser, download the latest free versions from: http://www.real.com, http://www.macromedia.com/shockwave and http://www.macromedia.com/flashplayer

Shockwave and **Flash** have become de facto standards for producing high-impact sites. Used properly, they're welcome, but mostly they get in the way – particularly when you strike lengthy animations on a site's front page. If you're not interested in viewing a tedious animated billboard, hit the "skip intro" link. Who knows – you might even get to the next page without crashing.

Once you have RealAudio, you can **sample CDs** before you buy at online music stores, listen to Internet concerts and tune into live and archived radio broadcasts from all over the world. Although Microsoft's **Media Player** is capable of playing Real

media, it supports only the older standards. So, when you install the **RealPlayer**, make sure it takes over as your default viewer for all Real media. You'll find the option under the RealPlayer's Preferences.

Meanwhile Microsoft is busy pushing its own streaming media standard, which is starting to gain ground. You'll find it on show at: http://www.windowsmedia.com

Media Player also supports the infamous **MP3** audio standard. For an introduction to online music and live Internet broadcasts, see p.283.

Don't buy into the dream that we're living it up in the cyberspace age. We're still struggling in the computing equivalent of the pre-transistor black-and-white TV era. These are very much the early days of mass-market Internet programs. So if you can run your browser for more than a few hours without some kind of strange error, you should consider yourself fortunate. If the glitches are minor or infrequent, don't bust your gut trying to solve them. Life is too short. But, if you're unable to browse, or can't get something to work, turn to the Net for assistance.

Helpful sites

For step-by-step instructions on using or configuring your browser, **refer to the Help menu**. Microsoft provides excellent help, including all manner of troubleshooting wizards. Netscape's is adequate for basic instructions. If you're experiencing frequent errors, search on the error code in:

Microsoft's Knowledge Base http://support.microsoft.com

Unofficial FAQ sites, however, are often more useful. For example, try:

ActiveWin http://www.activewin.com/faq/

IE Infosite http://www.ieinfosite.co.uk

IE Security Center http://www.nwnetworks.com/iesc.html

And, for tips, news and general troubleshooting, try:

CNet http://www.browsers.com

ZDNet http://www.zdnet.com/zdhelp/

Peer support newsgroups

The very best place to seek advice on Internet Explorer, however, is in Microsoft's **peer support newsgroups** (for more on newsgroups, see p.212). You'll find the full set on Microsoft's own public news server at: msnews.microsoft.com

Just start a new account in Outlook Express, or your preferred newsreader, and join any of the groups that look appropriate. You can also browse and post through this Web interface, but it will be slower: http://communities.microsoft.com/newsgroups/

Before you post a question, first search the Usenet archive at **Google Groups** (http://groups.google.com) to see if it's already been answered. Try coining a unique term from the error code or your problem.

While you might strike the odd Microsoft employee in these groups, most participants are volunteers, so be polite and appreciative. You'll no doubt encounter the **MVP** gang (Microsoft Valued Professionals) on your travels. They don't work for Microsoft (officially, anyway), but come with the Microsoft seal of approval. While you might find their cult-like loyalty to Microsoft irksome, you can usually trust their advice. Their personal sites are also good sources of FAQs on Internet Explorer, Windows and other Microsoft products:

MVPs.org http://www.mvps.org/links.html

For help with Netscape, try:

Netscape NUGgies http://help.netscape.com/nuggies/
UFAQ http://www.ufaq.org

Crashes and lockups in Windows

Because Internet Explorer is so tightly woven into Windows, problems with one can affect the other. You'll soon discover that when a browser crash takes out your System tray or freezes your system. It's impossible to give a blanket solution for Internet

Explorer's misbehaviour, but it's usually possible to recover when it stops responding to your mouse clicks. Just give Windows the **three-fingered salute** – hold down the **Ctrl**+**Alt**+**Del** keys. If the "Close Window" dialog box appears, you should be able to restore sanity without rebooting. Select the Internet Explorer entry, click on "End task" and wait a few seconds. Either a window will appear asking if you'd like to close the program, or it will close automatically. If that doesn't help, or you have a phantom screen that won't go away, do the same with the Explorer entry. This normally restores everything to normal – except when Explorer reboots, you'll notice some icons missing from the System tray, including the one to disconnect.

Disconnecting when the icon's missing

To disconnect after an Explorer reboot has removed the icon from the System tray, double-click on your connection shortcut to bring up the connection dialog box. If that doesn't work, open Outlook Express and choose "Work Offline" from the File menu. When it asks if you'd like to hang up your modem, answer "Yes."

Common culprits

The most common cause of Internet Explorer problems is **bad programming** within the browser itself. There's not much you can do about that, except keeping it up-to-date. Unfortunately, problems often arise from the layering of version upon version. This is particularly the case with installing Windows ME over Windows 98. Not only is it preferable to install Windows ME onto a cleanly formatted hard drive, if you install a lot of software your system will run better if you format once a year or so and reinstall everything from scratch. Don't forget to back up first (see p.115).

Next in the line-up is so-called "**spyware**" – software sponsored by advertisements such as the dreaded **Comet Cursor** and **Netsonic**. See p.278 for advice on how to avoid and remove these bugs. But commercial software can be just as meddlesome, and sometimes harder to troubleshoot. Worst of all are the programs that run in the background and promise to accelerate your connection, remove pop-up banners or save passwords. They're closely followed by the "crashguard", disk cleanup and speed utilities. Steer clear, and disable your virus scanner from launching at startup (p.162).

Finally, make sure your **video and sound card drivers** (check the manufacturer's website) are up-to-date, and uninstall any software you don't need – through Add/Remove Programs in the Control Panel only.

AOL and CompuServe browsers

Although AOL's software is Internet Explorer underneath, what it adds over the top tends to get in the road. If its software is playing up on your system, call AOL support for assistance – or switch to a normal ISP. Don't forget to **completely uninstall AOL**; otherwise it could still interfere, whether or not you use its service.

Upgrade, repair and reinstall

If you already have the latest release, updating it won't solve anything. Instead try "**repairing**" or "**reinstalling**" it. If any of the installation files are corrupt, that could involve going online and picking up a few pieces. Prepare to log on, if prompted.

Close all running programs. Open "Add/Remove Programs" in Control Panel, highlight Microsoft Internet Explorer and Internet Tools, and hit the button. You'll see three options. Choose "Repair".

Reboot your computer. Open "Add/Remove Programs" again, and this time uninstall Outlook Express. Reboot again when asked.

Next, go back to the Internet Explorer and Tools entry in "Add/Remove Programs", and this time rather than "Repair" choose "Add a component". Add Outlook Express. Reboot.

If that didn't solve anything, try the "Reinstall" option.

Backing up and transferring your data

If you're moving machines, formatting your hard drive to reinstall Windows or just worried about losing data, you'll need to find all the bits and pieces you've created so that you can restore them. Microsoft, unfortunately, hasn't made this task simple. The most important files and settings to locate are your **Favorites**, **Address book**, **mail store** and **mail account settings**. Here's how:

➡ To **save your Favorites**, choose "Import/Export" from under the File menu in Explorer. Follow the prompts to export them to a Bookmark file on your Desktop, and then move them to a floppy disk or email them to yourself. To import them later, follow the same procedure – except this time you import. You can export your cookies under the same process but it's easy to live without them. It will only mean logging into a couple of sites again so they recognize you.

➡ To **export the Address book**, choose "Export" from under the File menu in Outlook Express and follow the prompts. To import it, choose "Import" in the same way.

➥ The **mail store** could be very large – and unlikely to fit on a floppy – so you'll somehow need to transfer it to a CD burner, second hard drive or a networked machine. To find where it's stored, go to the Maintenance tab under Outlook Express's Options, and click on the "Store folder" button. You'll need to move this entire folder. To restore your mail store, move it into place and assign it as the mail store when you install Outlook Express (or later using the "Store folder" button), or import the messages through the Import under the File menu in Outlook Express.

➥ Your **mail account settings** aren't so important – you can always enter them again. Nonetheless, you can export and import them under "Accounts" in the Tools menu.

A much easier way to back up is to automate the whole procedure with a special utility, which will catch other data such as your mail rules and preferences, and export everything, all as a single file. Test-drive some here:

http://www.ajsystems.com/oexhome.html

http://www.genie-soft.com

http://www.outlook-express-backup.com

For more information on **backing up and restoring mail**, see: http://www.tomsterdam.com/insideoe5/

5

Email
Like regular mail – only better

If you only need one good reason to justify getting online, email should do the trick. Once you get used to corresponding by email, you'll wonder how you lived without it. You'll write more, respond faster, and discover something similar to the joy of old-fashioned letter-writing. But beware – it's easy to get addicted, and because it's so easy to copy (cc) a message to everyone in your address book, you might invite more mail than you can handle …

Why email will change your life

Email is such an improvement on the postal system it will revolutionize the way and the amount you communicate. You can send a message to anyone with an email address anywhere in the world – instantly. In fact, it's so quick that they could receive your message sooner than you could print it.

All you need to do is **type an address**, or choose it from your **email address book**, write a brief note and click **Send**. No letterheads, layout, printing, envelopes, stamps or visiting the post office. And once you're online, your mail program can automatically check in at whatever interval you like. You needn't wait for the postie to arrive. Email arrives 24 hours a day, seven days a week, every day of the year.

Email is also better than faxing. It's always **a local call to anywhere, at any time**. No busy signals, paper jams or failed attempts. Plus you receive the actual text and not a photocopy, or an actual image file and not a scan, which means you can send **high-resolution colour** and **editable documents**. As a matter of fact, each edition of this book has been submitted and edited via email.

Email even **beats the phone** at times. You can send a message to a part of the world that's asleep and have a reply first thing in the morning. No need to synchronize phone calls, be put on hold, speak to voicemail or tell some busybody who's calling. With email, you take the red-carpet route straight through to the top. And you don't have to make small talk – unless that's the purpose of the message.

Replacing the post and fax is not email's only strength. You can also **attach any computer file to a message**. That means you can forward things like advertising layout, scanned images, spreadsheets, assignments, tracks from your latest CD, links to webpages or even programs. And your accompanying message need only be as brief as a note.

What's more, with email **everything you send and receive can be filed** in a relatively small amount of disk space. No filing cabinets, no taped phone calls, no yellowing fax paper. All in writing, and instantly searchable for later reference.

Brief, yet intimate

Out with stuffy business letters, in with email. As email messages are (for the most part) simply text files, there's no need to worry about fonts, letterheads, logos, typesetting, justification, signatures, print resolution or fancy paper. It distils correspondence down to its essence – words – and this encourages people to get to the point, allowing you punch out more letters and deal with more people than ever before. For a rundown of business email etiquette, see: http://www.emailreplies.com

Conversely, email is also putting personal correspondence back into letters rather than phone calls. Most new users remark on this – and the way it often seems to spark off a **surprising intimacy**.

Avoiding viruses

One potential downside of email is that messages can harbour **viruses** (see p.158). However, as long as you take the necessary precautions you're very unlikely to have any problems. If you update Windows with the latest security patches (p.58), the only way you'll catch a virus from email is by clicking on an infected attachment (a file attached to a message). For a rundown on the measures you should take, see p.142.

Choose carefully

Once you have an **email address**, no matter where you roam people can reach you. You might shift house, business, city or country, but your email address need never change. Whether you're **at home**, **at work**, **out shopping** or **on holiday**, if you can get online, you can get your mail (turn to p.151 to find out how). So, take care when choosing your address – it might become your virtual home for years to come.

Your new address

Before you can become a card-carrying member of the Internet generation, you'll need to get yourself an email address. That's no problem, as they're very easy to find. However, before you grab the first one that comes your way, determine which type would suit you best. The main types of accounts you'll strike are **webmail, POP3, IMAP4** and **mail forwarding**. Let's look at the pros and cons of each in turn.

Webmail – usually free and easy, but slow

As the name suggests, webmail accounts work through the Web. Rather than use an email program, you simply **log into a website** to collect, write and send your mail. Your messages are stored on a remote server (a computer belonging to the email provider) until you decide to delete them. That means you can **access all your email, past and present, from any computer with a Web browser** – and no matter what computer you're on you won't need to change any settings. Also, as you can give any details you like when signing up for a webmail account, you can **stay anonymous** (though abusers can still be traced by their IP address).

However, Web accounts have their downsides. First, since you're doing everything online – through the Web – things can become **painfully slow** if you're using a poor connection. And, because your messages are stored online, you'll only be allocated a **specific amount of space**, and once you've filled this you'll have to delete some messages (or download them to a computer) before you can receive any more. Most accounts provide enough space for hundreds of text-only messages, but when people start sending you emails with files attached your quota of megabytes can go pretty quickly. Further, webmail addresses also carry **zero prestige**, so try not to use one as your permanent business address.

Webmail accounts are everywhere, and **usually free**. Just about every major site will give you one in an attempt to get you to return. Usually they're very easy to set up – you simply log in, give a few details and you'll have an account in seconds.

Microsoft's **Hotmail** (http://www.hotmail.com) is the most popular, and is heavily featured with junk-mail detection and automatic virus scanning. However, with their market domination secure, Microsoft have implemented a policy of "freezing" accounts that haven't been used for just thirty days. To "reactivate" you have to sign up again, and you'll lose all your old messages and addresses – and any mail sent to you in this time will be rejected. And unless you pay an annual subscription, this will happen again and again. Furthermore, the free accounts have a measly 2MB storage limit.

So if you do want a webmail account, you'd be well advised to look elsewhere. **MyRealBox** (http://www.myrealbox.com) and **FastMail** (http://www.fastmail.fm), for example, have good reputations for simplicity, speed and reliability. Or, if you'd rather get a more distinctive address, you could try

Another.com (http://www.another.com).

While you can collect webmail with Outlook Express 5+ and Netscape 6+, you'll find it tediously slow to send and receive compared to a POP3 account from an ISP. **If you have your own computer and ISP account, POP3 is the way to go**.

One is never enough

Need an email address that you can keep for as long as you like without paying a penny, or signing up for Internet access? Perhaps you already have one through work, but you'd like an alternative for personal mail – one that your boss can't read. Or you need a second one for junk mail. Or to take on vacation. No problem. You can score one (or more) online within minutes and it needn't cost you a thing, though you might have to suffer a little advertising. For thousands of free email providers, see:
http://www.fepg.net
http://www.emailaddresses.com
http://www.internetemaillist.com

POP3 – a better option

Most ISPs will provide at least one **POP3 email account** with your Internet access. If not, you shouldn't sign up with them. Without getting into the superior technical aspects of the **Post Office Protocol** (POP3), the main distinction as far as you're concerned is that POP3 email is normally handled by a mail program (eg Outlook Express), rather than a browser. Dedicated email programs give you far more power, especially for filing, handling attachments and dealing with large quantities of mail. Still, if you prefer to use a browser, you should also be able to send and receive your POP3 mail through the Web, on any computer, either by visiting the ISP's website or by using **Mail2Web** (http://www.mail2web.com).

The one disadvantage of using a POP3 account from your ISP is that if you ever close your account you'll lose the address. However, you can buy POP3 mail-only accounts, which leave you free to switch ISPs. Ask any ISP, or try a mail specialist such as **NetIdentity** (http://www.netidentity.com).

You can get **free POP3 accounts**, but they're not as common or as good. Apart from being  slower and less reliable, free POP3 accounts usually aren't as convenient, as you normally have to check your mail before you can send – and Outlook Express likes to do it the other way around. The ideal solution is to specify your ISP's SMTP server as the outgoing mail server.

IMAP4

If you like the idea of organizing your mail into folders on a remote server, rather than storing it locally (on your own machine), **IMAP4** might be for you. When you log onto the server with your mail program it will synchronize your computer with the server, and download all the new mail headers (who it's from, the subject, etc). Clicking on the message will download the body, but not delete it from the remote server. The most obvious advantage is you can access your mail archives from different machines. The disadvantage is that it might become a bit cumbersome over a dial-up connection. Ask your ISP if it's available.

Mail forwarding

Perhaps you already have an email address and simply want something funkier. If so, you can get one ending in anything from @struth.com to @donkeylover.com through a forwarding service. What's sent to this address gets redirected to wherever you choose. You're then free to switch providers, while retaining a fixed address. Such addresses are readily available free from such sites as **Mail.com** (http://www.mail.com) and **V3** (http://www.v3.com). Be careful, though, because adding a relay between your incoming mail and your inbox is only going to **slow it down** and expose you to new risks such as outages. So if you take your mail delivery seriously, you won't want to go near these types of accounts.

Your email program

As your **email program** will become the workhorse of your Net kit, you should choose it as carefully as your browser. Still, that need only be one decision – Internet Explorer's **Outlook Express** and Netscape's **Mail** (called **Messenger** in earlier versions) lead the pack by a length and a half. Outlook Express acts like an independent mail program, whereas Mail clings closely to Navigator, and is every bit as buggy.

If it comes down to nitpicking between the two, **Outlook Express** starts quicker, is more stable and handles multiple mail accounts superbly. What's more, **if you have any version of Windows since 98, you already have it**. It even supports Hotmail, treating it like an IMAP server. In fact, if you don't have an email address you can start a Hotmail account on the spot through Accounts in the Tools menu. Not too surprising, this, if you consider that Microsoft owns Hotmail.

Netscape Mail concentrates more on getting the basics perfect than trying to be clever. That means there's never a hitch carrying out simple everyday tasks such as replying to a message or forwarding it to someone else. It also gives you greater hands-on control of your formatting. Outlook Express isn't quite as well-polished in this regard, as we'll explain later. Mail does have some annoying quirks of its own, though, as you'll soon find out: going online to pick up ads isn't its most endearing quality.

Support for multiple accounts, including AOL mail and Netscape webmail, has been added in version 6.

It's not worth trying to mix the browser suites, as neither Outlook Express nor Netscape Mail can be installed without their respective browsers. **So ultimately, if you're browsing with Internet Explorer, use Outlook Express**. Simple as that.

Other mail programs

Microsoft put out various email programs in the early years. **Exchange** (built into Windows 95) was a real stinker and should be avoided at all costs. Yet **Internet Mail & News**, which accompanies IE3, is simple, elegant, and ample for the task if you're strapped for disk space.

More recently, their flagship email program has been **Outlook** (not to be confused with Outlook Express), which ships as part of Microsoft Office. Outlook has seen numerous versions: **97** (part of Office 97 and terrible), **98** (an improved version of 97), **2000** (part of Office 2000) and **2002** (part of Office XP). Compared to Outlook Express, Outlook is more business-orientated and offers various features such as contact, calendar and task-management tools, in addition to some neat features such as mapping and return receipt. However, you can safely get by without this extra bulk.

If you'd prefer a stand-alone non-Microsoft email program, Eudora (http://www.eudora.com) remains the choice option. You can have it for free, but you'll have to view a few ads.

Where to get email programs and tools

If these options can't satisfy your email appetite, you'll find plenty of alternative mail programs and tools at:

DaveCentral http://www.davecentral.com (PC)

Download.com http://www.download.com (Mac and PC)

Hotfiles http://www.hotfiles.com (Mac and PC)

These include utilities for polling your accounts and download-ing just the headers, selectively deleting mail from your server and attaching all sorts of multimedia such as video and voice. You're unlikely to need them, though.

And, for dozens of AppleScripts to enhance **Outlook Express** and **Entourage** on the Mac, see:

AppleScript Central http://www.applescriptcentral.com/paul/

Setting up Outlook Express

Before you can start sending and receiving email using an email program, you'll need to fill in a few **configuration details** for whoever supplied your email account (usually your ISP). Even if this process is automated by a wizard or your ISP's software, take some time to understand your email profile so you can enter it on other machines. For more on email addresses, see p.23.

You might also like to **change a few of the default settings** (see p.128), as they're not always the best for everyone.

Starting a new account

You can't even open Outlook Express 5+ without an account. It simply won't let you. So at some stage, either during the Internet Setup Wizard routine or when you first try to open the mail pro-gram, you'll have to fill in the blanks. Of course, you'll need all the details first. To **start a new account in Outlook Express**, open "Accounts" from the Tools menu, choose "Add Mail" and follow the prompts. To change the settings of an account, select it from the list and choose "Properties". Even if you set it up through a wizard, it wouldn't hurt to go in and check the details.

Let's say you're Anton Lavin and your email address is **anton@leisureprince.com**

Open your settings in any mail program and here's what you'll strike: **Name**: Anton Lavin (Who or what will appear as the sender of your mail.) **Email Address**: anton@leisureprince .com (Where mail you send will appear to come from.) **Return Address**: anton@leisureprince .com (Where replies to your mail will go. Most users opt for their regular email address, but you could divert it to a work account, for example.) **Outgoing Mail (SMTP)**: mail.leisureprince.com (The server to handle your outgoing mail – usually your own provider.) **Incoming Mail (POP3)**: mail.leisureprince.com (Where your mail is stored. This should be the same as the last part of your email address, though often with **pop.** or **mail.** added at the start.) **Account Name**: anton (The first part of your email address.) **Password**: ★★★★★★ (Careful: don't let anyone see you enter this one.)

Adding a second account

You can collect and send from as many accounts as you like through Outlook Express. To add another account, simply click on "Accounts" under the Tools menu, and then "Add Mail". While it's almost impossible to go wrong, there are a couple of options worth checking. Once you've finished, select the account, and choose "Properties". If you'd rather not check this account every time you collect your mail, uncheck the box "include this account when receiving mail or synchronizing". Under the Servers tab, make sure you have the right **outgoing mail server**. This should **match your ISP**, not the provider of the mail account. If you have **more than one ISP account**, under the Connection tab, uncheck the box "always connect to this account using". Otherwise it might drop your connection if you try to collect on the other account.

Options – tweaking the settings

If you leave Outlook Express with its default settings, a couple of features might annoy you. Even if they don't, it's worth going through the various options, checking each and deciding what you'd prefer – you'll inevitably discover lots of things you didn't know about. On the PC, select "Options" from the Tools menu. As ever, **the Mac versions are completely different**, and somewhat cut back on features. Here the settings are located **under "Preferences" in the Edit menu**.

We won't go through all the options here, as they should be pretty self-explanatory. Also, if any items confuse you, you can right-click on the text and click on "**What's This**?" Clear any boxes you accidentally check in the process, and vice versa. It's bound to happen.

The options that cause the most problems are under the **General** tab, in the "Send/Receive" section. If you have a standard dial-up connection, it's best to clear "**Send and Receive messages at Startup**" and "**Check for new messages every x minutes**". Otherwise it will try to go online whenever you have the program open. Instead, send and receive manually (p.130). It's not a big inconvenience. And, unless you use MSN instant messenger (p.255), clear the box "**Automatically log on to MSN**".

Under the **Send tab**, clear the box "Automatically put people I reply to in my address book" unless you think it would suit you. It probably won't.

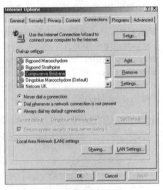

Under the **Connections tab**, make sure "**ask before switching connections**" is checked and "**hang up after sending and receiving**" is cleared (unless you regularly forget to disconnect after sending your mail). Click on the "Change" button under the Internet Connection settings to reach Internet Explorer's connection options. "**Never dial a connection**" is preferable, as otherwise you'll find it trying to go online at inopportune moments – such as when you're reading HTML mail (see p.139) offline.

Email basics

Using email is usually very simple. You don't even have to be online to write, or "**compose**", an email message. Simply open your mail program, start a new message, add an address (either manually or by selecting a name from your address book), add a subject, write the note and then click **Send**.

Send and Receive

In Outlook Express, if you're not already online, your new message will be automatically stored in a folder called the **Outbox**, until you connect to the Internet and click "**Send and Receive**". As well as sending your messages, this will also check for new ones. It's possible, if necessary, to separate sending and receiving under "Send and Receive" in the Tools menu. This is also the place to check for new messages on accounts that don't receive automatically (something you can set up under "Accounts" in the Tools menu).

Other programs

Most mail programs work in a fairly similar way to Outlook Express, but there are some differences. For example, if you're using Netscape Mail and you finish a message but don't want to send it immediately because you're offline, you'll have to choose "Send Later" from the message's File menu. It will then go to the Unsent Messages folder until you go online and choose "Send Unsent Messages" from the File menu. To check for new messages in Netscape Mail, select "Get new Messages" from the File menu.

You have mail!

Incoming mail arrives in the **Inbox** (unless you set "filters" or "Message Rules" to dump it elsewhere; see p.145). When it arrives, you'll hear a sound, get a message and/or see a little envelope in your System Tray. That depends on what you configure in your options (see p.128). You can **change the new mail sound** in Windows under Sounds in the Control Panel.

Offline/Online

If your provider or phone company charges by the minute to stay connected, it's best to **compose and read your mail offline** (when you're not connected by phone). That way, while connected you're actually busy transferring data and getting your money's worth. All email programs allow you to send your messages immediately or place them in a queue, as well as to collect mail at regular intervals or on request.

Unless you're always online, you should choose: **not to send mail immediately**; **to check manually** (not every x minutes); and **not to check for messages at startup**. Otherwise your software will try to send and collect when you're offline. It's best to go online, collect your mail, upload your unsent mail, reply to anything urgent, log off, deal with the rest and send your new bag of letters next time you go online.

If you have **unsent messages** it will ask you if you wish to send them whenever you open or close the program. Choose "**No**" if you're offline.

Messages that haven't been read yet will appear in bold and the **little envelopes next to them will be closed**. Outlook Express helpfully displays a number beside each folder to tell you how many unread messages it contains.

Creating a new email

Open your mail program. Click on the **Create Message** icon on the toolbar, or choose "New Mail Message" from the File menu. You'll see a line starting with **To:**, which is where you type in your **recipient's address**. Internet email addresses should be something along the lines of someone@somewhere where **someone** is the recipient's account name and **somewhere** identifies the server where they collect their mail. It will end in .com, co.uk, .com.au, .net or another domain (p.24).

If you submit a wrongly constructed or a nonexistent address, your message should bounce back to you with an **error message** saying what went wrong. This tends to happen within a matter of minutes. Sometimes, however, mail bounces back after a few days. This usually indicates a physical problem in delivering the mail rather than an addressing error. When it occurs, just send it again.

The address book

Despite first appearances, Internet email addresses aren't so hard to recall. Their name-based components are stacks easier to remember than telephone numbers and street addresses. However, there's no real need to memorize them, nor do you have to type in the whole address every time. Not when you have an **address book**.

Open the address book in Outlook Express from under the Tools menu or by clicking on the book icon. In Netscape Mail it's under the Communicator menu. Start your address book by putting yourself in – simply choose "**New Card**" or "**New Contact**" and fill in the blanks. It's worth spending a few minutes getting familiar with the various options that the address book offers.

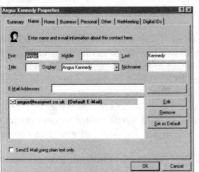

To add an address of someone who has send you a message, simply right-click the message (or Ctrl-click on a Mac) and choose "**Add Sender to Address Book**" from the menu. If the address is already there, it will tell you.

You can **send a message to someone in your address book** in several ways. In Outlook Express, when you have the address book open, you can select the person and click "Send Mail" from "Actions" (on the toolbar or in the Tools menu). Other programs let you **click** or **double-click** on addresses to create new mail, and Netscape **drag and drop addresses** into the **To**: or **CC**: (Carbon Copy) fields of a new message.

Alternatively, you can simply create a new message and start typing the address, name or nickname of the person you want mail. You should only have to enter a few letters before the program finds a match from your address book and suggests the rest. Just be careful it does enter the right address – otherwise it could prove embarrassing.

It's worthwhile experimenting to see which way you prefer. Understanding your address book's capabilities will save you time and tedium in the long run. But the simplest way to address a message is by replying to a previous one.

Sending to more than one person

If you want to send two or more people the same message, you have two options.

When you don't mind if the recipients know who else is receiving it, one address will have to go in the **To**: field, and the other addresses can also go in this field or in the **CC** field.

Put recipients in the **BCC** (**blind carbon copy**) field if you want their names and addresses masked from all others. However, everyone, including those in BCC, can see who the message is addressed and copied to. To send a bulk mailer without disclosing the list, put yourself in the To: field and everyone else in BCC.

If you don't see a BCC option in Outlook Express, open a new message and tick "All Headers" under the View menu.

Send from another account

To send a message from an account other than your main (default) account, simply start a new message, click on the down arrow at the end of the **From:** bar, and select your other account.

The subject

Let your email recipients know what your message is about. Put something meaningful in the **Subject:** heading. It's not so important when they first receive it – they'll probably open it even if it's blank. However, if you send someone your CV and you title it "Hi, dude", two months down the track when they're looking for talent, they'll have a hard time weeding you out of the pile.

Filling in the subject is optional when replying. If you don't enter anything, it will retain the original subject and insert **Re:** before the original subject title to indicate it's a reply.

Replying

Another way to send an email to someone – and probably the way you'll use most – is to **reply to a message** they've sent you. Simply select it and click on the **Reply** button or choose **Reply** from the Message menu (or the right-click mouse menu). You can also choose **Reply all**, which addresses your message not only to the sender but also to all recipients of the original. This can be very useful, but it's not something you'll always want to do.

One great thing about replying is that you can quote from the received mail. When you press Reply, the **original message will appear** – depending on your settings (see box) – with quote tags (**>**) prior to each line, in a different colour or underneath a dotted line. It will also contain the **header** of the original message, detailing the sender, subject and delivery date.

You can **keep parts or the entire original message**, including the subject, or you can delete the lot. So when someone asks you a question or raises a point, you're able to include that section and answer it directly underneath or above. This saves them having to refer back and forth between their message and your answer. It also saves keying in their address.

Don't fall into the habit of including the **entire contents of the original letter** in your reply. It wastes time for the receiver and its logical outcome (letters comprising the whole history of your correspondence) hardly bears thinking about.

You can normally tell if a message is a reply because the **subject will start with "Re:"**.

chapter 5

Setting the quote style

To change the quote style in Outlook Express, go to the Send tab in **Options** (in the Tools menu), and play with the "Mail Sending Formats". Start by setting the Send format as "**Plain Text**" – not all mail programs understand HTML. Then you can select to send HTML on a per-message basis under the Format menu of the new message's window.

Unfortunately, **formatting and wrapping replies** is Outlook Express's biggest shortcoming. Six generations into the program and it still creates orphans (single-word lines) throughout the message, making it look very messy indeed. It also has difficulty indenting some formats of replies with quote tags. Luckily, help is now at hand thanks to the Quotefix add-on (**http://jump .to/oe-quotefix/**), which corrects the problem on the fly. Another little utility, MessageCleaner, lets you tidy up the messages already in your archive (**http://www.roundhillsoftware.com**). It's not an issue with Netscape, nor any other mail program.

Netscape Mail gives a far greater depth of control over reply formatting. Its settings are within "Preferences" under the Messages and Formatting tabs in Mail & Newsgroups.

Forward a message

If you'd like to share an email with someone, just **forward it on**. Forwarded messages are like replies, except they're not addressed to the original sender. You'll have to add the address-es manually. Unfortunately, Outlook Express treats forwarded messages under the same rules as replies. That means if your replies come with quote tags, your forwarded messages will follow suit. It's better to forward them **inline** – that is, **beneath a dotted line**. The only way to switch over in Outlook Express is to re-enter Options. That's quite a pain. Alternatively, you could **forward the message as an attachment**. This isn't a bad option.

To forward, select a message and either select "**Forward**" or "**Forward as an attachment**" from the mouse menu, toolbar, or under the Message menu. The same goes for Messenger, except it differentiates between Forward Quoted and Forward Inline (three cheers!).

You can tell if a message has been forwarded to you because the subject line will start with "**Fwd:**" or "**Fw:**".

Resend a message

There isn't a menu option to resend a message in either Outlook Express or Messenger, so the easiest way to open a message is to right-click it and choose "select all". Then copy and paste the text into a new message and re-enter the subject and recipients.

Signatures and vCards

All mailers let you add your personal touch at the end of your composition in the form of a **signature**. This appears automatically on the bottom of your email, like headed notepaper. It's common practice to put your address, phone number, title and perhaps round off with a recycled witticism. There's nothing to stop you adding a monstrous picture, frame or your

```
   /////\        //|| \\        //\| \\        ///|| \
  /`0-0'`        ` @ @\        //o o//         a a
   ]               >           ) | (          _)
   -               -            -             ~
  John           Paul         George         Ringo
```

initials in ASCII art (pictures made up of text characters). Except you have more taste than that.

To **create and manage your signatures**, click on the Signatures tab in Outlook Express's Options, or under Identity in Netscape Mail's Mail & Newsgroups Preferences.

A **vCard** is an address book entry with as much contact details as you care to disclose. You might like to attach a copy to your mail so your recipients can add it to their address books. To set it up in Outlook Express, edit the "Business card" section under the Compose tab in Options. In Messenger, choose "Edit Card" under Mail & Newsgroups Preferences.

Return receipts

If you'd like to know if your mail has been delivered and/or opened, you could try requesting a "**delivery receipt**" and/or "**read receipt**". Delivery receipts verify that your message has arrived safely on your recipient's mail server, but only if it supports the Delivery Service Notification (DSN) standard. If it doesn't support it, you'll get no reply. Read receipts notify you that your message has been opened. But again, the recipient must be using a mail program that supports the Message Disposition Notification (MDN) standard. Not only that, even if their mail program supports it, when they receive your message a box will pop up asking whether they'd like to acknowledge receipt. If they say no, you'll get no receipt. In other words, it's not a reliable system and really **not worth the bother**.

Still, if you feel like experimenting with it, you can easily enable either or both types in Messenger – on a per-message or per-recipient basis. Outlook Express only supports read receipts. For instructions, search on the keyword "receipt" in Help.

If you're serious about confirmation, you should ask them to reply, send a follow-up, make a phone call or use a third-party confirmation service such as: http://www.itraceyou.com

Rich Text (HTML) and sending Web pages

Not long ago, email was a strictly plain text affair. Microsoft Exchange introduced formatting, but it didn't really make an impact until Netscape introduced **HTML mail** as a new standard. Today, if your mail program lacks HTML support you'll feel a bit out of it. Surprisingly, some still do – so you might get the odd complaint if you habitually send in **Rich Text** (HTML).

HTML mail blurs the distinction between email and the World Wide Web, bringing Web pages right into your email. This means Web publishers, particularly magazines and news broadcasters, can send you regular bulletins formatted as webpages complete with links to further information. It also means you can send webpages by email. Either drag and drop them into a message or choose "Send Page" from under the File menu. Just make sure your recipient also has an HTML-compliant email program; otherwise they'll get all the formatting as a useless and time-wasting attachment.

To **change the font, size or colour of your message** text or add a **background colour, picture or sound**, choose "Rich Text (HTML)" under the Format menu of a new message, and experiment with the various options along the toolbar and under the Format menu.

Although the concept of fancying up your email with **stationery** and a business logo might seem more professional, it's unnecessary and perhaps even inappropriate. It actually detracts from one of email's strongest features – simplicity. So don't spend too much time worrying about the appearance of your email. Just get the words right.

For lessons on using Outlook Express HTML mail and stationery, see: http://lettermanstationery.tripod.com

Your first email

So you've set up your mail account (see p.120) and program (see p.124), and you're ready to send your first email? OK, let's go. The best way to start is to **send yourself some email**. That way you'll get to both send and receive something. If you have a standard dial-up connection, start this exercise offline with your mail program in **offline mode** (click "Work Offline" from the File menu).

1. Open a new message, enter your email address either manually or from the address book (see p.132), give the message a subject, enter something in the body and click **Send**. The message will be placed in a queue to be sent once you go online, or it might try to send it immediately, depending on your program and settings.

2. Now connect to the Net (see p.74). Once you're online (and not before), click on the "Send and Receive" icon on the toolbar to send your outgoing mail and check your server for new incoming mail. Outlook Express will pop up a progress window to tell you what's going on – except on the Mac, where it reports the activity in the bottom right-hand corner.

3. Once you've sent yourself the message keep checking every 30 seconds or so until you receive it. It shouldn't take more than a few minutes.

Find an email address

By far the best way to find out someone's email address is to **ring up and ask.** Don't know their phone number? Then try one of the online phone directories (p.182). Alternatively, if you know where they work, look up their company's webpage.

However, if they fall into the long-lost category, it might be possible to trace them though the Web. You could start by searching **Google** (p.170) for leads; it will help if their name is reasonably unique. You might find their name mentioned somewhere on the Web, and perhaps even their personal website. If not, you could try the people-finding services.

People finders

Your email address should be private unless you instruct someone to list it in a directory or make it public in some other way. Unlike the telephone networks, there are no official public email registries. There are, however, a few independent **people search services** that boast huge email address databases – sometimes combined with street addresses and phone numbers. Unfortunately, you'll find most of the email addresses are out-of-date. Still, if you're trying every angle to locate a long-lost childhood sweetheart, they might be worth a look as a last resort. It mightn't hurt to list yourself, either – that way *they* might find *you*!

Bigfoot http://www.bigfoot.com

Classmates http://www.classmates.com

ICQ Email directory http://www.icq.com/search/email.html

InfoSpace http://www.infospace.com

Internet Address Finder http://www.iaf.net

Switchboard http://www.switchboard.com

WhoWhere http://www.whowhere.com

Yahoo! PeopleSearch http://people.yahoo.com

The people-finding features built into Windows, Mac OS, Outlook Express and Netscape Messenger are supposed to tap into these databases, but rarely work well – if at all. Instead, to query several at once, try:

Copernic http://www.copernic.com

Help

Need to brush up your Net detective skills? See the **FAQ on finding email addresses** (http://www.qucis.queensu.ca/FAQs /email/finding.html) and **Yahoo!'s email search directory** (http://dir.yahoo.com/Reference/Phone_Numbers_and_Addresses /Email_Addresses/)

Attachments

Suppose you want to email something other than just a text message – such as a **word processor document, spreadsheet or an image**. It's a piece of cake. In **Outlook Express,** simply compose a message, click on the paperclip icon or choose "File attachment" from the Insert menu. Then locate the file and click "attach". Or, even simpler, drag and drop the file (or files) from its (their) location into the message window.

Encoding

Well, it's almost that simple. Both parties' mail software needs to support a common encoding standard, otherwise it will appear in gibberish. The most used methods are **MIME** and **UUencode**. MIME is gaining acceptance across all platforms (it's all that Netscape's older mailers recognize), so you'll probably never have to think about encoding. But if you do have problems getting a file to someone, refer to your Help file on how to specify an encoding method. Eudora for Macs includes **Binhex**, **Apple Single** and **Apple Double**. Always choose Apple Double.

If your mail program doesn't automatically decode attachments, ditch it for one that does. It's not worth the bother. Old office systems like early Microsoft Mail and AOL mail are notoriously fussy. And if you're not allowed to use an email program that handles attachments with grace at work, consider getting a new job.

Opening attachments – beware viruses

Before you click on that attachment, consider that it might contain a virus. Ignore the advice on p.158 at your peril.

Big attachments

You shouldn't ever send an attachment of more than a few hundred kilobytes without prior warning or agreement. Large attachments can take ages to download, and even crash, meagre machines. It's no way to make friends.

When they bounce

Servers at both ends can strip or bounce messages, if the size of the attachment exceeds the server's relay limit or if storing it would exceed the mailbox's size limit. If the mail server rejects the attachment, it will normally bounce an error message back to you. You can usually get around mail server restrictions by splitting your messages into smaller chunks. Open "Accounts" under the Tools menu in Outlook Express, and click on the Advanced tab. Check the box to "Break apart messages larger than", and specify an arbitrary size – say, 1000 kilobytes.

To compress or not compress?

If you're sending something large, you can reduce the byte size using a **compression program**. Smaller files take less time to download, so the person on the other end might be thankful. Or, if you're sending a lot of small files, you could bundle them all into one. How you'd go about it depends on the type of file and where it's going.

The most commonly used archive format on the PC is **ZIP** and, on the Mac, **Stuffit** (.SIT). As a rule, **don't send Stuffit files to PC users** – they won't be able to open them without downloading Stuffit Expander, a program they wouldn't otherwise need. Stuffit for the Mac, however, can unzip ZIP files. For more on archiving, see p.273.

There's nothing to be gained, however, by archiving JPEG images, MP3 audio files or any movie formats. They're already compressed. If you're sending an image over about 500 KB, you might consider reducing it by either converting it to a JPEG, resizing it or reducing the quality. It depends whether quality is more important than speed. See p.315 for more on **compressing images for the Web**.

Funny programs that end in .EXE

Before you send that "funny" program or circulated greeting card to a friend, are you sure it's not a virus? Don't forward it on unless you're certain (and likewise, don't open one sent to you). Checking it with a virus scanner isn't enough. See p.157.

How to send a CD track

If you'd like to share a tune from your new CD, try encoding it as an MP3 or Windows Media Format file and attaching it to a message. All your friend will need is an MP3 (or Windows Media) player. For instructions, see p.285.

Faxes and Voicemail

Although thanks to email the days of fax are clearly numbered, not everyone is quite up to speed. So what do you do if your fax is in Houston and you're in Hochow? **Efax** (http://www.efax.com) and **J2** (http://www.j2.com) have the answer. They can allocate you a phone number in the US or UK for free, or in about a hundred cities worldwide for a small charge. Faxes sent to these numbers are converted to email attachments, redirected to your email address or online mailbox, and type can be converted into copyable, editable text by OCR software. Callers can also leave voice messages, which are forwarded as compressed audio files. Sending faxes from your desktop is also a breeze, and the whole thing can even integrate with your mobile Internet toyphone. **So forget fooling around with faxmodem software – this is the way to go.**

Managing your mail

Just as it's a good idea to keep your work desk tidy and deal with paperwork as it arrives, try to keep your email neat. Most programs can organize your correspondence into **mailboxes** or **folders** of some sort, and offer you the option of automatically filing sent mail into a **Sent Mail** folder.

It's good discipline to use several folders for filing your mail (family, work, etc), and to transfer your sent mail into periodic archives. Otherwise you'll create unwieldy, hard-to-open folders containing thousands of messages. Similarly, when you've dealt with mail, either delete it (and empty the Deleted Messages folder regularly) or put it into a topic-specific folder.

Sorting

To **sort your messages** by date, sender, size or subject, click on the bar at the top of each column. Click again to sort in the opposite order. Sorting by date makes the most sense – you can instantly see what's most recent.

Filtering – message rules

Your mail program can **filter** incoming mail into designated folders, either as it arrives or afterwards. It looks for a common phrase in the incoming message, such as the address or subject, and transfers it to somewhere other than the default inbox. This is indispensable if you subscribe to a lot of mailing lists (see p.226) or get a ton of junk office email.

To set up your filters in Outlook Express, open "Message Rules" under the Tools menu. In Messenger, the "Message Filters" are located under the Edit menu.

Tracking replies

Transfer email that needs attention into a special folder until it's dealt with, so you can instantly see what's urgent. Do the same with your Sent box – transfer mail that's awaiting replies.

Alternatively, "**flag**" it for attention. Clicking in the flag column to the left of the sender in the mail folder will toggle a red flag on and off. Click on the top of the flag column to sort the folder, and instantly see what's outstanding.

As email is quick and people tend to deal with it immediately, if you don't get a reply within a few days you'll know you have to follow it up. Once you've received your reply, you can either archive or delete your original outgoing message.

Important – back up your mail

People sometimes forget when backing up essential files on their computer to do the same for their email archive and address book, though losing this data can be catastrophic. For instructions on how to **back up and restore your email**, address book and mail rules, see p.100.

Stop the junk!

If you start receiving piles of unsolicited mail (commonly called **spam**), contrary to popular advice **there's not a lot you can do about it**. You can set up Message Rules (filters) to shuffle them into folders, but it probably won't save you any time. It's just as quick to delete them directly from your inbox.

What's spam?

Unlike most Internet slang, "**spam**" isn't an acronym or abbreviation, nor is there any logical relationship between junk email and spiced meat. According to Net folklore, the word probably came from a Monty Python sketch. On the Internet, "to spam" means to send bulk email to a list gathered by unscrupulous means, or to post (usually commercial) messages inappropriately across multiple newsgroups (p.212). The messages themselves are also called "spam".

What's not spam?

Although some of the mail you receive might be delivered in bulk or seem irrelevant to you, it's not spam if you've granted permission for someone to mail you. For example, you might've given your email address when you registered with a website and checked a box to keep you informed of special deals, or given the OK for them to pass your details onto their partners. This is known as **opt-in** or **permission-based** email. The difference between this and spam is you should be able to get off the list by "**unsubscribing**". If there isn't an unsubscribe instruction within the email, contact the site's support address and demand to get off the list. With genuine spam, however, you can't get off the list, and the return addresses are almost always bogus.

How spammers get your address

The main ways spammers can get your address are: **guessing it**; **harvesting it from the Web, chat or Usenet**; **tricking you into giving it to them through a website**; **or buying it from a mailing list merchant**. Once they have your address, you can be sure they'll try to sell it to someone else. That means once you start receiving the junk, it's not likely to stop. In fact, it will probably get worse.

Prevention – the only cure

So how do you stop it? The short answer is: once it starts, you can't. The best you can do is prevent them from getting your address in the first place.

Guessing is surprisingly common. They simply take a dictionary of names, append it to a list of domains, run a test mailing and perhaps cull any that bounce. So if your address is **john@**

a major ISP, there's not much you can do to stop them. You can, however, prevent them from getting your address through **Usenet, chat** and on the **Web**. Here's how:

1. **Set up a secondary email address** for registering with websites. Never give your main address to any website, unless you're making a credit card purchase or you're sure they're reputable. If you do give your main address, ask **not** to be sent any occasional offers from their "associates".

2. Never post messages to Usenet, or in a chat forum **under your main address**. Either use a fictitious alias, your secondary account or mask your real address (see p.232).

3. Don't enter your main email address in **competitions** or hand it out at **trade shows**. Use a separate account.

4. Don't use your main email address when logging into **FTP sites**.

5. Don't **register software** under your main address. Use your secondary account.

Setting filters

If you feel like trying to beat them at their game, make a new mail folder called "**Junk Mail**", and experiment with filters ("**Message Rules**" under the Tools menu) to redirect emails containing typical spam words within the message or address. It won't take you long to spot them, but you'll find it impossible to catch them all.

Complaining

Spammers know they're **detested**, but that doesn't bother them. It's a numbers game. They know there'll always be **someone stupid enough to send them money**. There's no point replying or asking to be taken off their list. They rarely use a valid email address, and if they do it's normally shut down almost instantly. Few ISPs will tolerate people spamming from their services. For that reason, the normal course of action is to complain to their ISP and the owners of any of the open mail relays involved. Don't expect them to thank you, though – you won't be alone in complaining. The easiest way is through **SpamCop** (http://www.spamcop.net), which can automatically pick through the fake headers and send off the complaint on your behalf. For more on the war against spam, see:

Cauce http://www.cauce.org

SpamCon http://www.spamcon.org

Whew http://www.stop-spammers.org

Email on the run

One of the really great things about email is that it's easy to pick up your messages wherever you are. And not just if you use a Web-based email account – there are various ways to pick up your POP3 mail too. The first thing you should know is that **your email address does not tie you to your ISP**. While your mail may be stored on your ISP's server, you needn't dial into your ISP to access it. All you need to do is get online through any means – at a **cybercafé**, a **friend's house** or even via a **WAP phone** – and access the server through the Net.

Through the Web

The simplest way to collect and receive your mail on someone else's machine is to use a Web interface. That means you won't have to go near their email program or configure anything. Of course, this is how you always use webmail accounts

such as Hotmail, so nothing changes there.

Many ISPs have a Web-based email interface on their website. You simply visit their site, find the email section, log in and you'll be able to read, compose and send messages. AOL users, for example, should visit: **http://www.aol.com/netmail/**

Even if your ISP doesn't offer this service, you should be able to access your POP3 or IMAP mail through **Mail2Web** (**http://www.mail2web.com**). Just enter your **long email address★** and password to collect and send your mail on the fly. There's no need to set up an account. Unless you choose to delete messages, they'll still be there next time you collect. That means you'll have to download your entire mailbox (headers only) afresh whenever you collect. If you like to keep a record of your outgoing mail, don't forget to CC yourself (see p.134), so you can file it later when you get back to your own machine. Just move the message from your Inbox to your Sent folder.

★ Your long email address is your mail account name @ your incoming mail server name. For example, the long email email address of **angus@easynet.co.uk** is **angus@mail.easynet.co.uk** (**mail.easynet.co.uk** is the incoming mail server address).

You can also configure some Web-based email accounts to collect your POP3 mail and retain the headers in your mailbox. With Hotmail, for example, you can choose, when setting up, whether to delete the messages from the server at the point of collection. It will also store your outgoing mail in the Sent folder. When you return to your machine, you can synchronize the Hotmail account with Outlook Express and file the messages into your usual archives. However, Hotmail is a much slower interface than Mail2Web. Of course, if you have temporary problems with HotMail, you can always switch to Mail2Web. The messages will still be there next time you check in with Hotmail.

Through a WAP phone

Your phone dealer should be able to show you how to send and receive email through your **WAP phone**. For example, you can read and reply to your POP3 mail through Mail2Wap:

Mail2Wap http://www.mail2wap.com

Use someone else's mail program

To collect mail using an email program on **another computer**, you need to set up a new account with your details (see p.126). Enter your **user name**, your **incoming mail server** address and your **password** when prompted. To send email you also need to enter your **identity** (who you want your mail to appear to have come from) and your **return address** (your email address). Although you can sometimes use your regular **outgoing mail server address if you collect your mail first**, you'll get a faster response if you use the one maintained by the ISP through which you're dialling. So if the machine you're using has one set, leave it be. Don't forget to delete your mail from both the Inbox and Sent items folder when you're finished; otherwise someone else might read it.

Through a portable

If you're **taking your computer with you**, it's doubly easy to collect your POP3 mail. You mightn't even have to change your mail settings – only your dial-up configuration and perhaps your outgoing mail server. If your connection's slow or difficult, you can **configure your mail program** to download the first kilobyte or so of each message and then select which you want to read. Alternatively, if your mail server supports **IMAP4** (see p.123), you can download just the headers. So, when you're up in a plane paying 14 cents per second to download at 2400 bps, you can leave all those massive mail-list digests for later. In such situations you'll also be thankful if you **maintain an alternative address for priority mail**. For tips on connecting your computer away from home, see p.48.

Through Telnet

Some universities and workplaces don't maintain POP3 mail accounts. If that applies to you, you might have to use **Telnet** to log in. Once you get over the indignity of not being able to point and click, it's not so bad. You can access Telnet in Windows by opening "Run" on the Start menu and typing: telnet

Collecting this way will involve logging into your mail server over the Net, supplying identification and typing commands into a UNIX mail program. **You can also read your POP3 email by Telnetting to your mail server** on port 110 (you'll have to add this in manually in Windows). Enter user, then your user name, separated by a space, and press Enter. Then do the same with pass and your password, and type list to view a list of all your messages. To read messages selectively, type retr followed by the message's number. This is also the best way to collect mail when you're operating over a **very low bandwidth**, under poor conditions, or are limited by software – for example, with a palmtop. Ask your ISP or systems manager for further instructions.

Privacy

Occasionally, when sending mail or joining a discussion (p.197), you might prefer to **conceal your identity** – for example, to avoid embarrassment in health issues. There are three main ways to send mail anonymously. As mentioned earlier (p.105), **web-mail** is one.

The second might seem less ethical. You can **change your configuration** so that it looks like it's coming from somebody else, either real or fictitious. If anyone tries to reply, their mail will attempt to go to that alias, not you. But be warned: it's possible to trace the header details back to your server, if someone's eager – and your national law enforcement agency might be exactly that if you're up to no good.

The third way is to have your IP address masked by a third party, such as an **anonymous remailer**. This can be almost impossible to trace. See:

http://www.andrebacard.com/remail.html

http://www.anonymizer.com

http://www.xganon.com

Snoopers – your boss could be one

Although there's been a lot of fuss about hacking and Net security, in practice email is potentially more secure than your phone or post. In fact, most new-generation email programs (including Outlook Express and Netscape Mail) have some kind of **encryption** built in. But it's not hackers who are most likely to read your mail – it's whoever has access to your incoming mail server and, of course, anyone with access to your computer. If it happens to be at work, then you can **assume your boss can read your mail**. In some companies it's standard practice, so don't use your work mail for correspondence that could land you in hot water. Instead, set up a private account and don't store your messages on your work machine. You can collect and send your POP3 mail from a Web interface (see p.151), or set up a free webmail account – the most private being **HushMail** (http://www.hushmail.com), which offers secure storage and encrypted messaging between users.

If you're serious about privacy, you may want to investigate **PGP (Pretty Good Privacy)**, a powerful method of encryption, which generates a set of public and private "keys" from a passphrase. You distribute the public key and keep the private key secure. When someone wants to send you a private message, they scramble it using your public key. You then use the private key, or your secret passphrase, to decode it. For more about PGP and other security add-ons, see: http://www.pgpi.org and http://www.slipstick.com/addins/security.htm/

Find out who's having an affair in your office

Want the hot gossip on who's seeing who in your workplace, who's looking for a new job, or who's talking about you behind your back? Get drunk with your office's mail server administrator. It'll make you think twice about what you send in future.

Digital signing and encryption

Internet Explorer, Netscape Communicator and their associated mailers already support emerging encryption and digital signing standards – but few use them.

Digital signing proves your identity via a third-party certificate. Here's how to get yours. First up, fetch a personal certificate from Verisign (http://www.verisign.com). You can't go wrong if you follow the instructions. Once it's installed, open your mail security settings and see that the certificate is activated. You may choose to sign all your messages digitally by default, or individually. Then send a secure message to all your regular email partners, telling them to install your certificate. Those with secure mailers can add your certificate against your entry in their address books. From then on, they'll be able to verify that mail that says it's from you is indeed from you. Don't use it flippantly, though, because **it's a pain for your recipients**.

Encryption works similarly, though you'll also need your email partners' certificates to encrypt messages to them. Also, as each certificate only works on one installation, you'll need a different one for work and home. This makes it a bit cumbersome if you're collecting mail on the road. It also means anyone with access to your machine could pretend they're you.

Yes, it's all a bit flaky at this stage. So spend a few minutes in your Help file figuring out the finer details, try it with your friends and decide among yourselves whether it's worth the bother.

Help

If you're frustrated with Outlook Express or Netscape Messenger, you'll find help on the same Web and Newsgroup circuits as their respective browsers (see p.111). Just follow the links. Again, the best place to find help with Outlook Express and Outlook is on the Microsoft support groups (see p.112). For tutorials, bug fixes and FAQs on Outlook Express and Outlook, try:

Outlook Express FAQ http://www.tomsterdam.com/insideoe5/faqs/
Outlook FAQ http://www.slipstick.com/outlook/faq.htm/

6

Play it safe
Now, not later

Picture this: you receive an email from your best friend, with an attachment demanding "You have to see this!" Because you trust them, you open it without a second thought. Nothing unusual happens. A few days later you notice that all is not well, and some of your documents won't open. Your friend says they had the same problem, which turned out to be caused by a virus – a new strain that your virus software didn't detect. After many frustrating hours, you manage to update your virus software and remove the infection. The damage, however, has already been done, and your computer can't be restored without technical knowledge. The easiest solution is to wipe your hard drive and reinstall everything from scratch.

Sounds extreme doesn't it? Regrettably it's not, and if you don't understand how viruses spread **you stand a very high**

chance of being infected. The first thing to know is that anti-virus programs might not protect you. In fact they often cause more problems than they solve. However, as long as you adhere to the few simple rules laid out in this section, it shouldn't be an issue.

The bad guys

Let's start by examining the various threats lurking beyond your network connection, and then set out a strategy to protect you against them.

Viruses

A **virus** is a program that infects other program files or floppy-disk boot sectors, so that it can spread from machine to machine. In order to catch a virus you must either run an infected program (possibly without your knowledge) or boot your machine with an infected floppy disk inserted fully into the drive. There are thousands of strains, most of which are no more than a nuisance, but some are capable of setting off a time bomb that could destroy the contents of your hard drive. A **macro virus** spreads by infecting Microsoft Word or Excel documents.

Worms

Worms, like viruses, are designed to spread. But rather than wait for an earthling to transfer the infected file or disk, they actively replicate themselves over a network such as the Internet. They might send themselves to all the contacts in your email address book, for example. That means worms can spread much faster than viruses. The "**email viruses**" that have made world news in recent years were, strictly speaking, worms – not viruses.

Trojans

A **Trojan (horse)** is a program with a hidden agenda. When you run the program it will do something unexpected, usually without your knowledge. While viruses are designed to spread, Trojans are usually (though not always)

designed to deliver a one-off pay packet. There are dozens of known Trojans circulating the Net, most with the express purpose of opening a back door to your computer to allow hackers into your system while you're online. A custom-built Trojan can be bound to any program, so that when you install it the Trojan will also install in the background. For a sobering insight into the power they can hand over to even the most inexperienced hackers, see: **http://www.sub7files.com**

Hackers

The term **hacker** is something of a fuzzy expression amongst the computerati (**http://www.happyhacker.org/define.shtml**). The popular definition is the one that concerns us here: someone who wants to break into, or meddle with, your computer. They might be a professional out to steal your secrets or a "script kiddy" playing with a prefab Trojan. They might be a vandal, a spy, a thief or simply just exploring. As far as you're concerned it doesn't matter. You don't want them, or their handiwork, inside your computer.

chapter 6

Marketeers

People who want to sell you something – or sell information about you – might be more annoying than threatening, but it won't take long before they get on your goat. Unless you keep your contact details to yourself, your inbox will receive an unstoppable flood of junk mail, and you can never be sure what information is being gathered about you by programs that "**phone home**" (see Spyware on p.261).

Get protected

Contrary to popular belief, antivirus software isn't the answer. While you should still install a virus scanner, it's more important to understand how viruses work and use caution (and an up-to-date system) as your first line of defence. Here's how:

Rule one – think before opening attachments
Assuming your system is presently clean and up-to-date, the only way you can be attacked by a virus or hacker is to introduce a program onto your computer. The obvious points of entry are floppy disks and installation CDs, but these are far less of a risk than in previous years.

The single most risky thing you can do is to open files attached to emails (p.126). The same, of course, applies to files attached to other forms of communication such as Instant Messaging, Chat and Usenet. **Unless you're 100**

percent certain that an attachment is safe, even if it's from your best friend, DON'T OPEN IT! Instead save it to your Desktop or a quarantine folder, and examine it carefully before proceeding (see p.164).

Treat the **gag programs** and **animated cards** that tend to circulate around the festive season with utmost caution. These are some of the favourite vehicles of Trojan distributors.

If everyone followed this basic rule, it would stop almost all viruses, worms and Trojans in their tracks, but if you don't trust yourself to act with due caution, you may want to investigate Script Sentry (http://www.jasons-toolbox.com).

Rule two – stay up-to-date
Rather than perfect their products before release, Microsoft and other software publishers prefer to rush out their programs and fight the ensuing security fires in the form of "patches" and "service releases". If you don't apply these minor software upgrades, you're prone to whatever blunder they've puttied over. For example, the version of Outlook Express (5.0) that shipped with Windows 98 Second Edition can be infected by the KAK worm, an email-borne virus that spreads simply by highlighting the message. But if you upgrade Outlook Express, or apply the appropriate security release from Windows Update, you'll be safe. For instructions on how to stay up-to-date, see pp.71 and 166.

Incidentally, if you receive a message that **contains an ActiveX control**, tell the sender they probably have the **KAK worm**. Scanning and cleaning isn't enough, as they could easily reinfect themselves. They'll need to update their browser first, and then run a virus scanner or KAK cleaner such as: http://www.getvirushelp.com

Rule three – don't run Office macros
The "macros" used to automate tasks in Microsoft Word and Excel are programs that can contain viruses. And more often than not that's all they do contain. So, as a rule, never accept to run a **macro** unless the creator assures you've put it in for a good reason. If you use **Microsoft Office**, read the security advice at: http://officeupdate.microsoft.com/Focus/Articles/virusres.htm

Rule four – go to the source

If someone sends you a program, script or registry patch (.REG or .INF) by email, **ditch it and ask them to send you a link to the source instead**. Only download directly from the software publisher or through a reputable file repository, such as those listed on p.265. If the source looks unprofessional, tread carefully.

Rule five – as a last resort, scan

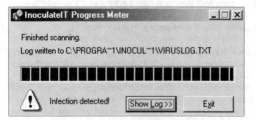

Before you open any incoming file, whether or not it looks safe, scan it with a virus checker (look under the right-click menu). It will only take a few seconds. However, don't put too much faith in the results, especially if it's out-of-date. Most scanners will pick up viruses, but their record with Trojan horses isn't so hot. Naturally, you'll need to install a virus scanner first. Try **AVG** (http://www.grisoft.com). It's as good as any, and free. New PCs typically come with McAfee's VirusScan or Norton AntiVirus. They're supposedly the best in the field, but often cause more problems than they solve, especially when left to run in the background (real-time protection). Instead, switch them off and simply scan all new arrivals. Most importantly, though, **don't forget to keep the signature file up-to-date** – check in every week or two. Refer to the help file for instructions.

If you suspect you're infected, and you have neither a scanner or the time to install one, visit http://housecall.antivirus.com to get an online diagnosis.

Or, if you suspect a program might contain a Trojan, try scanning it with **The Cleaner** (http://www.moosoft.com).

Rule six – become invisible with a firewall

As a line of defence against hackers, install a security firewall. For
PCs you need look no fur-
ther than the excellent, and
free, **ZoneAlarm**
(http://www.zonelabs.com).
It will let you choose which
programs can access the
Net and effectively make
your PC invisible to out-
siders – thus protecting you
against inquisitive hackers
and Trojans that open
remote-control back doors
into your computer. Don't
stop to think about it. Just
do it.

Windows XP has its own
built-in firewall feature; to
activate it, right-click your connection's icon in the Network
Connections folder and select "Properties". Under the Advanced
tab, check the "Firewall" box and click "OK".

Rule seven – beware "spyware"

Protect your privacy and prevent crashes by avoiding software that
is supported by advertisements or which tracks your movements.
ZoneAlarm (see above) can help by telling you if a program is trying to "phone home"; **Ad-aware** (http://www.lavasoft.de) can
remove the bugs left behind after uninstalling. For more on so-
called "Spyware", see pp.264 and 278.

Rule eight – go undercover

Don't feel guilty about giving an alias when you download software or register at a website. It won't upset the company's statis-
tical records, but it will offer you a buffer of privacy and reduce
your junk mail. Simply set up an alternative email address (see
p.122).

Rule nine – don't forward virus warnings
Although there are plenty of real concerns out there, any email
that insists you forward it on to "everyone you know" is almost
certainly a hoax. Do us all a favour and break the chain.
See: http://www.vmyths.com and http://www.urbanlegends.com

How to examine an attachment

Any program entering your computer is a risk until proven
otherwise. So to protect yourself, you'll need to learn how to
recognize danger.

Windows uses "**file extensions**" to distinguish between various types of files. These come at the end of the file name. For
example, Microsoft Word creates documents that end in: **.DOC**

A file ending in **.JPG** is a JPEG image, while one ending in
.EXE is an executable, the most common type of program file.
You should be able to tell whether a file is a program simply by
looking at its file extension.

To make computing seem simpler for newbies, Windows hides
file extensions by default. It would be wise to change this, however. Set all your folders to "Details view" and **unhide all the
hidden files and extensions** as follows. Double-click on My
Computer. Choose "Details" under the View menu. Go to the
View tab under "Folder Options" in the Tools menu. Tick
"Show hidden files and folders" and clear the tick from "Hide
file extensions for known file types". Then click on either "Like
Current Folder" or "Apply to All Folders" to make these your
default folder settings.

Alternatively, if you like your extensions hidden, create a new
folder on the Desktop to quarantine incoming files and apply
these changes to it alone.

Good attachments, bad attachments

Most attachments aren't capable of carrying viruses. The trouble is that you have to be able to pick the odd one that can. The following (and most commonly attached) file types are always safe:

Plain text (.TXT)
Images (.JPG, .GIF, .BMP, .TIF, .WMF)
Movies (.AVI, .MPG, .MOV, .WMV)
Portable documents (.PDF)

Warning –
don't be fooled by fake extensions

Before you click on that attachment that appears to be a safe music, movie, image or document file, **check the icon** that comes with it. Is it the right one for that type of file? If not, you might find a long series of spaces inserted between the fake extension and the real one, for example:

Read this message.TXT   .PIF (The real extension is **.PIF**).

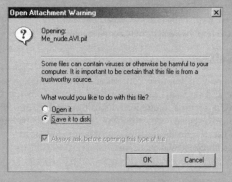

Always double-check: it's the way most viruses spread.

Audio (.MP3, .WAV, .WMF)
Internet Shortcuts (.URL)
Email and Web pages (.EML, .HTM, .HTML) are normally safe. Though it's possible to wreak havoc with scripts, it's not something to worry about.

The following file types are **highly suspect and should never be opened** unless you're certain they're safe: .BAT, .COM, .EXE, .INF, .JS, .JSE, .PIF, .REG, .SCR, .SHS, .VBE, .VBS, .WSF and .WSH.

More on viruses

Some ISPs automatically scan your mail attachments for viruses. It's another factor to consider when shopping around for a provider. To see what's presently top of the virus pops, check the scanning stats at: http://www.star.net.uk

You'll find everything you need to know about viruses at:

About.com http://antivirus.about.com

Alt.comp.virus FAQs http://www.faqs.org/faqs/computer-virus/

Computer Associates http://www.cai.com/virusinfo/

Symantec http://www.symantec.com/avcenter/

Play Catchup

A good way to improve your security, keep your software up-to-date and find any adware on your system is to use **CNet's CatchUp service**. Download a small program from their site, and once installed, each time you return you'll be presented with a list of relevant updates available for download.

CatchUp http://catchup.cnet.com

7

Find it

Without losing your mind

T he art of **finding something** pinned up on the world's biggest scrapboard is, without doubt, **the most valuable skill** you can glean from your time online. If you know how to use the Net to find an answer to almost anything quickly and comprehensively, you'd have to consider yourself not only useful, but pretty saleable too. Most people, including many Net veterans, simply **bumble their way around**. Yet it's a remarkably basic skill to master. So read this section, then get online and start investigating. Within an hour or two you'll be milking the Net for all it's worth.

How it works

The Net is massive. Just the Web alone houses around three billion pages of text, and many millions more are added daily. So you'll need some serious help if you want to find something.

Thankfully there's a wide selection of **search tools** to make the task relatively painless. The job usually entails keying your **search terms** into a form on a webpage and waiting a few seconds for the results.

Over the next few pages, we'll introduce you to search tools that can locate almost anything: on the Web; linked to from the Web; or archived into an online Web database, such as email addresses, phone numbers, program locations, newsgroup articles and news clippings. Of course, first it has to be put online and public access granted. So just because you can access US government servers doesn't mean you'll find a file on DEA Operative Presley's whereabouts.

Your weapons

There are three main types of Web search tools: **search engines**, **hand-built subject directories** and **search agents**. Apart from the odd newspaper archive, they're usually free. Because they're so useful and popular, a few years ago there was a trend towards tacking other services onto the side and building so-called **portals**, **communities** and **hubs**. More recently, that trend has begun to reverse, with the launch of several skeletal search tools free of fancy overheads. Irrespective of which you use, ignore the quantity of froufrou and concentrate on the quality of the results. The next few pages discuss each category in detail and show you how to torture them for answers.

Search engines

The best way to find just about anything online is to start with a **search engine**. The good thing about search engines is they can search through the **actual contents** of webpages (and file servers), not just descriptions. The better search engines can riffle through **billions of webpages** in a fraction of a second. You simply go to the search engine's website and submit **keywords** – search terms to you and I. It will query its database and, almost instantly, return a list of results or "**hits**". For example, if you were to search on the expression "Rough Guides", here's what might come up on top:

Rough Guides Travel
ROUGH GUIDES.COM features online coverage of thousands of travel destinations, plus music reviews of every genre. Read our text ...
Description: travel and music guide publishers; includes an online guide to destinations throughout the world,...
Category: Recreation > Travel > Publications > Magazines and Ezines
www.roughguides.com/ - 24k - 24 Jun 2002 - Cached - Similar pages

In this case the top line tells us the name of the page or site, and it's followed by some text excerpted from the page and some more info including a description and the page's address. If it suits, click on the link to visit the site.

Tip: Don't just click on a result then hit the Back button if it's no good. Instead, run down the list and open the most promising candidates in new browser windows. It will save you tons of time, as you can read one while the others are loading. Do this by holding down the **Shift key** as you click (or the **Apple key** on Macs), or by using the right-click mouse menu.

The reason it's so quick is that **you're not actually searching billions of webpages**. You're searching a **database** of webpage extracts stored on the search engine's server. This database is compiled by a program that periodically "crawls" around the Web looking for new or changed pages. Because of the sheer size of the Net and a few factors relating to site design, it's not possible for the crawlers to find every site, let alone every word on every page. Nor is it possible to keep the database completely up-to-date. That means you can't literally "search the Web";

you can only search a snapshot taken by a search engine. So, naturally, different search engines will give you different results depending on how much of the Web they've found, how often they update, how much text they extract from each page and how well they actually work.

So, which search engine?

There are dozens of search engines, but only a few are worth trying. In fact, you'll rarely need more than one. But, since you'll be using it often, make sure it's up to speed. You'll want the **biggest, freshest database**. You'll want to **fine-tune your search** with extra commands. And you'll want the most hits you can get on one page with the most **relevant results on top**. Right now, that's **Google**:

Google http://www.google.com

This completely free service has an uncanny knack of getting it right in the first few hits, both from within its search engine database and through  its association with the **Open Directory** (see p.177). It also provides access to **"caches"** of pages that have disappeared since its crawl, or are otherwise unavailable. This is great when you can't get a link to load. Click on "cached" under a search result to see how this works.

If Google falls short, try **All the Web** and **AltaVista**. They're also big, fast, clutter-free and can deliver lots of relevant hits:

All the Web http://www.alltheweb.com

AltaVista http://www.av.com

As for the rest? Just because an engine isn't the biggest or best doesn't mean it's worthless. Even the smallest engines can find unique hits. Still, unless you're after extra hits, you're unlikely to need them. They might improve, of course:

Excite http://www.excite.com

HotBot http://www.hotbot.com

Lycos http://www.lycos.com

If you notice some engines give identical or very similar results, it might be because they share technologies. **HotBot** and **MSN**, for example, currently use the **Inktomi** system, and **AOL** have recently licensed Google's technology.

But if you seriously need **more results**, rather than visit several engines in turn, query them simultaneously using an agent such as **Copernic** (see p.180). You can tell how each engine ranks from the results. For more detailed analysis, see:

Search Engine Showdown http://www.searchenginesshowdown.com

Search Engine Watch http://www.searchenginewatch.com

Search Engine World http://www.searchengineworld.com

Search Lore http://www.searchlore.org

These sites keep tabs on all the finer details such as who owns what, how they tick and who's currently biggest – essential reading for budding webmasters. They also report on technologies that are in the pipeline. To see what Google are experimenting with, go straight to the source:

Google Labs http://labs.google.com

Limitations

Search engines aren't the be-all and end-all of what's on the Web. **They're only as good as their most recent findings**, which might be just a small proportion of what's actually there – and which could be months old. So, just because you can't find it through a Web search doesn't mean it's not there. If you're after something brand-new, for instance, they're not always the best choice. You might be better off searching **Usenet** (see p.229) or a news service.

How to use a search engine

OK – this is important. Get searching right and your whole relationship with the Internet will improve tenfold. The trick is to think up a **search term** that's unique enough to get rid of junk results, but broad enough not to miss anything useful. It will depend entirely on the subject, so be prepared to think laterally.

A typical search

Let's start with a complex example. Suppose we want to search for something on the esteemed author **Angus Kennedy**. Let's see how you'd do it in most of the major search engines.

A few years ago, if you entered **angus kennedy** you would get a list of pages that contained the words "angus" or "kennedy", or both. Fine, but it meant you'd get loads of pages about Angus cattle and JFK. These days most search engines will automatically look for pages containing **both words**.

Unfortunately, though, there's no guarantee that they'll be next to each other. What we really want is to **treat them as a phrase**. A simple way to do this is to enclose the words within quotes, like this: **"angus kennedy"**

Now we've captured all instances of Angus Kennedy as a phrase, but since it's **a person's name** we should look for **Kennedy, Angus** as well. However, we want to see pages that contain either of these terms, rather than only those that contain both. We usually do this by inserting an upper-case "OR" between the terms (or, at All the Web, by inserting the terms in brackets). So let's try **"angus** kennedy" OR "kennedy angus"

You may have noticed that we left out the comma of "kennedy, angus", and that we haven't bothered using capital letters. This is because most search engines ignore such details.

By now we should have quite a few relevant results, but they're bound to be mixed up with lots of irrelevant ones. So we should narrow the search down further and exclude some of the excess, such as pages that contain a different person with the same name.

Our target writes books about French literature, so let's start by getting rid of that pesky Rough Guide author. To **exclude a term**, place a **minus sign** ("-") in front of it. Let's ditch him, then: "angus kennedy" OR "kennedy, angus" -"rough guide"

Know your engine

That's about all you need to know in most instances. However, there are exceptions to these rules, so you might have to adjust your search terms slightly, depending on the engine, to get the best results. There are still search engines, for example, that require you to use a **plus sign** ("+") to state that the page must contain a word (eg +angus +kennedy). The same applies to online stores, encyclopedias, newspaper archives and anything else you can search.

So at some point it's worth reading the instructions. You should find a link to a "FAQ", "Search Tips" or "Help" section on the front page. A few minutes' study could save hours of weeding through poor results.

Observe how the engine interprets **capitals**, **dashes** between words, **brackets**, **wild cards**, **truncations** and **Boolean operators** such as AND, OR, NEAR and NOT.

Also watch out for "**stop words**". These are words that are normally ignored. In Google, for example, common words like "the" and "it" are not included in your search unless they're part of a phrase (eg **"the beatles"**). If you really want to include a common word in a non-phrase search, place a plus sign in front of it (eg **+the beatles**).

Advanced searches

Any decent search engine will offer you a whole range of advanced tools. For example, you could look for only those pages that include your search term in their **titles**, **URLs** or **domain names**; pages written in a **specific language**; files with a particular **file format**; or pages **updated within a certain time frame**, such as within the last year. These are very valuable – once you've used them, you'll wonder how you ever found anything before.

Certain engines put some of these tools on **dropdown menus** on the search homepage, but for a full list look for an "**advanced search**" link. These tools can also usually be accessed using codes in your search – in Google, for example, entering **"Jimmy White" site:bbc.co.uk** would bring up pages from **http://www.bbc.co.uk** that contained everyone's favourite snooker star. This is extremely useful considering how many sites have poor internal search engines.

> **Tip:** You'll be using your favourite engines often, so drop their addresses onto your browser's **Links** bar (see p.92). But, rather than save the front page, favour the "Advanced search" page, which will feature a wide assortment of boxes for fine-tuning.

Results per page

There's nothing more annoying than getting loads of results from a Web search but only being shown ten of them per page, which is the default for many search engines. In the advanced search options you should find a "results per page" option, and some engines allow you to **set a new default**. At Google, for example, click on "Preferences", selected your preferred options from the lists, and they will be stored in your cookies.

Translations

If your results include foreign-language sites, Google and AltaVista can **translate them** (albeit pretty roughly) into English or a different language. Just click on "translate".

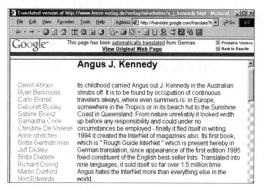

Seaching for images

Some major search engines, including AltaVista and Google, now offer **image-specific searches**, which can prove very handy. However, they are far less reliable than text searches because of the way that pictures are named and so on. So just because a photo of you doesn't appear when you tap your name into an image search, it doesn't mean you're not adorning a webpage somewhere. Try running a normal search too, and browse the hits for relevant photos.

> **Tip:** If you want instant access to Google, you could download the **Google Toolbar** and put all the search engine's advanced features close at hand. That way you can do Web, Usenet and image seaches immediately, without having to go to Google's homepage first. Some other sites offer similar tools. However, beware that browser add-ons can make your computer more likely to crash, and always check the privacy small print, to be sure you're not installing spyware (see pp.264 and 278).

Can't find it?

Just because search engines can't find something doesn't mean it's not on the Web. It just means their trawlers haven't visited that site yet. Which means you'll have to turn to another, maybe fresher, source. Read on.

Subject directories

It's sometimes more useful to browse a range of sites within a topic or region rather than throw darts at the entire Web. For this you should turn to a **subject directory**. These aren't compiled by machines trawling the Web; **they're put together by human beings**. Everything is neatly filed under various categories, like a phone directory or library, making it easy for you to drill down to what you're after. This is particularly useful if you're looking for a listing of services in an area – your home town, say.

You usually have the choice of browsing directories by **subject group** and sometimes by other criteria such as **entry date** or **rating**. Often you can search the directory itself through a form, rather like a search engine. Unlike search engines, directories don't keep the contents of webpages but instead record titles, categories and sometimes comments or reviews, so adjust your search strategy accordingly. Start with broad terms and work down until you hit the reviews.

General directories

The Internet doesn't have an official directory, but it does have several broadly focused listings that will help you on your way to most subject areas. The **best general directories** are:

About.com http://www.about.com

Open Directory http://dmoz.org

Yahoo! http://www.yahoo.com

Yahoo! is the closest the Net has to a central directory. If the Web had seven wonders, it would probably be the first. Apart from the massive site directory, it also has loads of added extras such as national and metropolitan directories, regional TV listings, weather reports, kids' guides, seniors' guides, Yellow Pages, sport scores, plus outstanding news and financial services. You should spend at least one session online exploring its reaches. Chances are you'll be back there every day. If you're located outside the USA, or looking for country-specific information, then switch to the relevant regional guide, if available. For example:

Yahoo! Asia http://asia.yahoo.com

Yahoo! Australia & NZ http://www.yahoo.com.au

Yahoo! Canada http://www.yahoo.ca

Yahoo UK & Ireland http://www.yahoo.co.uk

The Open Directory is a relatively recent project, though it has grown at an alarming rate. It's compiled by tens of thousands of volunteers and served through several sites including Google. While it lacks Yahoo!'s armada of added services, its directory is better maintained in many areas. It pays to look at both.

About.com deserves a special mention because, unlike most broad directories, its topics are presented by expert guides. This makes it an excellent jumping-off point. If you like this approach, **Suite101** (http://www.suite101.com) attempts the same sort of thing.

There's no shortage of alternatives. These might prove useful if the above fail, such as:

AltaVista http://www.av.com

Excite http://www.excite.com

LookSmart http://www.looksmart.com

Lycos http://www.lycos.com

But broad subject directories aren't always the best at digging up everything within a category or giving you expert guidance. For that you need a specialist directory – or, as the suits call them, **vortals**.

Specialists

Whatever your interest, you can bet your favourite finger it will have several dedicated sites and another that keeps track of them all. Such **specialized directories** are a boon for finding new, esoteric or local interest pages – ones that the major directories overlook. How do you find a specialist directory? You could go straight to Google with a very specific search, but in this case it would make more sense to seek a helping hand. Try **About.com** first. It maintains specialist directories on most common interests. Next try **Yahoo!** and the **Open Directory**. If there's more than a couple of Web directories on the subject, they'll put them in their own section. You might also glean something from consulting a directory that specializes in listing specialist directories, such as:

Complete Planet http://www.completeplanet.com
Directory Guide http://www.directoryguide.com
GoGettem http://www.gogettem.com
Search Bug http://www.searchbug.com
Search Engine Guide http://www.searchengineguide.com
Search IQ http://www.searchiq.com
Webdata http://www.webdata.com

Specialist sites often maintain a **mailing list** to keep you posted with news and, in some cases, run **discussion lists** or

bulletin boards so you can discuss issues with other visitors. If you feel you can contribute to the site, just email the webmaster. That's how the Web community works. You'll find hundreds of specialist sites throughout our Web guide (see p.331).

Search agents

Search agents, or **searchbots**, gather information live from a limited number of sites – for example, to find new information, to compare prices or stock, or combine the results from several search engines. **Shopping agents** (p.212) like Shopper.com scan online stores for the best deals.

"**Metasearch**" sites that query multiple search engines and directories simultaneously – such as Metacrawler, Vivisimo,

Dogpile, Mamma and Ixquick – are close to useless. You will get better results, faster, by going directly to Google.

You'll find the same goes for the bewildering layers of **search aids built into Internet Explorer** and the **Windows Start menu**. These make a search form appear on the left-hand side of your browser. Clicking "Customize" lets you choose from an impressive array of search engines, directories, email databases, maps and more – but though it looks promising you'll probably get better value at the source. Similarly, only use Apple's metasearch agent, **Sherlock**, if you feel you need a handicap.

But all is not lost. For serious research, try **Copernic** (http://www.copernic.com). It's a stand-alone program that can query hundreds of search engines, directories, Usenet archives, shops and

email databases at once. It filters out the duplicates, displays the results on a single page in your browser, and even retrieves them automatically for offline browsing.

There are also dozens of ways to monitor search engines, individual sites and newsgroups for changes. For example, **Spyonit** (http://www.spyonit.com) can notify you by email, pager, SMS or ICQ whenever your search term comes up on an auction, TV listing, directory or search engine. And **Tracerlock** (http://www.tracerlock.com) will let you know when your keywords come up on AltaVista, Usenet or the online personals.

For more on searchbots, see **BotSpot** (http://bots.internet.com).

Finding stuff

General search engines and directories are great, but they don't always strike gold first time. As you get more familiar with the run of the Net, you'll gravitate towards specialist sites and directories that index more than just webpages, add their own content and shine in specific areas. What's best depends largely on what you're after. When you find a useful site, **store it in your Favorites or Bookmarks** so you can return. Here's how to:

Find someone's email address

Not as simple as you might think. See p.140.

Find local information

You'll sometimes want to find sites that cater to a very specific region. Say, for example, you want to look up film screenings across your city, or select a honeymoon suite in Tamanrasset. Although it might seem logical to use a local search engine to find local sites or information, it's often not the most efficient method. **Always start your searches with Google** and then move on if that fails. Most small local search engines simply aren't very good.

Directories, however, can be another matter. Try Yahoo! and the Open Directory and see what's listed in the region. Your target location might be filed under the country, state or province rather than the town or suburb, so start broad and then drill down from there. You should soon find the major specialist directories relevant to your region. For a directory of regional directories, see:

Search Engine Colossus http://www.searchenginecolossus.com

Find a local business or phone number

While online residential and business telephone directories can be kept more current than their paper equivalents, they're not usually as easy to browse. Apart from the phone companies' offerings, you'll also find a raft of private directories in competition. Some even deliver a book as well. If you haven't been exposed to their advertising, don't expect too much. Investigate a few of the major services listed below and see what they offer in your area, and keep your eye out for advertisements in your local press. They should come looking for you, not vice versa.

Australia
CitySearch http://www.citysearch.com.au
White Pages http://www.whitepages.com.au
Yellow pages http://www.yellowpages.com.au

United Kingdom
192 Enquiries http://www.192enquiries.com
192.com http://www.192.com
BT PhoneNet http://www.bt.com/directory-enquiries/
Scoot http://www.scoot.co.uk
Yellow Pages http://www.yell.co.uk

USA & Canada
Anywho http://www.anywho.com
CitySearch http://www.citysearch.com
Infospace http://www.infospace.com
SuperPages.com http://www.superpages.com
Switchboard http://www.switchboard.com

To find a phone number in almost any country:
World Pages International Directories http://global.wpz.com

Find answers to the most common questions

Where else would you look for answers to the most Frequently Asked Questions than **the repository for Usenet FAQs**? If the answer's not in **http://www.faqs.org**, try Usenet itself (see p.229).

Find out what others think on Usenet

There's no better place to find opinions and personal experiences than **Usenet** (see p.226), but there's a lot of text to scan. Although it's sorted into subject bundles, if you had to find every instance of discussion about something, it could take you days. And, if it was tossed around more than a couple of weeks ago, the thread might have expired.

With **Google Groups** (http://groups.google.com), however, not only can you scan close to all Usenet now, but two decades of its history as well. You can pursue entire threads and profile each contributor. Which means you can follow a whole discussion, as well as check out who's who and how well they're respected. On top of that, you can identify which groups are most likely to discuss something, join them and even post messages once registered. You'll get to the bottom of even the most obscure subject.

Find computer help

Enter a couple of unique phrases from your error or computer problem in Google Groups. Try a normal Web search, too. If your question isn't answered, join a relevant newsgroup and post it there. See also the Computer section of our Web guide (p.353).

Find games, hints and cheats

Try one of the big games sites such as **Games Domain**, **Gamespot** or **Happy Puppy**, which are listed along with many others in our Web guide games section (see p.383). Alternatively, search Usenet as explained above. Stuck on a level? Look for a walkthrough, or ask in Usenet. Alternatively, try a file-sharing network (see p.293).

Find a product review or an online shop

See our Shopping chapter (p.193).

Find product support

Whenever you purchase something – especially electrical goods – see if the company has a website offering **follow-up support** and **product news**. If it's not on the accompanying literature, try putting the company's name between **www** and **.com**. If that doesn't work, use a search engine to look for it. Most companies offer some kind of online product support and registration, but if you want advice from other users go to Usenet.

Find the latest news, weather, finance, sport, etc

Apart from hundreds of newspapers and magazines, the Net carries several large **news-clipping archives** assembled from all sorts of sources. Naturally there's an overwhelming amount of technology news, but also an increasing number of services dedicated to what you would normally find on the newsstands – and it's often fresher on the Net. They occasionally charge, though usually only for archives.

For pointers, check our Web guide under News, Fashion, Finance, Weather and so forth (see p.334). The best place to start would be **Moreover** (http://www.moreover.com), where you can search or browse headlines from thousands of newsfeeds and then link to the story. **Yahoo! Daily News** (http://dailynews.yahoo.com) is also good.

Find out about a film or TV show

See our Film & TV site guide (p.368) or try the entertainment section of any major directory for leads to specialist sites. The **Internet Movie Database**, for example, is exceptionally comprehensive and linked to Amazon in case you're tempted to order the video.

Find the latest software

See our Download Software chapter (p.260).

Find new and interesting websites

Try one of the numerous sites dedicated to listing, ranking or reporting sites that are new, "cool" or popular. For lists, picks and weblogs, see p.333.

Find health support

Start by searching the Web. Try Yahoo! for listings of organizations and so forth, and then Google for mentions on webpages. Chances are they'll refer you to useful mailing lists and discussion groups. If not, try Google Groups to see if – and in which groups – your target subject is being discussed on Usenet. Ultimately, though, you'd probably be best to join a mailing list.

Find a mailing list

The best place to find mailing lists is through a well-worded Web search (that includes "mailing list" and the topic), or through the small-list directories at:

PAML http://www.paml.net

List Universe http://www.list-universe.com

Liszt http://www.liszt.com

If that's not satisfactory, try Google Groups and check the FAQs from groups with hits.

Find something you've forgotten

Don't give up if you can't remember where you saw that hot tip last week. Just open Internet Explorer's History and search your cached pages (see p.94). So long as it hasn't been deleted, you should even be able to recall it offline.

Find advice

If all else fails – and that's pretty unlikely – you can always turn to someone else for help. Use Google Groups to find the most appropriate newsgroup(s). Summarize your quest in the subject heading, keep your message concise, post, and you should get an answer or three within a few days. Alternatively, try a mailing list or one of the "expert" advice services (some free, some not), such as:

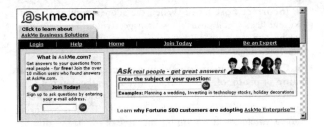

Abuzz http://www.abuzz.com
AllExperts http://www.allexperts.com
AskMe.com http://www.askme.com
Google Answers http://answers.google.com
LiveAdvice http://www.liveadvice.com

Finding the right Web address

It won't be long before you come across a **Web link or address that won't work**. It's very common and usually not too hard to get around. Many of the addresses in this book will be wrong by the time you try them – not because we're hopeless; just because they change. That's the way of the Net. The most useful thing we can do is show you how to find the correct address.

Error codes

When something goes wrong, your browser will **display a page with an error message** – or nothing will happen, no matter what you try. To identify the source of the problem, get familiar with the various types of errors. Different browsers and servers will return different error messages, but they'll indicate the same things. Here are the most common errors:

➥ **Incorrect host name**. When the address points to a non-existent host, you'll probably get a page saying, "The page cannot be displayed" or "DNS lookup error". Test this by keying: http://www.rufgide.com

➥ **Illegal domain name**. When you specify an **illegal host name** or **protocol** – for example, if you miss the dots out of an address – your browser may alert you to the problem, or it might simply say, "This page cannot be displayed". Try this by keying http://wwwrufguide. If you simply miss one of the slashes after the http: (eg http:/www.ibm.com), Internet Explorer should automatically detect and correct the error.

➥ **File not found – 404 error**. If the file (the bit of the address after the last slash) **has moved**, **changed name** or you've overlooked **capitalization**, the server will tell you the file doesn't exist, or send you back to the front page. It differs between servers. Test this by keying a valid address with a bogus path, such as: http://www.bbc.com/bogus/ and http://www.cnn.com/bogus/

➥ **Request timeout**. If it's taking too long to retrieve a page, the operation may be terminated. It's worth trying again when this happens, as it might just be that the site was temporarily busy.

➥ **Not authorized to view this page**. Some sites, or files within sites, require a password to be accessed, or can only be reached if you're on a certain server – for example, within that company.

➥ **Busy host or host refuses entry**. Occasionally you won't succeed because the site's server is either overloaded with traffic or temporarily (or permanently) off limits. This sometimes happens when a site is heavily promoted or makes the news.

Locate the problem

Now that you're on speaking terms with your browser, you're set to troubleshoot that problem address. First check your **connection** by trying another site, like: http://www.yahoo.com

If that works, you know it's not your connection, and you can continue try to locate the correct address (see p.190). However, if you can't connect to any website, **close and then reopen your browser**. It might only be a software glitch. Otherwise, it's most likely a problem with your Net connection or proxy server (if you're using one).

Check your mail. If that fails, log off then back on. Check it again. If your mailer connects and reports your mail status normally, you know that the connection between you and your ISP is OK. But there still could be a problem between it and the Net or with your proxy server. Check you have the right proxy settings and, if so, disable them (see p.104). If it still doesn't work, **ring your ISP** and see if there's a problem at their end or diagnose it yourself.

To do this, test a known host – say, www.yahoo.com – with a **network tool** such as **Ping**, **TraceRoute** or **NetMedic** (see p.82). If this fails, either your provider's connection to the Net is down or there's a problem with your **Domain Name Server**. Get on the phone and sort it out.

If you've verified that all connections are open but your browser still won't find any addresses, then the problem must lie with your **browser setup**. Check its settings and reinstall it if necessary.

When a page won't display

You'll sometimes find a page or frame inside a page instantly comes up blank. You can tell your browser hasn't tried to fetch the page because it happens too quickly. In this case hit the

"**Refresh**" button. If that doesn't work, reboot your browser and re-enter the address. Failing that, open your "Internet Options" and clear your Temporary Internet Files or browser cache. Finally, if you're still having problems and it appears to be related to Internet Explorer security – such as the acceptance of an ActiveX control at an online banking site – check your security settings within Internet Options, disable **Content Advisor** and consider adding the site to your Trusted Sites.

When one address won't work

If only **one address fails**, you know the address is wrong or the site has server problems. Now that you're familiar with error messages, you can deduce the source and fix that address.

Web addresses disappear and change all the time, often because the address has been simplified – for example, from http://www.netflux.com/~test/New_Book/htm to http://www.newbook.com

Sometimes they'll leave a **link to the new page** from the old address, but that too might be out-of-date. Since the Web is in a constant state of construction, just about everything is a test site in transit to something bigger and more glorious. And, when a site gets serious, it might change hosts and discard the old address.

If you're convinced the address is fine, then **try it later** – perhaps even days later. The site might be down for maintenance or experiencing local problems. If you can reach it on another machine but not yours, the problem might lie with your Windows Hosts file – especially if you've ever installed any browser acceleration software. If so, first get rid of the offending program properly through the "Add/Remove" applet in the Windows Control Panel. Then locate the file called **Hosts** in your Windows folder. It will have no file extension. Open it with Notepad and remove any lines not starting with **#** except for the **localhost** entry. Save the file and exit.

Finding that elusive address

The error messages will provide the most helpful clues for **tracking elusive addresses**. If the problem comes from the host name, try **adding or removing the www part**. For example, instead of typing **http://roughguides.com**, try **http://www.roughguides.com**. Other than that you can only guess. It may only be that the host is busy, refusing entry or not connecting, so **try again later**.

If you **can connect to the host but the file isn't there**, there are a few further tricks to try. Check capitalization, for instance: **book.htm** instead of **Book.htm** Or try **changing the file name extension** from .htm to .html or vice versa (if applicable). Then try **removing the file name** and then each subsequent directory up the path until finally you're left with just the host name. For example:

http://www.roughguides.com/old/Book.htm
http://www.roughguides.com/old/book.htm
http://www.roughguides.com/old/book.html
http://www.roughguides.com/old/
http://www.roughguides.com

In each case, if you succeed in connecting, try to locate your page from whatever links appear.

May the search engine be with you

If you haven't succeeded, there's still hope. Try **submitting the problematic address into Google**, and you may find that, though the actual page is no longer available, you can still access Google's cached copy.

If that doesn't work, you could try searching in the relevant demain for a keyword from the name of the file or from what you expect the file to contain. So, continuing the above example, you could search with Google for: **Book.htm site:roughguides.com**

Also remember that you can use a search engine to look only within URLs (addresses). So if the elusive file has an unusual name, let's say **worldcupstats.html**, you could search the Web for URLs contain that term. At Google you would enter: **allinurl: worldcupstats.html**

Get sidetracked

If everything else fails, try searching on related subjects, or scanning through relevant sections of **Yahoo!** or the **Open Directory**. By this stage, even if you haven't found your original target, you've probably discovered half a dozen similar (if not more interesting) pages, and in the process figured out how to navigate the Net more effectively.

8

Shopping
Have your credit card handy

Welcome to the world's biggest bazaar. Whether you're after a ticket to the **monster trucking safari** (http://www.ticketmaster.com) or a **midget tourist submarine** (http://www.ussubs.com), just step right up and click.

So is it merely catalogue mail order made complicated by computers? Sometimes, maybe, but that's only part of the story. The Net hasn't entirely killed off catalogues just yet, but it already blitzes them in many ways. To start with it's interactive, not static. That means you can sift large inventories in seconds, and get the latest information – be it new releases, stock levels or recommendations based on your tastes. So, if you're shopping for music, for example, you could plough through a performer's entire back catalogue, listening to samples as you read what other customers have to say about each album. Plus you can **visit several stores in different parts of the world all at once**, simply by opening multiple browser windows. Or send a search engine to forage for the best prices or availability across hundreds of shops simultaneously. Catalogues don't even come close.

But **you might be concerned that it's unsafe**. Fair enough, but you needn't worry too much. As long as you follow the advice here you'll find it's considerably less risky than the offline world.

Pros and cons

The Net isn't as neatly arranged as your average shopping centre, but it does offer some advantages – particularly when you can't find something as cheaply locally (if at all). Nonetheless, while you can't rule anything out completely, some products are definitely more suited to selling online. **Books** and **CDs**, for example, fit the bill because you can sample and read reviews before you buy. If you don't like your purchase, too, you can return it for a refund (and you won't have blown your life savings if you can't be bothered). Clothes, on the other hand, are much trickier. You might squeeze by on generics like jeans and T-shirts, but anything that requires trying on will cause problems. While you can always return them if they don't fit, it's a hassle involving extra postage costs and monetary risk.

In essence, the Net isn't suitable if: you need to examine the goods; the weight or size makes shipping too costly; they can't deliver in time; or it costs more without being more convenient. **So, just because you're on the Net doesn't mean you'll never have to leave the house again.**

Shop safe

Without wishing to scare you unduly, beware that sharks do lurk out there. Not that many, but certainly enough to keep you on your toes. Contrary to the popular notion, the biggest threat isn't some young hacker sneaking off with your card number – they mostly only break into sites to show off. In the unlikely chance one does get your number, they probably won't even use it. Besides, **there are far easier ways to nab your credit details**. Like getting a part-time job in a shop, for instance.

On the other hand, with **organized online crime** on the rise it's not impossible that your card details could fall into the wrong hands and be used in an unauthorized transaction. Of course, regardless of whether you use credit online, you should always check your statement each month and report any discrepancies to your issuer immediately.

Still, you should be more concerned with con artists running seemingly legitimate sites or approaching you by unsolicited email. Ignore the following warnings at your own peril:

➡ If anything at all seems fishy, don't shop there.

➡ If a site hasn't gone to the effort of registering its own domain name, then don't expect it to be professional in any other way. **Merchants using free servers like Geocities should be regarded as classified ads** rather than shops. And regard any business operating out of a collective shopping mall as a **market stall**.

➡ **Never deal with a site that doesn't give a street address** and phone number. An email address isn't enough. And a free email address, like Hotmail, spells trouble. Mind you, failure to display a phone number doesn't make them instantly dodgy. It's an all-too-common omission on even the best-known sites. And some, such as Amazon, bury their contact details at the bottom of a help file. **Feel free to abuse them about it**. Tell them we sent you.

➡ Any site or email that uses **LOADS OF BOLD UPPER CASE TEXT** isn't to be trusted.

➡ Always **switch to a secure connection** when modifying your account details or checking out. When a connection becomes secure, the beginning of the address will change from **http://** to **https://** and a closed lock will appear in the bottom bar of your browser. If a shop doesn't offer secure purchasing, it's not serious about its online presence. Shop elsewhere, or phone through your order. **Never send your credit card details by email**.

➡ To make an online purchase you should only need to provide your name, billing address, delivery address, credit card number, account name, expiry date and shipping preferences. **You should never need any other form of identification** such as your social security, health insurance, driving licence, savings account or passport number.

➡ The **username/password combination** you choose for a site applies to that site only. Never give it to another site, or to anyone by email or phone. Avoid using the same combination at every site, and especially don't use your mail or dial-up connection password.

➡ **Don't respond to spam** (unsolicited email; see p.147). Those "get paid to surf", "stock tips", "work from home", "recruit new members", "clear your credit rating" and various network-marketing schemes **are** too good to be true. It should go without saying that ringing a number to claim a prize will only cost you money.

➡ Read this government bulletin before following **investment advice** found online, whether on the Web or through a newsletter. See: http://www.sec.gov/investor/pubs/cyberfraud.htm/

➡ **Don't install free browser or mouse cursor enhancements** – including so-called Web accelerators – or let any site make itself your "homepage". They're only interested in collecting marketing data. Your browser is fine just the way it is.

➤ Avoid any site that pops up a new window when you try to leave, or spawns multiple windows. Don't deal with, or download software from, any site that seems to consist of top lists of other sites, which in turn point you to more lists. These are merely trying to milk click-through referrals. It mightn't cost you anything, but it wastes your time.

➤ It has to be said: **almost all online scams revolve around porn sites.** More than is let on, because their victims are often too embarrassed to own up. **Don't pass over your credit details to adult sites unless you're prepared to be stung**. And whatever you do, don't download any connection software, picture viewers or browser add-ons from adult sites. These have been known to drop your line and redial somewhere like Vanuatu, racking up a massive phone bill in the process. If you must delve in porn, go and wallow in the binary newsgroups.

➤ Consider giving your money to charity rather than an **online casino**.

➤ Never accept **ActiveX controls** unless you're absolutely positive they're from a reputable firm.

➤ Beware free trials and **subscription services** that require your credit details – such as AOL. You might find it harder to cancel than you anticipated. Or they might bill you whether you use the service or not. Check your bill carefully each month for discrepancies, and make sure the subscription doesn't renew itself automatically.

➤ Don't believe everything you read. As much as the Net is the greatest source of consumer advice, it's also **a great source of misinformation**. Look for a second opinion before you fork out cash on the basis of a recommendation.

➤ And don't forget: **keep a record of your order**, so you can balance it against your bank statement.

Are you covered?

Credit and debit cards provide varying degrees of **protection against fraud**. You'll need to read the fine print on your agreement for specifics, but normally you're only liable for a set amount. You also might be able to pay a yearly surcharge to fully protect your card against fraud. Ask your bank, along with what to do if you suspect you've been wrongly charged. Some sites also offer to pick up the balance if you can show they're at fault.

Help

For more advice and information on online fraud, see:

WWW.CYBERCRIME.GOV

Computer Crime and Intellectual Property Section (CCIPS) of the Criminal Division of the U.S. Department of Justice

CyberCrime http://www.cybercrime.gov
Cyber Criminals http://www.ccmostwanted.com
Fraud Bureau http://www.fraudbureau.com
Internet Fraud Complaint Ctr https://www.ifccfbi.gov
Scambusters http://www.scambusters.com

Know your product

Whether you're buying online or off, the Net is an invaluable mine of consumer advice. However, consumer written reviews can often be more anecdotal than scientific, and somewhat prone to rigging. So while you can't take it all at face value, the more you know, the better your chance of a happy purchase. Usenet (p.229) is often the best place to ask advice, but search **Google Groups** (http://groups.google.com) first to see if it's already been discussed. For buying guides, customer opinions, ratings and product reviews, try:

Amazon http://www.amazon.com

Ciao http://www.ciao.com (UK, EUR)
Consumer Guide http://www.consumerguide.com
Consumer Reports http://www.consumerreports.org
Consumer Review http://www.consumerreview.com
Consumer Search http://www.consumersearch.com
Dooyoo http://www.dooyoo.com (UK, EUR)
Epinions http://www.epinions.com
eSmarts http://www.esmarts.com
Rateitall.com http://www.rateitall.com
Review Board http://www.reviewboard.com

You could also query Yahoo!, the Open Directory or a search engine to locate trade magazines or sites that specialize in your desired product category. Such as:

Computers http://www.zdnet.com
Digital Cameras http://www.dpreview.com
Gadgets http://www.the-gadgeteer.com
Hi-fi http://www.audioreview.com

Or perhaps try one of the consumer organizations, like:

Choice http://www.choice.com.au (AUS)
Consumers Int. http://www.consumersinternational.org (INT)
Which? http://www.which.net (UK)

These can also alert you to problem products and recalls, as will:

Recall Announcements http://www.recallannouncements.com (INT)
Product Recalls http://www.recalls.gov.au (AUS)

But if you need hands-on experience you should examine the goods in a shop first, and then check whether you can get a better deal online.

Buying foreign

With the entire Net at your fingertips, you're empowered to shop the world. And placing an order with a foreign store should be no harder than doing it locally, especially if you're paying by credit card. But it does require a little more effort on the vendor's part, and certain products aren't suitable for export – the result being that many stores, particularly in the US, won't accept foreign orders. You can usually find this out fairly quickly by looking up the store's shipping and handling section.

Before you leap on a bargain, **ensure it will work at home**. Phone or power plugs can be adapted quickly, but if the conversion involves something complex like replacing a power transformer, question if it's worth the effort. Other things that may differ between countries include: DVD region codes; console games; TV and video devices (check whether they're PAL or NTSC); PC keyboard layouts; software editions; and, of course, anything where measurements could cause confusion – such as recipes, clothing and space exploration vehicles.

Finally, when applicable, ask if it's covered by an **international warranty**, whether spares are available locally, where you'd have to send it for repairs and who's responsible for shipping.

But is it really a steal?

Sure, you can save money by shopping abroad, but if saving cash is your primary motive you'll need to do your figures carefully. To start with you'll need to work out what it costs in your own currency. Call your bank for the going foreign exchange rate less transaction charges, and compare it with the wholesale rate at **http://quote.yahoo.com**. Then you'll be able to work it out in future.

Next, balance the shipping costs against transit time. Heavy items will naturally cost more, and cheaper shipping options will take longer. How long can you wait? If you need it pronto, you'd better check they have it in stock.

And, not least, the **sticky issue of tax**. The ideal scenario is to buy duty-free and have it arrive untaxed by local customs. That can happen, but it will depend on the countries involved, the nature of the product, what it's worth and whether anyone can be bothered to chase it up. The US is the most complex situation due to its state taxes. Technically you should be able to buy duty-free between states as long as the shop doesn't have an office in your home state. If you need more info on your tax laws, call your local post office or customs helpdesk. Or if you live in the UK, US or Australia, try unpicking some sense from this lot:

Australian Customs http://www.customs.gov.au
HM Customs & Excise http://www.hmce.gov.uk
US Customs http://www.customs.ustreas.gov

Auctions

Whether it's new or used, collectable or disposable, if it can be sold, you can bet it's up for sale somewhere in an online auction. Unlike much of what's happening online, auctions aren't an overnight fad. With millions of goods in thousands of categories changing hands every day, they're definitely here to stay. You really won't believe what's up for grabs:

Who Would Buy That? http://www.whowouldbuythat.com

chapter 8

How they work

You know how auctions work: the sale goes to the highest bidder, as long as it's above the preset reserve price. Or, in the case of a Dutch auction, the price keeps dropping until a buyer accepts. Well, it's the same online, but less stressful. Most obviously, you don't have to drive across town and waste a day.

It generally works like this: when you see something you want, submit a **maximum bid** that is higher than the current bid or any minimum bid the seller may have set. The auction site will then bid incrementally on your behalf, raising your bid – up to your specified maximum – to fend off other bidders. If your bid is the highest when the auction's clock stops ticking, the deal is struck.

Once the deal's been settled, it's up to the buyer and seller to arrange delivery and payment, though both can be arranged via trusted third parties. The auctioneer typically takes a cut of the vendor's taking.

As long as you take the time to read the new user's section and follow the prompts from there, you should have no problem getting started.

Paying up

Many choose to settle their auction transactions with a cheque in the post. If the seller is a trader you could also use a credit card, but employ the same caution you would in a regular online store. The other alternative is to sign up with an **Internet Payment System**. You set up an account, place funds into it and then electronically forward payment to the seller. Though it sounds straightforward enough, there have been some reports of fraud and hacked accounts – so check out the articles and reviews on sites like ZDNet (**http://www.zdnet.com**) and AuctionWatch (**http://auctionwatch.com**), and read the small print carefully before signing up. And avoid those that demand a hefty commission.

A couple of the more commonly used systems can be found integrated into the big auction sites:

Billpoint (eBay) http://www.billpoint.com

PayDirect (Yahoo!) http://paydirect.yahoo.com

Finding an auction

You've probably already heard of **eBay** – it was the first auction house to take the Net by storm and has had very prominent ad campaigns. Hundreds of other auction sites have appeared since its launch, but eBay (with branches in over twenty countries) remains the biggest and best known. You should investigate it first:

eBay http://www.ebay.com

If you like what you see but aren't satisfied, try a few more. Such as:

Amazon http://www.amazon.com (or one of their local branches)

QXL http://www.qxl.com (US, UK, EUR)

Sold.com.au http://www.sold.com.au (AUS)

Yahoo! http://auctions.yahoo.com (or local branch)

While these carry most items, some objects, such as art and antiques, are better suited to a specialist dealer. For a more comprehensive list, try Yahoo!, the Open Directory or a dedicated auctions directory:

Bidfind http://www.bidfind.com

Internet Auction List http://www.internetauctionlist.com

Open Directory http://dmoz.org/Shopping/Auctions/

Tools and twists

To search across hundreds of auctions simultaneously, try **Auctionwatch.com**, **BidXS** or one of the many auction programs – search for "auction" at **Download.com** or **Tucows** (http://www.tucows.com). And check out **Esnipe**, which can help you get a better price at eBay by waiting until the last minute to bid.

The Net has also added a load of new twists to the bidding game. At **Priceline**, for example, you state how much you'd like to pay for a particular service and wait to see if a vendor bites. **MyGeek** approaches merchants on your behalf looking for the best deal, and **LetsBuyIt.com** uses collaborative buying power to clinch lower prices. At **NexTag** you can compare the going prices of new against used and add yours to the marketplace, while at **Webswappers** you can exchange your goods for something other than money.

Ventures like these attract ample press, so watch the shopping and Internet sections of your newspaper for further leads. But be warned: although they promise the world, don't be surprised if you end up lumped with a so-so deal.

Auctionwatch.com http://www.auctionwatch.com

BidXS http://www.bidxs.com

Esnipe http://www.esnipe.com

LetsBuyIt.com http://www.letsbuyit.com

myGeek http://www.mygeek.com

NexTag **http://www.nextag**
Priceline **http://www.priceline.com**
Webswappers **http://www.webswappers.com**

Auction tips

➡ Entering an auction at the very last minute with a clinching bid can be both exciting and profitable, but **don't succumb to the thrill of the chase**. Decide on a realistic highest bid and stick to it.

➡ Ebay and many of the other auction sites **rate buyers and sellers** according to feedback from other users. Some sellers decline to accept bids from punters without a certain score; conversely, you should glance at the rating of a seller before committing yourself with a bid. If you're asked to leave feedback by a seller, do so, and make sure they return the compliment. These ratings can also be a useful means of sizing up your opponents during an auction.

➡ **Take advantage of the tools at your disposal**: on eBay, for example, you can email sellers to clarify sketchy details about an item; "watch" items you are interested in without actually bidding; and view an auction's "bid history", which should give you an idea of the competitors.

Classified ads

Online classifieds need no explanation. They're like the paper version, but easier to search and possibly more up-to-date. In fact most papers are moving their classifieds onto the Net, though you might have to pay to see the latest listings. Here's just a small selection, but as they tend to work on a local level check your home-town papers or your regional Yahoo!:

Excite Classifieds **http://www.classifieds2000.com**

Half.com http://www.half.com

Loot http://www.loot.com (UK)

Loot http://www.lootusa.com (New York)

Newsclassifieds http://www.newsclassifieds.com.au (AUS)

Trader.com http://www.trader.com (INT)

Trading Post http://www.tradingpost.com.au (AUS)

Zshops http://www.zshops.com

Let's shop!

Shopping's the same the world over: you collect your booty, head to the checkout, fix the bill and carry it home. As you'd expect, that's also how it works online. While the intricate details might differ between sites, once you've used one, the rest should fall into place. Let's use **Amazon** as an example.

A journey through Amazon.com

Getting online and not visiting Amazon would be like going to Cairo and skipping the pyramids. Although the company only recently reported its first net profit, it's without argu-ment the very model of online shopping excellence. Since launching in 1995 as a not-so-humble bookshop – allegedly the world's biggest – it's blossomed into a massive department store carrying music, DVDs, electronics, furniture, cosmetics, toys, tools, the next biggest auction house after eBay, classifieds and loads more – even cars. But as you'll soon see, it's not the sheer bulk of stock alone that makes it so special. Amazon has branches in:

France http://www.amazon.fr
Germany http://www.amazon.de
Japan http://www.amazon.co.jp
UK http://www.amazon.co.uk
US http://www.amazon.com

Although their inventories and editorials overlap, they're all separate outlets with local stock and distribution hubs. The US operation is ahead of the rest, stocking a wider range of products and features. But, wherever you are, it's worth checking both the UK and US operations – especially if you're after music.

Sifting the inventory

Point your browser at **http://www.amazon.com**. Everything's linked from the front page, so save it into your Favorites, then take a look around. You can either search the inventory using the form at the top left, or browse through the categories. Information about the vendor (including shipping and help) is located at the bottom of the page – standard practice at all well-designed sites. After you've clicked a little, it will soon become clear how everything works, even though it might take you an hour or two to fully appreciate the range on offer. We'll leave that up to you.

But for now, try clicking the "music" tab and searching for your favourite performer. Within seconds it will return a list of entries – click on any title to display the album details. Sometimes this will include a full track listing, along with editorial and customer reviews. Track entries that look like links are short RealAudio samples. Clicking on the performer's name will bring up a listing of their entire works, or at least those that Amazon carry. Now that you've worked that out, you should have no trouble navigating the rest of the site.

The shopping basket

Although you can't actually purchase anything until you set up an account, you can add items to your "**shopping basket**". This does exactly what you'd expect: if you see something you like, drop it into your basket by clicking the "add to basket" button. (All good sites use this system.) **Don't worry about how much you add** – you're not committed to buying anything until you move the items through the checkout and pay for them. So you can always take out items later, or simply leave them there for another time. To return to shopping, hit your back button or start another search. You can return to your basket at any time by clicking on the basket icon at the top of the screen or on the link at the bottom of the page.

Starting an account

When you're ready to buy, go to your basket and examine its contents. At this point you can remove items, change the quantities or save them for later. Again, don't worry because you'll be given the chance to do all this again. Clicking "**proceed to checkout**" will bring up the "**signing in**" page. If it's your first visit you'll need to create a new account. Just choose "**I am a new customer**" and follow the prompts. You can change your account details later by clicking on "your account" at the top of the page, or when you're checking out. Once you move into the account phase, the server goes into **secure mode** – the address changes to **https://** and a closed lock appears on the bottom bar. If your browser doesn't support secure purchasing, then either download one that does or don't shop online!

Your privacy

Whenever you give your details to any site, it will ask whether you'd like to receive mail from them or associated parties. **Say no.** You don't need junk mail from them, nor anyone else.

Checking out

Once you've logged in with your password, checking out is as straightforward as following the prompts. The most difficult part will be deciding between the various shipping options. If you've bought more than one item you'll have to decide whether to ship them all at once or as they arrive at the warehouse. One item might take weeks to arrive, for instance, delaying the rest of the order. You'll see an indication of how long Amazon thinks each item will take to arrive underneath its entry in the basket. The rest should be all self-explanatory – just read the help files if you're unclear.

Confirmation

Almost all shops send you an instant email confirming your order. Some shops need a reply to confirm acceptance, though Amazon doesn't. Keep all your orders and shipping notices together in a separate folder so you can refer to them later if something goes amiss.

Tracking

To check the status of each item in your order at Amazon, click on "your account", sign in and look under "**order history**". Some sites can give you order tracking details right down to the shipping hubs. If your package fails to arrive, report it to customer support. They should send you a replacement without question.

Your next visit

Next time you arrive at Amazon it will welcome you by your name. This will only work if you're using the same computer, though, as it stores your ID in a cookie file. This isn't a bad thing generally – the system learns from your purchases and attempts to recommend stuff you might like. It's not a security concern, as you still have to sign in with your password to make a purchase or change your account details.

Find a shop

We listed individual shops in earlier editions of this book, but there are now so many it's no longer practical to do so. So many, in fact, that there's now a *Rough Guide to Shopping Online* and several others like it. But even these guides are feeling the strain: listing all the online shopping options will soon be like attempting to replicate the *Yellow Pages*. Even so, you might find such a guide useful if it's well-researched and can save you time.

Otherwise it's tough to advise you where to start. It depends where you live, what you're after and, of course, what you like. The major search portals like **Yahoo!**, **Excite** and **AltaVista** index shopping sites within their normal directories, but they don't make it easy for you to get to them. Instead, when you click on "Shopping" you're shunted towards their own hybrid shopping malls favouring their partnered vendors. Still, if you're looking for a specific product rather than a type of shop, this can be a good way to go. The **Open Directory** (http://dmoz.org), on the other hand, treats shopping like any other category, making it much easier to browse.

Shopping directories

There are also hundreds of specialist shopping directories. None, however, can claim to list every shop, and even with the few they do carry, they make browsing hard work. Such as:

Buyersguide **http://www.buyersguide.to**

InternetMall **http://www.internetmall.com**

Internetshopper **http://www.internetshopper.com**

InternetShopping **http://www.internetshopping.com** (UK)

MyTaxi **http://www.mytaxi.co.uk** (UK)

Ozshopping **http://www.ozshopping.com.au** (AUS)

Premierstores **http://www.premierstores.com**

ShopEthical **http://www.shopethical.co.uk** (UK)

ShopSmart **http://www.shopsmart.com** (UK)

UKShopping **http://www.ukshopping.com** (UK)

For more, see: **http://dmoz.org/Shopping/Directories/**

Most directories provide a description, but if you'd rather look at a rating or review, see:

Bizrate **http://www.bizrate.com**

Gomez **http://www.gomez.com**

Planet Feedback **http://www.planetfeedback.com** (US)

Shopping Sites **http://www.shopping-sites.com** (UK, US)

Special needs

If your needs are more specialized, or you know the exact product or model you're after, try searching the Web with **Google** (p.170). You'll really need to refine your searching skills, though, as it's likely to return pages of hits. Your best bet might be to locate the manufacturer's site and work from there. Or, if you need advice, scan **Google Groups** (**http://groups.google.com**) for an appropriate newsgroup. For example, if you ask about coffee grinders in **alt.coffee**, you'll get the rundown on various brands and vendors and be pointed to several FAQs. A shopping directory is less likely to be so helpful.

Given the wealth of information online, this might sound like an odd suggestion, but the best way to keep up with what's hot in online shopping is to follow the regular media – especially the full-page ads in the glossy magazines.

Prefer it on paper?

Then drive your postie crazy by ordering every catalogue in the world:

Buyer's Index http://www.buyersindex.com

Catalog Site http://www.catalogsite.com

Google Catalogs http://catalogs.google.com

Try our Web guide

You'll find short guides to buying music, cars, books, travel, financial services, groceries and more in our Web guide, which starts on p.331. Or if that doesn't slake your thirst, get hold of the *Rough Guide Website Directory*.

Find the best deal

Comparing prices across shops is the craze amongst shopping portals. Whether they're called comparison engines, **shopping bots** or bargain finders, they more or less do the same thing. You enter a product or keyword and they return a list of prices and availability across a range of retailers. Sounds great, but unfortunately few seem capable of keeping their databases consistently current. Which kind of defeats the point of the exercise.

Generally, the bots that specialize in one product group do better than the all-purpose variety, particularly if they scan a lot of shops, including all the big names. Take **Shopper.com** and **Pricewatch.com**, for example. If you're after anything computer-related, they're definitely the best place to start.

But it also depends on the shops queried and whether they're passing out correct information. You'll find some – for example, AltaVista's **Shopping.com** – query a lot of products, but across a very limited and often obscure selection of shops. In the end you might get a better deal at Amazon.

So again, like the shopping directories, it's a hit-and-miss affair. Try a few and see what works for you:

AddAll http://www.addall.com (books worldwide)

Best Book Buys http://www.bestbookbuys.com (books)

Buy.co.uk http://www.buy.co.uk (UK utilities)

Deal Time http://www.dealtime.com (US, UK, DE, JP)

Egg http://shopping.egg.com (UK)

Genial Comparison http://www.genialcomparison.com

InfoChoice http://www.infochoice.com.au (flights, utilities) (AUS)

Kelkoo http://www.kelkoo.com (UK, EUR, Latin America)

My Simon http://www.mysimon.com (US, FR, DE)

ShopSmart http://www.shopsmart.com (UK)

Or, for a software option, try **Copernic Shopper** (http://www.copernic.com), which can also express prices in your own currency and hunt for product reviews.

9

Discussions

Make friends, get answers

Whatever you do, don't think the Net starts and ends with the World Wide Web. If you miss the discussion areas – particularly Usenet – you've barely scratched the surface. In this section you'll find out how to use the Net to interact with other people, and not just pages.

It's all talk

As outlined earlier (p.5), the main forms of online discussion are Mailing Lists, Usenet, Chat and Instant Messaging. **Mailing list** (p.226) discussions are carried out in private by email. In **Usenet** (p.229), your messages form part of an ongoing dialogue on a public notice board. Whereas **Chat** (p.245) and **Messaging** (p.254) are instant, like a conversation. You can chat with complete strangers on the **Web** (p.252), or in an **Internet Relay Chat (IRC)** room (p.247), while to natter among your friends you may find **instant**

messaging more appropriate. You can speak by **Internet telephone** (p.257), place a **PC call to a normal telephone** (p.258) or even set up a **videoconference** (p.295). You'll never feel alone again.

But before you jump head-first into the rough and tumble of online forums, make sure you're familiar with some of the **accepted codes of conduct**.

Rules of the game

When you sign up with any kind of access provider – whether it's for the complete works or a Usenet-only account (p.231) – you'll have to agree to a few **terms and conditions** in the fine print. These are the **formal rules that apply to your Internet connection** and, needless to say, they're too boring to read. They're not there to make the Internet a safer place; they're there to protect your provider from being responsible if you run riot. About all you need to know is that if you breach the rules, your provider might cut off your access and force you to look elsewhere for a connection. Or, worse, if your provider happens to be your office, school or library, you might find yourself out of work, expelled or banned.

The law of the land

Although the Net itself has no law, you're still bound by the laws of your country or state (p.9). So being online doesn't grant you permission to threaten, steal or libel.

Flame throwers

People who **make complete pigs of themselves** in discussions sometimes get reported to their ISP or news provider, which might result in them losing their account, or even being sued. The address for reporting someone is generally **abuse@ serviceprovider** where "serviceprovider" is the name of their news server or ISP. Mostly, however, offenders just get ignored or **abused**. On the Net, personal abuse is called **flaming**. You don't have to do much to get flamed – just expressing a contrary or naive opinion should do the trick. When things degenerate into name-calling, it's called a **flame war**. Just about every busy group will have a war in progress within one of the threads, and sometimes, for example in the **alt.flame.** hierarchy, that's about all that's in there. You'll probably be spitting insults yourself before too long. It's all part of the fun.

Netiquette

Apart from your **provider's contract**, the Net has no formal rules. Instead, there is an established and developing code of conduct known as **Netiquette** (Net-etiquette). This is usually associated with Usenet (p.229), though notions of Netiquette can equally be applied to messaging and even email.

You won't go to jail for breaching the stiff, and often overly proper, codes of conduct that fall under the banner of "**netiquette**" but you'll certainly be lectured. And any protest on your behalf will inevitably lead to a long, heated debate. The first thing to know is, as long as you're not breaching your **terms of service** or **laws of your land**, you can do whatever you like. However, you might find yourself ostracized for exercising your rights. On the other hand, if you stick to the following rules, you'll spare yourself the pain and be treated better by the group. It's your choice.

Read the Frequently Asked Questions (FAQs)

Most newsgroups (p.229) have at least one **FAQ** (Frequently Asked Question) document. This should describe the newsgroup's charter, give guidelines for posting, and compile common answers to questions. They should always be your first source of information. FAQs are periodically posted and usually updated every few weeks. You can usually find them by searching **Google Groups** (p.183) or the:

FAQ archive http://www.faqs.org

Post to the right group

It's wise to **get the feel of a newsgroup** before posting. If it's a big group, one session should do, but don't be in a hurry. Be sure your messages aren't old hat – some newsgroupies are not too tolerant of repeats. But that's no rule.

Next, make an effort to **post in the most relevant group**. If you were to ask for advice on fertilizing roses in rec.gardening you might find yourself politely directed to rec.gardening.roses but if you want to tell everyone in talk.serious.socialism about your favourite Chow Yun Fat film, don't expect such a warm response.

Use descriptive subjects

Sum up your Usenet post in the **Subject line** (p.238) so busy people can instantly see whether they'll want to read or reply. The more detail you can squeeze into the fewest words, the better.

Warn if you might spoil a surprise

If your Usenet message reveals something that might spoil a surprise, such as the plot of a film or the score in a sports match, it's good manners to start the subject line with the word "**Spoiler**" or "**Warning spoiler**".

Mark off-topic posts

When you want to post something that **might interest the group**, but it **doesn't directly relate to the topic** of the group, start the subject with "**OT**" (off-topic).

Be tactful

Before you call someone a retard or question their intelligence, consider that they might indeed have a mental handicap, and being able to part in an online discussion on their favourite sport or hobby might be an achievement in itself.

Bite your tongue

Never post in anger. You'll regret it later, especially when everything you send is archived at Google Groups. And beware of **Trolls**. These are baits left to start arguments or make you look stupid. If someone asks something ludicrous or obvious, says something offensive or inappropriate, or attacks you personally, don't respond. Let it pass. Tread carefully with sarcasm, too, as not everyone will get it, especially those nationalities with no sense of irony. (This is meant to be a joke, but how can you be sure?) As much as you might **frown on smileys** (p.224), they're better than being misunderstood.

Mind your language

Nothing will get you on the wrong side of a discussion faster than **swearing**. You can swear freely (almost) in everyday life, so you might think the same should apply online. You're welcome to try, but it probably won't work in your favour. It's not so much that you'll stand to offend; it's that you'll be set upon by the pious, who'll furthermore delight in complaining to your ISP. Yet if you reduce your obscenity to an obvious abbreviation, such as F or F★★★, you'll not hear a peep of protest. Remarkable.

Watch your words

Unless you're on a private mailing list, you should consider discussions to be **in the public domain**. That means they could end up archived on the Web. This isn't the case with most mailing lists, and may not even be legal, but it's safer not to test it. What this means is that whether or not you appear anonymous, if you threaten or maliciously defame someone, it will be possible to trace and prosecute you under your local laws. Take care not to say anything you wouldn't like to see next to your name on the front page of your local paper.

Don't use all UPPERCASE

NEVER POST IN UPPERCASE (ALL CAPS) unless you're shouting (emphasizing a point in a big way). It makes you look rude and ignorant.

Respect confidentiality

Don't post email you've received from someone else without their consent. Apart from being rude, it's an illegal **breach of confidence**.

chapter 9

Keep it simple

Express yourself in plain English (or the language of the group). Don't use **acronyms** or **abbreviations** unless they reduce jargon rather than create it. And avoid overusing **smileys** and other **emoticons** (p.224). They spell "newbie". And keep your **signature file** short and subtle. Three to five lines, no ASCII art. Got it?

Don't be a grammar pedant

Everyone makes spelling mistakes and grammatical errors online – sometimes every time they post. You don't need to point it out, especially when they're not posting in their first language.

Use plain text

Although most email programs and newsreaders can display HTML and Mime Quoted Printable format, you may get a lecture if you send a message to a newsgroup or mailing list in anything but plain text. That said, HTML is sometimes more appropriate – for example, if you're pasting a long URL – so have a look to see what others do in the group or list.

> **Tip:** One good way to send a long URL – or give one out over the phone – is to visit **ShorterLink** (http://shorterlink.com). Enter a long address and you'll immediately be given a shorter link that will forward to it.

Posting ads

Having such a massive captive audience pre-qualified by interests is beyond the dreams of many marketeers. Consequently, you will frequently come across **advertisements and product endorsements** crossposted to inappropriate newsgroups.

Spamming (p.147) is the surest way to make yourself unpopular in Usenet. Try and you'll be bombed with hate mail and more than likely reported. In other words, it's not good publicity. As a rule, no one who uses this technique to advertise is reputable – as with those who send mass emails.

If you'd like to make **commercial announcements**, you could try the groups in the **.biz** hierarchy; after all that's what they're for. The catch is no one reads them because they're chock-full of the usual network marketing schemes. In other groups, tread more carefully with mentions of your new book, CD or whatever; otherwise you might come in for a hard time. You can do it, but only in the right groups and in the right context.

Curiously, nobody minds what you put in your **signature**. So if you put in some business details and include your Web address, it's sure to attract a few visitors.

Chat Netiquette

IRC is so diverse that you're as likely to encounter a channel full of Indian expats following a ball-by-ball cricket commentary as a couple of college kids flirting. So long as no one rocks the boat too much, coexistence can be harmonious. Of course, there's bound to be a little mayhem now and then, but that usually just adds to the fun of the whole event.

However, some actions are generally frowned upon and may get you kicked from channels, or even banned from a server. These include dumping large files or amounts of text, harassment, vulgarity and inviting people into inappropriate channels.

Get in there

These warnings aside – and they're pretty obvious – don't hold back. If you can forward a discussion in any way, contribute. That's what it's all about. **Post positively** and invite discussion rather than make abrasive remarks. For example, posting "Hackers are social misfits" is sure to get you flamed. But: "Do hackers lead healthy social lives?" will get the same point across and invite debate, yet allow you to sidestep the line of fire.

Overall it's a matter of courtesy, common sense and knowing when to contribute. Remember: you're a complete stranger until you post. You'll be known through your words and how well you construct arguments. So if you want to make a good impression, think before you post, and don't be a loudmouth. If you're a real stickler for rules, read:

Albion Netiquette http://www.albion.com/netiquette/

Or, if you'd prefer a less conservative approach:

Emily Postnews http://www.psg.com/emily.html
Guide to Flaming http://www.advicemeant.com/flame/
Usenet Tomfoolery http://www.elsop.com/wrc/humor/usenet.htm

Net language

Before the Internet became a public thoroughfare, it was **overrun with academics**. These greasy geek types could be found chatting and swapping shareware on the bulletin-board networks. As the Internet was popularized this culture collided with the less digitally versed general public. While the old-school types are now in the minority, their culture still kicks on – as witnessed by the continued use of their **abbreviated expressions**.

Low transfer speed, poor typing skills and the need for quick responses were among the pioneers' justifications for keeping things brief. But using Net lingo was also a way of showing you were in the know. These days, it's not so prevalent, though you're sure to encounter acronyms in IRC and, to a lesser extent, Usenet and Mailing Lists. Chat is a snappy medium, messages are short, and responses are fast. Unlike with CB radio, people won't ask your "20" to find out where you're from but they might ask your **A/S/L** – age/sex/location. Acronyms and abbreviations are mixed in with normal speech and range from the innocuous (BTW = by the way) to a whole panoply of blue phrases. But don't be ashamed to stick with plain English, Urdu or whatever. After all, you'll stand a better chance of being understood.

Shorthand: Net acronyms

AFAIK As far as I know
AOLer AOL member (rarely a compliment)
A/S/L Age/Sex/Location
BBL Be back later
BD or **BFD** Big deal
BFN or **B4N** Bye for now
BOHICA Bend over here it comes again
BRB Be right back
BTW By the way
CUL8R or **L8R** See you later
CYA See ya
F2F (S2S) Face to face (skin to skin)
FWIW For what it's worth
g Grin
GR8 Great
HTH Hope this helps
IAE In any event
IM(H)O In my (humble or honest) opinion
IOW In other words
IYSWIM If you see what I mean

LOL Laughing out loud
MOTD Message of the day
NRN No reply necessary
NW or **NFW** No way
OIC Oh I see
OTOH On the other hand
POV Point of view
RO(T)FL (MAO) Roll on the floor laughing (my ass off)
RTM or **RTFM** Read the manual
SOL Sooner or later
TIA Thanks in advance
TTYL Talk to you later
WRT With respect to
WTH? or **WTF?** What the hell?
YMMV Your mileage may vary

Smileys and emoticons

Back in the old days, potentially contentious remarks could be tempered by tacking **<grins>** on the end in much the same way that a dog wags its tail to show it's harmless. But that wasn't enough for the E-generation, whose trademark smiley icon became the 1980s peace sign. The same honed minds who discovered that **71077345** inverted spelled Greenpeace's *bête noire* developed the ASCII smiley. This time, instead of turning it upside down, you had to look at it sideways to see a smiling face. An expression that words, supposedly, fail to convey. At least in such limited space. Inevitably this grew into a whole family of **emoticons** (emotional icons).

The odd smiley might have its use in defusing barbs, but whether you'd want to use any of the others is up to your perception of the line between cute and dorky. The nose is optional:

:-) Smiling	X-) I see nothing
:-D Laughing	:-X I'll say nothing
:-o Shock	:-L~~ Drooling
:-@ Screaming	:-P Sticking out tongue
:-(Frowning	(hmm)Ooo.. :-) Happy thoughts
:'-(Crying	(hmm)Ooo.. :-(Sad thoughts
;-) Winking	O:-) Angel
:-I Indifferent	}:> Devil
X= Fingers crossed	(_)] Beer
: =) Little Hitler	:8 Pig
{} Hugging	\o/ Hallelujah
:* Kissing	@}-`—,—- Rose
$-) Greedy	8:)3)= Happy girl

A few others, mostly Japanese anime-derived, work right way up:

@^_^@ Blushing	^_^; Sweating
*^_^* Dazzling grin	T_T Crying

Emphasis

You could also express actions or emotions by adding commentary within < and > signs. For example:

<flushed> I've just escaped the clutches of frenzied train spotters
<removes conductor's cap, wipes brow>

Or by using asterisks to *emphasize* words. Simply *wrap* the appropriate word:

Hey, everyone, look at *me*.

el33t h4x0r duD3

When your mouse misleads you into young and impressionable realms you might encounter language that looks like this: "l00k

4t ME. I'M @n eL33t h4x0r dUD3." ("Look at me. I'm an elite hacker dude.") To translate, see:

http://www.geocities.com/mnstr_2000/

Or, better still, get out of there.

For more

If you come across an abbreviation you don't understand, ask its author. Don't worry about appearing stupid – these expressions aren't exactly

common knowledge. Alternatively, consult one of the many online references, such as:

Acronym Finder http://www.acronymfinder.com

Emoticon Universe http://emoticonuniverse.com

Jargon and Hacker style http://www.tuxedo.org/~esr/jargon/html/

Microsoft lexicon http://www.cinepad.com/mslex.htm

NetLingo http://www.netlingo.com

Slang Zone http://www.sabram.com/Slang/slang.html

Mailing lists

If you want email by the bucketload, join some mailing lists. This will involve giving your email address to someone and receiving whatever they send **until you beg them to stop**. Mailing lists fall into two categories: closed (one-way) or open. **Closed lists** are set up by some sort of authority or publisher to keep you informed of news or changes – anything from hourly weather updates to product release announcements. They're **one-way**

only: you don't contribute. What comes through an **open list**, however, is **sent by its members** – and, yes, that could be you.

The purpose of most lists is to broadcast news or encourage discussion about a specific topic – anything from alien abductions to Zimbabwean zoos. In some cases, the list itself forms a group, like a social club, so don't be surprised if discussion drifts way off topic or into personal and indulgent rants. You'll see. But you'll also find lists are an easy way to keep up with news and to meet a few peers – maybe in person, too. People just like you, in fact:

Flame Warriors http://www.winternet.com/~mikelr/flame1.html

How it works

Each mailing list has two addresses: the **mailing address** used to contact its members, and the **administrative address** used to send commands to the server or maintainer of the list. Don't mix them up or everyone else on the list will think you're a dill.

Most lists are **unmoderated**, meaning they relay messages immediately. Messages on **moderated** lists, however, get screened first. This can amount to downright censorship, but more often it's welcome, as it can improve the quality of discussion and keep it on topic by pruning irrelevant and repetitive messages. It all depends on the moderator, who's rarely paid for the service.

Certain other lists are moderated because they carry messages from one source, such as the US Travel Warnings. Such lists often have a parallel open list for discussion.

If you'd rather receive your mail in large batches than have it trickle through, request a **digest** where available. These are normally sent daily or weekly, depending on the traffic.

As discussions are conducted entirely by email, **the only software you need is your everyday mail program**.

Climbing aboard a list

Joining should be simple. In most cases, you **subscribe** by email or through a form on a webpage. It depends who's running the list. Once you're on an open list, you'll receive all the messages sent to the list's address, and everyone else on the list will receive whatever you send. Your first message will either welcome you to the list, or ask you to confirm your email address (to stop prank subscriptions). **Keep the welcome message**, as it should also tell you how to **unsubscribe**, and set other parameters such as ordering it in **digest format**. You'll need to follow the instructions to the letter. Don't bother **writing a courtesy letter**, as it will only confuse the automated list manager.

Finding lists

Most busy sites publish **newsletters** (one-way lists) to keep you up-to-date with what's happening in their world – just look for an option to provide your email address. To find open discussion lists, see p.186.

Starting your own list

If you'd like to **create your own public list, private list or discussion group**, see:

Coollist http://www.coollist.com

Topica http://www.topica.com

Yahoo! Groups http://groups.yahoo.com

They're free, and are simple to manage from the Web. Or, if you want to get serious, ask your provider or network manager to set you up a **Listserv**, **Listproc** or **Majordomo** account on their server.

Coping with the volume

Before you set off subscribing to every list that takes your fancy, consider using **separate email**

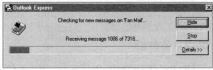

addresses for mailing lists and personal mail. Apart from the obvious benefits in managing traffic and filtering, it protects your personal account from evil **spammers** (p.147). If nothing else, you should at least **filter** your list messages (p.145) accordingly, so your high-priority mail doesn't get buried amongst the junk. Remember when posting to select whichever identity you want from the dropdown menu in the "**From:**" bar of your mail program.

Vacation alert!

If you're trotting off from your mail for a while, consider **unsubscribing from your high-volume lists**. Otherwise you might face a serious mail jam when you return, especially if you have a meagre account size such as the one provided by Hotmail.

Newsgroups

Would you like a **deep and meaningful discussion** on the matters closest to your heart; an **answer to a question** that's been bugging you forever; to **share your expertise** with others; or just hook up with **people who think like you**? If so, the place for you is **Usenet news**, the Net's prime discussion area. Don't be confused by its name – it's not about delivering news as you know it. In this context, "news" relates to the messages stored in around 100,000 discussion groups. These groups are called "**newsgroups**", and each one is dedicated to a specific topic.

How it works

A **Usenet newsgroup** is a bit like a **free public notice board**. When you send (post) a message to a newsgroup, everyone who reads that group can see it. They can then **contribute to the discussion publicly** by posting a reply and/or **contact you privately** by email. Normally, however, it's like a public conversation that anyone can join. You can't tell who's reading your messages unless they post a reply. It's possible to read any message, in any group, as long as it remains on your news provider's system, which could be anywhere from a few days to a month depending on the policy it has set for each group. Anything older can be dug up in Google Groups (see p.183).

Web discussions

You'll also come across discussion groups in various guises on the Web. They might be called **message boards**, **guestbooks**, **bulletin boards**, **egroups**, **communities** or **forums**, but they work in much the same way as newsgroups; that is, they allow you to post a message for other people to read. You shouldn't need help in figuring them out. If it's not immediately obvious, there'll normally be instructions somewhere nearby. You'll find thousands indexed at:

Tile.Net http://www.tile.net/lists/

You can set up your own Web discussion group in minutes at:

Yahoo Groups http://groups.yahoo.com

What you'll need

All you really need to get Usenet happening on your machine is an Internet connection and a Web browser, as you can access Usenet via the Web at **Google Groups** (see p.183). However, if you're looking to wet more than just your big toe, you'll want to employ a **newsreader** – a program used to view and post to newsgroups – and get access to a **news server**.

You'll already have a newsreader if you've installed Outlook Express or Netscape. And, as most ISPs maintain a news server as part of the package, you should be ready to go. Just refer to the support section of your ISP's homepage, or call your ISP's support line, to find the address. If your ISP doesn't carry Usenet, go with Google or seek an account with a specialist news provider such as **Tera News** (http://www.teranews.com), which offer free, uncensored access to all groups. The folks at Berlin University also offer a free service (http://news.cis.dfn.de).

Choosing a newsreader

If you're using **Outlook Express** for email, you might as well start with it as your newsreader. It's not the most powerful option, but you'll find it the easiest. **Netscape**'s newsreading software is OK, too, but a little more cumbersome and unstable. It's only worth considering if you use Netscape as your browser. If you're using **Outlook**, you'll need to install Outlook Express or another newsreader.

Apart from these there are several **dedicated programs** that will give you a little more control over your sessions, in exchange for at least twenty minutes of complete confusion as you try to unravel their unique ways of doing things. You will definitely need to spend some time in the help files.

For **PCs**, try **Agent** from Forté (http://www.forteinc.com). It has two versions: Free Agent, which is gratis; and Agent, the registered, fully featured edition. On the **Mac**, go straight for **MT NewsWatcher** (http://www.smfr.org/mtnw/).

Setting up your newsreader

To start out, you'll need to specify your **news server**, **identity** and **email address**. It should be part of your initial setup routine. If not, to add a new Usenet service in **Outlook Express**, open "Accounts" from under the Tools menu, select "Add News" and follow the prompts.

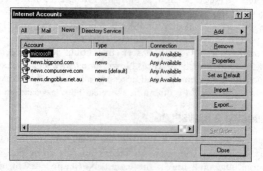

Most newsreaders offer a whole bunch of options for how long you want to keep messages after you've read them, how much to retrieve, how to arrange your windows and so forth. Leave those in the default settings and go back when you understand the questions and know your demands. Right now, it's not so important.

Very important – mask your address!

Spammers regularly extract all the email addresses from Usenet to add to their bulk mail databases. Consequently, all savvy users doctor their addresses in an obvious way to fool bulk mailers, but not genuine respondents. For example, **henry@ plasticfashions.com** might enter his address profile as **henry@ die-spammer-die.plasticfashions.com** or **henry@remove-this-bit. plasticfashions.com**

It's essential to do the same before you post your first message; otherwise you'll be **bombarded with junk email** for years to come. Alternatively, you could **use a second address**, perhaps under a pseudonym, for privacy's sake. It'll only take you a few minutes (p.122).

Building a group list

Before you can jump in, you'll need to compile a list of the **newsgroups** available on your server. Your newsreader should do this automatically the very first time you connect to your news server. It's a big file, so expect to wait a few minutes.

As the newsgroups arrive on your list, they'll either appear in a window entitled "**New Groups**" or go straight into the main list (commonly called "All Groups"). **To compile your newsgroup list** in Outlook Express, go online and click on your news server entry at the bottom of your mail folder list.

Downloading Newsgroups from news.compuserve.com

Downloading the list of newsgroups available on the server. This only needs to be done once, and it may take a few minutes if you have a slow connection.

Downloading newsgroups: 28054 received...

Cancel

Understanding newsgroup names

Newsgroups are divided into specific topics using a simple naming system. You can usually tell what a group's about by looking at its name. The first part is the **hierarchy** (broad category) under which it falls. Here are just some of the top-level and most popular (asterisked) hierarchies:

Hierarchy	Content
alt.	Alternative, anarchic and freewheeling discussion*
aus.	Australian
bionet.	Biological
bit.	Bitnet LISTSERV mailing lists*
biz.	Commercial bulletins
can.	Canadian
comp.	Computing*
de.	German
k12.	Education through to grade 12
microsoft.	Microsoft product support
misc.	Miscellaneous*
news.	About Usenet itself*
rec.	Hobbies and recreational activities*
sci.	All strands of science*
soc.	Social, cultural, and religious*
talk.	The most controversial issues*
uk.	British

You'll notice **newsgroup names** contain dots, like domain names. But they work differently: the name tells you what the group discusses, not its location.

The top of the hierarchy is at the far left. As you move right, you go down the tree and it becomes more specific. For instance, **rec.sport.cricket.info** is devoted to information about the compelling recreational sport that is cricket. Also, though several groups may discuss similar subjects, each will have its own angle. Thus while **alt.games.gravy** might have light and anarchic postings, **biz.gravy.train** would get right down to the business.

Browsing the groups

If your ISP has a decent newsfeed, you should be faced with a list of at least 20,000 groups. Don't be put off by the volume: your newsreader can sift through them in a flash. But before you start filtering, scroll down and see what's on offer.

In **Outlook Express**, click on your news server's entry in the folder list in the left-hand frame. If you aren't yet subscribed to any of the server's groups, you will be prompted to view its list. Alternatively, summon the list by clicking "Newsgroups" in either the main window, the news server's right-click mouse menu or under the Tools menu. The "Newsgroup Subscriptions" window will appear. To browse the groups, click into the Newsgroups list and scroll up and down using your arrow keys or mouse wheel. To filter on the fly, click in the box marked "Display newsgroups which contain" and enter your search term. There's also a further check box option to search the brief descriptions that accompany some groups. You might as well check that box, though if the descriptions weren't downloaded with the groups list, Outlook Express will spend several minutes retrieving them from the server.

Find the right group

Unlike the Web, newsgroups aren't scattered across the Net in a chaotic mess. Your newsgroups list is effectively a complete directory of Usenet – or at least the part of it that your news provider carries.

By browsing and filtering, you should see a few groups that look interesting at first glance. However, you won't know whether they contain active discussions, or whether they're appropriate, until you subscribe and check them out. Although you can generally tell what groups are about just by looking at their names and descriptions, sometimes it's not always so obvious.

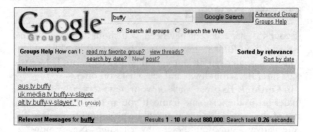

There might also be several groups that appear to discuss the same thing. You'll find, though, there will always be some distinction, or a dominant group. While filtering and browsing is fine for locating groups by their name, it's not always the quickest route. To fast-track the process, run a keyword search at **Google Groups**, take note of the "relevant groups" at the top of the page, and then locate them in your newsgroups list.

Don't overlook the local hierarchies (**aus**, **can**, **uk**, etc) for regional topics such as TV, politics, for sale, employment and sport. For instance, if you want to find out what happened last week to Buffy in the UK, you might find **uk.media.tv.buffy-v-slayer** more up your street than **alt.tv.buffy-v-slayer**

Subscribe to a group

The newsgroup list contains only the group names, not the actual messages. You have to retrieve the messages you might first need to subscribe to the group.

To **subscribe to a group in Outlook Express**, open the "Newsgroup Subscriptions" window (see p.232). When the list appears, select a group (or multiple groups by holding down the Ctrl key as you select), click "Subscribe" and then "Go to" to commence downloading the message **headers**. These contain the message subject, posting date and contributor's name. They can be threaded (bundled together) by subject, or sorted by date or contributor. Once all the headers have arrived, **clicking on a message will download its body**. You can then read it in the preview panel. If you wish to read the group again, just select it from under the news server folder and wait for the new headers to arrive. To **remove a newsgroup**, choose "**Unsubscribe**" from its right-click menu.

Other news-readers use a different combination of menu choices to go through the same motions. Refer to the help file for instructions.

Download older messages

Your newsreader might not bring down all the headers from the news server, only a preset amount – in Outlook Express the default is set to download the newest 300. To download older messages, select the newsgroup and repeatedly choose "**Get next 300 headers**" from under the Tools menu, or click the "**Get next headers**" button on the toolbar (if you've got one). You can change the setting to download more, or everything, under the "Read" tab in Options.

Bundle the threads

When someone posts a message with a new subject, it's called **starting a thread**. Replies to that initial message add to this thread. You'll find it a lot easier to follow discussions if you bundle these threads together. In Outlook Express, place a tick next to "**Group messages by conversation**" under "Current View" in the View menu.

Watch a thread

In Outlook Express and most other newsreaders, **unread messages** will have bold headers like unread emails. Once you group the conversations, you'll know when someone's replied because the top message will appear bold. An even better way to tell is to "watch the thread (conversation)". Select any message in the thread, and click on the column to the immediate left with the glasses on top, or choose "**Watch conversation**" from the Message menu. This will turn the headers red. When someone replies to your watched threads, the newsgroup entry will also appear **bold red** until you've read the messages. To **mark messages as read**, examine the options under the Edit and right-mouse button menus.

You can also flag the threads, or sort by sender, date, subject and so forth, in the same way as email (p.130).

Posting

Posting is like sending email – and equally simple. You can start a new thread, follow up an existing one and/or respond privately by email.

To **post a new message in Outlook Express**, enter a group and click on the "New Message" toolbar icon or select "New Message" from under the Message menu. Most programs automatically insert the newsgroup you're reading in the "Newsgroups:" line.

If you're **starting a thread**, enter a subject that outlines the point of your message. That way it will catch the eye of anyone who's interested or can help. The subject line will then be used to identify the thread in future.

To **crosspost** (post a message to more than one group), just add those groups after the first group, separated by a comma and then a space. Replies to crosspostings are displayed in all the crossposted groups. Crosspost to the wrong groups, or too many groups, and you're sure to get abuse – or cancelled by one of the roving cancelbots.

Send a test post

Feel free to post whatever you like to any group with **test** in the name, such as **alt.test**, or **misc.test**, but remember not to use your real email address as it might generate a pile of responses, some unwelcome.

Replying

Replying (or responding) is even easier than posting. You can send your contribution to the relevant newsgroup(s) and/or email the poster directly.

It's sometimes appropriate **to reply by email as well as post**, so the original poster gets it instantly. It's also more personal and saves scanning the group for replies. Don't forget to edit the address if they've masked it. But, of course, if they've used an obviously bogus address – which is very common – and provided no clue to their real one, there's no point sending an email.

Like email, you also have the option of **including parts or the entire original message**. This can be quite a tricky choice. If you cut too much, the context could be lost when the original post is deleted. If everyone includes everything, it creates a lot of text to scan. Just try to leave the main points intact.

In all newsreaders you'll find the various reply options beside or below your **New Message** menu entries.

chapter 9

Reply above or below?

It used to be taboo to reply at the top of a message ("top posting") until Microsoft made it the default setting. Now only Usenet fundamentalists will chastise you for it. In some ways it makes sense to post on top as it saves having to scroll through lines of quoted text. On the other hand, it prevents you from replying to points within the message. Microsoft has also made replying messy by mucking up the indenting and wrapping so that orphans (single-word lines) are created through the replies. This can be remedied, though, by downloading the **Quotefix add-on** (http://jump.to/oe-quotefix/).

As a rule of thumb, **follow the format of the previous poster**, otherwise you'll upset the logical thread of the conversation.

Cancelling a message

If you've had second thoughts about something you've posted, select it in the newsgroup and choose "**Cancel Message**" from under the Message menu in Outlook Express. Unfortunately, it won't be instantly removed from every server worldwide so someone still might see it.

Blocking nuisances

If you don't like a certain person on Usenet, you can "plonk" them. If your newsreader has a **kill file**, just add their email address to that, or use your **Filters**. Then you'll never have to download messages they've posted again. You can also trash uninteresting threads in the same way, by setting a delete filter on the subject. But don't make it too broad or you might filter out interesting stuff as well. See:

http://www.kibo.com/kibokill/

Reading offline

Reading articles one at a time online is convenient, but not if it's costing you to stay connected or you're tying up your only telephone line. Consider **downloading the article bodies along with the headers** to read offline at your leisure.

This is simple in **Outlook Express**. Before you go online, choose "Work Offline" from under the File menu, select the group, open its "Properties" from under the File or mouse menu, and make your selection under the "Synchronize" tab. Click on the group when you're next online, and choose "Synchronize" from the Tools menu to retrieve whatever you've sent. Now when you're disconnected and back in Offline mode, you can browse the articles as if you're online.

Decoding binaries (pictures, programs, audio, etc)

As with email, Usenet can carry more than plain text. Consequently, there are entire groups dedicated to the posting of **binary files** such as images, sounds, patches and even full commercial programs. Such groups should have **.binaries** in their address.

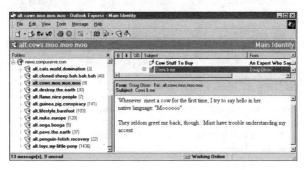

Again like email, binary files must be processed, most commonly in UU encoding or MIME, before they can be posted or read. This is something you needn't think about, as your newsreader will do it automatically. Sometimes larger files like movies get chopped into several messages. Each part will have the same subject heading followed by its number. The problem is that sometimes parts go astray, which makes it impossible to reassemble the file.

Depending on your newsreader, to **retrieve a binary file** you might have to highlight all the parts and decode them in one go. Agent and Free Agent recognize a set when you click on just one part. **Messenger** and **Outlook Express** both decode automatically within the window, but are very slow. You'd be better off with Agent or one of the many newsreaders dedicated to binary decoding.

To decode a multi-part attachment in Outlook Express, select the components and choose "**Combine and Decode**" from the Message menu. For other newsreaders, it's best to read your Help file to get it straight.

To **post a binary**, just attach it as in email and your newsreader will look after the rest.

> **Warning:** Virus check any programs you download from Usenet –
> or, better still, don't go near them. The same goes for Word
> documents with macros. And just because you can find full
> PlayStation CDs posted to **alt.binaries.cd** doesn't make it legal for
> you to burn them to disc – even for your own use.

Getting access to more groups

No news server carries every group. Some groups are restricted to a local geographical area or one ISP's network. Other groups which are deemed unpopular or irrelevant by your newsfeeder might be cut to conserve disk space, or they might have a policy to ban certain groups and hierarchies – it's their call.

This is not entirely a bad thing, as it takes less bandwidth to keep the Usenet file up-to-date and thus reduces the general level of Net traffic. And **most providers are flexible**. If, say, your provider has arbitrarily decided to exclude all foreign-language and minor regional groups, and you're interested in Icelandic botany and Indian plumbing, you might be able to get the **groups added to the feed** simply by asking. However, sometimes omissions are due to **censorship**. Many providers remove groups on moral grounds, or to avoid controversy. The usual ones to get the chop are the **alt.binaries.pictures.erotica** (pornography), **alt.sex** and **alt.warez** (software hacking and piracy) hierarchies.

If you can't get the groups you want from your provider, your account doesn't come with a newsfeed (for example, at work), or you have privacy concerns, you needn't resort to another ISP. You could sign up for a **news-only account** with a Usenet specialist, such as:

http://www.newsguy.com

http://www.supernews.com

http://www.usenetserver.com

For help in choosing a **commercial newsfeed provider**, see:

http://www.newsreaders.com

http://www.exit109.com/~jeremy/news/providers/

http://members.tripod.com/~newscompare/

Publicly accessible newsfeeds are rare and short-lived:

http://www.newzbot.com

http://home1.gte.net/docthomp/servers.htm

Unless you're chasing binaries, you'd do better at **Google Groups**.

chapter 9

Searching Usenet

See p.183.

How it gets from A to B

Although Usenet messages seem like email, they actually belong to a separate system called **NNTP** (Network News Transport Protocol). Your Usenet provider (for example, your ISP) maintains an independent database of Usenet messages, which it updates in periodic exchanges with neighbouring news servers. It receives and dispatches messages anything from once a day to instantly. Due to this pass-the-ball procedure, messages might appear immediately on your screen as you post them, but propagate around the world at the mercy of whoever's in between. Exactly how much newsfeed you get, and what you see, depends on your provider's neighbours and how often they update their messages. These days, most of the time, it's almost as fast as email.

Starting your own newsgroup

With Usenet already buckling under the weight of 85,000-plus newsgroups, you'll need fairly specialized tastes to get the urge to start another – plus a smattering of technical know-how. For instructions, see: http://www.geocities.com/nnqweb/ncreate.html

Further help

For beginners' guides, and more on Usenet in general, see:
http://www.geocities.com/nnqweb/nnqlinks.html
http://www.newsreaders.com
And, for tips and hacks to **enhance Agent**:
http://www.skuz.net/madhat/agent/patch.html

Chat – join the party

You won't really feel the full impact of having instant access to a cast of millions until you **jump into your first chat session**. You might even find it a touch spooky at first – you can type something in, and within seconds someone replies. Even if chat doesn't quite sound like your sort of thing, at least give it a go once or twice, just for fun.

You'll find Internet chat opportunities at almost every corner, particularly within the Online Services, and increasingly, on the Web. AOL and CompuServe are known for their **chat forums**, which often host interviews with notable **celebrities**. You have to be a member, though, to join in. But don't let that bother you because there are ample **chat forums on the Web** (p.252), and way more again within an entirely separate system called **IRC** (p.247). Or, if you'd prefer to chat among your circle of friends, you might prefer to install an **instant messenger** (p.254) or even try your hand at **Internet telephony** and **videoconferencing** (p.257). The possibilities for communication are endless.

If you're only chatting in text, you won't need a particularly fast connection, nor a powerful computer. Voice and video are another matter: the more speed you throw at them, the better they work. Ideally, you don't want to be paying timed **online charges**, because once you're hooked you'll end up squandering hours online.

How it works

Unlike Usenet and email, on Internet chat **conversations are live**. Joining a **chat channel**, **chat room** or **chat forum** is like **arriving at a party**. It could be full of people, or you might be the first to arrive. Whatever you say in that channel is instantly broadcast to everybody else on the same channel, even if they're logged into a server on the other side of the world. And you can expect them to reply as instantly as if they were in the same room.

Some channels (chat rooms) are obviously dedicated to **specific topics** but most are merely **informal chat lines**. While chat might have business potential in areas such as customer support, it's overwhelmingly orientated to **social banter.** Such idle natter between consenting strangers can lead to the online equivalent of seriously heavy petting, and inevitably makes it particularly attractive to teens. It can also make it unnervingly confrontational, so tread with caution.

Take precautions

Of all the Net's corners, chat is the one most likely to trip up newbies – mainly because you can't hide your presence. For example, on Usenet, unless you jump in and post, no one can tell you've been following the discussion. However, the second you arrive in an IRC channel **you'll be announced** to all, and your nickname will remain in the names list for as long as you stay.

If you select someone's name in your channel, and click the right button, you'll be able to find out a little bit about them. So bear in mind that others might be checking you out in the same way.

Whatever you do, **don't click on files sent to you** by a stranger. This is the most common way of spreading **Trojans** (p.159), which can do all sorts of damage – such as opening your PC to outsiders. While its file extension might say it's a harmless JPEG image, it's possible that after the **.jpg** there are about a hundred spaces followed by an **.exe**. In other words, it could be a program in disguise. And **don't rely on your virus checker** to pick them up. The kids on IRC are smarter than that.

As an extra precaution against attacks, install a personal **fire-**

wall (p.163). It will protect you from anyone trying to access your computer from outside, and alert you to any stealth programs trying to access the Internet from your machine.

For the same reasons, **don't enter any unfamiliar commands at the request of another person**. If someone is bothering you privately, protest publicly. If no one defends you, change channels. If they persist, get them kicked out by an operator.

IRC

Because **IRC** (**Internet Relay Chat**) predates the World Wide Web, chatting online required specialized software until recently. With the advent of the Web and clever use of Java, new users seem to be overlooking the somewhat more arcane world of IRC in favour of the instant gratification of Webchat (p.252) and the instant messaging programs (p.254). Nonetheless, in many ways IRC is the technically superior system. The software gives you far greater control than you could ever expect from a simple Web interface. For this reason it's preferred by **techie types**, particularly file traders and Linux eggs. So, if you're hoping to meet your perfect match in IRC, expect them to be at one with computers. Perhaps too much so.

Choosing your chat software

Net software bundles often omit a standard IRC program. But that's no problem – you can download one in a few minutes. **mIRC** (http://www.mirc.co.uk) is by far the most popular under Windows, while **Ircle** (http://www.ircle.com) rules on the Mac. For more, check any of the major software archives (see p.280).

chapter 9

Getting started

There's not much to configure. First, you'll need to think up a **nickname** for yourself. That's something that will identify you in the channel, so if you make it something rude you can expect to be ignored or treated accordingly. Next, you'll have to decide what to enter as your **real name** and **email address**. For privacy's sake and to avoid potential embarrassment, stick to an alias. Finally, enter a **chat server address**. You'll probably be offered a choice from a dropdown menu, either within your user options or upon connecting. Experiment with a few and settle on whichever takes your fancy.

If it's not obvious where to enter your details refer to the program's Help files. In fact, it wouldn't hurt to run through any tutorials either. It might sound a bit pedestrian but it will pay off. Chat programs have an array of cryptic buttons and windows that are less intuitive than most Internet programs. Before you start randomly clicking on things to see what they do, **remember that people are watching**.

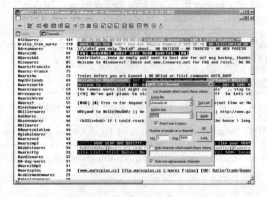

The servers

There are hundreds of open IRC hosts worldwide, many of them linked together through networks such as **Undernet**, **DALnet** and **EFnet**. To ease the strain on network traffic, start with a **nearby host**. The best place to get a fresh list of servers, or indeed any information about IRC, is from the **alt.irc** newsgroup. Alternatively, try **http://www.irchelp.org/irchelp/networks/**

For starters, choose a host from your chat program's "Connect Setup" menu or try: **us.undernet.org** on port 6667.

IRC commands

IRC has **hundreds of commands**, but you can safely get by only knowing a few. However, the more you learn, the more you can strengthen your position. You can almost get away without learning any commands at all with modern programs, but it won't hurt to know the script behind the buttons, and you may even prefer it. Your client won't automate everything, so each time you're online, test a few more. The Help file should contain a full list. If not, try any of the Chat help sites, such as:

IRC Help http://www.irchelp.org

Chatcircuit http://www.chatcircuit.com

IRC-Chat.org http://www.irc-chat.org

There are far too many commands to list here, but those below will get you started. Note that **anything after a forward slash (/) is interpreted as a command**: if you leave off the slash, it will be transmitted to your active channel as a message and you'll look like a dork.

/AWAY <message> Leave message saying you're not available

/BYE Exit IRC session

/CLEAR Clear window contents

/HELP List available commands

/HELP <command> Return help on this command

/IGNORE <nickname><*><all> Ignore this nickname

/IGNORE <*><email address><all> Ignore this email address

/IGNORE <*><*><none> Delete ignorance list

/JOIN <#channel> Join this channel

/KICK <nickname> Boot this nickname off channel

/LEAVE <#channel> Exit this channel

/LIST <-MIN n> List channels with minimum of *n* users

/MOP Promote all to operator status

/MSG <nickname><message> Send private message to this nickname

/NICK <nickname> Change your nickname

/OP <nickname> Promote this nickname to operator

/PING <#channel> Check ping times to all users

/QUERY <nickname> Start a private conversation with this nickname

/TOPIC <new topic> Change channel topic

/WHO* List users in current channel

/WHOIS <nickname> Display nickname's identity

/WHOWAS <nickname> Display identity of exited nickname

Step by step through your first session

By now, you've configured your client, chosen a **nickname you'll never use again** and are raring to go. The aim of your first session is to connect to a server, have a look around, get a list of channels, join one, see who's on, say something public, then something private, leave the channel, start a new channel, make yourself operator, change the topic, and then exit IRC. The whole process should take no more than about ten minutes. **Let's go**.

➡ Log on to a server and wait to be accepted. If you're not, keep trying others until you succeed. Once aboard, you'll be greeted with the MOTD (message of the day) in the server window. Read the message and see if it tells you anything interesting.

➡ You should have at least two windows available: one for input, the other to display server output. Generally, the two windows form part of a larger window, with the input box below the output box. Even though your client's point-and-click interface will replace most of the basic commands, since you probably haven't read its manual yet you won't know how to use it. So instead just use the commands.

➡ To see what channels are available, type: **/LIST** You'll have to wait a minute and then a window will pop up, or fill up, with thousands of channels, their topics, and the number of users on them. To narrow down the list to those channels with six or more users, type: **/LISTMIN 6** Now you'll see the busiest channels.

➡ Pick a channel at random and join it. Channel names are always preceded by #, so to join the lard channel, type: **/JOIN #lard** and then wait for the channel window to appear. (Clicking on its name should have the same effect in most programs.) Once the channel window opens, you should get a list of the channel's occupants in yet another window. If not, type: **/WHO*** for a full list including nicknames and email addresses.

➡ Now say something clever. Type: **Hi everyone, it's great to be back!** This should appear not only on the screen in your channel window, but on the screen in every other person's channel window. Wait for replies and answer any questions as you see fit.

➡ Now it's time to send something personal. Choose someone in the channel and find out what you can about them first, by typing: **/WHO** followed by their nickname. Your client might let you do this by just double-clicking on their nickname in the names window. Let's say their nickname is Tamster. To send a private message, just type: **/MSG Tamster Hey Tamster, I'm a clueless newbie, let me know if you get this so I won't feel so stupid.**

➡ If Tamster doesn't reply, keep trying until someone does. Once you're satisfied you know how that works, leave the channel by typing: **/LEAVE** Don't worry, next time you go into a channel you'll feel more comfortable.

➡ Now to start your own channel. Pick any name that doesn't already exist. As soon as you leave, it will disappear. To start a

channel called lancelink, just type: **/JOIN #lancelink**. Once the
window pops up, you'll find you're the only person on it. Now promote yourself to operator by typing: **/OP** followed by your nickname. Others can tell you have channel operator status because
your nickname will appear with an @ in front of it. Now you're an
operator – you have the power to kick people off the channel,
change the topic, and all sorts of other things that you can find
out by reading the manual as recommended. To change the topic,
type: **/TOPIC** followed by whatever you want to change the topic
to. Wait for it to change on the top of your window and then type:
/BYE to exit IRC.

That's it, really – a whirlwind tour, but enough to learn most
things you'll need. Now before you can chat with other chat-
ters, you'll need to **speak their lingo**. See p.222.

IRC games

Some chat channels are dedicated to **games**. You might play
against other people, but more commonly you're up against programs called **bots.** Such programs are written to respond to
requests in a particular way, and even learn from the experience.
You'll also come across bots in standard chat channels. It might
even take you some time to recognize you're not talking to a
human.

For more about IRC games, see: **http://dmoz.org/Games/
Internet/Chat/IRC/**

Webchat

Like almost every other aspect of the old-world Internet, chat
too has moved onto the Web. **Webchat** doesn't require a special
IRC program – all you need is your Web browser. Because of
this, it's becoming more popular than IRC, especially among
new arrivals.

Simple Webchat isn't as instant as IRC, as you have to wait a little while for the page to refresh to follow responses. However, most decent Webchat is done through Java, ActiveX or a small program download, which makes it just like a crippled but fool-proof version of the real thing. And in some cases you can circumvent the Web interface and log onto the server directly with your dedicated chat program. You only need find out the server address, and then enter the channel name.

Just about all the top-line portals have strong chat facilities, divided by interest and region, coupled with planned events guides and links to chat elsewhere.

About.com http://chatting.about.com
Excite http://chat.excite.com
Lycos http://chat.lycos.com
MSN http://chat.msn.com
Yahoo! http://chat.yahoo.com

You'll also find chat (or at least a bulletin board) at any site that's attempting to create a community around their content, such as most investment, gaming and newspaper sites. For more, browse the chat sections of the following directories:

LookSmart http://www.looksmart.com
Open Directory http://dmoz.org/Computers/Internet/Chat/
Yahoo! http://www.yahoo.com

What's on

Although most of what goes on in chat rooms is spontaneous, they also play host to loads of organized events, including

celebrity interviews and topical debates. The big ones tend to hide behind the Online Service curtain, but the Net still attracts its share. For a calendar of what's planned across all forms of Internet chat, including the structured Web-based alternatives, such as **Talk City** (http://www.talkcity.com), see **Yack** (http://www.yack.com). Also check the **events guides** at the various portals, such as: http://guide.yahoo.com

Chat worlds

There's no doubt virtual reality can look quite cute, but there's not much call for it. The best applications so far seem to be among the **chat worlds**, **virtual cities** and **avatars**. These tend to work like IRC, but with an extra dimension or two. So rather than channels, you get rooms, playgrounds, swimming pools and so forth. To switch channels, you might walk into another building or fly up into the clouds. You might be represented by an animated character rather than a text nickname and be able to do all sorts of multimedia things such as build 3D objects and play music.

This all sounds pretty futuristic and it's certainly impressive at first, but whether you'll want to become a regular is another matter. The most popular are:

The Palace http://www.thepalace.com

World's Chat http://www.worlds.com

If it's action and hi-tech graphics you're after, however, head straight to the world of **Online Gaming**. See p.300.

Instant Messaging (IM)

IRC, Webchat and Online Service forums are fine for meeting complete strangers, but they're not the best for talking privately amongst friends. If you'd like to corner your pals as soon as they pop online, consider an instant messaging (IM) program – but bear in mind the downsides mentioned on p.256.

How they work

Installing an IM program is a bit like joining a club. Once you're on board you can **send messages**, **trade files** and set up **impromptu chat sessions** with other members. Although this sounds a bit like email, it goes a few steps further. For example, once you add someone to your contact (or buddy) list, you can instantly tell when they go online – unless they've chosen to hide their presence. So you can send them a quick note and expect an immediate reply, or a text, voice or video chat session. If they're not online, you can send a note for them to receive

the second they log on. While they're undoubtedly popular amongst the same gossipy set as other chat programs, Internet messengers are also beginning to find their place in the office as serious business tools.

Which one?

You're certainly not starved for choice when it comes to IM software. AOL commands the lion's share of the market with **AOL Instant Messenger (AIM)** and **ICQ**, the two most heavily featured and used systems, and these are followed in popularity by MSN and Yahoo!'s respective messengers. All are crammed with goodies – ICQ, for instance, can send SMS messages to mobile phones – and none will cost you any money. They will, however, take up plenty of your time time installing, figuring out how they work and, of course, playing message ping-pong.

AOL Instant Messenger http://www.aol.com/aim/

ICQ http://www.icq.com

MSN Messenger http://messenger.msn.com

Yahoo! Messenger http://messenger.yahoo.com

At the time of writing, none can communicate with the other, so if your friends have already taken the dive in one direction, you might as well go the same way. However, if your mates are split between two or more, you might prefer a free program that can connect to all of them, such as **Imici** or **Trillian**:

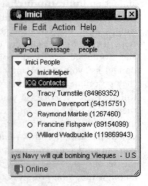

Imici http://www.imici.com

Trillian http://www.trillian.cc

If you're running Windows XP, don't even try downloading MSN Messenger – it won't work. XP comes with its own utility, **Windows Messenger**, pre-installed. It can be found on the Start menu. For help with Windows Messenger, see http://messenger.jonathankay.com

The downside

Once the novelty subsides, you might find instant messengers to be more of a **nuisance than they're worth**. AIM and ICQ would have to be two of the most notoriously buggy and meddlesome programs in mass circulation. If you find them crashing too often, popping up windows, interfering with your online activities and/or slowing down your system, disable them from loading at startup. If you tire of being perpetually buzzed by your friends as you're trying to work, opt to hide your presence (invisible mode). And, finally, when you're ready to give them the flick, be sure to uninstall them completely through "Add/Remove Programs" in the Control Panel.

Apart from their nuisance potential and drain on your system resources, they also introduce a new security risk. As with any other medium, never run any files sent to you by strangers, and preferably operate behind a firewall such as **ZoneAlarm.** If you install ICQ, at least read the following:

http://www.icq.com/features/security/

Internet telephony

The concept of using the **Internet as an alternative to the telephone network** is getting some quarters quite frisky – mainly because it can **cut the cost of calling long distance** to that of a local call plus Internet charges (at both ends). It works but don't expect the same fidelity, convenience or reliability as your local regular phone network. In other words, give it a go for curiosity's sake, but don't invest any money in it.

To place a Net call through your computer, you need a **soundcard**, **speakers** and a **microphone** – standard multimedia fare. Alternatively, pick up a **hands-free headset** with a built-in microphone, and if you want to try videoconferencing (p.259) you'll obviously need a **webcam**. If your soundcard permits duplex transmission (is able to encode and decode sound simultaneously), you can hold a regular conversation like an ordinary telephone; otherwise it's more like a walkie-talkie where you take turns to speak. A modem is generally ample for the task, but the higher the bandwidths at each end, the better your chance of decent sound quality.

Phone programs

You have plenty of choice in **Net phone programs**. Some, like **Internet Phone**, are similar to IRC – you log into a server and join a channel. Others, such as **WebPhone**, are more like an ordinary phone and start a point-to-point connection when you choose a name from a directory. Check into any software archive for a selection (see p.280).

Most regard **Microsoft NetMeeting** as the pick of the pack. It has **real-time voice and videoconferencing**, plus things like collaborative application sharing, document editing, background file transfer and a whiteboard to draw and paste on. Even better, it's free. Grab the latest version through Windows Update, or from:

http://www.microsoft.com/netmeeting/

Internet to telephone

It's also possible to initiate a call from your PC to a normal telephone at the other end. With **DialPad** (http://www.dialpad.com), you can talk as long as you like to any number in the US from anywhere in the world entirely free, and call phones worldwide at a cut-price rate. **Net2Phone** (http://www.net2phone.com) is similar, but charges within the US.

Calling a phone rather than a PC is a lot more convenient as it means you can call almost anyone worldwide, whether or not they're online. Of course, it's not as convenient as using a telephone at your end, so compare the price with a **discount calling card** and decide whether it's worth the added bother.

Alternatively, there's **Aplio Phone** (http://www.aplio.com), which looks like an ordinary telephone and works similarly except it automatically initiates a call through each end's ISP. The sound is passable, albeit with slight delay, but you'll need to tally the combined cost of both party's Internet access and local call charges, and factor in the cost of the units at each end, to tell whether it's cheaper than a discount calling card. At the moment it seems unlikely.

Videoconferencing

You might like the idea of seeing who you're talking to, but you'll need serious bandwidth to make **Internet videoconferencing** anything more than a slide show. But, if it means seeing live footage of a loved one across the world, perhaps it's worth it. All you need's a relatively cheap webcam and **Netmeeting**.

10

Download software

So many programs, so little time

Whether you need a browser upgrade, the latest Quake patch or some obscure CD mastering software, the Internet is the very first place to look. Just about every program that's released nowadays finds its way onto the Net, and most of the time you can download a full working copy. If not you should be able to order it on disk by email direct from the publisher – at the very least.

What you certainly will be able to find is all the **Internet software** you'll ever need. And the good news is you can download the pick of the crop, for free. Not only that, but you can often upgrade your system and existing software for free. So don't be afraid to replace your starter kit. Once you're online, you can use whatever you like.

File transfer – defined

The operation of copying a file – such as a program, image, movie or even a webpage – from one machine to another is called a **file transfer**. When it's headed for your machine, it's called a **download**. Normally, downloading simply "**copies**" the file to your hard drive, leaving the original undisturbed. An **upload** is a transfer in the other direction. You need special permission from the server to delete, upload or change files (p.270).

What you'll need

You won't need any special software to start downloading; you can do almost everything with your Web browser. However, you may need some **decompression software** to get the downloaded file to install (see p.273) and, as your demands increase, you might like to investigate the range of dedicated file transfer (**FTP**), sharing, archiving and download management utilities. We'll discuss these in the following pages.

Where to start

The very first thing to do once you've read what follows is to drop into **Windows Update** (p.71) and pick up the latest browser, mail software, drivers and security patches (p.161). Next, peruse our list of recommended programs (p.276), and then hit the software guides for more (p.280).

Free and almost free

While the Internet might be a veritable clearing house of freely available software, it's not all genuinely free. There are five types of programs you're allowed to use, at least for a while, without paying. They're known as **freeware, adware, shareware, betas** and **demo programs**.

Freeware

Freeware is provided by its author(s) at no cost to you. It could be a complete program, a demonstration sample with crippled features, a patch to enhance another program or an interim upgrade. If you like the program, write and thank the developers. It's the least you can do in return.

Adware

Adware is freeware that serves you advertising banners. The banners themselves aren't usually a hindrance, but sometimes the mechanism of getting them to you can cause nasty crashes. Then there's the question of whether they're spying on you. See p.264.

Shareware

Shareware comes with strings attached, which you accept when you install or run the program. Commonly, these may include the condition that you must pay to continue to use it after an initial free trial period, or that you pay if you intend to use it commercially. Sometimes a shareware program, while adequate, is a short form of a more solid or better-featured registered version. You might upgrade to this if you like the shareware, usually by paying a registration fee, in return for which the author or software distributor will mail you a code to unlock the program or its upgrade.

Betas

Betas (and Platform Previews) are distributed as part of the

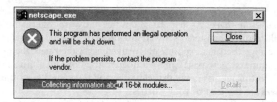

testing process in commercial software development. You shouldn't pay for them as they're not finished products. But they're often good enough for the task, and usually right at the cutting edge of technology. Take Netscape and Internet Explorer betas, for example. They've been the most popular programs ever to hit the Net.

With all betas, expect to encounter **bugs and quirks** now and again and don't be too upset about having to restart the program (or your computer) occasionally – it's all part of the development process. Do report recurring faults to the developers: that's why they let you have it for free. If it's just too buggy, get an alternative.

Demo programs

Demo software is crippled or stripped back to the point that you can see what it does, but if you want to use it, you'll need to order the full program.

Protect your privacy

It seems few people will pay for software if they can avoid it. Run a search on "crack" or "serial no" in any search engine, or check into **AstaLaVista** (http://www.astalavista.com) or **Share Reactor** (http://www.sharereactor.com) and you'll soon see how rife pirating has become. As a result, Internet software developers have been forced to prostitute their programs to ad-serving networks and marketing sharks. At first glance this free "**adware**" alternative to full-featured registered software might seem a happy marriage – the advertisers get exposure, the marketers get their stats, the programmers get paid and you get the product for nix. Unfortunately, it's rarely that clear cut, and those **pesky ad banners** are the least of your worries.

Gibson Research (http://grc.com/optout.htm/), for example, has gone as far as labelling it "**spyware**", accusing the ad hustlers of all sorts of privacy infringements, including tracking your online activities and calling home with the results. At the time of writing these allegations are a little on the wild side, and have little concrete supporting evidence, but they're still plausible.

Invasion of privacy, however, is only half the story. Adware is also notorious for **crashing your system**. And some leave behind active remains after they're uninstalled, further adding to your woes.

On an even more cynical note, the adware concept has also sparked off a rash of **useless programs** that are little more than purpose-built ad servers or data collectors. You can usually spot them because they sound like "as-seen-on-TV products" – that is, they're designed to sell, not to use. Don't even consider installing anything that claims to **accelerate your browser**, **optimize your modem**, enhance your **mouse cursor** or **serve extra information on the sites you visit**. Your browser is touchy enough as it is, without adding more junk to it. You especially do not need **search aids that integrate into the browser**.

You'll find **RealNetworks** and **AOL/Netscape** will aggressively thrust third-party software your way during updates. Say no to it all. Read independent reviews before you download anything, and get it straight from the source.

If the prospect of browsing the Web entirely ad-free sounds appealing, try **Adfilter** (http://www.adfilter.co.uk) or **WebWasher** (http://www.webwasher.com). They can automatically cull ad banners and pop-ups, which might even speed up your session. The downside is they could also cut useful information, or disable critical tasks like Windows Update. Take care.

Plunder the Web

Most of your downloads will come from the Web. For instance, if you were to read a review of a computer game you can bet your back door it will contain a link to download a demo. To retrieve it, all you should need to do is **click on the link and follow the prompts**. You might have to supply a bit of information, but it all should be self-explanatory. Your Web browser will take care of everything. Well, almost everything – as you'll soon find out.

The download process

Webpages typically consist of several images laid out on a page of text. So when you load one, you're actually kicking off multiple file transfers – a separate transfer for each element of the page. Your Web browser recognizes that the elements are parts of a webpage and displays them in your browser. Now let's say you click on a link to a file that's not normally an element of a webpage, such as a program. When your browser locates the file, it will examine its file type (see p.274) and decide that it's not meant to be displayed. Because it

84% of dap43.exe Completed

Saving:
dap43.exe from download1.speedbit.com
Estimated time left: 44 sec (964 KB of 1.13 MB copied)
Download to: C:\WINDOWS\Desktop\do...\dap43.exe
Transfer rate: 4.40 KB/Sec
☑ Close this dialog box when download completes

Open | Open Folder | Cancel

doesn't know what to do, it will ask you whether to **open or save it**.

You would only choose "Open" if you want to play or display the file as it downloads; for example, if you're downloading a movie or sound file over a high bandwidth connection.

Otherwise, choose "**Save**" and browse to where you'd like to put it on your computer. The Desktop is usually the most convenient location (see p.270). Once that's done, a new window will appear with a running estimate of the transfer rate and time until completion.

The **Mac version of Internet Explorer** automatically places all your downloads in one place (the Desktop unless you specify otherwise in the Internet section of the Control Panel). It also features a useful **Download Manager** window, which lets you view all your current and recent downloads simultaneously.

What if it tries to open the file?

If you want to save a file to your hard drive but your browser insists on trying to open it or display it as a page, rather than click on the link, right-click and choose "Save Target As" from the mouse menu. This often happens with movies and PDF (Adobe Acrobat) files. You can prevent it from happening in future by adjusting the offending program's settings.

Carry on surfing

There's no reason to down tools while you wait for the download to finish. You can continue to browse the Web, and even start more downloads. Bear in mind, however, that webpages will take longer to load with a download going on in the background.

FTP or HTTP – huh?

You don't need to understand the protocols used for transferring files on the Internet, but you're sure to bump into the terminology. The two most used for downloading are **HTTP** (HyperText Transfer Protocol) and **FTP** (File Transfer Protocol). About all you need to know is that HTTP is handled by a **Web server**, and FTP by an **FTP server** (see p.268). If you're presented with alternative links for either protocol, flip a coin.

Resume downloads

As downloads can take some time – hours, even, if it's a big program and your link is slow – it's helpful if your transfer program supports **resume downloads**. Then if you drop out, you can go back and pick up where you left off. That's a real lifesaver if you're ninety percent through downloading a 35MB game demo. Netscape and Internet Explorer are supposed to support resume downloads, but it doesn't always work in practice. All the more reason to get a dedicated **download manager**.

Download managers

If you're serious about downloads, get a download manager such

as **Download Accelerator Plus** (http://www.downloadaccelerator .com), which is available free of charge, or **Mass Downloader** (http://www.metaproducts.com), which is shareware. Both integrate into your mouse button menu, but Mass Downloader is a little more powerful in that it can leech all the links in one action. You can assign them to take over whenever they detect a file download of a certain type, such as **.zip**, **.exe** or **.mp3**.

They can search for alternative locations and tell you which one is quickest, and speed up downloads considerably by setting up parallel transfer streams. And if you break the transfer it can take over where it left off (as long as the server supports resume downloads). Experiment with the option of letting them monitor your clipboard and browser clicks. But you might find they get in the way and prefer to just call them up as needed. There are plenty of similar products, but steer clear of **Go!Zilla**, which causes nasty crashes in Internet Explorer.

FTP servers

Only a couple of years ago, most of your downloads would come from dedicated FTP servers. They still exist, but more and more files are being stored on the Web. Nonetheless, FTP still plays an important role in storing and moving files about the Internet.

FTP programs

While you can use your Web browser or download manager to handle your FTP downloads, serious FTP heads prefer dedicat-

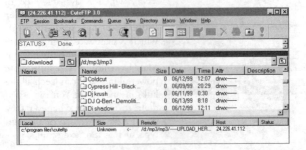

ed FTP programs, especially if they're **uploading files** such as webpages. You'll find a wide choice on offer at any of the major file archives (p.280). None are anywhere near as easy as using a Web browser. You'll definitely need to **read the Help file**.

FTP addresses

FTP domains are often prefixed by **ftp.** but that's not a rule. When you're supplied a file location it could be in the form **ftp.fish.com/pub/dir/jane.zip** That tells you that the file **jane.zip** is located in the directory **pub/dir** on the **ftp.fish.com** server. You can enter that address directly into your Web browser to start the download process. If the file isn't there, you'll see some kind of error message. You can try browsing the server to see if it's moved by removing the file's name (**jane.zip**) from the end of the address – in the same way you'd look for a missing webpage (p.190). However, not all servers will let you browse. You'll soon find out.

Logging into an FTP server

Unless you've been granted special permission to log into an FTP server to transfer files, you'll have to use one that permits **anonymous FTP**. Such sites follow a standard log-in. Once you're in, you can look through the contents of a limited number of directories and transfer files to, and sometimes from, your computer.

Many **Net servers** have areas set aside for anonymous FTP. Some even carry massive specialist **file archives**. And most **software houses** provide updates, patches and interim releases on their own anonymous FTP sites. No single server will have everything you need, but you'll soon find favourites for each type of file. Your ISP should have an FTP area, too, where you can transfer files for updating webpages, download access software and exchange files with colleagues.

Browsing an FTP server

You can browse an FTP server in much the same way as your own hard drive, except under the restrictions set by the administrator. Once you're accepted onto the server, you'll see a listing of the initial directory's contents. Look for a contents file called **readme**, **index** or the like. That should tell you what's in the folder.

Uploading files

Unless the owner has specifically granted you permission, you won't be able to upload, rename, delete or move files on a remote server. This is called "**read only**" access. In essence, this means you can "read" but you can't "write" or delete. Site administrators can fine-tune these permissions in all sorts of ways. For instance, if you're building your own website and you need to upload new pages, you'll have to enter a password to gain "write" access.

You can upload through your Web browser, but it's simpler with a dedicated program. You'll need to log into the site, probably with a legitimate username and password, switch to the directory and start the transfer. With most programs it's as simple as dragging and dropping the file. Check your Help file if it's not obvious.

Set up your folders

Before you start installing every Internet program you can find, sort out your folders. Otherwise you'll make a jungle of your hard drive.

Hard drives are organized into tree-like structures. On Macs and in Windows this tree comprises a hierarchy of **folders** (or

directories in DOS, UNIX and Windows 3.x), which contain further folders and, of course, your files.

In Windows the primary hard drive is generally labelled "**C:**" and can be found in My Computer; on the Mac it sits on your Desktop. No matter what system you're running, you'd be well advised to use the following folders to manage your downloads (it's best not to lob things straight into the drive at the highest – **root** – level). These folders can be found in your primary hard drive, or you can create them yourself:

Download

Configure your **browser, newsreader and download managers** to download to a common **Download folder** and create a shortcut (alias) on your desktop to open it. Think of it as an in-tray and clear it accordingly. Alternatively, save files onto your **Desktop** but deal with them straight away.

Temporary

When opening a compressed program download, extract it to a **Temporary folder** ready for installation. Once done, delete the contents of the Temporary folder.

chapter 10

Programs

Install all programs into their own separate subfolders within your operating system's main programs or applications folder. In Windows this folder is called **Program Files**, and most programs will install themselves by default to it (it's wisest to take this choice where possible, as it's less likely to cause problems later).

Archive

Keep all the original installation files you've downloaded in an **Archive folder** in case you need to reinstall them later. Make sure there are enough subfolders to make it easy to find things again. If space is an issue, delete older archive versions of a program when you download a new one, though older versions can be useful where you find the newer edition to be either too buggy or not to your taste.

You could open your archive to your peers through an FTP server or a file-sharing program like **Gnutella** (http://www .gnutelliums.com). And, where possible, back up all your installation files on a CD or elsewhere.

Folders in Windows XP

Windows XP features a first-level folder called "Documents and Settings" that contains a named folder for each "User" and a folder for "Shared Documents". If several people use your machine, and all have their own downloads to manage, use these named folders to house everyone's "Download", "Temporary", "Document" and "Archive" folders. But take note that everyone still shares the same Program Files folder.

File types and compression

Don't expect your browser or operating system to be able to open every type of file you throw at it. You might need some more software to decompress or make sense of many downloads. For our pick of the essentials, see p.276.

Compression

Files available for downloading are very often **compressed**. There are two very good reasons for this. One is to decrease their transfer times (and storage space), and the other is to bundel a selection of files into a single "**archive**". After you download a compressed file, you must decompress it to get it to work. Before you can decompress it, you need the right program to do the job.

PC compression software

Most PC archive files end in the extension **.exe** or **.zip**. The **.exe** files are usually **self-extracting archives**, which means they unpack themselves when double-clicked. Others will only open if you have the necessary software.

Recent versions of Windows (Me and XP) have decompression – and compression – tools for **.zip** and some other formats built-in. Simply right-click the file or folder and look for the "Extract All" option. But if you're on an older PC platform, or struggling to open a specific file, you'll need to download a program or two. **WinZip** (http://www.winzip.com) is probably the most popular option, though you'll be able to handle most files with a freeware utility such as **UltimateZip** (http://www.ultimatezip.com). It's also worth downloading Aladdin's **Stuffit Expander** for Windows (http://www.aladdinsys.com), which will let you deal with files compressed on Macs.

Mac compression software

Compressed Macintosh files usually end in .bin, .cpt, .sit, .sea or .hqx. The .sea files **self-extract** when you click on them; the rest do so by opening with **Stuffit Expander**.

If you're **expanding a Mac file for PC use**, set the options under Cross Platform to "convert text files to Windows format when the file is known to contain text" and "never save files in MacBinary Format".

Internet Explorer will automatically decode MacBinary and BinHex files unless you specify otherwise within "Download Options" in Preferences.

File extensions and their programs

The following table shows some common **file extensions** and the **programs needed to decompress or view them**. For a list of every file format in the world, see:

http://whatis.techtarget.com/fileFormatA/

Extension	File type	Program to decompress or view
.ace	ACE	archiveWinAce, WinRAR
.asf	Advanced	Windows Media Player streaming format
.bin	MacBinary	MacBinary, usually automatic in Macs
.bmp	Bitmap	Graphics viewer
.cab	Cabinet file	WinZip
.cpt	Mac Compact	Compact Pro, Stuffit Expander Pro archive
.doc	MS Word	Word processor such as MS Word document or Wordpad
.exe	PC-executable	Self-executing from DOS or Windows

.gif	Graphic	Graphics Interchange Format
.hqx	Mac BinHex	BinHex, Stuffit Expander
.jpg	Compressed graphic	Graphics viewer
.mov	Quicktime movie	Quicktime Player
.mp3	MP3 audio file	Media player
.mpg	Compressed video	Media player
.pls	MP3 playlist	Media player
.pdf	Portable Document File	Adobe Acrobat
.pit	Mac PackIt	PackIt
.ra, .ram	RealAudio	RealPlayer
.rar	RAR compressed archive	WinRAR, WinACE
.sea	Mac self-extracting	Click on icon to extract archive
.sit	Stuffit compressed	Stuffit Expander archive
.txt	Plain text	Notepad, text editor, word processor
.wav	WAV audio file	Media player
.wma	Windows media file	Windows Media Player
.uu, .uue	UU-encoded	WinZip, Stuffit Expander
.zip	ZIP compressed archive	WinZip, Stuffit Expander

Watch out for viruses

Remember always to examine incoming files for bogus extensions (p.165) and scan for viruses before opening (p.162). You don't need to scan your whole system, just the file.

Installing it

Downloading a program from the Net should be relatively painless. Just go to its developer's website, read about it first, decide whether it sounds useful and, if so, fill in any required details, and pick the **appropriate version** for your system – Windows,

Mac, UNIX, DOS, etc. If the choice isn't there, you can usually tell which platform a given download is for by looking at the file type (see p.274).

Most files will **self-extract**, so installation should be as simple as following the prompts. If not, you'll need a decompression program (see p.273) to extract the installation files. Once extracted, read the accompanying text files for installation instructions. It's usually a matter of clicking on a file called "install.exe" or "setup.exe" in Windows, or on an install icon on the Mac.

Uninstalling

If the program doesn't float your boat, remove it from your hard drive so you don't clog up your system with rubbish. In Windows, that means deleting it from within **Add/Remove Programs** in the Control Panel. If there's no entry in there, look for an uninstall icon in its Start menu folder. If neither exists, it will be safe to delete the file directly from its folder. Note that some programs will hijack your file associations, so to get file types to open automatically with a previous program you might have to go into that program's settings or simply reinstall it.

Updates

Most programs now offer the option to check for updates automatically. However, it's a common source of **mystery crashes**, so switch it off and check manually.

Software roundup

Now that Web browsers have become such Internet software lucky dips, it's no longer so important to scout around for accessories, and you certainly needn't pay for some "Internet made easy" kit. All the same, even though you can get by with the bare minimum, there's no reason to rough it.

One way to stack up with Net software is to install it from the free CDs given away with PC rags. A better way is to **get the latest versions fresh from the Net**. You could start by poking your snout into the software troughs listed on p.280. But before you trot off there, read this section, and get set with the crucial downloads first. They're all free – at least for a limited time – though some have superior commercial versions.

Windows Update – browser update

Your first concern will be to make sure your system has what it takes to dial up, connect to your ISP and jettison you onto the Web. Your next operation should be to **update your browser** to its latest version, bring your operating system up-to-date, and, if you like, gradually try some added extras. If you're running Windows with Internet Explorer, you can do it all through Windows Update (see p.71). Check back at least once every couple of weeks:

Windows Update http://www.windowsupdate.com

Update your drivers

To get the best from your hardware, grab all the latest device drivers – especially for your video card and modem. You'll find the newest drivers at the component manufacturer's website, or sometimes at your PC maker's site. They're normally located in the support section. Look for "files", "downloads" or "drivers", and follow the prompts. Alternatively, try one of the driver guides (see p.282).

chapter 10

Detect and remove "spyware"

The nastiest side effect of so-called spyware is that their parasites often remain on your system even after you've uninstalled the overlying product. These often cause weird behaviour such as crashes and improper shutdowns. If your system is playing up, it wouldn't hurt to clean out any spyware to see if it helps. Look no further than **Ad-aware** (http://www.lavasoft.nu). It can scan your memory, registry and hard drives for known spyware, and allow you to selectively remove the ad systems. Of course, removing the ad systems might disable the associated program, so before you remove them you'll have to weigh up the alternatives. To keep Ad-aware up-to-date, you'll also need to download **Refupdate** from the same address.

Wrap up in a security blanket

As mentioned tirelessly throughout this book, unless you want to expose yourself to a multitude of security risks, you'll need to keep your system up-to-date, run all incoming files through a fine-tooth comb and install a firewall (p.163). Just follow the instructions starting on p.157.

Tidy up your OE messages

If you use Outlook Express for email or newsgroups, download OE-Quotefix (http://jump.to/oe-quotefix/). Once installed, your messages will no longer be full of impossible-to-read quotes with single-word lines.

PDF – portable document files

You're sure to encounter the odd portable document file (PDF), particularly at government sites. These are like laid-out brochures, and can be viewed – either within your Web browser or in a separate window – once you've installed **Adobe's Acrobat Reader** (http://www.acrobat.com). If you're having problems viewing PDF files inside your browser, you can download the file to your hard drive and open it from there (right-click or Ctrl-click the link, choose "Save target as" from the menu and save to your Desktop). Alternatively, set up the Acrobat Reader to always open in a separate window (run the program, choose "General" under "Preferences" in the File menu and uncheck the box "Web browser integration") or launch the "Save as" box ready for downloading. This can be done in "Folder Options" in the Control Panel: select the File Types tab, select "Adobe Acrobat" under the Registered File Types, then uncheck "Browse In Same Window" and check "Confirm open after download" under the Edit or Advanced options.

Sort out your media players

Next sort out your media players, image viewers and plug-ins. For both PC and Macs, grab the latest versions of:

QuickTime **http://www.quicktime.com**

RealPlayer **http://www.real.com**

Shockwave **http://www.macromedia.com/shockwave/**

Windows Media Player **http://www.windowsmedia.com**

This will cover all the popular music and video formats at least twice over, but you might still prefer to switch programs. You'll be able to assign what plays what within each program's settings. Alternatively, if you'd like a program to take over, just reinstall it. For a rundown on the various music players, see p.286.

It's also handy to have some **image viewing and editing**

software so you can flick through saved pictures and fool around with them. Try **ACDSee** (http://www.acdsee.com) as a viewer and set it to associate with all image formats. The full release becomes inoperative after thirty days, whereas the Classic version merely nags you to register. **Irfanview** (http://www.irfanview.com) is a free alternative, but is not quite as polished. If your editing demands run a bit higher, try **Paint Shop Pro** (http://www.jasc.com), the next best thing to Adobe's professional, though somewhat overpriced, PhotoShop.

Other Internet software

Despite Microsoft, AOL, Netscape and Real Networks, there's still competition left at the boutique end of the Internet software trade. You'll find numerous standout programs mentioned within the relevant sections throughout this book, but of course there are many more, and new strains appear daily. So don't take our word for it. If you become embroiled in Usenet, for instance, investigate several newsreaders and ruthlessly toss them out if they fail to meet your expectations. Check into any of the following software guides and you'll be sure to leave with a few downloads in progress!

Software guides

When it comes to software, your biggest problem won't be finding it, but **narrowing down the choices**. That's why you'll need to turn to a software guide for assistance. These sites **list, review and rate programs** and sort them into various **categories** to make it easier to find the best tool for each job.

So where do you start? Try one of the megasites such as **Download.com**. You might be best browsing through a different one every session to see what you can find. None of them will list every program, even within one category, nor can they hope to keep up with the features changed in every release. That means the reviews are prone to going out of date or being superseded by a more recent program. Nonetheless, they do make an effort, and usually it's enough. If you're looking for something specific, it may also be worth trying some **file-sharing networks** (see p.293)

Megasites – all platforms

CNet Download.com http://www.download.com
Jumbo http://www.jumbo.com
Software Vault http://www.softwarevault.com
Version Tracker http://www.versiontracker.com
ZDNet Downloads http://www.hotfiles.com

PC-only

Rocket Download http://www.rocketdownload.com
Simtel http://www.cdrom.com
Slaughterhouse http://www.slaughterhouse.com
Winfiles http://www.winfiles.com

chapter 10

Mac-only
Chez Mark http://www.chezmark.com
Hyperarchive http://hyperarchive.lcs.mit.edu
Mac Orchard http://www.macorchard.com
Pure Mac http://www.pure-mac.com

Internet software
Dave Central http://www.davecentral.com
Stroud's http://www.stroud.com
Tucows http://www.tucows.com

Freeware
Freeware http://www.freewarehome.com
Freeware Guide http://www.freeware-guide.com
Moochers http://www.moochers.com
No Nags http://www.nonags.com

Tweaking your system
Tweakfiles http://www.tweakfiles.com

Locating hardware drivers
The Driver Forum http://www.driverforum.com
DriverGuide.com http://www.driverguide.com
PC Drivers HeadQuarters http://www.drivershq.com
WinDrivers http://www.windrivers.com

Find an alternative site
If you know the name of the file, or you need an alternative download location, try searching:
CNet Shareware.com http://www.shareware.com
Copernic http://www.copernic.com
FTPfind http://www.ftpfind.com
Lycos http://ftpsearch.lycos.com

11

Turn on the music

Listen live or play it later

Y ou can learn a lot about someone by riffling through their records and CDs, which might explain why back in the early days of vanity homepage publishing, when the Web was anarchistic and thoroughly geeky, listing your entire music collection was deemed cooler than posting your résumé.

Back then it wasn't practical to put audio samples online. Digitized music eats buckets of bytes, which makes it time-consuming to download – especially with old 14.4Kbps modems. But since then technology has advanced, both in the speed at which we connect and in the way we store music. As a result, people can now make their collections available online – much to the anguish of the music biz.

But there's more to online music than just flicking through other people's favourite songs and creating your own MP3 collection: Internet radio stations abound, many online stores (such as Amazon) feature music clips to help you choose, and numerous band sites offer exclusive tracks for their fans to download. And there's a multitude of audio players and jukebox programs available, many of which are free.

How it works

Music as it's stored on CD is too bulky to put online. A minute of sound needs roughly 10MB of disk space, which means a four-minute track would take more than three hours to download with a 56K modem. Thankfully there are several techniques that compress the music into more **space-efficient formats such as MP3**, which are quicker to transfer. These files can either be "streamed" (played straight off the Web) or downloaded to your computer and listened to at your leisure. For more, see: http://www.howstuffworks.com/mp3.htm/

Stream it live

Getting music to play in real time over a modem connection takes some pretty clever footwork in the **audio compression** department. Put very simply, this involves stripping out the bits that matter least to your ears. The catch is obvious: the more you take out, the worse it sounds.

Often files are encoded at a fixed rate low enough to cater for the average connection speed, so just because you have a clean, fast connection doesn't mean you'll get better sound. Sometimes, though, there'll be separate choices for low and high bandwidth connections. If you choose high bandwidth with a regular modem, you won't be able to download the data fast enough to play it live – it will take ages to load and drop out frequently. The same will happen if you choose low bandwidth and there's too much traffic between you and the server. Because heavy traffic is a way of life on the Net, most players "**buffer**" data in advance to cover up intermittent hiccups. You can adjust the buffer size in your player's options. But normally, once you've entered your connection speed at setup, you shouldn't need to worry about it again.

As you can imagine, this amount of audio compression takes its toll on fidelity. For example, when you tune into **Radio Nova** (http://www.novaplanet.com) across the Net, it won't sound as good as straight off the radio in Paris. But you might be surprised that it doesn't sound too bad, either. **Somewhere between AM and FM is a fair comparison.**

Play it again with MP3

Tinny sound might be OK for taste-testing CDs at Amazon or when it's your only chance of hearing a foreign station, but there are better options if you have time to download the tracks. Downloaded formats (usually **MP3s**) sound much better than streaming audio because they don't need to be as compressed.

The compression level of an MP3 file is expressed as a **bitrate**, which tells you the average number of bits used to store one second of audio data. The more bits you use, the better it sounds but the longer it takes to download. Most MP3s on the Net are encoded at a bitrate of **128Kbps**. This isn't far off **CD quality** – you won't be able to tell the difference over tinny PC speakers, but you might if you play it through your home stereo. A four-minute track recorded at 128Kbps would need 3.8MB. So with a 56K modem, this should take less than twenty minutes to download.

MP3s can be encoded at a range of rates, depending on the quality required. Many sites offer a choice of **hi-fi MP3s** (for download) or **lo-fi MP3s** (for streaming) – the latter are generally recorded at around 32Kbps.

Here's the catch

While it's fine to rip MP3s from your own CDs and listen to them on your PC or portable MP3 player, unless the artist or publisher has granted you express permission, it's illegal to distribute these copies or post them to your website. That means most of what you find through file-sharing agents is in flagrant breach of copyright – as Napster learned very publicly. In practice, if you're caught lobbing a few MP3s onto your Web site you might simply be told to pull them down. But if you're caught attempting to profit from them, you'll almost certainly be prosecuted. So irrespective of whether you believe exposure through illegal copying might increase sales to the benefit of all, beware that it could land you in the stew. If you need the point belted into you, see: http://www.riaa.com and http://www.bpi.co.uk

Load up with software

Before you can listen to anything, you'll need the right playing software. See what you already have and then build from there. The main formats you'll be playing, in order of popularity, are **RealMedia**, **MP3**, **Windows Media**, **QuickTime**, **Streaming MP3** and **Liquid Audio**. The annoying part is that the main players will happily take over playing all these formats (and more), but they most likely won't do them all justice. You're better off installing a few players and assigning the formats to whichever player handles them best. You might already have enough to get started, as most players are optional browser add-ons. While some of the ones mentioned below have commercial versions, you should download the free options first.

RealMedia

 RealMedia incorporates both **RealVideo** and **RealAudio**, the formats most commonly used for live radio and television broadcasts, as well as music samples at online CD stores. Until 2002, to play these formats you downloaded **RealPlayer**, though this is now called the **RealOne** player – it incorporates the media player, library and jukebox functions that used to be provided by a separate program, **RealJukebox**. (It's also tied in with an optional subscription service; see p.293.) The result is a program that looks and feels quite similar to Windows Media Player. To get the RealOne player, either update your current version of RealPlayer (via the option in its Tools menu), or visit http://www.real.com and look for the **Free RealOne Player** (not the free trial!).

Windows Media

 If you're running Windows, update **Windows Media Player**. It's the native player for a variety of new streaming formats. They should be supported by other programs such as the RealPlayer and **WinAmp**, but Media Player will do them better. Again, it can handle all sorts of other formats, including WAV, AU and MP3, as well as play your CDs. However, **leave RealPlayer to handle Real Media**.

You can get the latest version through **Windows Update**, by clicking the option under the Help menu in Windows Media Player, or by downloading it from the **Windows Media guide** (http://www.windowsmedia.com). There's also a version for the Mac (http://www.mactopia.com). For help, try the Microsoft newsgroups (see p.112) or this FAQ:

http://www.nwlink.com/~zachd/pss/pss.html/

QuickTime

Next, stop by Apple's **QuickTime** Guide (http://www.quicktime.com) and see if you can play what's on offer. Don't be surprised if Windows Media Player or RealPlayer attempts to open the file but gives you a useless error message. If so, download the QuickTime player and assign it to **associate with only the native Macintosh file types** – under "Preferences", "Registration" then "File Type Associations". While the QuickTime player can handle other formats, it's pretty rustic compared to the competition and persistently nags you to pay. Still, Apple's video technology is widely used for online movie clips and promos (see p.290) so it's worth having support for it, especially if you have a **high bandwidth connection**.

Shoutcast and streaming MP3

Shoutcast is another streaming audio format, and it lets you turn your MP3 library into an online radio station within about thirty minutes of reading and tweaking. It's supported by most leading MP3 players – though best by **WinAmp**, the original force behind the technology. You can listen by logging into http://www.shoutcast.com and choosing a station. If you like what you hear, grab **RadioSpy** (http://www.radiospy.com) to help find other stations.

Liquid Audio and other formats

 By now you should be able to play everything that comes your way. Apart from the main formats, there are a few less popular alternatives such as **Liquid Audio** (http://www.liquidaudio.com). Generally, all you'll need to play them is a downloaded RealPlayer plug-in, offered when you check for new updates. But, generally, if you strike an unsupported format somewhere, you'll probably see a link to its player nearby.

What plays what

The worst part of installing a new media player is that it'll try to hijack all your media settings. Once you've established a preferred player for a format, go through its "Options", "Preferences" then "Settings" and specify that you'd like it to be the **default for that media type** – it's something that's often well-hidden. If you can't find the option, refer to the help file, try the publisher's support page or ask in Usenet.

Choose your MP3 jukebox

If you've been paying attention, you'll have at least one program that can play MP3s. But once you start to accumulate a large MP3 collection, you'll appreciate a **full-blown MP3/CD jukebox** – such as WinAmp, RealJukebox, Sonique, Windows Media Player, RealOne or MusicMatch Jukebox. Typically, these all-in-one jukeboxes can play your music CDs, automatically look up the track listings at Gracenote's **CDDB database** (http://www.cddb.com), rip tracks from a CD and encode them into MP3s, play streaming broadcasts, search your hard drive for media files and catalogue your music library into **playlists**. Most players are available in some form to download for free. But if you pay to

chapter 11

Online video and animation

As connection speeds have increased, streaming video and animation have become a major presence on the Net, and everything from short clips to full-length movies can be found to download and view in a media player.

The video formats you're most likely to encounter online are RealVideo (for streaming with RealOne), the various members of the MPEG family and QuickTime (for use with the QuickTime player). Compared to music streams and downloads, video file sizes tend to be much bigger, so they take longer to download and are usually of pretty poor quality. But things are improving fast, thanks to new technologies such as DivX, an MPEG-4 standard that can be played using the dedicated DivX player or Windows Media Player (visit http://www.divx.com to download the necessary codec).

Animations created in programs such as Flash (see p.319) are, unsurprisingly, much smaller than actual video, so they stream much better and download quicker, though you'll need the appropriate player to watch them. For Flash, visit:
http://www.macromedia.com.

So, whether you want to check out trailers to the latest movies (http://www.film.com) or watch a wild martial arts animation (http://home.earthlink.net/~woowoody/), start searching for links. And if you fancy getting your own home movies online, or just want to find out more about the formats, try:
http://www.deliveryourmedia.com
http://www.mediastreamnetwork.com/faqs.htm/

upgrade to the full version you might get more features, such as being able to encode your own MP3s at a higher fidelity. Try a few before you settle, but once you've made a choice completely uninstall the rejects (except Windows Media Player) so they don't interfere. Alternatively, save yourself the bother, and just download the best:

MusicMatch Jukebox http://www.musicmatch.com

For more music software

You'll find hundreds of music players and utilities for free download through:

Download.com http://www.download.com

MP3.com http://www.mp3.com

MP3 for the Mac http://www.mp3-mac.com

Shareware Music Machine http://www.hitsquad.com/smm/

ZDNet http://downloads-zdnet.com.com/

Find the music

Go to any search engine, type in "MP3" and it'll soon seem like the format is taking over the Net – you won't have any trouble finding MP3s. Like any search, though, you might need to try a few places if you're after something very specific or obscure. And, of course, it has to be online in the first place.

MP3 hubs

The MP3s you'll strike will fall into three main categories: **free previews** authorized by the artist or publisher; tracks you can **pay to download**; and illegal **bootlegs**. Free previews tend to be from acts that can't get radio airplay and are eager for exposure, but that's not necessarily the case. You can usually preview pay tracks in a lo-fi format, such as RealAudio or streaming MP3, before purchasing. Here are a few commercial sites that have both free and pay-to-download **legal MP3s**:

Artist Direct http://www.artistdirect.com

AudioGalaxy http://www.audiogalaxy.com
ClickMusic http://www.clickmusic.co.uk
Dmusic http://www.dmusic.com
Emusic http://www.emusic.com
Epitonic http://www.epitonic.com
iCrunch http://www.icrunch.com
IUMA http://www.iuma.com
Launch.com http://www.launch.com
Liquid Audio http://www.liquid.com
Listen.com http://www.listen.com
MP3.com http://www.mp3.com
MP3.com.au http://www.mp3.com.au
Peoplesound http://www.peoplesound.com
RioPort http://www.rioport.com
Vitaminic http://www.vitaminic.co.uk

Once you hit the search engines and file sharing agents, you'll start seeing the contraband. That's not to say they only index bootleggers – they don't. But don't be impressed by an engine just because it returns hundreds of hits. You might find they're mostly dead links. To search using a webpage front end, try:

AudioFind http://www.audiofind.com
AudioGalaxy http://www.audiogalaxy.com
FindMP3 http://www.findmp3.org
Look4MP3 http://www.look4mp3.com
Lycos http://music.lycos.com
MP3Board http://www.mp3board.com

Several software agents can also poll multiple search sites at once. They're OK, but not outstanding. Try:

Copernic http://www.copernic.com

Finally, try using a normal search engine to find **fan pages**, which might lead you to all sorts of gems like outtakes, rare singles and live bootlegs.

Subscription services

Especially since the Napster debacle, the major labels have been vying for a profitable presence on the Net, and the result has been the growth of subscription services that let you stream, download and sometimes burn songs to CD. The big guns are **Pressplay** (http://www.pressplay.com) and **MusicNet** (http://www.musicnet.com), which feeds AOL and RealOne. However, these services have their flaws – such as limiting the number of songs you can download and play per month. And often, if you stop subscribing, you'll lose all your songs. Unsurprisingly, they've failed to displace the (less legal) file-sharing options.

File-sharing networks

Much to the alarm of artists and labels, most of the activity in MP3 isn't happening at the commercial and official sites, but at the underground file-sharing or **P2P** (peer-to-peer) networks made notorious by **Napster**. File-sharing programs enable you to share your own library online and, of course, pick through everyone else's.

Continuous legal action saw Napster bludgeoned into submission. A similar fate befell **Scour** – except it was because of movie rather than audio sharing. At the time of writing, however, both Napster and Scour are preparing to be reborn with commercial sensibilities.

Napster http://www.napster.com
Scour http://www.scour.com

As a result of their difficulties, serious MP3 hounds have migrated onto other networks. One of the best at present is **WinMX**, which can search personal servers running its own Peer Networking Protocol, plus networks using the OpenNap and Napster protocols. In English, that means it's still open season, despite the court cases.

WinMX http://www.winmx.com

While most of the alternatives aren't as fast or heavily populated as WinMX, they might turn up something different. **KaZaA Lite** is especially reliable, and shouldn't be confused with KaZaA, which harbours spyware.

Filetopia http://www.filetopia.com

Gnutella http://www.gnutella.co.uk

KaZaA Lite http://www.kazaalite.com

Limewire (Gnutella clone) http://www.limewire.com

The following are riddled with spyware (p.264) and, unless you're desperate, probably best avoided:

AudioGalaxy Satellite http://www.audiogalaxy.com

Bearshare (Gnutella clone) http://www.bearshare.com

iMesh http://www.imesh.com

Sharing more than music

Peer-to-peer file-sharing networks can be used for a whole lot more than music. Any file can be made available and downloaded, including programs, images, videos, documents and more. One of the most popular networks is **EDonkey** (http://www .edonkey2000.com). For news, reviews and everything else related to file sharing, visit **Zeropaid.com** (http://www.zeropaid.com).

Trading over Usenet and IRC

Set your **newsreader to filter on MP3** and you'll uncover a bevvy of groups dedicated to posting music binaries, though again they're predominantly bootlegs. As always, **read the FAQ first**: http://www.mp3-faq.org

IRC (p.247) isn't only used for idle chatter. It's also a hotbed of file trading, thanks to the **DCC** command and mIRC scripts like **Multimedia Jukebox** (http://spr.darkrealms.org). Log onto any server, and list the channels and topics that match MP3. But don't accept any programs – they'll be Trojans for sure.

Streaming music – radio and more

Real-time audio comes in two forms: **live** broadcasts and **on-demand** pre-recordings. Tapping into a live broadcast is like switching on a radio, except you have a lot more choice. For starters, you're not restricted to your local reception area, meaning that you can tune into real world stations from right around the globe. And as anyone can set up a broadcast without a special licence, there are also thousands of "stations" you won't hear anywhere else. On top of that there are loads of special events and concerts being piped online. All you need to know is where to look. To help you on your way, see the Radio and Webcasts section of our Web guide (p.439) or *The Rough Guide to Internet Radio*.

The difference with on-demand audio is the material is pre-recorded. So, no matter when you join, the clip will start at the beginning. You might come across the odd archived radio broadcast, but its biggest use is for **previewing CDs** at online music stores like Amazon. There's no better way to shop for music – as long as your credit card can handle the pressure. For a guide to **CD shopping**, see p.414.

Listen

Unless you have a very fast connection, you'll need to download hi-fi MP3s to your machine in order to play them. If clicking on a link to an MP3, or other large media file, starts your player rather than a download, right-click and choose "**Save Target As**" (on the Mac, Ctrl-click and choose "**Download Link to Disk**"). Adjust your player's settings to prevent it from happening in future.

Think about where you'd like your music to arrive. It makes the most sense to set up an incoming folder dedicated to audio downloads. Then, once you've listened to them, transfer them into your main music library under sensible subfolder names. Still, your jukebox won't mind if you lump them all in together, as it should be able to separate them by their internal ID (naming) tags.

As MP3s are big files, it's wise to relegate transfers from the Web or an FTP server to a **download manager** that can resume downloads (p.267). However, if you're using a file-sharing program such as WinMX (p.293), this won't be necessary – they look after the entire download process.

Turn on the broadcast

Clicking on a streaming audio (or lo-fi MP3) link should call up the appropriate player. After a few seconds of buffering, you should hear the clip or broadcast. If you can't hear any sound, but it appears to be playing, check the player's volume control. If that's up full, try your master volume settings. You can reach these in Windows by clicking on the speaker in your system tray. If nothing opens when you click on the link, or a player opens but fails to recognize the format, you'll either need to reset the file associations in the preferred player or reinstall it.

Roll your own MP3s

If your CD drive supports **DAE** (digital audio extraction) – and it should – you can extract MP3s from your own CDs. Technically this is a two-step process that involves "ripping" an audio track from the CD into a WAV file, then encoding it into an MP3. But most ripper/encoder programs can copy straight from the CD into MP3. The program you choose – and its associated compression algorithm – could make a difference to the sound quality, so read some reviews and try a few before coding up your entire CD collection.

Still, the bitrate will always be the **biggest determinant of sound quality**. Although **128 Kbps** has become the de facto standard online, if you intend to convert them back to WAV files to create a **compilation CD**, encode them at **upwards of 192 Kbps** – on a decent sound system you'll probably notice the difference. For better sound still, also consider ripping your CDs into WAVs before encoding into MP3.

If you can't seem to rip a crackle-free copy, try:

Exact Audio Copy http://www.exactaudiocopy.de

For more on encoding, see:

http://www.mp3-converter.com
http://www.r3mix.net

Keep your CDs online

If you'd like access to your CD collection from any computer online, beam your CDs to **My MP3** (http://www.mp3.com). You simply insert your CD and it will look it up in its database. If it has the album in its library, it adds the tracks to your personal collection. You can then access them at any time without ever having to upload any MP3s. And any CDs bought from their online music store partners can be beamed across instantly. Incredible, but true.

MP3 hardware

Part of MP3's recent surge in popularity has been due to the proliferation of Walkman-like **portable players**. They can be a little inconvenient in that to "change a disk" you have to upload tracks from your computer (either into an onboard memory or a removable memory stick), though the latest models can hold thousands of tracks, so you won't need to do this too often.

Here are some things to check out when shopping around:

➥ **USB, USB2 or IEEE uploads?** IEEE 1394 (also known as FireWire and iLink) and USB2 are both super-fast, but your computer may not support them.

➥ **Supports your system?** Check that the model you buy is compatible with your operating system.

➥ **Memory?** Figure on about one megabyte per minute of music. Is it expandable and how much does it cost to add extra storage?

➥ **Power?** What's the battery life and does it come with a charger?

➥ **Upgradable?** Not being able to upload software upgrades could render the unit obsolete before its time.

➥ **Display?** Does it display track names?

➥ **Size?** Smaller might mean a short battery life.

For opinions on the latest models, try the computer press, techno toy mags like *Stuff* and *T3*, or sites with consumer reviews such as **Epinions**, **MP3.com** and **Amazon** (see p.198).

Burning to a CD

If you want to play your MP3s or Windows Media files on a regular CD player, you'll need to convert them to the WAV format and burn them to CD (unless you have a special MP3 CD player). However, most modern CD burning programs will do this automatically once you've specified that you're creating an audio CD (as opposed to a data CD). For more on converting and burning, see:

CDR FAQ http://www.cdrfaq.org

CDR Info http://www.cdrinfo.com
CDR Labs http://www.cdrlabs.com
CDRW Central http://www.cdrwcentral.com
CMJ http://www.cmj.com/mp3/

For instructions on how to rip your vinyl collection, see:
http://homepages.nildram.co.uk/~abcomp/lp-cdr.htm/

For more

If the following FAQs
http://webhome.idirect.com/~nuzhathl/mp3-faq.html
http://www.mp3-faq.org
don't answer your questions, try the newsgroup
alt.music.mp3

For the latest news and reviews on MP3 and streaming audio, drop by any of the MP3 supersites (p.291) or:

About.com http://mp3.about.com
DailyMP3 http://www.dailymp3.org
MP3 for Macs http://www.mp3-mac.com
ZDNet http://music.zdnet.com

You'll find still more by searching **Dmoz.org** or **Yahoo!** for "MP3".

Rather buy the CD?

Then see our guide to buying music online (p.414).

12

Play games

Rule the planet

Taking on the computer in games like **Quake**, **Half-Life** and **Serious Sam** isn't much of a challenge. But over the Internet, playing against real people – even strangers – means that games take on a whole new dimension. In fact, once you've played in multi-player mode, you'll never want to play alone again.

Multi-player capability has become standard in most new games, and not just in the action genre. Almost any computer game that can be played by two or more people can, in theory, be played online.

Hooking up

To bring in another player to a computer game, you'll need to connect to their machine. The simplest way is to link two computers in the same location together with a **direct cable connection** (usually serial or USB). You can do something similar using modems and a telephone cable, though your gaming speed will be limited.

To conscript more victims, you need a proper network. A **local area network (LAN)** is best – that's where you connect all the machines via network PCI cards and cables. Specific gaming network kits are readily available these days.

If you'd like to experience network gaming at its fastest and fairest, drop by a cybercafé (p.28) that caters for gamers. However, the most popular way to find an opponent, even at 4am, is via the **Internet**.

The problem with Internet gaming

Although it's the easiest way to meet other players, the Net has its drawbacks for games that require split-second reactions. **Latency** – the length of time it takes data to reach its destination – is the biggest issue. If it takes too long, it makes a fast game such as Quake unplayable. Then there's **packet loss** – where segments of data fail to reach the other end and must be retransmitted. This has the same slowing effect as high latency.

Online games use latency correction algorithms that attempt to predict likely moves. However, players with lower latency (ping) times – usually those close to the server – will always be at a distinct advantage.

Obviously things are better with a **broadband connection**, but even if you're dialling up with a standard modem it's worth considering signing up to an **ISP that runs gaming servers**. This will massively reduce lag time.

What you'll need

If you're **running a PC**, 3D games (and these are the most popular) appreciate every bit of speed you can throw at them. As well as a zippy joystick or gamepad – a mouse just won't do – you'll need a fat connection, a fast processor, plenty of RAM and, most of all, 3D video acceleration. In fact, serious gamers obsess about their video cards and the driver software associated with rendering the images, and overclock their PC chips to melting point (see http://www.overclockers.com). If you'd like to improve your gaming frame-rate (sometimes at the expense of stability), experiment with the latest video drivers. If you're running anything with an Nvidia chip, you'll find a whole assortment of official releases and "leaked" betas. For advice, consult the **alt.comp.periphs.videocards** newsgroup that discusses your chipset (see p.229).

Macs have never quite cut the gaming mustard, but PCs are now being challenged by a new breed of console machines, which are not only cheaper but have superior graphics. **Sega Dreamcast** (http://www.dreamcast.com), **Sony PlayStation 2** (http://www.playstation2.com), **Nintendo GameCube** (http://www.gamecube.com) and **Microsoft XBox** (http://www.xbox.com) are all Net-enabled. Dreamcast comes with a modem, PlayStation 2 can connect via a USB modem or broadband card, the Xbox has both USB and Ethernet ports and Nintendo offer 56K and broadband connection adaptors for the GameCube.

Let's rock!

Once you're armed, online and ready to duel, you'll need to track down some willing chumps. That's usually not too hard, but how you go about it depends on what game you're playing.

Most recent games – such as **Tribes II**, **Serious Sam** and the basic board games that come with **Windows Me and XP** – include in-built support for finding, and chatting to, opponents, but many still require a third-party program.

The best way to start is to download **GameSpy Arcade** (http://www.gamespy.com) and **Kali** (http://www.kali.net). They

enable you to find the closest games, with the lowest lag times, and then automate the connections.

Once you've found your game, you'll either be able to jump on board straight away, or will get sent to some kind of lobby to wait for a new game to start.

Quake

id Software's **Quake** was the first major game designed primarily for online play. Over a network, it's usual to switch off the "monsters" and fight with or against other players. Serious Quakers form clans, complete with their own custom-designed outfits, called skins. Clan members compete side by side against other clans or individuals.

Quake III303304 comes with its own Netplay support. For more, see http://www.bluesnews.com and http://www.quake.com

Team play

The most recent trend is not to pit you against the world, but to **join a team**. The first generation of teamplay arrived in Quake's Team Fortress add-on, where you had to choose a team, pick a character type and battle against one or more opposing teams. But there are now many more mission types such as **Capture The Flag**, where the goal is to raid the other team's base and pinch their flag.

Breaker, breaker!

Want to chat with your teammates or opponents as you play? Try **Roger Wilco** (http://www.resounding.com). It works like an Internet telephone, but uses so few resources it shouldn't interfere with your game. Or if you'd like to step it up a notch, try

Microsoft's Game Voice (http://www.microsoft.com/sidewinder/) headset, which also enables voice activation of commands such as switching weapons.

Where to find the real eggs

Remember those ancient **text-based games** where you'd stumble through imaginary kingdoms looking for hidden objects, uttering magic words and slaying trolls? Believe it or not, they're still going strong, and are now multi-player, with some 100,000 players entwined in more than 3000 gaming worlds, like **Wheel of Time** (http://wotmud.org), **Lord of the Rings** (http://mume.pvv.org) and **Discworld** (http://discworld. imaginary .com).

What sets these apart from conventional arcade games is their community spirit and the level of character involvement as players become absorbed in their alter egos. This can make them especially addictive. If it sounds like your bag, see http://www .mudconnector.com and the newsgroup hierarchy rec.games.mud

Somewhat up the evolutionary ladder graphically, but along similar lines, **Ultima Online** (http://www.uo.com), the latest in the Ultima fantasy series, throws you into a continually evolving

virtual world, complete with day and night. The idea is to create not only a battleground, but a social community for thousands of players. As does **EverQuest** (http://www.everquest. com), creating a spectacular fantasy world in the process.

For games – and more info

Many of the best games around are so big that you'll balk at the prospect of downloading even the demo versions. So check out the gaming magazines, such as **PC Gamer** (http://www .pcgamer.com), **GameSpot** (http://www.gamespot.com) and **PC Zone** (http://www.pczone.co.uk). They're often the best place to find out what's hot in online gaming, not just because gaming companies send them software evaluations early, but because they invariably come with a **free CD-ROM full of games**. It's a worthy saving in download time. Especially when you'll get rid of most of them after a few minutes.

On the Net, the best sources of news and downloads are the main games websites (p.383).

13

Your first webpage

Stake your claim

It won't be long before you want a crack at your own webpage. You don't need to be anyone particularly important or a company with something to sell. If you have something to say or display, there's plenty of room for you on the World Wide Web. As long as it's not against the law, you can publish whatever you like – anything from how to build a **psychotronic mind-control deflector** (http://zapatopi.net/afdb.html) to your **navel fluff collection** (http://www.feargod.net/fluff.html).

What's involved?

Publishing a webpage is a three-phase operation. You need to **create your site in HTML** (p.308), find somewhere to **park**

it on the Web (p.320), and finally **transfer all the pages** from
your computer to your newfound Web server (p.324). However,
before you do anything you should acquaint yourself with
HTML, the Web's markup language.

HTML – a code for all browsers

The formatting commands used to style and position the
images, text and other components within a webpage belong to
a relatively simple language called HTML (**H**yper**T**ext **M**arkup
Language). The HTML tags (p.311) tell the Web browser how
to display the contents of the page.

In theory, any machine that can browse the Web should be able
to display the page as intended by the author. This isn't always
the case in practice, however, as the leading browser companies
(Microsoft and Netscape) have done their own thing rather than
adhere to the standards specified by the **W3C** (http://
www.w3c.org). So a page that displays perfectly in IE6 for the PC
might look wonky in Netscape 4.7 on the Mac, and vice versa.
Consequently, most professional developers test their pages on a
number of browsers before setting them live.

Where do I start?

Even if you build your pages with a **WYSIWYG** (What-You-
See-Is-What-You-Get) editor that hides all the code, at some
point you'll probably need to go in and tweak the raw HTML.
The best time to learn the basics behind HTML is right now,
before you build your first page. Read on.

Build your site

Once you've worked out what to say on your site, the next
thing to decide is how to convert your thoughts into HTML.

Let's examine some of your options, starting with the easiest first.

Nothing to pay – no need to learn HTML

If you need to get something online quickly, without learning HTML and don't mind that it looks a bit prefabricated, head straight to one of the **free Web hosting services.** In most cases, you can build your entire site though a drag-and-drop site builder, a step-by-step wizard, or by simply filling in a set of templates. You won't need any software or to hunt around for a hosting service, as they provide the lot all rolled into one. Just read the instructions and follow the prompts. While it's almost impossible to go wrong, don't expect to create a work of art. See p.320.

Grow your own HTML

HTML is simpler than computer programming in general, but it's even more repetitive and tedious. Once you understand how it works, you'll probably prefer to do most of your construction in a site editor that automates much of the coding process. With a basic grounding in HTML under your belt, you can tweak the code afterwards. And trust us – you will need to tweak.

Dozens of programs can convert text to HTML in some fashion, often in a WYSIWYG manner, meaning that you don't have to look at any of the underlying code. This way of doing things isn't just restricted to the dedicated site editors. Microsoft Office programs such as **Word**, for example, can save your documents as HTML ready for shipment onto the Web. Nonetheless, a dedicated website editor will do a far better job. These come in two main flavours: WYSIWYG and HTML.

A **WYSIWYG editor** is a little like a desktop publishing program. You work with objects and boxes rather than raw code. Some also allow you to directly edit the code as well.

With an **HTML editor**, on the other hand, you work directly on the code behind the page, either manually or through
automated shortcuts. While the editor itself can add all the
appropriate code around your text, you'll still have to understand what you're doing. That means you'll definitely need to
learn HTML, or at least the basics. The good news is **it should-
n't take you more than an afternoon** to get the gist of it.

Select your site editor

The quickest way to get familiar with HTML is to **create a
simple page from scratch**. You won't even need a site editor
– a simple text editor like **Notepad** or **SimpleText** will do.
That said, an **HTML editor** will make the process far less
laborious.

There are plenty of editors to choose from, but your choices
will narrow when you know what kind of website you want to
create, and how much you're willing to spend on software. In the
meantime, you might as well start with something free, such as:

1st Page 2000 (HTML) http://www.evrsoft.com

AceHTML (HTML) http://www.visicommedia.com

Arachnophilia (HTML) http://www.arachnoid.com

Coolpage (WYSIWYG) http://www.3dize.com

HTML Kit (HTML) http://www.chami.com/html-kit/

The next best thing about these programs is they all come
with helpful HTML tutorials. After the couple of evenings it
will take you to figure them out, you'll be well and truly versed
with the basics of building a website. For more options, along
with ratings and reviews, see:

Builder.com http://www.builder.com

Dave Central http://www.davecentral.com/webauth.html

Tucows http://www.tucows.com

ZDNet http://www.zdnet.com/downloads/webauthor.html

If you don't mind paying, **Microsoft FrontPage** (http://www.microsoft.com/frontpage/), which comes on its own or with certain versions of Microsoft Office, makes the transition from familiar Office products like Word and Excel relatively painless. It's capable of producing highly professional-looking sites, but is often criticized for generating bulky code.

Serious projects, however, demand serious editors. These pack in full support for Cascading Style Sheets, DHTML, ASP and other curiosities you really don't need to know about unless you're intent on doing it for a living. If you do, you'll want nothing short of **DreamWeaver**, a powerful industry-standard WYSIWYG and raw-code editor. Download the free trial:

Macromedia http://www.macromedia.com

Once you read around, you'll quickly discover that – whatever the price – not one WYSIWYG editor offers full control over HTML. So, whether you like it or not, you'll eventually end up **grappling with raw code**. In other words, resign yourself to learning the lingo.

Play tag – the basis of HTML

Next time you're online, examine the raw HTML code that makes up any webpage. To do this, simply choose "**View Source**" from under your browser's right-click mouse menu, or "**Source**" from under the View menu. The first thing you'll notice is that the text is surrounded with comments enclosed between less-than and greater-than symbols, like this:

```
<BOLD>My head hurts</BOLD>
```

These comments are known as **tags**. The tags shown above make the text appear **bold** when displayed in a browser. **Most tags come in pairs** and apply to the text they enclose. A forward slash signals the end of their relevance, as in: **</BOLD>**

Your first page

Let's dive straight in and make a simple page. Create a new blank page in a text editor like **NotePad** or **SimpleText**, and then type in the following:

```
<HTML>
<HEAD><TITLE>My First Page</TITLE></HEAD>
<BODY>I am a genius</BODY>
</HTML>
```

The paired **<HTML>** and **</HTML>** tags signify that the document is (yes, you guessed it) an **HTML file**, and that it has a beginning and an end.

And with that, bravo – you've finished! Next close your editor, save the page onto your Desktop with the name **index.html**, and then double-click on it to open it in your browser.

You'll see your page has two parts: a **head** and a **body**. The head contains the title, which is displayed in the top bar of your browser. The body defines what appears within the browser window. Everything else is a refinement.

Save your pages

When you call up a webpage by entering the domain name (such as **http://www.roughguides.com**) into your browser, it actually retrieves a file called **index.html** or **index.htm**, which is stored on the website's host server. It's the same as entering:
http://www.roughguides.com/index.html

So when you save the front page to your site you should call it: **index.html or index.htm** – all in lower case. That way you'll have a shorter Web address to hand out. The rest of your pages should also use the same extension (**.htm** or **.html**). Name them in a way that relates to their contents. Unless you have a very good reason, save all your filenames in lowercase, as it's less likely to cause confusion. And don't use names containing spaces (use dashes or underscores) or non-English language characters.

Take a tutorial in HTML

Rather than explain a smattering of HTML tags, we suggest you try an **online tutorial** or two, and perhaps print one out for reference. Alternatively, consult the tutorials and help files that accompany your site editor. You'll find just about everything you need to know about site-building at:

About.com http://html.about.com

Builder.com http://www.builder.com

HTML Goodies http://www.htmlgoodies.com

HTML Writers Guild http://www.hwg.org

W3C http://www.w3.org/MarkUp/Guide/

Web Developers Library http://www.stars.com

WebMonkey http://www.webmonkey.com

And try the newsgroup: **alt.html**

Plundering the Web

Once you're comfortable with the logic behind basic HTML, you can glean advanced techniques by analysing other webpages or plundering their code. Just find a page you like and call up "**View Source**". You can cut and paste selections into your own pages, or save the file and tweak it with a text or HTML editor.

If you see a feature you like on a site and you can't work out how it's done by looking at the source code, ask the site's Webmaster, or search the Web for a good DIY document. There are plenty of books on the subject, but beware – the technology's moving so fast that they date quickly.

Prepare your images

As you know, webpages can contain more than just text. In fact, placing and preparing graphics is half the art of Web design. If they're too big, for example, your pages will take too long to load. Here's how to get them right.

Getting an image onto your computer

There are three ways to produce a digital image. Talents permitting, you could create one on your computer with **drawing software**. You'll find various paint programs through the software guides (p.280), but they pall in comparison with professional-level products such as:

Adobe Illustrator http://www.adobe.com

CorelDraw http://www.corel.com

Macromedia Fireworks http://www.macromedia.com

You could import a copy of a slide, photograph, magazine page or drawing – just about anything two-dimensional – into your computer with a computer peripheral called a **scanner**. It works a bit like a photocopier, except instead of printing, it sends a digital image directly to your hard drive. Or you could take a photograph with a **digital camera** – or a still from a **digital video camera** – and import it into your computer. For advice on buying a scanner or digital camera, consult the consumer guides in our Shopping section (p.198) or *The Rough Guide to Personal Computers*.

Reduce its size for online consumption

Before you post your digital image on the Web (or attach it to an email; see p.142), you might need to reduce its size in bytes, otherwise it will take too long to download. You can do this in two ways:

➡️You can reduce the **dimensions of the image in pixels**, making the picture itself smaller. For example, if it measures 1024x768, you could reduce it to, say, 800x600. This would reduce the file size, but not affect the quality of image.

➡️You can convert it to a **compressed image format**. Images saved in formats such as **BMP** or **TIFF** are uncompressed, which means they take up more disk space. Converting (or saving) them to a compressed format such as **JPEG**, **GIF** or **PNG** will reduce the byte size dramatically. However, this saving comes at the cost of image quality and, depending on the level of compression, things might start to look a little blocky or blurred. Packages like **Adobe PhotoShop** (see p.317) let you set the compression level when you convert the image, allowing you to try various different options and strike a good balance between image quality and file size.

GIF or JPEG?

The two most popular image formats on the Web are JPEG (JPG) and GIF. They both lend themselves to online use because of their relatively small file sizes, though their uses and characteristics are quite different. GIFs can only display 256 colours, while JPEGs can display 16 million. JPEGs also permit a greater degree of compression, which makes for smaller image files. For these two reasons, most photographs and finely detailed images are best saved as JPEGs.

GIFs have their uses, though. If an image contains a relatively small number of colours or has large expanses of the same colour, a GIF is often more efficient. GIFs can also be animated like a slideshow, and can have transparent backgrounds. Consequently, they're often used for bars, icons, banners and backgrounds. Experiment for yourself and you'll soon see what's what.

Processing your images – tips

First of all, you need to plan the layout of your page so you know what size images you'll need. Keep in mind the average size of computer screens when you're laying plans – the last thing you want is for your images to appear either too small or overblown in a browser. You can reduce the size of images by cropping (chopping off excess from the edges), or resizing the entire image. Any basic image editor will offer these options. Just keep a copy of your original image, in case you make a mistake!

Whenever you save in a compressed format, you run the risk of losing a little quality. So, rather than make incremental changes to the compressed image, complete any touch-ups and cropping in the uncompressed format, and then experiment with different levels of compression until you're happy with quality and how it relates to size. You'll find the quality, or compression levels, offered as an option when you convert or save the image as a JPEG.

Online photo galleries

Like to show off your happy snaps, and perhaps even sell the prints? Upload them here and wait for the orders to roll in:

Club Photo http://www.clubphoto.com
Kodak Ofoto http://www.ofoto.com
PhotoLoft http://www.photoloft.com
Photopoint http://www.photopoint.com
Yahoo! Photos http://photos.yahoo.com

Remember: the fewer images you use on your webpage and the smaller they are in bytes, the quicker your page will load. So if you plan to display a large number of high-quality photos, consider linking the actual images from **thumbnails** (small, reduced-quality versions). Dozens of programs can do this automatically.

Image-processing software

Start by downloading an image viewer/editor (p.280) such as **Irfanview** so that you can flip through images quickly, convert between formats and make minor adjustments:

Irfanview http://www.irfanview.com

With practice, you can reduce byte size considerably without noticeably sacrificing quality. Almost any image viewer/editor can do the job, but you can skip all the trial and error by using a dedicated file-reduction program such as **JPEG Optimizer**:

JPEG Optimizer http://www.xat.com

For serious touching-up, however, you'll need something more powerful such as **PaintShop Pro**, or the professional's choice – **Adobe PhotoShop**. Both also have a range of Web compression tools, such as automated gallery generators:

PaintShop Pro http://www.jasc.com

PhotoShop http://www.adobe.com

You'll find an ample range of free Web graphics programs through the software guides listed from p.280. For help using them, see:

About.com http://graphicssoft.about.com

Open Directory http://dmoz.org/Computers/Graphics/

Pinoy7 http://www.pinoy7.com

Make it "usable"

If the point of your website is to convey some message about you, your business or your clients, make sure it's not a bad one. The first step in that direction is to present your site in a way that's **easy to navigate**, and your pages so they're **easy to read**. The further you move away from the tried-and-tested **black text on a white background**, the harder you'll make it for your readers. After all, how many **successful magazines** or newspapers have you seen use coloured print over a patterned background? Or which make it hard to get past the front page? The same goes for the Web. Almost all the successful sites stick to a similar minimal structure. The buzzword for this is "**use-ability**". You can read all about it here:

Alertbox http://www.useit.com

SpiderPro StyleGuide http://www.spiderpro.com/pr/pri.html

Usable Web http://usableweb.com

A more entertaining way to learn how to design a good web-site is to see examples of what not to do, and ensure you don't make the same mistakes:

GBU http://www.mcli.dist.maricopa.edu/webhound/gbu.html

Web Pages That Suck http://www.webpagesthatsuck.com

If, after all that, you're still considering a patterned back-ground, at least spare a thought for the colour-blind:

Vischeck http://vischeck.com

Beyond HTML

There are almost no bounds to the things you can do with a webpage. As you move up the levels of sophistication, you'll start to move out of the basic HTML domain into **DHTML**, **XML** and more complex scripting and programming languages such as **JavaScript**, **ActiveX**, **Shockwave**, **Java**, **PERL**, **CGI** and **Visual Basic**. You may also need access to the special class of storage space reserved for Web programs, known as the **cgi-bin directory**.

If you see a feature you like and you can't work out how it's done by looking at the source code, ask the site's Webmaster or search the Web for a good DIY document. There are plenty of books on the subject – but beware, the technology's moving so fast that they're quickly out-of-date.

Flash

Flash is a nifty little program that lets you create colourful interactive animations in very small files. A ten-second clip might only take up 10KB, for example. But beware – the greatest design crime online is the use of flatulent Flash animations to welcome you to a site. It's about as likely to impress your visitors as making them walk across broken glass to read your mission statement. Apart from the obvious blunder of putting an obstacle between your guest and where they want to go, it might even crash their browser and

lock them out of your site altogether. For more appropriate applications, visit **Macromedia** (http://www.macromedia.com) and, for tips, tools and more, see:

Flash Kit http://www.flashkit.com

Flazoom http://www.flazoom.com

Java

Java isn't a mark-up code like HTML, but a serious programming language designed to be interpreted by any computer. That makes it perfect for the Web as you can place an **applet** (Java program) on your site and activate it from your webpage. Most browsers have in-built Java interpreters, so visitors don't need any extra software to view it. Some useful online calculators, translators and interactive quizzes are powered by Java, but then so are countless useless applications that slow your browsing for no good reason. As for writing applets yourself, if you think C++ is a chuckle it's probably right up your alley. Good luck.

JavaScript

JavaScript, a Netscape innovation, extends the Java concept to HTML. Because it sits entirely within the HTML of the web-page, you can pinch the code from other pages, just like regular HTML. It can add tricks, which (with the odd exception such as form creation) are just that: tricks. But if you want to create personalized messages for each visitor to your site, display a clock, or spawn twenty pop-up windows, try:

JavaScript Source **http://javascript.internet.com**

WebCoder **http://www.webcoder.com**

Just bear in mind that most of your visitors would rather you didn't.

Park your pages

Once your webpages and images are ready to go live, you'll need to find a server to house your handicraft. While it might seem logical to use the free space that came with your ISP account, consider what might become of your site if you switch providers. You stand to lose not only the space, but the Web address as well. Not to worry – free Web space is plentiful.

Hundreds of sites will give you all the space you need, plus home-building tools to ease the process of editing and uploading pages. The big names include:

Freeservers **http://www.freeservers.com**

Moonfruit http://www.moonfruit.com

Tripod http://www.tripod.com

Yahoo! Geocities http://www.geocities.com

There are even a few without the usual hindrances associated with free space, such as pop-up windows and ad banners. For more options, and help in choosing, check out the reviews at:

Homestead http://www.homestead.com

Or, to read how to **remove ads** from your free space (you shouldn't really, and in theory you might get kicked off), check out: http://www.cexx.org/diepop.htm

For more options, and help in choosing, check out the reviews at: http://www.freewebspace.net

But before you settle on a server, whether free or otherwise, first decide if you should **register your own domain name**.

Master of your own domain

Say you run a shop called Top Clogs and you want to flog your clogs over the Web. Don't even consider an address like: http://members.tripod.com/~clogs/topclogs.htm

To be taken seriously, only http://www.topclogs.com – or something region-specific like http://www.topclogs.co.uk (see p.322) – will do.

Of course, if someone else has already taken your ideal name, you'll have to think of another – or offer to buy it from them. Any domain registry will instantly confirm if it's available, and register it for you within a matter of minutes. Such as:

Domain Direct http://www.domaindirect.com

DomainMonger http://www.domainmonger.com

Register.com http://www.register.com

Part of the registration process involves allocating **two DNS servers** to direct traffic to the Web server where you will eventually put your pages. If you do it through the above mentioned, they will park your site and supply the DNS servers until you

choose a hosting service. Alternatively, flick through any Internet or computing magazine for hundreds of alternative registries.

Once you've registered, you'll need to find some some permanent space. Compare prices and services listed at **Top Hosts**, **Find a Host**, or (again) any computer magazine. *Internet Magazine*, for example, tests and ranks British hosts.

Check out the bandwidth and support thoroughly. You don't want to be stuck on a slow server. Generally, the best deals are in the US. However, it helps to locate close to your target audience, as that way your pages will load quicker.

Find a Host http://www.findahost.com

Internet Magazine http://www.internet-magazine.com

Top Hosts http://www.tophosts.com

Identify with your own country

If you would prefer an association with a country other than the USA, consider registering a regional domain ending in a country code. See the list of available codes and relevant contacts at:
http://www.uninett.no/navn/domreg.html

You can register a wide range of countries at **Register.com**.

Alternatively, to register UK names, try http://uk2.net or http://www.thename.co.uk – and, for Australian ones, visit http://www.netregistry.com.au

Almost your own domain

Netidentity (http://www.netidentity.com) will rent you a cheap personalized Web/email address combination from a range of more than 12,000 domains. Or, if you don't want to spend a penny but still want a short, memorable Web address, try a re-direction service, such as:

http://www.v3.com
http://beam.to
http://www.iscool.net

Free domain hosts

A few operations will host your domain free, but don't expect the same level of service, speed, reliability, life span, support or credibility that you'd get from a good commercial service. They include:

Freeservers http://www.freeservers.com
Virtual Avenue http://www.virtualave.net

Before you commit, read the reviews at:

Domain Hosting http://www.webweaver.nu/domain.htm
FreeWebSpace http://www.freewebspace.net

Warning – don't use your main address

Nothing will attract more junk email from scam merchants than registering a domain name. So rather than submit your main email address, set up an alternative account just for this purpose (p.122). Don't forget to check it occasionally for legitimate messages from your domain registrar, domain host, or perhaps even people wanting to buy your domain name.

Uploading your site

The usual way to deliver files to a Web server is by **FTP**, where you use a special program to copy your pages onto one of your host's computers. This process requires a user ID, password and FTP address for your pages. Ask your hosting service if you're unsure.

Most HTML editing packages incorporate FTP software, or some kind of site-uploading wizard. They can also synchronize the content to ensure you have the same files live (available on the Web) and locally (on your computer), as well as check for broken links and dead files. You'll find instructions in the Help menu.

Versions of Windows since 98 also have a simple FTP tool built-in, in the form of the **Web Publishing Wizard**. To launch it, click the Start menu, select "Programs", "Accessories", then "Internet Tools". You'll also find a link for it on the File And Folder Tasks panel of XP's Windows Explorer.

But if you're building a serious site with a basic HTML editor and want a tool that caters to all servers and upload conditions, consider an easy drag-and-drop FTP client like **FTP Voyager** and a **link validator**, such as **Linkrunner** or **SiteManager**, to scan your pages for broken links.

Alert Linkrunner http://www.alertbookmarks.com/lr/

Astra SiteManager http://www.mercuryinteractive.com

FTP Voyager http://www.ftpvoyager.com

You can check whether your site is compatible with various browsers at:

Website Garage http://www.websitegarage.com

Site tools

Once your site has settled on your server, you might like to enhance it with some free, or inexpensive, add-on accessories. For instant quizzes, polls, chat rooms, bulletin boards, guest books, visitor counters, tracking statistics and much more, see:

Be Seen http://www.beseen.com
Extreme Tracking http://www.extremetracking.com
My Computer http://www.mycomputer.com
Free Site Tools http://www.freesitetools.com
Free Tools http://www.freetools.com
WebSite Toolbox http://www.websitetoolbox.net

To add a free search engine to your site, try:

Free Find http://www.freefind.com
Google http://www.google.com/services/

A Web or FTP server at home

Most people store their webpages on a dedicated Web-hosting service. However, once your computer's connected to the Net, it can also act as a Web or FTP server just by running the right software. You can even run your own server on a regular dial-up account, though of course your pages or files will only be accessible while you're online – and you'll have a different IP address each time you log in, so you won't be able to pass it on until you're online. This is functional enough if you just want to demo a couple of webpages to a colleague or friend. However, if you want a serious Web presence, you'll need a permanent connection to run your own server. You'd also be well advised to use a stable and secure operating system such as Windows 2000 or XP rather than an earlier version.

Servers are remarkably simple to install – read the Help file and you'll be up within half an hour. But take the time to set up your security options to allow only appropriate access to appropriate directories. That means things like making your webpages read-only and your FTP incoming write-only. If you don't, you might get hacked. Also, note that some ISPs don't allow you to use your connection as a server – they may even try and charge you a fine if you try – so check the details of your contract first.

The most popular web server software is made by **Apache** (http://www.apache.org). It's open-source and downloadable for free. For more on server software, check out **ServerWatch** (http://serverwatch.internet.com).

Get your site noticed

Once you've published your page and transferred it to your server, the real problems begin. How do you **get people to visit it?**

People will arrive at your site in two main ways: by taking a link from another site, or by typing in the address. That means if other pages link to yours, or people can find your address written somewhere, you'll stand a chance of getting traffic.

To increase the links to your site, contact other sites similar to yours and suggest swapping links. Most will oblige, especially if you offer them useful content to put on their site. This sometimes starts a wonderful relationship (and it will also increase your ranking on Google; see opposite). If you want to move up a step to sell or buy commercial syndicated material, visit:

iSyndicate http://www.isyndicate.com

Also, generate some off-Web interest. Announce your site in relevant **newsgroups** and **mailing lists**. Make sure it's relevant, though; otherwise, you might only generate bad publicity. And don't forget about the non-cyber world, either. **Include the address** on your stationery, business cards, *Yellow Pages* entry and in all your regular advertising. Finally, if it's genuinely newsworthy, send a press release to whatever media might be interested, and throw a party with free food, drink and T-shirts for journos.

Get spotted by search engines

The best publicity machines of all, of course, are the search engines and directories. The biggest services should eventually find your site, but there's no need to wait. Visit each site in turn and look for a link to "submit your site", or similar, and follow the prompts. Alternatively, several services such as **AddMe!** http://www.addme.com and **Broadcaster** http://www.broadcaster .co.uk can send your details to multiple engines and directories at once. You'll get better results if you do it yourself, though.

Raise your ranking

When you enter keywords into a search engine, it will return a list of results in the order it deems most relevant. And the ones that appear near the top of the list are inevitably the ones that get clicked. Different engines work in different ways, so even if two engines find the same sites, they might present the results in a different order. Consequently, if you care about your site's **ranking** – and you should – you should go directly to each search engine and directory and find out **how it works**. Establish whether it accepts brief reviews, scans your page for keywords or indexes your site in full. If what you're doing is **new**, Yahoo! might even create you a new category. For a list of the top referring search sites, see:

http://www.useit.com/about/searchreferrals.html

Links, links, links

Google is the search engine of the moment, in no small part due to the "**PageRank**" technology that helps it find the most relevant results. Integral to this is the ability to look at a page in terms of who is linking to it. The more sites that link to yours, the better your Google ranking will be – especially if the sites linking to you are ranked highly themselves. This means that one of the best ways to increase your ranking is to contact sites (especially well-established ones) and encourage them to have a look at yours and consider linking to it.

chapter 13

Page titles and meta tags

You can also improve your search engine rankings by **dotting appropriate words and phrases in key places** in your HTML code. Most importantly, make sure your page titles are relevant. This is usually the main determinant of keyword ranking, followed by the contents of any "**meta tags**". Here's an example of how the top of your page might look in HTML:

```
<TITLE>Heavy Breathing Hamsters do Honolulu</TITLE>
<META NAME="DESCRIPTION" CONTENT="Furry friends get
fresh."> [This will appear in search listing results]
<META NAME="KEYWORDS" CONTENT="ham, pineapple,
mozzarella, david attenborough"> [Should increase your
ranking in searches for these keywords]
```

It also doesn't hurt to add keywords to the <alt> tags behind graphics. Whatever you do, don't respond to spam that claims to be able to "raise your ranking". These schemes rarely work. Instead, do your own homework into the black art of search engines:

About.com http://html.about.com/cs/metatags/
Search Engine Tutorial http://www.northernwebs.com/set/
Search Engine Watch http://www.searchenginewatch.com

And finally, to measure your success, see:

Did It Detective http://www.did-it.com
LinkPopularity http://www.linkpopularity.com
Web Position Agent http://www.webposition.com

Part two

The guide

Website directory

14

Website directory

No one can tell exactly how many addresses are accessible from the Web. If you were to try to work it out you'd have to factor in not only every webpage, but all the off-Web links as well. That means every newsgroup on every news server, every chatroom, every music sample and potentially every computer hooked to the Internet in any way. The Web proper, though, is the most popular part, and it's what we'll deal with in this guide. As you'll see from the following listings, it's more than just the world's biggest library; it defies explanation.

Technically, website addresses start with the prefix **http://** – anything else, although accessible from the Web, really belongs to another system. What sets the Web apart is the way you can move around by **clicking links**. Most websites have links to other sites strewn throughout their pages. As a bonus, they might even devote a section to listing similar sites (or simply ones they think might interest you). Just look for a section called "Links". Of course if you take such a link, you'll arrive at another site that could link to even more related sites. So although we only list a couple of thousand sites in the following pages, they'll lead you to millions more.

How to get there

To reach a site, carefully enter its **address** (taking note of any capital letters) into your browser's **Address bar**. This is normally located directly underneath the menu bar. Although formal Web addresses start with **http://**, you don't need to enter this bit unless you have a very old browser. **So if the address is listed as** http://www.abc.com, **simply type:** www.abc.com

How to find a site again

When you see something you like, save its address to your **Favorites**, **Bookmarks** or **Links** bar. To find it later, simply click on its name in the list. You could also read it offline by saving the page to disk or switching to offline mode. For instructions, see p.95.

When it's not there

Some of the following sites will have moved or vanished altogether, but don't let that deter you. For advice on how to track them down, see p.191.

Website directory

So far no one has succeeded in creating a Dewey Decimal System for websites, and chances are they never will. Some websites sit across several categories, while others almost defy categorization. We've had a go at sorting them under sensible headings, but you still might need to use your lateral thinking a little. So check under a few categories, especially "Reference" before giving up hope. To search the Net by subject or keyword, try out some of the entries in "Find it" (p.167).

If you're still looking for more destinations to browse, *The Rough Guide Website Directory* should point you in the right direction(s).

Just browsing ...

If you're merely browsing, rather than looking for information about a particular area, you might like to try the sites dedicated to listing, ranking or reporting sites that are new, "cool" or popular – or amusingly bad. They come in many guises, from the top hundred busiest sites in various categories to daily doses of extreme weirdness. **Weblogs** (blogs) are generally kept like diaries, with daily postings on whatever's attracted the author's interest over the last 24 hours. To find hundreds, run a search on "weblog" at **Dmoz.org**. And for some light entertainment, shuffle through the following selection:

100 Hot Websites http://www.100hot.com
MemePool http://www.memepool.com
Cruel Site of the Day http://www.cruel.com
Netsurfer Digest http://www.netsurf.com/nsd/
Portal of Evil http://www.portalofevil.com
Losers.org http://www.losers.org
Useless Pages http://www.go2net.com/useless/
Worst of the Web http://www.worstoftheweb.com
Yahoo!'s picks http://www.yahoo.com/picks/

Subjects

Websites

Subject guide

Amusements

Looking for a chuckle or perhaps to extend your lunchbreak into the late afternoon? Click through the following directories to enter a whole new dimension of time-wasting:

Humor Sites http://www.ranks.com/home/fun/top_humor_sites/
Open Directory http://dmoz.org/Recreation/Humor/
Yahoo! http://dir.yahoo.com/Entertainment/Humor/

If you have a high bandwidth connection, or are blessed with abnormal patience, you might like to investigate the world of online animation. Offerings range from clones of old-school arcade games to feature-length Flash cartoons from renowned cartoonists such as the creators of *Ren and Stimpy* (**http://www.spumco.com**). Pursue the galleries and links from:

About Animation http://animation.about.com
Animation http://dmoz.org/Arts/Animation/
Flashkit http://www.flashkit.com

Flazoom http://www.flazoom.com

Shockwave http://www.shockwave.com

Assassin
http://www.newgrounds.com/assassin/
Toast a few excess celebrities.

Brain Candy
http://www.corsinet.com/braincandy/
Riddles, jokes, insults and general wordplay.

Burn Maker
http://toy.thespark.com/burn/
Convert weak platitudes into powerful vitriol.

Cartoon Bank
http://www.cartoonbank.com
Every cartoon ever published in the *New Yorker*.

Comedy Central
http://www.comedycentral.com
Download full *South Park* episodes, listen to comedy radio and see what's screening across the network. More of a station promo than a source of laughs.

Comic Book Resources

http://www.comicbookresources.com
http://www.zapcartoons.com • http://www.cartoon-links.com
http://www.geocities.com/Area51/Aurora/2510/greatest_comics/
Comic and cartoon sites, shops, fanfare – and the hundred greatest?

Complaint Letter Generator

http://www-csag.ucsd.edu/individual/pakin/complaint/
Punch in a name for an instant dressing-down.

Dean and Nigel Blend In

http://www.deanandnigel.co.uk
Witness the gentle art of urban camouflage.

Funny Forwards

http://www.ilovebacon.com • http://www.collegehumor.com
http://www.mrjoker.net • http://www.millerinc.com
http://www.goofball.com • http://www.allfunnypictures.com
Most of the sight gags that arrive in your inbox courtesy of your caring
friends will, sooner or later, wind up in these or similar archives – usually before your friends see them. Don't go near the galleries if you're a
bit sensitive.

Horrorfind

http://www.horrorfind.com
A helpful hand into the darkness.

In the 70s/80s/90s

http://www.inthe70s.com
Re-enter the landscape that wallpapered your childhood memories.

Japanese Engrish

http://www.engrish.com
Copywriters wanted, English not a priority.

Jester: The Online Joke Recommender

http://shadow.ieor.berkeley.edu/humor/
It knows what makes you laugh.

Joke Jukebox

http://www.uselessjokes.com • http://www.humordatabase.com
http://www.humournet.com • http://www.humor.com
http://www.jokeindex.com • http://www.looniebin.mb.ca
http://www.jokecollection.com • http://www.twistedhumor.com
http://www.tastelessjokes.com
So many jokes it's not funny.

Liners Archive

http://www.newsmax.com/liners.shtml
Last night's openers from US chat-show hosts.

Matoox

http://www.matoox.com
Say something contentious by anonymous email or postcard.

National Lampoon

http://www.nationallampoon.com
Daily humour from the satire house that PJ built. Not what it was in the
1970s, as you'll see from the vault.

Newspaper Comic Strips

http://www.kingfeatures.com • http://www.comics.com
The entire works of the Phantom, Mandrake and friends.

The Onion
http://www.onion.com
Unquestionably the finest news satire on or off the Net, and source of inspiration to:
http://www.satirewire.com
http://www.herdofsheep.com (UK)
http://www.chaser.com.au (AUS)
http://www.strewth.org.au (AUS)
For breaking satire headlines, visit: http://www.gagpipe.com

Pocket Internet
http://www.thepocket.com
Gadgets, games, greeting cards, cartoons and more, updated daily.

Pranksta's Paradise
http://www.ccil.org/~mika/
All the practical jokes from alt.shenanigans.

Rec.humor.funny
http://www.netfunny.com/rhf/
Archives of the rec.humor.funny newsgroup, updated daily.

Sissyfight
http://www.sissyfight.com
Scratch, tease and tattle your way to playground supremacy.

Stick Figure Death Theater
http://www.sfdt.com
Stick city citizens meet their sticky ends.

UnderGround Online
http://www.ugo.com
Vigilante gang of counterculture sites – close to the antithesis of AOL.

Art, Museums and Photography

If you're an artist, photograph your work (preferably with a digital camera) and post it online. It's cheap gallery space that your disciples can visit at any time without even leaving home. But don't expect them to stumble across it randomly: you'll need to hand out its address at every opportunity. And, don't forget to include news of your exhibitions and contact details.

Like the real world, finding art online is very much a click-and-miss affair, and of course entirely a matter of taste. Most major galleries are finding their feet online with limited exhibitions, and any artist who's at all switched on will have their work on the Web. If you're up for clicking, these link banks will locate just about everything that could be considered a bit arty:

ADAM http://adam.ac.uk
Artcyclopedia http://www.artcyclopedia.com
World Wide Arts Resources http://www.wwar.com

Or if the prospect of an art portal sounds more like your scene:
Art Advocate http://www.artadvocate.com
Artnet.com http://www.artnet.com
Artstar http://www.artstar.com

To find museums:
MuseumNetwork.com http://www.museumnetwork.com
Museums Around the World http://www.icom.org/vlmp/world.html
24 Hour Museum (UK) http://www.24hourmuseum.org.uk

To set up your own free **online photo gallery**, see p.295.

24 Hours in Cyberspace
http://www.cyber24.com
One thousand photographers save the day.

3D Artists
http://www.raph.com/3dartists/
Art that looks too real to be real.

AllPosters.com
http://www.allposters.com • http://www.allaboutart.com
Plaster over the cracks in your bedroom walls.

American Museum of Photography
http://www.photographymuseum.com
Exhibitions from back when cameras were a novelty.

The American Museum of PHOTOGRAPHY™

CHOOSE AN EXHIBITION!

Click here to go to the Exhibits Floor

Or choose any of these shortcut links to current shows:

• AN EYE FOR THE WORLD Photographs by Shotaro Shimomura, 1954-1935, Rediscovered. Sponsored by The Film Shop

• AT EASE Informal Portraits from the Dawn of Photography

• SMALL WORLDS The Art of the Carte de Visite

Amico.org
http://www.amico.org
Thumbnails from the top North American galleries.

Anime Web Turnpike
http://www.anipike.com
http://anime.about.com
Today, Japan; tomorrow, a schoolyard near you.

The Art Connection
http://www.art-connection.com
Buy Brit art.

Art Crimes: Writing on the Wall
http://www.graffiti.org
Spray-can art from around the world.

ArtMuseum
http://www.artmuseum.net
Infrequent exhibitions of modern US classics.

Censored Cartoons
http://www.toonzone.net/looney/ltcuts/
Find out what was removed from your favourite classic cartoon.

Core-Industrial Design Resources
http://www.core77.com
Get a hand with industrial design.

Design Addict
http://www.designaddict.com
Ergonomic paradise.

Dia Center for the Arts
http://www.diacenter.org
Web exclusives from "extraordinary" artists, plus the lowdown on the NY Dia Center's upcoming escapades.

Digital Photography Review
http://www.dpreview.com
Considering a new camera? Read on. To learn how to use it, see:
http://www.photographytips.com

Elfwood
http://www.elfwood.com
Sketches and tales from a gaggle of junior fantasy and sci-fi buffs.

The Exploratorium
http://www.exploratorium.edu
Kid-friendly online exhibitions from San Francisco's Exploratorium.

Great Buildings Collections
http://www.greatbuildings.com
Shuffle knowingly through 3D models of some 750 of the world's most notable structures.

Grove Dictionary of Art Online
http://www.groveart.com
Freeload on the definitive art reference for a day.

Interactive Collector
http://www.icollector.com
Bid on art and collectibles like celebrity castoffs. No luck? There's always eBay (p.203).

Labelcollector.com
http://www.labelcollector.com
Salute the golden era of fruit crates and jars.

Library of Congress
http://www.loc.gov
Research tools, exhibitions, library services, current hot bills and an unparalleled multimedia showcase of American history.

Life
http://www.lifemag.com
View *Life* magazine's picture of the day, then link through to some of the world's most arresting photographs. There's even more at:
http://www.newsphotos.com.au
http://www.thepicturecollection.com
Or, for drunken celebrities: http://www.wireimage.com

Museum of Modern Art NY
http://www.moma.org
Not quite like being there in person, but a fair sample of what's on show.

One Model Place
http://www.onemodelplace.com
Window-shop for photographers and models.

Photodisc
http://www.photodisc.com
Plunder these photos free, or pay for the hi-res versions.

Soda Connector
http://sodaplay.com/constructor/
Train ingenious spring models that obey the laws of physics and the whims of your idle mind.

Stelarc

http://www.stelarc.va.com.au
No artist has given his body to the Net like Prof Stelarc. More hanging around at:
http://www.suspension.org

Vincent Van Gogh Gallery

http://www.vangoghgallery.com
Where else could you see his entire works in one place?

Year in the Life of Photojournalism

http://www.digitalstoryteller.com/YITL/
Tag along with voyeuristic pros and see what they do in their day-to-day.

Books and Literature

If a squillion webpages aren't enough to satisfy your lust for the written word, then maybe you should use one to order a book. You'll be spoiled for choice, with hundreds of shops offering millions of titles for delivery anywhere worldwide. That includes bumper showings from most of the major chains alongside exclusively online book havens such as **Amazon** and **BOL**. The superstores typically lay on all the trimmings – user ratings, reviews, recommendations, sample chapters, author interviews, bestseller lists, press clippings, publishing news, secure ordering and usually giftwrapping.

Major chains

Barnes & Noble (US) http://www.bn.com
Blackwell's (UK) http://bookshop.blackwell.co.uk
Book Passage (US) http://www.bookpassage.com
Collins (AUS) http://www.collinsbooks.com.au
Dymocks (AUS) http://www.dymocks.com.au
Hammicks (UK) http://www.thebookplace.com

McGills (AUS) http://www.mcgills.com.au
Ottakar's (UK) http://www.ottakars.co.uk
WHSmith (UK) http://www.bookshop.co.uk

Only on the Web

Alphabet Street (UK) http://www.alphabetstreet.com
Amazon (UK) http://www.amazon.co.uk
Amazon (US) http://www.amazon.com
Amazon (other countries) http://www.amazon.com/international/
BOL (UK, Europe, Asia) http://www.bol.com
Buy.com (US, UK) http://www.buy.com

Not listed here? Try browsing or subject-searching this directory of booksellers worldwide: **http://www.bookweb.org/bookstores/**

For a rundown on British online booksellers, visit: **http://www.books.co.uk**

While Barnes & Noble and Amazon may rightly jostle over the title of "world's most ginormous bookstore", you'll find all the biggies offer a staggering range, usually at substantial discounts. But because books are heavy, any savings could be offset by freight. And, naturally, the further away you are and the sooner you want it, the more it adds up. So, before you check out in a frenzy, see that you have the best deal:

AddAll (INT) http://www.addall.com
Best Book Buys (US) http://www.bestbookbuys.com
BookBrain (UK) http://www.bookbrain.co.uk
BookFinder (US) http://www.bookfinder.com
Zoomit (UK, EUR, Latin America) http://www.zoomit.com

If the hype is to be believed, one day we might be downloading all our books into palm-sized electronic readers. You can already buy various brands of **eBook** (electronic book) readers at most electronic outlets, but as yet they're not exactly sending the paper mills broke. To find digital tomes, try the big bookshops such as Amazon or a specialist:

eBooks http://www.ebooks.com

eBook Palace http://www.ebookpalace.com

And, for news about eBook software and gadgets, see:

Electronic Books http://www.electronic-books.com

eBooks 'N' Bytes http://www.ebooksnbytes.com/

Absolute Shakespeare

http://absoluteshakespeare.com • http://shakespeare.palomar.edu
The Bard unbarred online. To download the works in PDF format, try:
http://www.hn.psu.edu/faculty/jmanis/shake.htm

Audible.com

http://www.audible.com
Why read when you could listen?

Banned Books Online

http://digital.library.upenn.edu/books/banned-books.html
Extracts from books that riled the righteous.

Bibliofind
http://www.bibliofind.com
Millions of old, used and rare books from sellers worldwide. Or, if you want to swap all your savings for a manuscript or first edition, try: http://www.bibliopoly.com

Book-A-Minute
http://www.rinkworks.com/bookaminute/
Knock over a classic in your lunch hour.

BookCloseouts
http://www.bookcloseouts.com
Lorryloads of books slightly past their shelf life – including this one's first edition!

Bookwire
http://www.bookwire.com
US book trade news, bestseller lists and author road schedules with content from *Publisher's Weekly* and *Library Journal*. For UK publishing news, see: http://www.thebookseller.com

CrimeBoss
http://www.crimeboss.com
Shock comic covers from the mid-20th century.

CRIMEBOSS
CRIME COMIC BOOKS
OF THE 1940s & 1950s

WELCOME
GALLERY
HISTORY
WANT LIST
LINKS
GUESTBOOK

From the cover of
Crimes By Women #2

Internet Classics Archive
http://classics.mit.edu
Hundreds of translated Greek and Roman classics. For more ancient and medieval literature, see: http://argos.evansville.edu

The Internet Public Library
http://www.ipl.org
Browse online books, magazines, journals and newspapers.

January Magazine
http://www.januarymagazine.com
Dissecting books and authors.

MysteryNet
http://www.mysterynet.com
Hmm, now what could this be?

Poetry Society
http://www.poetrysoc.com (UK) • http://www.poets.org (US)
Halfway houses for budding poets and their victims.

Project Gutenberg
http://www.gutenberg.net
Copyrights don't live forever; they eventually expire. In the US, that's 75 years after first publication. In Europe, it's some 70 years after the author's death. With this in mind, Project Gutenberg is gradually bringing thousands of old texts online, along with some more recent donations. Sounds great, but you might prefer the convenience of hard copy. See also: http://digital.library.upenn.edu/books/

Pure Fiction (US, UK)
http://www.purefiction.com
For pulp worms and writers alike. Not a word of it is true.

The Slot: A Spot for Copy Editors
http://www.theslot.com
Soothing words of outrage for grammar pedants.

Word Counter
http://www.wordcounter.com
Paste in your composition to rank your most overused words.

The Word Detective
http://www.word-detective.com • http://www.quinion.com/words/
Words never escape him.

The Yarn
http://www.theyarn.com
A story that offers you the choice of two paths at the end of each chapter. If one leads you to a dead end, you're asked to contribute.

Business

AccountingWeb
http://www.accountingweb.co.uk
Safe playpen for British bean-counters.

Ad Critic
http://www.adcritic.com • http://www.superbowl-ads.com
Make a cuppa while you wait for this year's best US TV ads. For the
best of the last twenty, see: http://www.commercial-archive.com
For Australian ads going back to the 1950s: http://www.tvc.com.au

Ad Forum
http://www.adforum.com • http://www.portfolios.com
http://www.sourcetv.com
Gateway to thousands of agencies, their ads and the humble creatives
behind them.

Bizymoms
http://www.bizymoms.com
Crafty ways to cash up without missing the afternoon soaps.

Business.com
http://www.business.com
Attempting to become the Yahoo! of business sites.
For more European sites and trade data, see:
http://www.europages.com

Clickz
http://www.clickz.com
The Web as seen by the marketing biz.

Cluetrain Manifesto
http://www.cluetrain.org
Modern-day translation of "the customer is always right". Read it or
perish. Alternatively, if you'd prefer an update on "never give a sucker
an even break", consult the Ferengi Rules of Acquisition:
http://www.psiphi.org/DS9/rules.html

Business Magazines

Most business magazines archive their past editions online, break news throughout the day and provide excellent starting points for company resource. For example:

Advertising Age	http://www.adage.com
Adweek	http://www.adweek.com
Barrons	http://www.barrons.com
Business 2.0	http://www.business2.com
Business Review Weekly (AUS)	http://www.brw.com.au
Campaign (UK)	http://www.campaignlive.com
Fast Company	http://www.fastcompany.com
Financial Review (AUS)	http://afr.com
Financial Times (UK)	http://www.ft.com
Forbes	http://www.forbes.com
Upside	http://www.upside.com
Wall Street Journal	http://www.wsj.com

See also News, Newspapers and Magazines (p.422) and Money (p.404).

Companies Online
http://www.companiesonline.com
Get the score on almost a million US companies.

Customers Suck!
http://www.customerssuck.com
Grumbly dispatches from the retail front.

Delphion Intellectual Property Network
http://www.delphion.com
Sift through a few decades of international patents, plus a gallery of obscurities. Ask the right questions and you might stumble across tomorrow's technology long before the media. For UK patents, see:
http://www.patent.gov.uk

Entrepreneur.com
http://www.entrepreneur.com
Get rich now, ask us how.

The Foundation Center
http://fdncenter.org
Companies who might happily spare you a fiver.

Fucked Company
http://fuckedcompany.com
Join the rush to gloat over startup shutdowns.

Garage.com
http://www.garage.com
Matchmaking agency for entrepreneurs and investors founded by
Apple's Guy Kawasaki. For more help milking funds for your online
white elephant, see: http://www.moneyhunter.com

Guerilla Marketing
http://www.gmarketing.com
Get ahead by – metaphorically – butchering your competitors' families
and poisoning your customers' water supply.

InfoUSA
http://www.infousa.com
Find likely Americans to bug with your presentation.

International Trademark Association
http://inta.org
Protect your brand identity.

IT Anthems
http://www.zdnet.co.uk/specials/2002/it-anthems/
What to whistle while you work.

Killer Internet tactics
http://www.killertactics.com
How to murder brain-dead Web surfers with HTML.

Patent Café
http://www.patentcafe.com
Protect your crackpot schemes and see them through to fruition.

Setting up an online shop

When you're ready to put your business online, you should seek advice from – and probably the services of – someone who knows what they're doing. Setting up an online shop is a lot more involved than whipping up a simple webpage (p.307). Start by looking for "ecommerce" software and shop-hosting service reviews in the computer, Internet, and business press so you know what's on offer. What's best for you will depend largely on the size of your inventory. You might find a quick solution in one of the hundreds of click-and-build stores, such as:

Amazon http://www.zshops.com
BigStep http://www.bigstep.com
Biz Infinity http://www.bizfinity.com
BT Ignite (UK) http://www.btignite.com
Click and Build http://www.clickandbuild.com
Demon (UK) http://www.demonpowertrader.com
Freemerchant http://www.freemerchant.com
Jumbostore http://www.jumbostore.com
Magic Moments (UK) http://www.magic-moments.com
Merchandizer http://www.merchandizer.com
Site America http://www.siteamerica.com
VirginBiz (UK) http://www.virginbiz.net
Yahoo! US http://store.yahoo.com

If your bank won't give you a merchant account for online trading, try a specialist PSP (Payment Service Provider). Compare the transaction costs, annual fees and international restrictions at:

BidPay http://www.bidpay.com
Checkfree http://www.checkfree.com
Datacash http://www.datacash.com
Netbanx http://www.netbanx.com
Secure Trading http://www.securetrading.com
WorldPay http://www.worldpay.com

Planet Feedback

http://www.complaintline.com.au (AUS)
http://www.howtocomplain.com (UK)
http://www.planetfeedback.com (US)
http://www.thecomplaintstation.com (US)
Let companies know what you think of their service.

Super Marketing: Ads from the Comic Books

http://www.steveconley.com/supermarketing.htm
The ads that kept you lying awake at night wishing you had more money.

The Wonderful Wankometer

http://www.cynicalbastards.com/wankometer/
Measure corporate hyperbole. Couple with:
http://www.dack.com/web/bullshit.html

Computing and Tech News

Every decent manufacturer of PCs or components brand has a site where you can download the latest drivers, get support and find out what's new. It won't be hard to find: usually it's the company name or initials between a **www.** and a **com.** So you'll find

Dell at **http://www.dell.com**, Gateway at **http://www.gateway.com** and so forth. Most of the big names also have international branches, which will be linked from the main site. Consult Yahoo! if that fails. If you're in the market for new computer bits, check out the best price across US online vendors:

AnandTech http://www.anandtech.com/guides.html
Price Watch http://www.pricewatch.com
Shopper.com http://www.shopper.com

Popular package software vendors include:
Amazon (UK, US) http://www.amazon.com
Buy.com (UK, US) http://www.buy.com
Chumbo http://www.chumbo.com
Jungle (UK) http://www.jungle.com

Bear in mind, if you live outside the US, that any imports might be taxed upon arrival.

Apple
http://www.apple.com
Essential drop-in to update your Mac, pick up QuickTime and be hard-sold the latest hardware. To top up with news, software and brand affirmations, see:
http://www.macaddict.com • http://www.appleinsider.com
http://www.tidbits.com • http://www.macintouch.com
http://www.macnn.com • http://www.macslash.com
Don't even think of looking at http://www.ihateapple.com. It will only upset you.

Bastard Operator from Hell
http://bofh.ntk.net
If you work in a big office, you know this man.

Troubleshooting

The best place to find an answer to your computer problems is usually on Usenet (p.229). Chances are it's already been answered, so before you rush in and post, search the archives through Google Groups.

Google Groups http://groups.google.com

That's not to say you won't find the answer on the Web. You probably will, so follow up with a Web search. You'll find a choice of engines at the very bottom of the results page. If you click on Google, for example, it will perform the same search in the Web database. Apart from Usenet, there are several very active computing forums on the Web, such as:

Computing.net http://www.computing.net
Tek Tips http://www.tektips.com

There are also hundreds of troubleshooting and Windows news sites, such as:

ActiveWin http://www.activewin.com
Annoyances http://www.annoyances.org
Common Problems
http://www.users.qwest.net/~careyh/fixes.htm
Help.com http://www.help.com
TweakXP http://www.tweakxp.com
Virtual Dr http://virtualdr.com
Windows XP tips http://www.winoscentral.com
WinOScentral http://www.tipsdr.com
XP Tweaks http://www.xp-erience.org

Don't forget to keep your hardware installation drivers up-to-date. You'll find the latest files for download direct from the manufacturer's website, or at driver guides such as these:

Driver Forum http://www.driverforum.com
Driver Guide http://www.driverguide.com
Drivers HQ http://www.drivershq.com
Windrivers http://www.windrivers.com

For browser-related trouble, see p.111.

Chankstore FreeFont Archive

http://www.chank.com/freefonts.htm
http://www.printerideas.com/fontfairy/
http://www.fontface.com

Download free fonts till your computer feels sick. If you know what you
want and don't mind paying, see:
http://www.fonts.com

Clip Art

http://webclipart.about.com

Bottomless cesspit of the soulless dross used to inject life into
documents.

CNET

http://www.cnet.com

Daily technology news and features, plus reviews, shopping, games
and downloads, along with schedules, transcripts and related stories
from CNET's broadcasting network. To automatically find and download
updates and security patches, and remove adware from your machine,
use their CatchUp service:
http://catchup.cnet.com

Desktop Publishing

http://desktoppub.about.com • http://desktoppublishing.com
Get off the ground in print.

The Dingbat Pages

http://www.dingbatpages.com
For when you just can't get enough symbol fonts.

Distributed Computing

http://www.aspenleaf.com/distributed/distrib-projects.html
Advance civilization by sharing your processor.

Easter Egg Archive

http://www.eeggs.com

A racing game in Excel 2000, a basketball game in Windows 95 and a
raygun-wielding alien in QuarkXPress? They're in there, but you'll never
find them on your own. Here's how to unlock secrets in scores of
programs.

Happy Hacker
http://www.happyhacker.org
Crash course in l33td00dz 101.

MacFix-it
http://www.macfixit.com
Diagnose what's ailing your Mac.

Microsoft
http://www.microsoft.com
If you're running any Microsoft
product – and the chance of that
seems to be approaching 100
percent – drop by this disorgan-
ized scrapheap regularly for
upgrades, news, support and
patches. That includes the latest
free tweaks to Windows, Office
and all that falls under the Internet Explorer regime.

Modem Help
http://www.modemhelp.com • http://www.56k.com
http://www.modemhelp.org
Solve your dial-up dramas for modems of all persuasions including
cable, ISDN and DSL. And be sure to check your modem maker's page
for driver and firmware upgrades, especially if it's X2 or K56flex.

Need to Know
http://www.ntk.net
Weekly hi-tech wrap-up with a sarcastic bite.

Newslinx
http://www.newslinx.com
Have the top Net technology stories, aggregated from around fifty
sources, delivered to your mailbox daily. Or for the highlights in a
digest: http://classifieds.news.com.au/ni/netnews/

Palmgear
http://www.palmgear.com
Know your palm like the back of your hand. For the Pocket PC, see:
http://www.pocketmatrix.com

PC Mechanic
http://www.pcmech.com/byopc/ • http://www.tweak3d.net
http://arstechnica.com/tweak/hardware.html
How to build, or upgrade, your own computer.

PC Tweaking
http://www.anandtech.com • http://www.arstechnica.com
http://www.pcextremist.com • http://www.pureperformance.com
http://www.sharkyextreme.com • http://www.shacknews.com
http://www.tomshardware.com • http://www.tweaktown.com
http://www.geek.com • http://www.mvps.org/serenitymacros/
How to overclock your processor into the next millennium, tweak your
bios and upgrade your storage capacity to attract members of the
opposite sex.

PCWebopedia
http://www.pcwebopedia.com
Superb illustrated encyclopedia of computer technology.

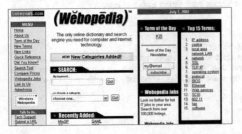

Programmers Heaven
http://www.programmersheaven.com
Code your way to eternal fulfilment in almost any language.

The Register
http://www.theregister.co.uk
Punchy tech news that follows its own tune.

Scantips
http://www.scantips.com
Become a scan-do type of dude.

Slashdot.org
http://slashdot.org
News for those who've entirely given up on the human race.

StreamLoad
http://www.streamload.com
Free storage space on the Net – perfect for backups and file transfers.

Techtales
http://www.techtales.com • http://www.helpdesktech.com
Customers – they might always be right but they sure do ask the darndest things.

Virus Myths
http://www.vmyths.com
If someone sends you an email insisting you forward it on to everyone you know, send them here instead. Build up your immune system by following the advice starting on p.157.

Wired News
http://www.wired.com
The Net's best source of breaking technology news, plus archives of *Wired* magazine.

Woody's Office Portal
http://www.wopr.com
Beat some sense out of Microsoft Office. For Outlook, see:
http://www.slipstick.com/outlook/faq.htm

Yahoo! Computing
http://www.yahoo.com/Computers/
The grandpappy of all computing directories.

ZDNet
http://www.zdnet.com
Computing info powerhouse from Ziff Davis, publisher of *PC Magazine*, *MacUser*, *Computer Gaming World* and scores of other IT titles. Each magazine donates content such as news, product reviews and lab test results – plus, there's a ton of Net-exclusive technochow. The best place to start researching anything even vaguely computer-related.

Education

Just about every tertiary institution in the world should be online by now, so don't expect to find any listed here. Just search in **Braintrack** (**http://www.braintrack.com**), or use **Google** or **Yahoo!**, to find their admission centres, staff listings, study guides and so forth. Most also place their lecture materials online, which makes the Net perfect for distance learning and – of course – skipping classes. Homework sites are also plentiful, but of questionable usefulness. You'd probably do better by keying your subject into a search engine. After all, the entire Internet is an education resource. Nevertheless, you might find a few shortcuts through the likes of:

About Homework http://homework.about.com

BBC Learning http://www.bbc.co.uk/learning

Bigchalk http://www.bigchalk.com

HighWired http://www.highwired.com

Homework Spot http://www.homeworkspot.com

Academic Info
http://www.academicinfo.net
Research directory for students and teachers.

Evil House of Cheat
http://www.cheathouse.com
Thousands of college essays, term papers and reports.

SearchEdu

http://www.searchedu.com
Search millions of university and education pages.

Study Abroad

http://www.studyabroad.com
Hop to greener grass.

Study Web

http://www.studyweb.com
Ideal school research aid with thousands of leads split by topic.

Web66: International School Website Directory

http://web66.coled.umn.edu/schools.html
Add your school's webpage if it's not already listed.

Employment

The Web is increasingly useful for those seeking employment. Lots of newspapers that are popular for vacancy listings put all their jobs ads online, and there are many Web-only services that list thousands of available posts, both local and international. Equally numerous are online job agencies (some of which specialize in particular areas), with which you can post your CV, to be contacted when suitable things come up. Bear in mind, though, that your boss could find you up there – embarrassing at the very least.

Further, the Net is great for finding out about companies that you fancy working for. Most sites have a link for "jobs", "opportunities" or "vacancies", or at least an email address that you can use to enquire. And it should go without saying that you should never interview with any company without fully surveying its website, along with its main competitors and other industry voices.

Here are some of the most popular job sites:

chapter 14 • website directory

INT

http://www.adecco.com
http://www.drakeintl.com
http://www.headhunter.net
http://www.monster.com
http://www.topjobs.com

AUS

http://www.careerone.com.au
http://www.seek.com.au

UK/EUR

http://www.fish4jobs.co.uk
http://www.gojobsite.com
http://www.jobsearch.co.uk
http://www.jobsunlimited.co.uk
http://www.peoplebank.com
http://www.reed.co.uk

US

http://www.ajb.dni.us
http://www.careerbuilder.com
http://www.flipdog.com
http://www.futurestep.com
http://www.hotjobs.com

Cool Works

http://www.coolworks.com
Seasonal jobs in US resorts, national parks, camps, ranches and cruise lines.

Expat Network

http://www.expatnetwork.co.uk
Subscription placement and settling service for working globetrotters.

Integrity Based Interviewing

http://www.interviewing.net
Ex-federal agents show you how to get to the truth without drawing blood.

i-resign.com
http://www.i-resign.com
Quit now – while you're ahead.

The Riley Guide
http://www.rileyguide.com
Messy, but massive, directory of job-hunting resources.

Salary Info
http://www.salary.com • http://jobsmart.org/tools/salary/
See what you're worth, and then how much you'd need in another
state: http://www2.homefair.com/calc/salcalc.html

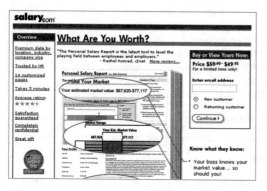

Yahoo! Careers
http://careers.yahoo.com (.co.uk, .com.au, etc)
As ever, Yahoo! is in on the act and, as ever, does it superbly.

Entertainment and Events

Finding out what's on in town, and booking your perch, has
never been easier – once you settle on a trusty online source. Your
local newspaper's site would be the first logical port of call. Then

see how these multi-city guides cater to your locale and interests:

Ananova (UK) http://www.ananova.com

CitySearch (US, AU and more) http://www.citysearch.com

Ninemsn (AUS) http://www.ninemsn.com.au

Time Out (INT) http://www.timeout.com

And if you find something you like, why not book tickets in advance? These sites are also good sources of infomation about upcoming events.

Aloud (UK) http://www.aloud.com

NME Tickets (UK) http://www.nmetickets.com

Tickets.com (US) http://www.tickets.com

Ticketek (AUS) http://www.ticketek.com.au

Ticketmaster (AUS) http://www.ticketmaster.com.au

Ticketmaster (UK) http://www.ticketmaster.co.uk

Ticketmaster (US) http://www.ticketmaster.com

Tickets Online (UK) http://www.tickets-online.co.uk

What's On Stage (UK)
http://www.whatsonstage.com
Find out what's on in the theatre, and then book online.

CultureFinder (US)
http://www.culturefinder.com
What's-on guide to classical music, theatre, opera, dance and visual arts in around a thousand US cities.

Music Festival Finder
http://www.festivalfinder.com
Upcoming North American outdoor gigs of all persuasions. For the UK, depending on your taste, see: www.virtual-festivals.com or http://www.artsfestivals.co.uk

Operabase
http://www.operabase.com
What's on where in worldwide opera, plus details of past performances and reviews.

Fashion

Unless it entirely erodes your reading time, the Net isn't likely to cut your guilty expenditure on glossy mags. While there's a spree of fledgling style zines and something of sorts from nearly all the big rack names, none of it compares to getting it in print (see p.422 for more):

Condé Nast (UK) http://www.condenast.co.uk
Condé Nast (US) http://condenast.com
Cosmo (INT) http://www.cosmomag.com
Elle (INT) http://www.elle.com
Esquire http://www.esquire.com
FHM (INT) http://www.fhm.com/international/
Flare (CAN) http://www.flare.com
GQ (UK) http://www.gq-magazine.co.uk
Marie Claire (INT) http://www.marieclaire.com
Vogue (INT) http://www.vogue.com

Nonetheless, they will certainly supplement your vice. What you will find the Net far better for is researching products, checking out brands and saving money on consumables like cosmetics at stores such as:

http://www.drugstore.com • http://www.gloss.com
http://www.ibeauty.com • http://www.perfumania.com
http://www.reflect.com • http://www.sephora.com

http://www.hqhair.com (UK) • http://www.thinknatural.com (UK)
http://www.theperfumeshop.com (UK)

Buying clothes is tough, but popular nonetheless. They're out there, if you know what you're doing, but you'll soon see why Boo.com failed. The best place to find fashion sites is in your regular glossies and newspaper's style section – both in editorial and ads. Label sites are sometimes interesting for new-season looks, stockists and, sometimes, direct ordering.

FashionBot
http://www.fashionbot.com
Search several UK high-street retailers' catalogues.

Fashion Information
http://www.fashioninformation.com
Pay for trend forecasting reports. Some free stuff, too.

Fashionmall.com
http://www.fashionmall.com • http://www.brandsforless.com
http://www.bluefly.com
Mail-order familiar – and mostly American – labels.

Fashion Net
http://www.fashion.net • http://www.efashion.com
Handy shortcut to the highest-profile shopping, designer, magazine, modelling and fashion industry sites, with enough editorial to warrant an extended stopover.

Fashion UK
http://www.fuk.co.uk
Minimal, but fresh, vanity monthly out of London.

Firstview
http://www.firstview.com
See what's trotting the catwalks – sometimes at a price.

I Enhance
http://www.ienhance.com
Address your imperfections without pills or creams.

InShop (US)
http://www.inshop.com
Track shop sales and promotions in your area.

The Lipstick Page
http://www.thelipstickpage.com
Cosmetic appliances for fun and profit.

Moda Italia
http://www.modaitalia.net
Patch through to the Italian rag-traders.

Mullets of the Gods
http://www.mulletgods.com • http://www.mulletjunky.com
Don't touch the back (or the sides): http://www.badburns.com

Solemates: The Century in Shoes
http://www.centuryinshoes.com
Stepping out in the 20th century.

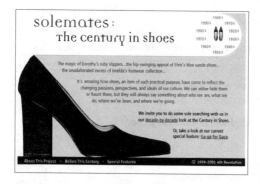

Victoria's Secret
http://www.victoriassecret.com
Order online or request the catalogue preferred by nine out of ten
teenage boys.

Film, TV and Stars

Most TV stations maintain excellent sites with all kinds of extras such as live sports coverage, program reruns and documentary follow-ups, often including live chats with the producers. We won't need to give you their addresses because they'll be flashing them at you at every opportunity. In any case, you'll be able to find links either at the channel's site, or via a search engine. Alternatively, try: **http://www.tvshow.com**

For personalized listings, perhaps delivered by email, try your local Yahoo!, or:
http://www.sofcom.com.au/TV/ (AUS)
http://www.tvguidelive.com (CAN)
http://www.radiotimes.beeb.com (UK)
http://www.digiguide.co.uk (UK)
http://www.ananova.com/tv/ (UK)
http://www.gist.com (US)
http://www.tvguide.com (US)
http://tv.zap2it.com (US)

For more options, and other countries:
http://www.tvshow.com/tv/scheds/

Or for an approach bordering on the libellous:
http://www.tvgohome.com

To be notified when something's on:
Spyonit http://www.spyonit.com

Several sites specialize in TV episode guides:
Epguides.com http://epguides.com
Hu's Episode Guides http://www.episodeguides.com
Television Without Pity http://www.televisionwithoutpity.com

But if you want obsessive detail along with picture galleries, scripts, spoilers and rumours, search Yahoo! or the Open Directory for a site dedicated to that show. If it's current and popular, you'll be confronted with hundreds of choices. For the strictly nostalgic:

TV Cream (UK) http://tv.cream.org

Yesterdayland http://www.yesterdayland.com

Or, if you'd prefer a video or DVD, you won't find a bigger range than:

Amazon http://www.amazon.com (.co.uk)

Black Star (UK) http://www.blackstar.co.uk

Reel.com http://www.reel.com

And to compare prices:
http://www.dvdpricesearch.com • http://www.formovies.com

For more on DVD hardware and software:
http://www.7thzone.com • http://www.dvdfile.com

When it comes to movies, one site clearly rules:
The Internet Movie Database http://www.imdb.com

To say it's impressive is an understatement. You'll be hard-pressed to find any work on or off the Net as comprehensive as this exceptional relational database of screen trivia from over 100,000 movies and a million actors. It's all tied together remarkably well – for example, within two clicks of finding your favourite movie, you can get full filmographies of anyone from the cast or crew, and then see what's in the cooker. Still, it's not perfect or entirely without competition. For example, you'll find a similar service with superior biographies and synopses at the colossal:

All Movie Guide http://www.allmovie.com

Or for more Chan, Li and Fat:
Hong Kong Movie Database http://www.hkmdb.com

They'll also direct you to external reviews, as will:
Movie Review Query Engine http://www.mrqe.com

But perhaps you'd prefer a summary:
Rotten Tomatoes http://www.rottentomatoes.com

Or a recommendation based on your tastes:
MovieLens http://movielens.umn.edu

While at least one site picks the all-time greats:
Greatest Films http://www.filmsite.org

Far more are content to trash:
Bad Movie Night http://www.hit-n-run.com
Filthy Critic http://bigempire.com/filthy/
Mr Cranky http://www.mrcranky.com
The Stinkers http://www.thestinkers.com

Roll in it:
Astounding B Monster http://www.bmonster.com
Bad Movie Report http://www.stomptokyo.com/badmoviereport/
Badmovies.org http://www.badmovies.org
Oh the Humanity http://www.ohthehumanity.com
Shock Cinema http://members.aol.com/shockcin/

Or just point out the blunders:
Movie Mistakes http://www.movie-mistakes.com
Nitpickers http://www.nitpickers.com

But none unveil box office evil like:
Childcare Action Project http://www.capalert.com
Movie Rat http://www.saunalahti.fi/~mitt/movierat.htm
Screen It! http://www.screenit.com

For whispers of what's in production:
Ain't It Cool News http://www.aint-it-cool-news.com
CHUD http://www.chud.com
Coming Attractions http://www.corona.bc.ca/films/
Dark Horizons http://www.darkhorizons.com
IMDB http://www.imdb.com/Sections/Inproduction/
Upcoming Movies http://www.upcomingmovies.com

Or use a film directory like **TD Film** to find everything from film schools to directors:
TD Film http://www.tdfilm.com

You can even download films and TV shows to watch on your computer. And not only amateur shorts like:
Atom Films http://www.atomfilms.com
Pixelfest http://www.pixelfest.com

But even full-length box office hits, TV archives:

Cinema Now http://www.cinemanow.com
CinemaPop http://www.cinemapop.com
iFilm http://www.ifilm.com
Intertainer http://www.intertainer.com
LikeTelevision http://www.liketelevision.com
MovieFlix http://www.movieflix.com
Moviefly http://www.moviefly.com
SightSound http://www.sightsound.com

To reach out to a star:

Celebrity Addresses http://www.writetoaceleb.com
CelebrityEmail.com http://www.celebrityemail.com

Every celebrity has at least one obsessive fan site
(**http://www.ggower.com/fans/**) in their honour. Finding them can
sometimes be tricky. If they're not listed in Yahoo!, try:

http://www.celebhoo.com • http://www.celebsites.com
http://www.csotd.com • http://www.webring.org
http://directory.google.com/Top/Arts/Celebrities/

Search engines tend to find porn scutlers who've loaded their
HTML meta tags with celebrity names – easy bait, when you
consider that most fans would be more than happy to catch a
glimpse of their idol in various states of undress
(**http://www.cndb.com**). If they succeed in catching your attention, at least have the sense not to pull out your credit card.
Adding **-naughty -naked -nude** to your search term, or

enabling an **adult filter** such as Google's SafeSearch (under Preferences), might help weed them out.

AsSeenonScreen
http://www.asseenonscreen.com
Buy stuff you've seen on TV or in movies.

BBCi
http://www.bbc.co.uk
Get your media fix direct from Auntie.

Drew's Script-O-Rama
http://www.script-o-rama.com • http://www.scriptshack.com
Hundreds of entire film and TV scripts. Need help writing or selling your own? Try here: http://www.scriptfly.com

E! Online
http://www.eonline.com
Daily film and TV gossip, news and reviews.

Empire Magazine
http://www.empireonline.co.uk
Reviews of every film showing in the UK.

Famous Birthdays
http://www.famousbirthdays.com
http://us.imdb.com/OnThisDay
See who shares your birthday.

Film Festival Guide
http://www.filmfestivals.com
All the news from all the festivals in all the world.

Filmmaking Net
http://www.filmmaking.net
Learn how to produce your own blockbuster. For more digital video, see: http://www.adamwilt.com/DV.html

Find a Grave
http://www.findagrave.com
See where celebrities are buried.

Friends Place

http://www.friendsplace.com

Every script of every episode ever. But if you have that much spare time it might make you wish you had some of your own.

Hollywood Reporter

http://www.hollywoodreporter.com

Tinseltown tattle, previews and reviews daily, plus a flick biz directory.

Internet Archive Movie Collection

http://www.archive.org/movies/

Thousands of archival films freely available for viewing and recycling.

Jump the Shark

http://www.jumptheshark.com

Named after that bit in *Happy Days* when the Fonz ski-jumped over – yup, you guessed it – a shark, this site chronicles the point when a TV series plot loses it.

Live TV

http://www.comfm.fr/live/tv/

Tune into live video feeds from hundreds of real world television stations. Or to record your favourite shows on your computer, try: http://www.snapstream.com

Lookalikes by Char

http://www.lookalikesbychar.com/

Impress your friends by having Jack Nicholson and Dolly Parton at your cocktail party.

Melon Farmer's Video Hits

http://www.dtaylor.demon.co.uk

Challenges British screen censorship.

Movie Clichés

http://www.moviecliches.com

Nothing unfamiliar.

Moviemags.com

http://www.moviemags.com

Directory of film print and ezines.

Movies.com

http://www.movies.com • http://www.universalstudios.com
http://www.realguide.com

Preview box office features and trailers direct from the major studios.

Movie Spoilers

http://www.themoviespoiler.com

Find out what happens at the end of films you can't be bothered to see. To ruin classic movies, see: http://www.moviepooper.com

Satco DX Satellite Chart

http://www.satcodx.com

Where to point your dish and what you can hope to get.

SciFi.com

http://www.scifi.com • http://scifi.ign.com

Science-fiction news, reviews and short films.

Screen Network Australia

http://www.sna.net.au

Gateway to Australian film and TV sites. For news, reviews and interviews, see: http://www.urbancinefile.com.au

chapter 14 • website directory

The Smoking Gun
http://www.thesmokinggun.com
http://www.apbonline.com/media/gfiles/
Celebrity shame dug up from police records, complete with the photo-copied sources.

Soap City
http://www.soapcity.com
http://members.tripod.com/~TheSoapBox/
http://www.soapweb.co.uk (UK) • http://www.soapdigest.com
Keep up with who's doing what to who, who they told, and who shouldn't find out, in the surreal world of soap fiction.

Soundtrack Collector
http://www.soundtrackcollector.com
If you can't get enough movie music, come here to research, review and share your collection.

TV Eyes
http://www.tveyes.com
Informs you when your search term is mentioned on TV.

TV Show
http://www.tvshow.com
Everything TV, from schedules of every station worldwide and links to just about every show ever made, to the technical aspects of produc-tion and broadcasting. Start your TV-related searches here.

TV Tickets
http://www.tvtickets.com (US)
http://www.bbc.co.uk/whatson/tickets/ (UK)
Secure your chance to clap on cue.

Variety
http://www.variety.com
Screen news fresh off the PR Gatling gun.

VCR Repair Instructions
http://www.fixer.com
How to take a VCR apart and then get all the little bits back in so it fits easier into the bin.

Who Would You Kill?
http://www.whowouldyoukill.com
So who would you toss into Dawson's Creek?

Food and Drink

Any decent search engine or recipe database will uncover more formulas for food than you could possibly cook in a lifetime. Start by casting your line into the Fish Finger king's collection:

All Recipes http://www.allrecipes.com
Cookbooks Online http://www.cook-books.com
Meals for You http://www.mealsforyou.com
Recipe Archives http://recipes.alastra.com
Recipedia http://www.lycos.com/search/recipedia.html

When following recipes, note where they're from so you don't mix up the measures. An Australian tablespoon is four, not three, teaspoons, for instance.

Beershots
http://micro.magnet.fsu.edu
/beershots/
Beers of the world put under a microscope.

Bevnet
http://www.bevnet.com
Know your new-age beverages.

RealBeer
http://www.realbeer.com
None of the usual beer yarns – here beer is treated with the dewy-eyed respect usually reserved for wine and trains. Like to find a UK pub, or send your chum a virtual beer? Stumble over to:
http://www.pubworld.co.uk

chapter 14 • website directory

Chile Heads
http://www.chileheadz.com • http://www.ringoffire.net
Get 'em while they're hot.

Chocolate Lover's Page
http://chocolate.scream.org
The good gear: where to find recipes and dealers.

Cigar Aficionado
http://www.cigaraficionado.com
Archives, shopping guides and tasting forums from the US glossy that sets the benchmark in cigar ratings.

Cocktails
http://www.barmeister.com • http://www.cocktailtime.com
http://cocktails.about.com • http://www.drinkboy.com
http://www.webtender.com
Guzzle your way to a happier home. Yes, do buy the book.

Cook's Thesaurus
http://www.foodsubs.com
Find substitutes for fatty, expensive or hard-to-find ethnic ingredients.

Curryhouse.co.uk
http://www.curryhouse.co.uk
Find a recommended biryani near you and, if you can't, then learn how to make your own.

Epicurious
http://www.epicurious.com
Online marriage of Condé Nast's *Gourmet*, *Bon Appetit* and *Traveller* magazines, crammed with recipes, culinary forums and advice on dining out worldwide.

The Espresso Index
http://www.espresso.com • http://www.espressotop50.com
Kick-start your morning with the FAQs on coffee.

Internet Chef
http://www.ichef.com
Over 30,000 recipes, cooking hints, kitchen talk and more links than you could jab a fork in.

Moonshine
http://moonshine.co.nz • http://homedistiller.org
Go blind (quite literally) on homemade spirits.

National Headache Foundation
http://www.headaches.org
Soothe the sore spot under your hat.

Buying groceries online

Your chances of being able to order home-delivered groceries online will be much higher if you live in a big city, but expect to pay a premium for the convenience. Although most of the following have physical stores, they mightn't offer their full range online:

Australia
http://www.colesonline.com.au
http://www.greengrocer.com.au
http://www.shopfast.com.au
http://www.woolworths.com.au

UK
http://www.iceland.co.uk
http://www.sainsburystoyou.com
http://www.somerfield.co.uk
http://www.tesco.co.uk
http://www.waitrosedeliver.com

US and Canada
http://www.egrocer.com
http://www.ethnicgrocer.com
http://www.netgrocer.com
http://www.peapod.com
http://www.telegrocer.com

An Ode to Olives
http://www.emeraldworld.net/olive.html
You'll never look at an olive ambivalently again.

Restaurant Row
http://www.restaurantrow.com
Key in your dining preferences and find the perfect match from hundreds of thousands of food barns worldwide.

Spice Advice
http://www.spiceadvice.com
Encyclopedia of spices covering their origins, purposes, recipes and tips on what goes best with what.

Tasty Insect Recipes
http://www.eatbug.com
http://www.ent.iastate.edu/misc/insectsasfood.html
Dig in to such delights as Bug Blox, Banana Worm Bread, Rootworm Beetle Dip and Chocolate Chirpie Chip Cookies (with crickets).

Tea & Sympathy
http://www.enteract.com/~robchr/tea/
Home of the Rec.Food.Tea FAQ.

Thai Recipes
http://www.importfood.com/recipes.html
Just click if you don't have an ingredient.

Tokyo Food Page
http://www.bento.com
Where and what to eat in Tokyo, plus recipes.

Top Secret Recipes
http://www.topsecretrecipes.com • http://www.copykat.com
At least one commercial recipe, such as KFC coleslaw, revealed each week. Many are surprisingly basic.

Vegetarian Society of the UK
http://www.vegsoc.org
Support for discerning consumers.

Wine Spectator

http://www.winespectator.com
Research your hangover.

Fortunes and Personality Tests

American Federation of Astrologers

http://www.astrologers.com
Impress your hairdresser by becoming a fully accredited seer by correspondence course.

Astrology – Atlas and Time Zone Database

http://www.astro.com/atlas/
Know exactly what was happening upstairs the second of your birth. Or, if you prefer your cold readings with a touch less pseudoscientific mumbo jumbo, try:
http://www.astrology.com • http://astrology.about.com
http://www.astrocenter.com • http://www.artcharts.com
Now see what old sensible shoes has to say:
http://www.skepdic.com/astrolgy.html
http://www.skepdic.com/coldread.html

Biorhythm Generator

http://www.facade.com/attraction/biorhythm/
Generate a cyclical report that can double as a sick note.

Dreamstop

http://www.dreamstop.com

Analyse your night visions, and jot them into a journal to share with your friends.

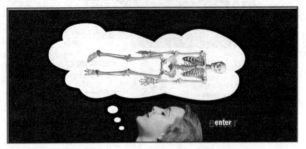

I Ching

http://www.facade.com/iching/

If the superior person is not happy with their fortune as told by this ancient Chinese oracle, one can always reload and get another one.

Psyche Tests

http://www.psychtests.com

http://www.keirsey.com • http://queendom.com/tests/

http://www.emode.com • http://buster.cs.yale.edu/implicit/

So what breed of dog are you? For the smug sceptics' angle, see: http://www.skepdic.com/myersb.html

RealAge

http://www.realage.com

Compare your biological and chronological ages.

The Spark

http://www.thespark.com

Are you the bitch or bastard they say you are, or merely a bit pregnant? Take the tests to find out.

What's In Your Name?

http://www.kabalarians.com/gkh/your.htm

The Kabalarians claim names can be boiled down to a numerical stew and served back up as a character analysis. Look yourself up in here and see what a duff choice your folks made. Then blame them for everything that's gone wrong since.

Games

Most multi-player games can be played across the Net. There are also thousands of simple table, word, arcade and music games as diverse as Chess, Blackjack, Connect 4 and Frogger that can be played on the Web courtesy of Java and Shockwave. In some cases you can contest online opponents for prizes. Peruse the selection on offer at:

Flipside http://www.flipside.com
FreeArcade.com http://www.freearcade.com
Gamesville http://www.gamesville.com
Playsite http://www.playsite.com
Pogo.com http://www.pogo.com
Real Arcade http://www.realarcade.com
The Riddler http://www.riddler.com
Shockwave.com http://www.shockwave.com
The Station http://www.station.sony.com
Web Games http://www.happypuppy.com/web/
Yahoo! Games http://games.yahoo.com

For reviews, news, demos, hints, patches, cheats and downloads for PC and console games, try the following:

Adrenaline Vault http://www.avault.com
Gamedex http://www.gamedex.com
Gamers.com http://www.gamers.com
Games Domain http://www.gamesdomain.com
Gamespot http://www.gamespot.com

Gamespy http://www.gamespy.com
Happy Puppy http://www.happypuppy.com
Hotgames.com http://www.hotgames.com
PSX Extreme http://www.psxextreme.com
Video Game Strategies http://vgstrategies.about.com

Or if you use a Mac:
Inside Mac Games http://www.insidemacgames.com
MacGamer http://www.macgamer.com

All Game Guide
http://www.allgame.com
From the same people as All Music Guide and All Movie Guide.

Blues News
http://www.bluesnews.com
Keep up with what's Quakin'.

Board Game Geek
http://www.boardgamegeek.com
Discuss, find, rate and swap non-cyber games.

ContestGuide
http://www.contestguide.com • http://www.contestlistings.com
http://www.iwon.com • http://www.loquax.co.uk (UK)

http://www.uggs-n-rugs.com.au/contests/ (AUS)
Get junk-mailed for life.

Game Downloads
http://www.fileplanet.com • http://www.freeloader.com
Stock up on gaming software.

GameFAQs
http://www.gamefaqs.com
Stuck on a level or just want to know more?

GameGirlz
http://www.gamegirlz.com
Team up with other game grrls and prepare to kick dweeb-boy butt right across their own turf. More reinforcement at:
http://www.womengamers.com

Kasparov Chess
http://www.kasparovchess.com • http://chess.about.com
Take tips from the Russian master and then find an opponent.

Vintage Gaming
http://www.vg-network.com • http://www.download.net
http://www.bhlegend.com • http://www.abandongames.com
Revive old-school arcade games like Xevious on your home PC.

Genealogy

Don't expect to enter your name and produce an instant family tree, but you should be able to fill in a few gaps – or dig up some dirt on your ancestors:
http://www.genhomepage.com • http://www.genealogylinks.net
http://www.genealogytoday.com • http://www.cyndislist.com
http://www.familytreemaker.com • http://www.familysearch.org
http://www.ancestry.com • http://www.surnameweb.org
http://www.rootsweb.com • http://www.genuki.org.uk (UK)

Once you've found a name, put a face to it:
Ancient Faces http://www.ancientfaces.com

Census Records (UK)
http://www.census.pro.gov.uk
Find out who lived in your house 100 years ago. If this site ever gets back up, that is.

Greetings Cards and Invites

If stretching the boundaries of good taste doesn't bother you, you'll find thousands of sites that will gladly speckle your message with multimedia tutti-frutti. Rather than forward your "card" directly, your victim will generally receive an invitation to drop by and collect it from the site. And, of course, being masked by a third party makes it perfect for harassing valentines and sending ransom notes. For hundreds of virtual card dispensers, see:

Card Lady http://www.cardlady.com
Free Greeting Cards http://www.freegreetingcards.org
Postcard Heaven http://www.postcard-heaven.com
Postcards.com http://www.postcards.com

But check out the most popular ones first:
Blue Mountain http://www.bluemountain.com
eGreetings http://www.egreetings.com
Hallmark http://www.hallmark.com
Pulp Cards http://www.pulpcards.com
Regards.com http://www.regards.com
Tackymail http://www.tackymail.com
Virtual Insults
http://www.virtualinsults.com
Yahoo! Greetings
http://greetings.yahoo.com

Digital Voodoo
http://www.pinstruck.com
Curse thy neighbour.

Hotpaper.com
http://www.hotpaper.com
Fill in the blanks to create handy everyday documents like greetings cards, references, eviction notices and credit card disputes.

Interflora
http://www.interflora.com
Punch in your credit card number, apology and delivery details, and land back in their good books before you get home. For thousands more flower vendors, drill down through your local Yahoo! or see: http://dmoz.org/Shopping/Flowers/Florists/
For advice on floral etiquette, history, meanings and choosing the right florist, see: http://www.aboutflowers.com

Invites
http://invites.yahoo.com • http://www.regards.com
http://www.egreetings.com
Throwing a slide night? Here's an easy way to create an instant email invitation and manage those thousands of RSVPs. For help planning: http://www.theplunge.com

IPrint
http://www.iprint.com • http://www.cardcorp.co.uk (UK)
Need some business cards or invitations fast? Design them online for snappy delivery either via email or on the paper of your choice. Naturally, the latter option costs.

Postcardland
http://postcardland.com
Confuse your parole officer by sending them a postcard from the other side of the world.

Virtual Presents
http://www.virtualpresents.com • http://www.it3c.co.uk
Why waste money on real gifts when, after all, it's the thought that counts?

Health

While the Net's certainly an unrivalled medical library, it's also an unrivalled promulgator of the 21st-century equivalent of old wives' tales. So by all means research your ailment and pick up fitness tips online, but – like the pill bottles say – check with your doctor before putting it to work. While you're with your GP, ask if they use the Net for research and, if so, which sites they recommend.

Don't expect to go online for first-aid advice. If it's an emergency, you simply won't have time. The Net is better for in-depth research and anecdotal advice, none of which comes quickly. But once you've spent a few sessions online studying your complaint, you'll be fully prepared to state your case. To find a doctor, dentist or specialist, try: **http://www.ama-assn.org/aps/** (US) or **http://www.netdoctor.co.uk** (UK).

WorldClinic (**http://www.worldclinic.com**) provides phone, fax or email response that could save your life on the road.

It's hard to say where to start your research. Perhaps try a directory: Yahoo! et al have seriously stacked medical arms, or you could try one of the specialist health portals:

Achoo http://www.achoo.com
Hospitalweb UK http://www.hospitalweb.co.uk
MedExplorer http://www.medexplorer.com
Patient UK http://www.patient.co.uk
SearchBug http://www.searchbug.com/health/

Or a government gateway:

Health Insite (AUS) http://www.healthinsite.gov.au
Health on the Net http://www.hon.ch
Healthfinder http://www.healthfinder.gov
NHS Direct (UK) http://www.nhsdirect.nhs.uk
US National Library of Medicine http://www.nlm.nih.gov

You'll find tons of excellent self-help megasites, though the presence of sponsors may raise ethical questions. Their features vary, but medical encyclopedias, personal health tests and Q&A services are fairly standard fare. Starting with the former **US Surgeon General's** site, try:

Dr Koop http://www.drkoop.com
HealthAtoZ.com http://www.healthatoz.com
HealthCentral http://www.healthcentral.com
HealthWorld http://www.healthy.net
Intelihealth http://www.intelihealth.com
Mayo Clinic http://www.mayoclinic.com
Netdoctor.co.uk http://www.netdoctor.co.uk
24Dr.com (UK) http://www.24dr.com
WebMD (US, CA) http://www.webmd.com
WebMD (Lycos) http://webmd.lycos.com
Yahoo! Health http://health.yahoo.com

Or, for lots of information and links about global health issues, approaches and research, turn to:
World Health Organization http://www.who.int

Most of the above are fluent in the needs of mothers-to-be, but if you're at that stage of your life when you can't get too much information on babies, try:
B4Baby (UK) http://www.b4baby.co.uk
Baby Center http://www.babycenter.com

Baby Centre (UK) http://www.babycentre.co.uk
Baby World (UK) http://www.babyworld.co.uk
Dr Greene http://www.drgreene.com
National Childbirth Trust (UK)
http://www.nctpregnancyandbabycare.com
Ninemonths (AUS) http://www.ninemonths.com.au
Parent Soup http://www.parentsoup.com
Parenthood Web http://www.parenthoodweb.com
Pregnancy Calendar http://www.pregnancycalendar.com

But for serious research go straight to **Medline**, the US National Library of Medicine's database. It archives, references and abstracts thousands of medical journals and periodicals going back to 1966. You can get it free at **PubMed**, but the subscription services may have access to more material. These are aimed more at health pros and students:

BioMedNet http://www.bmn.com
Medscape http://www.medscape.com
Ovid http://www.ovid.com
PubMed http://www.ncbi.nlm.nih.gov/PubMed/

Despite first appearances, Martindale's maintains an outstanding directory of medical science links:

Martindale's Health Science guide
http://www-sci.lib.uci.edu/HSG/HSGuide.html

If you know what you have and you want to contact other suf-
ferers, use a search engine (**http://www.google.com**) or directory
(**http://dmoz.org**) to find organizations and personal homepages.
They should direct you to useful mailing lists and discussion
groups. If not, try Google Groups (**http://groups.google.com**) to find
the right newsgroups, and PAML (**http://www.paml.org**) for mailing
lists.

Alex Chiu's Eternal Life Device
http://www.alexchiu.com
Live forever or come back for your money.

All Nurses
http://www.allnurses.com
Springboard to chat groups, research data, professional bodies, jobs
and other nursing resources. In the UK, visit: http://www.rcn.org.uk.

Alternative Medicine
http://altmedicine.about.com • http://dmoz.org/Health/Alternative/
http://www.wholehealthmd.com • http://www.alternativedr.com
http://www.alternativemedicine.com
Part of the Net's ongoing research function is the ability to contact people who've road-tested alternative remedies and can report on their
efficacy. Start here and work your way to an answer. See also the entry
for **Quackwatch** (see p.393).

Aromatherapy
http://www.aromaweb.com
Pseudoscience it may be (http://www.skepdic.com/aroma.html), but
you'll be on the way to smelling better. And surely that can't be a bad
thing.

Ask Dr Weil
http://www.drweil.com
Popdoctor Andrew Weil's eagerness to prescribe from a range of bewildering, and often conflicting, alternative therapies has seen him called
a quack in some quarters, but not by Warner. *Time* put him on the front

cover and gave him a job peddling advice beside vitamin ads. Whether or not you believe in food cures, his daily Q&As are always a good read.

Ask the Dietitian
http://www.dietitian.com
Eat yourself better.

Cancer Research Project
http://www.ud.com/cancer
Use your computer to help find a cure for cancer.

Colour Vision Test
http://www.umist.ac.uk/UMIST_OVS/UES/COLOUR0.HTM
Do you dress in the dark or are you merely colour-blind?

Dr Squat
http://www.drsquat.com • http://www.weightsnet.com
Avoid getting sand kicked in your face through deep full squats.

Drugs
http://www.erowid.org • http://www.lycaeum.org
http://www.trashed.co.uk • http://www.bluelight.nu
http://www.perkel.com/politics/issues/pot.htm
http://www.neuropharmacology.com
http://www.druglibrary.org
Everything you ever wanted to know about the pleasure, pain and politics of psychoactive drugs and the cultures built around them.

GYN101

http://www.gyn101.com

Swot up for your next gynaecological exam. But if you're after honours,
go straight to: http://www.obgyn.net

Gyro's Excellent Hernia Adventure

http://www.cryogenius.com/mesh/

Holiday snaps from under the knife.

HandHeldMed

http://www.handheldmed.com • http://medicalpocketpc.com
http://www.pdamd.com

Arm your pocket computer with medical software and references.

Medicinal Herb FAQ

http://ibiblio.org/herbmed/

If it's in your garden and it doesn't kill you, it can only make you
stronger. More leafy cures and love drugs at:
http://www.algy.com/herb/
http://www.botanical.com
http://www.herbal-ahp.org

Mental Health

http://www.mentalhealth.com

Guaranteed you'll come out of this site convinced there's something
wrong with you. Worry your way along to:
http://www.anxietynetwork.com

Museum of Questionable Medical Devices

http://www.mtn.org/quack/

Gallery of health-enhancing products where even breaks weren't bundled free.

Nutritional Supplements

http://www.nutritionalsupplements.com

First-hand experiences with vitamins, bodybuilding supplements and
other dubious health-shop fodder.

Quackwatch

http://www.quackwatch.com • http://www.ncahf.org
http://www.hcrc.org • http://nccam.nih.gov

Separating the docs from the ducks. Don't buy into any alternative remedies until you've read these pages.

Reuters Health
http://www.reutershealth.com
Medical newswires, reviews, opinion and reference.

RxList
http://www.rxlist.com • http://www.virtualdrugstore.com
Look up your medication to ensure you're not being poisoned.

Spas Directory (UK)
http://www.thespasdirectory.com
Locate a British spa or health resort.

Talk Surgery
http://www.talksurgery.com
Discuss your operation with people who appear interested.

The Virtual Hospital
http://www.vh.org
Patient care and distance learning via online multimedia tools such as illustrated surgical walk-throughs.

The Visible Human Project
http://www.nlm.nih.gov/research/visible/
Whet your appetite by skimming through scans of a thinly filleted serial killer, and then top it off with a fly-through virtual colonoscopy. For higher production values, see the Virtual BodyMap: http://www.medtropolis.com

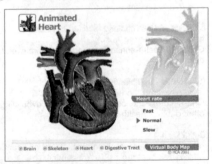

What Have I Got?
http://www.whathaveigot.net
Worry yourself sick through self-diagnosis.

Wing Hop Fung
http://www.winghopfung.com/winghopfung/herbs.html
Chinese cures by mail order.

World Sexual Records
http://www.sexualrecords.com
Go for gold in slap and tickle.

Yoga
http://www.timages.com/yoga.htm
Stretch yourself back into shape with a personalized routine. For more
bendy sites, see:
http://www.yogadirectory.com
http://www.yogasite.com

Home and Garden

Ask the Master Plumber
http://www.clickit.com/bizwiz/homepage/plumber.htm
Save a small fortune by unblocking your own toilet.

Buy.co.uk
http://www.buy.co.uk/Personal/
Clinch the best deal on British utilities (plus loans and more).

Carnivorous Plants FAQ
http://www.sarracenia.com/cp.html
Erect your first line of defence.

Feng Shui
http://www.qi-whiz.com • http://www.fengshui-fanzine.co.uk
Recreate the ambience of a Chinese restaurant.

GardenWeb
http://www.gardenweb.com
Hosts a multitude of gardening forums both here and on its European and Australian sister sites, plus a gardening glossary, plant database, calendar of garden events, plant exchange and plenty of meaty articles. Here's more:
http://www.gardensonline.com.au (AUS)
http://www.gardenguides.com
http://gardening.about.com
http://www.gardening.com
http://www.e-garden.co.uk (UK)
http://www.expertgardener.com (UK)
For even more gardening sites, try the Open Directory:
http://dmoz.org/Home/Gardens/

Gothic Gardening
http://www.gothic.net/~malice/
Grow a little greenhouse of horrors.

Home Improvement Network
http://www.improvenet.com (US)
http://www.improveline.com (UK)
http://www.homepro.com (UK)
Peruse the latest design ideas and find someone to do the job. You can even screen your local builders against public records and find the one least likely to quaff all your home-brew and sell your nude holiday snaps to the *National Enquirer*.

Home Sewing Association
http://www.sewing.org
Unpick hints from a bunch of sew and sews.

Home Tips
http://www.hometips.com • http://www.askthebuilder.com
http://www.doityourself.com • http://www.naturalhandyman.com
Load your toolbox, roll up your sleeves and prepare to go in.

How to Clean Anything
http://www.howtocleananything.com
Just add elbow grease.

Internet Directory for Botany
http://www.botany.net/IDB/ • http://botany.about.com
http://dmoz.org/Science/Biology/Botany/
Starting points for serious plant-life research. For greenery down under, visit: http://www.anbg.gov.au

Postcode Plants Database (UK)
http://www.nhm.ac.uk/fff/
Find the right native trees, shrubs and flowers for your area.

This to That
http://www.thistothat.com
So what would you like to glue today?

Kids (mostly)

It's your choice whether you want to let them at it headlong or limit their experience through rose-coloured filters. But if you need guidance, or pointers towards the most kidtastic chowder, set sail into these realms:

American Libraries Association
http://www.ala.org/parentspage/greatsites/

Cybersmart Kids Online
http://www.cybersmartkids.com.au

chapter 14 • website directory

Kids Click http://www.worldsofsearching.org
Kids Domain http://www.kidsdomain.com
Internet Detectives http://www.madison.k12.wi.us/tnl/detectives
Lightspan http://www.lightspan.com
Open Directory: Kids http://dmoz.org/Kids_and_Teens/
Scholastic International http://www.scholastic.com
Surfing the Net with Kids http://www.surfnetkids.com
Yahooligans (Yahoo! for Kids) http://www.yahooligans.com

The search engines Google, AltaVista and All the Web can also be set to filter out adult content. For encyclopedias and dictionaries, see p.442.

Bonus
http://www.bonus.com
Answers to typical kid questions from "why poo is brown" and "why farts smell" to "why your voice sounds different on a tape recorder" and "why the TV goes crazy while the mixer is on".

The Bug Club
http://www.ex.ac.uk/bugclub/
Creepy-crawly fan club with newsletters and pet-care sheets on how to keep your newly bottled tarantulas, cockroaches and stick insects alive.

Bullying Online
http://www.bullying.co.uk
Advice and support channels for bullied children and their parents. Perhaps a few sessions of self-defence might be a good place to start: http://www.blackbeltmag.com/bbkids/

Children's Literature Web Guide
http://www.ucalgary.ca/~dkbrown/
Critical roundup of recent kids' books and links to texts.

Club Girl Tech
http://www.girltech.com
Encourages smart girls to get interested in technology without coming across all geeky.

Cyberteens

http://www.cyberteens.com
Submit your music, art or writing to a public gallery. You might even win a prize.

Decoding Nazi Secrets

http://www.pbs.org/wgbh/nova/decoding/ • http://www.thunk.com
Use World War II weaponry to exchange secret messages with your clued-in pals.

Disney.com

http://www.disney.com
Guided catalogue of Disney's real-world movies, books, theme parks, records, interactive CD-ROMs and such, plus a squeaky-clean Net directory. For an unofficial Disney chaperone, see:
http://laughingplace.com

eHobbies

http://www.ehobbies.com
Separating junior hobbyists from their pocket money.

Funbrain

http://www.funbrain.com
Tons of mind-building quizzes, games and puzzles for all ages.

Funschool

http://www.funschool.com
Educational games for preschoolers.

The History Net

http://www.thehistorynet.com • http://www.historybuff.com
Bites of world history, with an emphasis on the tough guys going in
with guns.

Kids' Games

http://kidsnetgames.about.com
http://dmoz.org/Kids_and_Teens/Games/
http://www.wicked4kids.com
http://www.kidsdomain.com/games/
http://www.randomhouse.com/seussville/games/
http://games.yahoo.com/games/yahooligans.html
Give the babysitter a break.

Kids' Jokes

http://www.kidsjokes.co.uk
http://www.users.bigpond.com/lander/default.htm
Reams of clean jokes, riddles and knock-knocks.

Kids' Space

http://www.kids-space.org
Hideout for kids to swap art, music and stories with new friends across
the world.

The Little Animals Activity Centre

http://www.bbc.co.uk/education/laac/
The second the music starts and the critters start jiggling, you'll know
you're in for a treat. Let your youngest heir loose here after breakfast
and expect no mercy until morning tea. As cute as it gets.

Magic Tricks

http://www.magictricks.com • http://www.trickshop.com
http://www.magicweek.co.uk
Never believe it's not so.

Neopets

http://www.neopets.com
Nurture a "virtual pet" until it dies.

Roper's Knots

http://www.realknots.com
It's not what you know; it's what knots you know.

Sing Along Midis and Lyrics

http://www.niehs.nih.gov/kids/musicchild.htm
Gather round for a spot of keyboard karaoke.

StarChild

http://starchild.gsfc.nasa.gov
Nasa's educational funhouse for junior astronomers. See also:
http://www.earthsky.com • http://www.starport.com

Star Wars Origami

http://ftmax.com/ArtLife/Origami/SW/sw.htm
Graduate from flapping birds to Destroyer Droids and Tie Fighters.
Prefer something that will actually fly? See: http://www.aircraft.com
For more paper-folding, see: http://www.origami.com

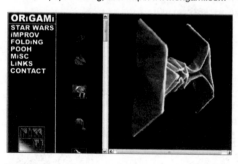

Toy Stores

http://www.faoschwartz.com • http://www.toysrus.com (.co.uk)
It's just like Christmas all year round.

The Unnatural Museum

http://www.unmuseum.org
Lost worlds, dinosaurs, UFOs, pyramids and other mysterious exhibits
from the outer bounds of space and time.

The Yuckiest Site on the Internet
http://www.yucky.com
Fun science with a leaning towards the icky-sticky and the creepy-crawly. But if you want to get thoroughly engrossed in the gross, slither right along to: http://www.grossology.org

Law and Crime

For legal primers, lawyer directories, legislation and self-help:
Australian Legal Info Inst http://www.austlii.edu.au
Compact Law http://www.compactlaw.co.uk (UK)
Delia Venables http://www.venables.co.uk (UK)
FindLaw http://www.findlaw.com (INT)
Free Advice http://www.freeadvice.com (US)
InfoLaw http://www.infolaw.co.uk (UK)
Law.com http://www.law.com (US)
'Lectric Law http://www.lectlaw.com (US)
Nolo.com http://www.nolo.com (US)
UKLegal http://www.uklegal.com (UK)

For more on criminal activities, trends, arrests and law enforcement, rustle through the following guides:
About Crime http://crime.about.com
Crime Spider http://www.crimespider.com
Open Directory http://dmoz.org/Society/Crime/

APBnews.com
http://www.apbonline.com
Highly acclaimed network news service focusing on crime, justice and safety.

Brutal.com
http://www.brutal.com
Bad news from around the world, as it breaks.

Burglar.com
http://www.theburglar.com
Profit from stolen goods that somehow happened into your possession.

Chilling Effects Clearinghouse
http://www.chillingeffects.org
Read about your (US) online rights, courtesy of some kindly academics.

Copyright Myths
http://whatiscopyright.org
http://www.templetons.com/brad/copyright.html
Just because it's online doesn't make it yours. For more, see:
http://www.copyrightwebsite.com

Crime Magazine
http://www.crimemagazine.com
Encyclopedic collection of outlaw tales.

CrimeNet (AUS)
http://www.crimenet.com.au
Pay to search a database of Aussie crims.

Cybercrime
http://www.cybercrime.gov
How to report online crooks.

Desktop Lawyer (UK)
http://www.desktoplawyer.net
Cut legal costs by doing it online.

Dumb Laws
http://www.dumblaws.com
Foreign legislation with limited appeal.

ECLS
http://www.e-commercelawsource.com
Global monitor and directory of online business law.

Money Claim Online
http://www.courtservice.gov.uk/mcol/
Get back what's rightly yours without leaving the comfort of your swivel chair.

chapter 14 • website directory

Overlawyered
http://www.overlawyered.com
Find out why American law sucks.

Police Officer's Directory
http://www.officer.com • http://www.cops.aust.com (AUS)
Top-of-the-pops cop directory with more than 1500 baddy-nabbing bureaus snuggled in with law libraries, wanted listings, investigative tools, hate groups, special-ops branches and off-duty home pages. To see who's in Scotland Yard's bad books: http://www.met.police.uk

PursuitWatch
http://www.pursuitwatch.com
Get paged when there's a live police chase on TV.

Texas Death Row
http://www.tdcj.state.tx.us/stat/deathrow.htm
Sobering reading from Bush's Land of the Free.

Money

If your bank's on the ball, it will offer an online facility to check your balances, pay your bills, transfer funds and export your transaction records into a bean-counting program such as Quicken or Money. If that sounds appealing and your bank isn't already on the case, start looking for a replacement. Favour one you can access via the Internet rather than by dialling direct. That way you can manage your cash through a Web browser whether you're at home, work or in the cybercafé on top of Pik Kommunisma. For help finding a true online bank:

Online Banking Report http://www.netbanker.com
Qualisteam http://www.qualisteam.com

As long as you can resist the urge to daytrade away your inheritance, the Net should give you greater control over your financial future. You can research firms, plot trends, check live quotes, join tip lists and stock forums, track your portfolio live, trade shares and access more news than is fit to read in a lifetime. By all means investigate a subscription service or two – at least for the free trial period – but unless you need split-second data feeds or "expert" timing advice, you should be able to get by without paying. Start here:

Yahoo! Finance http://quote.yahoo.com

Or go for a local counterpart such as:
Yahoo! Australia http://quote.yahoo.com.au
Yahoo! UK http://quote.yahoo.co.uk

Apart from housing the Net's most exhaustive finance directory, Yahoo! pillages data from a bunch of the top finance sources and presents it all in a seamless, friendly format. Enter a stock code, for example, and you'll get all the beef from the latest ticker price to a summary of insider trades. In some markets stocks have their own forums, which, let's face it, are only there to spread rumours. In other words, be very sceptical of anything you read or that's sent to you in unsolicited email. For more, see:

Investment Scams http://www.sec.gov/investor/pubs/cyberfraud.htm

chapter 14 • website directory

Yahoo! is by no means complete, nor necessarily the best in every area, so try a few of these as well:

ABC http://www.abc.net.au/news/business/ (AUS)

Ample http://www.iii.co.uk (UK)

Bloomberg http://www.bloomberg.com (INT)

CBS MarketWatch http://cbs.marketwatch.com

Egoli http://www.egoli.com.au (AUS)

Free Real Time Quotes http://www.freerealtime.com

Gay Financial Network http://www.gfn.com

MetaMarkets http://www.metamarkets.com

Microsoft MoneyCentral http://moneycentral.msn.com

Money Extra http://www.moneyextra.com (UK)

Muslim Investor http://www.muslim-investor.com

Quicken http://www.quicken.com (.au) (US/AUS)

Raging Bull http://www.ragingbull.com

The Street http://www.thestreet.com

Thomson Financial Network http://www.thomsonfn.com (INT)

Wall Street City http://www.wallstreetcity.com

Wall Street Research Net http://www.wsrn.com

You'll no doubt be after a broker next. As with banking, any broker or fund manager who's not setting up online probably doesn't deserve your business. In fact, many traders are dumping traditional brokers in favour of the exclusively online houses. **E★Trade** (http://www.etrade.com), for example, offers discount brokerage in at least nine countries. But traditional brokers are catching on. Many have cut their commissions, and offer online services in line with the Internet competition, so it pays to shop around. You might find you prefer to research online and trade by phone. To compare US brokers:

Gomez.com http://www.gomez.com

Ms Money http://www.msmoney.com

Smart Money http://www.smartmoney.com

If you're outside the US, try your local Yahoo! for leads. A word of warning, though: some online brokers have experienced outages where they were unable to trade. So if the market crashes in a big way, it mightn't hurt to play safe and use the phone instead.

BigCharts

http://www.bigcharts.com • http://www.stockcharts.com
http://www.tradesignals.com • http://www.livecharts.com
Whip up family-sized graphs of US stocks, mutual funds and market indices.

Clearstation

http://www.clearstation.com
Run your stock picks through a succession of gruelling obstacle courses to weed out the weaklings, or simply copy someone else's portfolio.

Earnings Whispers

http://www.earningswhispers.com
When a stock price falls upon the release of higher-than-expected earnings, chances are the expectations being "whispered" amongst traders prior to open were higher than those circulated publicly. Here's where to find out what's being said behind your back. For the biggest surprises, see: http://biz.yahoo.com/z/extreme.html

Financial Times
http://www.ft.com
Business news, commentary, delayed quotes and closing prices from
London. It's free until you hit the archives.

Foreign Exchange Rates
http://quote.yahoo.com • http://www.xe.net/ucc/full.shtml
Round-the-clock rates, conversion calculators and intraday charts on
pretty close to the full set of currencies.
To chart further back, see: http://pacific.commerce.ubc.ca/xr/plot.html

Hoovers
http://www.hoovers.com
Research US, UK and European companies.

iCreditReport
http://www.icreditreport.com
Dig up any US citizen's credit ratings.

Insider Scores
http://www.insiderscores.com
Get the inside on US and Asian directors' trades.

Investment FAQ
http://www.invest-faq.com
Learn the ropes from old hands.

InvestorWords
http://www.investorwords.com
Can't tell your hedge rate from your asking price? Brush up on your
finance-speak here.

Island
http://www.island.com
See US equity orders queued up on dealers' screens.

Missing Money
http://www.missingmoney.com • http://www.findcash.com
Reclaim those US dollars you're owed.

MoneyChimp
http://www.moneychimp.com
Plain English primer in the mechanics of financial maths.

Money Origami
http://www.umva.com/~clay/money/
It's much more fun when you can make something out of it.

Motley Fool
http://www.fool.com (.co.uk)
Forums, tips, quotes and sound advice.

One Share.com
http://www.oneshare.com
Gain favour by giving tiny slices of the American dream as presents.

Paypal
http://www.paypal.com
Arrange online payments through a third party.

RateNet
http://www.rate.net • http://www.bankrate.com
Tracks and ranks finance rates across over 11,000 US institutions in
175 markets. Also links to thousands of banking sites and investment
products. For UK and Australian rates, see:
http://www.blays.co.uk • http://www.buy.co.uk
http://www.bankchoice.com.au

Tax and Accounting Sites Directory
http://www.taxsites.com (US)
http://www.taxationweb.co.uk (UK)
Links to everything you need to know about doling out your annual
pound of flesh.

Technical Analysis Tutorials
http://www.e-analytics.com/techdir.htm
Beginners' guide to fortune-telling the markets using charts and indicators.

Wall Street Journal Interactive
http://www.wsj.com
Not only is this online edition equal to the print one, its charts and data

archives give it the edge. That's why you shouldn't complain that it's not free. After all, if it's your type of paper, you should be able to afford it, big shot.

Where's George?
http://www.wheresgeorge.com
Put a tail on your greenback.

Music

If you're at all into music, on the Web you've certainly come to the right place. Whether you want to hear it, read about it or watch it being performed, you'll be swamped with options. If you're after a specific band, search with Google, or try the Ultimate Band List on **Artists Direct**:
Ultimate Band List http://www.ubl.com

For biographies, CD reviews and recommendations covering rock, classical and world music, see our very own:
Rough Guide to Music www.roughguides.com/music/

Or try **All Music Guide**'s astoundingly complete database, spanning most popular genres, with bios, reviews, ratings and keyword crosslinks to related sounds, sites and online ordering:
All Music Guide http://www.allmusic.com

If you want hundreds of sites covering a particular genre, label or instrument, try one of the following directories:

About.com http://home.about.com/arts/
Open Directory http://dmoz.org/Arts/Music/
SonicNet http://www.sonicnet.com/allmusic/
Yahoo! http://music.yahoo.com

But, for searching through discographies of practically every album ever released on CD, nothing comes close to **Gracenote's CDDB database**, which provides the track listings in most computer CD players. It's fantastic for finding out who performed a certain song, or what album it was on. OK, maybe **Amazon** comes close, though:

Amazon.com http://www.amazon.com
Gracenote http://www.gracenote.com

Feel like singing along, but don't know the words? Try tapping the song, performer or author into **Songfile** for a hyperconnected rundown on everyone concerned with the tune, and often the lyrics, sheet music and a link to buy it on CD. If it doesn't stock the sheet music, try Yahoo! for another dealer.

Songfile http://www.songfile.com

Or, for rapping rhymes:
Original Hip Hop Lyrics Archive http://www.ohhla.com

Much of the mainstream music press is already well established online. For the latest music news:
Artists Direct http://artistsdirect.com

You'll find thousands of archived reviews, charts, gig guides, band bios, selected features, shopping links, news and various sound artefacts courtesy of these familiar beacons:

Billboard http://www.billboard-online.com
Blues and Soul http://www.bluesandsoul.co.uk
Dirty Linen http://kiwi.futuris.net/linen/
Folk Roots http://www.frootsmag.com
NME http://nme.com
Q http://www.q4music.com
Rolling Stone http://www.rollingstone.com
The Source http://www.thesource.com
Spin http://www.spin.com
Vibe http://www.vibe.com

And, if your concentration is up to it, **MTV**:
Americas http://www.mtv.com • http://www.mtvla.com
Asia Pacific http://www.mtvasia.com
Europe http://www.mtveurope.com
UK http://www.mtv.co.uk • http://www.mtv2.co.uk

Don't buy a stereo component until you've consulted the world's biggest audio opinionbases:

AudioReview.com http://www.audioreview.com

AudioWeb http://www.audioweb.com

eCoustics http://www.ecoustics.com

What Hi-Fi http://www.whathifi.com

Or if you wouldn't settle for less than a single-ended triode amp:

Audiophilia http://www.audiophilia.com

Stereophile http://www.stereophile.com

Consult these directories for manufacturers, shops and other audio sites:

AudioWorld http://www.audioworld.com

Hifiheaven.com http://www.hifiheaven.com

UK Hi-Fi Dealers http://hifi.dealers.co.uk

Addicted to Noise
http://www.addict.com (.com.au)
Monthly news and reviews with a heavy bias towards the rowdy end of the pop-rock spectrum.

Art of the Mix
http://www.artofthemix.org
"If you have ever killed an afternoon making a mix, spent the evening making a cover, and then mailed a copy off to a friend after having

made a copy for yourself, well, this is the site for you." Kind of says it all, really.

Buying records online

Shopping for music is another area where the Net not only equals but outshines its terrestrial counterparts. Apart from the convenience of not having to tramp across town, you can find almost anything on current issue, whether or not it's released locally, and in many cases preview album tracks in RealAudio. You might save money, too, depending on where you buy, whether you're hit with tax and how the freight stacks up. Consider splitting your order if duty becomes an issue.

The biggest hitch you'll strike is when stock is put on **back order**. Web operators can boast a huge catalogue simply because they order everything on the fly, putting you at the mercy of their distributors. The trouble is that your entire order might be held up by one item. The better shops check their stock levels before confirming your order, and follow its progress until delivery – and some let you choose whether to dispatch those in stock immediately or wait for the full order.

As far as where to shop goes, that depends on your taste. **Amazon** stands out by profiling your preferences, recommending selections, providing customer and editorial reviews, and serving up samples. But then you can't go too far wrong with most of the blockbusters:

Amazon http://www.amazon.co.uk (UK)
Amazon http://www.amazon.com (US)
AudioStreet http://www.audiostreet.co.uk (UK)
BOL http://www.bol.com (INT)
CDNow http://www.cdnow.com (US)
CD Universe http://www.cduniverse.com (US)
Chaos http://www.chaosmusic.com (AUS)
HMV http://www.hmv.com (AUS, JP, UK, US)
Sam Goody http://www.samgoody.com (US)
Tower Records http://uk.towerrecords.com (UK)
Tower Records http://www.towerrecords.com (US)

Or, if you're after something more obscure, you'll find no shortage of options under the appropriate Yahoo! categories or at:
http://www.offitsface.com/links.html
Like these, for example:

CyberCD
http://www.cybercd.de • **http://www.musicexpress.com**
German outfits with enormous catalogues, though they're not cheap.

Dusty Groove
http://www.dustygroove.com
Soul, jazz, Latin, Brazil and funk on vinyl and CD.

Funk45
http://www.funk45.com
Rare 1970s funk and soul.

Global Electronic Music Market
http://gemm.com
One-point access to over two million new and used records from almost two thousand sources. See also: **http://www.secondspin.com**

Hard to Find Records (UK)
http://www.htfr.com
Record-finding agency that specializes in house, hip-hop, soul and disco vinyl.

Penny Black
http://www.pennyblackmusic.com
Indie pop, punk and electronica.

Record Finder
http://www.recordfinders.com
Deleted vinyl, including over 200,000 45s.

Rockinghorse Records (AUS)
http://www.rockinghorse.net
Indie, dance and Australian obscurities.

For a listing of price comparison agents, see Shopping (p.212).

Band Names Registry
http://www.bandname.com
Register your bandname, post some press releases, find a soundtrack deal and then look for someone to play all the instruments.

Canonical List of Weird Band Names
http://www.geminiweb.net/bandnames/
Just be thankful your parents weren't so creative. Here's the story behind a few: http://www.heathenworld.com/bandname/

Classical Music on the Net
http://www.musdoc.com/classical/
Gateway to the timeless. See also:
http://dmoz.org/Arts/Music/Styles/Classical/
http://www.gmn.com/classical/
http://www.roughguides.com/music/

The Dance Music Resource
http://www.juno.co.uk
New and forthcoming dance releases for mail order, UK radio slots and a stacked directory.

Dancetech
http://www.dancetech.com
One-stop shop for techno toys and recording tips. For more on synths, look up:
http://www.sonicstate.com
http://www.synthzone.com

Dial-the-Truth Ministries
http://www.av1611.org
So why does Satan get all the good tunes?

DJ University
http://dju.prodj.com
Become a wedding spinner.

dotmusic
http://www.dotmusic.com
Top source of UK and global music news, weekly charts and new releases in RealAudio. See also: http://www.music3w.com

Getoutthere.bt.com
http://www.getoutthere.bt.com
Expose your talents or listen to other unsigned acts.

Guitarists.net
http://www.guitarists.net
Guitar resources, reviews and chat boards. For live lessons, or to offer
your latest riff to the world, see:
http://www.riffinteractive.com
http://www.wholenote.com
Or, to find the tab for any tune you've ever heard, try:
http://www.tabrobot.com

Harmony Central
http://www.harmonycentral.com
Product reviews, directory and headspace for musicians of all
persuasions.

Independent Underground Music Archive
http://www.iuma.com
Full-length tracks and bios from thousands of unsigned and indie-label
underground musicians.

Jazz Review
http://www.jazzreview.com • http://www.allaboutjazz.com
http://www.downbeat.com
Bottomless drawer of beard-stroking delights.

Kareoke.com
http://www.kareoke.com
Sing along in the privacy of
your own home.

Launch.com
http://www.launch.com
Thousands of music videos,
audio channels, record reviews
and chat forums.

Live Concerts
http://www.liveconcerts.com
Major gigs live in RealAudio.

MIDI Farm
http://www.midifarm.com
Synthesized debasements of pop tunes, TV themes and film scores.
Cheesy listening at its finest.

Minidisc.org
http://www.minidisc.org
Keep in tune with Sony's troubled Minidisc format.

Mr Lucky
http://www.mrlucky.com
Get smooth with rhythm 'n' booze.

PC Music Guru
http://www.pc-music.com
If you fancy making music with your computer, the Guru will show you
the way, with hardware and software recommendations and more.

Rap Network
http://www.rapnetwork.com • http://www.hiphopsite.com
http://www.scratch.dk • http://www.360hiphop.com
Fresh phrases rhymed daily.

Shareware Music Machine
http://www.hitsquad.com/smm/
Tons of shareware music players, editors and composition tools for
every platform.

Show and Tell Music
http://www.showandtellmusic.com
Albums much cooler than anything you own.

Sonic Net
http://www.sonicnet.com
Big-name live cybercasts, streaming audio and video channels, chats,
news and reviews.

Sony

http://www.sony.com

Think about everything that Sony flogs. Now imagine it all squeezed under one roof.

Soul City Limits

http://www.soulcitylimits.com

Listen to hundreds of '60s and Northern Soul clips.

Sounds Online

http://www.soundsonline.com

Preview loops and samples, free in RealAudio. Pay to download studio quality. If it's effects you're after: http://www.sounddogs.com

SS7x7 Sound System

http://www.ss7x7.com

http://www.jotto.com/bubblesoap/mixer.html

Mix your own tracks in Shockwave. Or have a bit of a scratch: http://www.turntables.de

Taxi

http://www.taxi.com

Online music A&R service. And guess what? You and your plastic kazoo are just what they're looking for.

Whammo

http://www.whammo.com.au

Directory of Aussie music news, releases, tours and acts.

For more music of the live streaming variety, fast forward to Radio (p.439) and for MP3s, see p.291.

Nature

3D Insects
http://www.ento.vt.edu/~sharov/3d/3dinsect.html
Whiz around a selection of 3D bugs. They're not real insects, but at least they don't have pins through their backs. For a bigger range of bug bios, see: http://insects.org

Bad Pets
http://www.badpets.net
Animal owners speak out.

Birding
http://birding.about.com
http://www.camacdonald.com/birding/
http://dmoz.org/Recreation/Birdwatching/
Birds are such regional critters that no one site could hope to cover them all. Use these to find the chirpiest one on your block.

Cliffy B's Cat-Scan
http://www.cat-scan.com
They love it – honest.

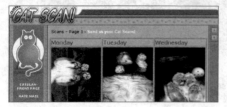

The Complete Hamster site
http://www.direct.ca/hamster/
Definitive guide to online hamsters and their inevitable obituaries.

Dog of the Day
http://www.dogoftheday.com
Submit a shot of the drooling retard that adores you unconditionally. Or, if it has its own webpage, enter it in Dog Site of the Day:
www.dogmark.net
No prizes for guessing what's at http://www.catoftheday.com and http://www.petoftheday.com

eNature.com
http://www.enature.com
Vibrant field guides to North American flora and fauna.

Environmental Organization Directory
http://www.webdirectory.com • http://www.eco-portal.com
Find primary production and green-minded sites.

F@rming Online
http://www.rpl.com.au/farming/ • http://www.farmwide.com.au
Gateways to (predominantly Australian) agricultural resources.

ForestWorld
http://www.forestworld.com • http://forests.org
Timber tales from both sides of the dozer.

Interspecies Telepathic Communication
http://www.cyberark.com/animal/telepath.htm
Relax, you're not hearing voices. It's merely your pets playing mind games.

Mr Winkle
http://www.mrwinkle.com
OK, so how cute is Mr Winkle? But is he really real?

Petsmiles (UK)
http://www.petsmiles.com
For all your feline and canine needs.

Pet Shops
http://www.petsmart.com • http://www.dogtoys.com
http://www.pets-pyjamas.co.uk (UK)
Seduce your mate with a rubber love-toy.

Planet Ark
http://www.planetark.org
Daily environmental news from Reuters. For more eco-news, try the
Environmental News Network: http://enn.com

Predator Urines
http://www.predatorpee.com
Bewitch neighbouring Jack Russells with a dab of bobcat balm or true-
blue roo poo: http://www.roopooco.com

Sea Turtle Migration-Tracking
http://www.cccturtle.org/satwelc.htm
Adopt a bugged sea reptile and follow its trail.

Veterinary Medicine
http://vetmedicine.about.com • http://netvet.wustl.edu
Take good care of your little buddy.

World Society for the Protection of Animals
http://www.wspa.org.au (INT) • http://www.rspca.org.au (AUS)
http://www.rspca.org (UK)
Help protect animals from cruelty and possible extinction. See also:
Australian Conservation Foundation http://www.acfonline.org.au
World Wildlife Fund http://www.wwf.org

News, Newspapers and Magazines

Now that almost every magazine and newspaper in the world
from *Ringing World* (**http://www.ringingworld.co.uk**) to the *Falkland
Island News* (**http://www.sartma.com**) is discharging daily content
onto the Net, it's beyond this guide to do much more than list a
few of the notables and then point you in the right direction for
more. The simplest way to find your favourite read would be to
look for its address in a recent issue. Failing that, try entering its
name into a subject guide or search engine. If you don't have a title
name and would prefer to browse by subject or region, try:
Open Directory http://dmoz.org/News/

Yahoo! http://dir.yahoo.com/News_and_Media/

Or a specialist directory:
AJR http://ajr.net
NewsLink http://newslink.org
Editor and Publisher http://www.mediainfo.com
Metagrid http://www.metagrid.com
NewsDirectory http://www.newsdirectory.com
Online Newspapers http://www.onlinenewspapers.com
Publist http://www.publist.com

Newspapers rarely replicate themselves word for word on the Web, but they often provide enough for you to live without the paper edition. Not bad, considering they're generally free online even before the paper hits the stands. Apart from whatever proportion of their print they choose to put up on the Web, they also tend to delve deeper into their less newsy areas such as travel, IT, entertainment and culture. Plus they often bolster this with exclusive content such as breaking news, live sports coverage, online shopping, opinion polls and discussion groups. In most cases they'll also provide a way to search and retrieve archives, though this might incur a charge. There are also a few sites that index multiple news archives – again, usually for a price. Such as:

Electric Library
http://www.elibrary.com
FindArticles.com
http://www.findarticles.com
NewsLibrary (US)
http://www.newslibrary.com

Northern Light http://www.northernlight.com

The best free services for searching current or recent stories across hundreds of international news sources are:
Moreover http://www.moreover.com
News Index http://www.newsindex.com

Like someone to monitor the Web and assorted newswires for mention of your product – or your misdeeds? Try:
Webclipping.com http://www.webclipping.com

Or you could go for a personalized news weblog:
Blogdex http://blogdex.media.mit.edu

To seriously improve your online newshound skill, why not visit some sites desgined for journalists:
Facsnet http://www.facsnet.org
Journalism Net http://www.journalismnet.com
USUS http://www.usus.org

A few of the more popular news bugles, to get you started:

Australia

The Age http://www.theage.com.au
The Australian http://www.news.com.au
Sydney Morning Herald http://www.smh.com.au

UK

Economist http://www.economist.com
Evening Standard http://www.thisislondon.co.uk
Express http://www.express.co.uk
Guardian http://www.guardian.co.uk

Independent http://www.independent.co.uk
Mirror http://www.mirror.co.uk
News of the World http://www.newsoftheworld.co.uk
Observer http://www.observer.co.uk
The Sun http://www.thesun.co.uk
Telegraph http://www.telegraph.co.uk
The Times http://www.thetimes.co.uk

US

The Atlantic http://www.theatlantic.com
Boston Globe http://www.globe.com
Chicago Sun Times http://www.suntimes.com
Chicago Tribune http://www.chicagotribune.com
Christian Science Monitor http://www.csmonitor.com
Detroit News http://www.detroitnews.com
Houston Chronicle http://www.chron.com
LA Times http://www.latimes.com
National Enquirer http://www.nationalenquirer.com
National Geographic News http://www.ngnews.com
New Republic http://www.tnr.com
Newsweek http://www.newsweek.com
New York Post http://www.nypost.com
New York Press http://www.nypress.com
New York Times http://www.nytimes.com
The Onion http://www.theonion.com
Philadelphia Newspapers http://www.philly.com
San Francisco Gate http://www.sfgate.com
San Jose Mercury http://www.sjmercury.com
Seattle Times http://www.seattletimes.com
Time Daily http://www.time.com
USA Today http://www.usatoday.com

chapter 14 • website directory

Village Voice http://www.villagevoice.com
Washington Post http://www.washingtonpost.com
Weekly World News http://www.weeklyworldnews.com

World

Arab News http://www.arabnews.com
Bangkok Post http://www.bangkokpost.net
Daily Mail & Guardian http://www.mg.co.za
Frankfurter Allgemeine Zeitung http://www.faz.de
The Hindu http://www.hinduonline.com
Independent Media Center http://www.indymedia.org
Irish Times http://www.ireland.com
Jerusalem Post http://www.jpost.com
Le Monde http://www.lemonde.fr
El País http://www.elpais.es
La Repubblica http://www.repubblica.it
St Petersburg Times http://www.sptimes.ru
South China Morning Post http://www.scmp.com
La Stampa http://www.lastampa.it
Straights Times http://www.asia1.com
Tehelka http://www.tehelka.com
Times of India http://www.timesofindia.com
Toronto Star http://www.thestar.com

Like much you do online, reading news is addictive. You'll know you're hooked when you find yourself checking into newswires throughout the day to monitor moving stories. Try these for a fix:

Breaking news

ABC http://www.abcnews.com

news, newspapers and magazines

ABC (AUS) http://www.abc.net.au/news/
Ananova (UK) http://www.ananova.com
Associated Press http://wire.ap.org
BBC (UK) http://news.bbc.co.uk
CBS http://www.cbsnews.com
CNN http://www.cnn.com
Fox http://www.foxnews.com
ITN (UK) http://www.itn.co.uk
NBC http://www.msnbc.com
News24 (SA) http://www.news24.co.za
Paknews (PAK) http://www.paknews.org
Reuters http://www.reuters.com
Sky (UK) http://www.sky.com
Sydney Morning Herald (AUS) http://www.smh.com.au/breaking/
Wired News http://www.wired.com

To tap into several sources simultaneously:

News aggregators

Arts & Letters Daily http://www.aldaily.com

Asia Observer http://www.asiaobserver.com
FastAsia (Asia) http://www.fastasia.com
Moreover (INT) http://www.moreover.com
NewsHub http://www.newshub.com
NewsNow (UK) http://www.newsnow.co.uk
Russian Story http://www.russianstory.com
TotalNews http://www.totalnews.com
Yahoo! News http://dailynews.yahoo.com

Most of the major portals – such as **Excite**, **Yahoo!** and **MSN** – also allow you to create a custom news page that draws from several sources, though none do it quite so thoroughly as **Crayon**. **Infobeat** does similar things but delivers by email.
Crayon http://www.crayon.net
Infobeat http://www.infobeat.com

While most magazines maintain a site, they're typically more of an adjunct to the print version than a substitute. Still, they're worth checking out, especially if they archive features and reviews or break news between issues. Again, check a recent issue or one of the directories for an address. If you'd rather subscribe to the paper edition, try:
http://enews.com • http://www.mmnews.com
http://www.acp.com.au (AUS) • http://www.magsuk.com (UK)

Then there are the "ezines" – magazines that exist only online or are delivered by email. However, as almost any regularly updated webpage fits this description, the term has lost much of its currency. Although most ezines burn out as quickly as they appear, a few of the pioneers are still kicking on. The best known, or at least the most controversial, would be the **Drudge Report**, the shock bulletin that set off the Lewinsky avalanche. A one-hit wonder perhaps, but still a bona fide tourist attraction on the info goat track. **Salon**, however, is the real success story. It spans the arts, business, politics, lifestyle and technology in a style that's both smart and breezy. Microsoft's long-suffering **Slate** marks similar territory, but succeeds more in being terribly dull.

Drudge Report http://www.drudgereport.com
Salon http://www.salon.com
Slate http://slate.msn.com

While most ezines operate independently, there is one network that will connect you to a slew of quality underground productions of almost opposite persuasions. You'll know instantly whether it's your scene:

UGO http://www.ugo.com

IGN (Internet Gaming Network) treads similar, though generally tamer, ground to UGO, partnering mostly with high-quality gaming, sci-fi, wrestling and comic sites:

IGN http://www.ign.com/affiliates/

For more, try browsing one of the directories listed at:
http://dmoz.org/News/Ezines/Directories/

People, Advice and Support

Adoption.com
http://www.adoption.com • http://www.adopting.org
http://www.bastards.org
Find a child or your original parents. Or, if you suspect Screaming Jay put a spell on your momma: http://www.jayskids.com

Alien Implant Removal and Deactivation
http://www.abduct.com/irm.htm
Discover, within a free three-minute phone call, how many times you've been abducted and which implants you're carrying. Then it's just a matter of surgically removing them (http://www.alienscalpel.com) and sorting out your mental health. Perhaps the latter is all that's needed.

Final Thoughts
http://www.finalthoughts.com
Plot your legacy.

Guy Rules
http://www.guyrules.com
Learn to conceal your latent femininity.

Miss Abigail's Time Warp Advice
http://www.missabigail.com
Solve modern dilemmas with old-school logic.

Random Access Memory
http://www
.randomaccessmemory.org
Store your treasured memories in a safe place.

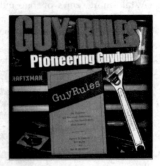

Politics and Government

Most government departments, politicians, political aspirants and causes maintain websites to spread the word and further their various interests. To find your local rep or candidate, start at their party's homepage. These typically lay dormant unless there's a campaign in progress but can still be a good source of contacts to badger. Government departments, on the other hand, tirelessly belch out all sorts of trivia right down to the transcripts of ministerial radio interviews. So, if you'd like to know about impending legislation, tax rulings, budget details and so forth, skip the party pages and go straight to the department. If you can't find its address through what's listed below, try:

Open Directory http://dmoz.org/Society/Government/
Yahoo! http://dir.yahoo.com/Government/
Or, better still, jump on the phone.

For the latest counts from the tally room, check the **breaking news sites** (p.426) on election night. Below is a selection of the most useful starting points in Australia, Britain and the US:

Australia

Democrats http://www.democrats.org.au
Electoral Commission http://www.aec.gov.au
Federal Government http://www.fed.gov.au
Labour http://www.alp.org.au
Liberals http://www.liberal.org.au
Nationals http://www.npa.org.au
Prime Minister http://www.pm.gov.au
State and Local Entry Point http://www.nla.gov.au/oz/gov/

UK

British Politics Links http://www.ukpol.co.uk
Government Portal http://www.open.gov.uk
Green Party http://www.greenparty.org.uk
Labour http://www.labour.org.uk
Liberal Democrats http://www.libdems.org.uk
National Assembly for Wales http://www.wales.gov.uk
Natural Law http://www.natural-law-party.org.uk
Northern Ireland Assembly http://www.ni-assembly.gov.uk
Prime Minister http://www.pm.gov.uk

Republican National Committee http://www.rnc.org
Scottish Parliament http://www.scottish-parliament.com
Sinn Féin http://www.sinnfein.ie
Socialist Party http://www.socialistparty.org.uk
Tories http://www.conservatives.com
Ulster Unionist Party http://www.uup.org

USA

Democratic National Committee http://www.democrats.org
Federal Consumer Info Center http://www.info.gov
FedWorld http://www.fedworld.gov
GovSpot http://www.govspot.com
Greens http://www.greenparty.org
House of Reps http://www.house.gov
National Security Agency http://www.nsa.gov
Political Index http://www.politicalindex.com
Political Resources http://www.politicalresources.com
SearchGov http://www.searchgov.com
Senate http://www.senate.gov
Thomas (search Congress) http://thomas.loc.gov
The White House http://www.whitehouse.gov

Amnesty International
http://www.amnesty.org
Join the battle against brutal regimes and injustice.

Antiwar
http://www.antiwar.com • http://www.iacenter.org
Challenges US intervention in foreign affairs, especially the Balkans and Middle East.

The Big Breach
http://www.thebigbreach.com
Download a free copy of the British MI6 spy-and-tell book.

The Black Vault
http://www.blackvault.com • http://www.abovetopsecret.com
File under X.

The British Monarchy
http://www.royal.gov.uk
Tune into the world's best-loved soap opera.

Center for the Moral Defense of Capitalism
http://www.moraldefense.com • http://www.aynrand.org
Is greed still good in the Y2Ks? Maybe not good, but legal, says
Microsoft's last bastion of sympathy.

Central Intelligence Agency
http://www.cia.gov
Want the inside on political assassinations, arms deals, Colombian
drug trades, spy satellites, phone tapping, covert operations, govern-
ment-sponsored alien sex cults and The X-Files. Well, guess what?
Never mind, you won't go home without a prize:
http://www.copvcia.com
http://www.magnet.ch/serendipity/cia.html

The Chairman Smiles
http://www.iisg.nl/exhibitions/chairman/
Stunning exhibition of communist propaganda posters.

Clandestine Radio
http://www.clandestineradio.com
Tune in to the voices of revolution.

Communist Internet List
http://www.cominternet.org • http://www.yclusa.org
Angry intellectuals and workers unite.

Conspiracies
http://www.conspire.com • http://www.conspiracy-net.com
Certain people are up to something and, what's worse, they're probably
all in it together. If these exposés of the biggest cover-ups of all time
aren't proof enough, then do your bit and create one that's more con-
vincing: http://www.turnleft.com/conspiracy.html

Council for Aboriginal Reconciliation
http://www.reconciliation.org.au
Unfinished business in the Lucky (for some) Country.

Disinformation
http://www.disinfo.com
The dark side of politics, religious fervour, new science and current affairs you won't find in the papers.

Fax Your MP (UK)
http://www.faxyourmp.com
Pester your local member through an Internet-to-fax gateway.

FBI FOIA Reading Room
http://foia.fbi.gov
FBI documents released as part of the Freedom of Information Act. Includes a few files on such celebrities as John Wayne, Elvis, Marilyn and the British royals. To get hold of top-secret gen (without signing your life away), try:
http://www.paperlessarchives.com

Federation of American Scientists
http://www.fas.org
Heavyweight analysis of science, technology and public policy, including national security, nuclear weapons, arms sales, biological hazards, secrecy and space policy.

Foreign Report
http://www.foreignreport.com
Compact subscription newsletter with a track record of predicting international flash points well before the dailies.

The Gallup Organization
http://www.gallup.com • http://www.pollingreport.com (US)
Keep track of opinion trends and ratings.

Gates Foundation
http://www.gatesfoundation.org
See where the world's richest man is spreading it around.

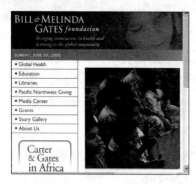

Gay and Lesbian Alliance Against Defamation
http://www.glaad.org
Stand up against media stereotyping, and discrimination, of those deviating from the heterosexual way.

Gendercide
http://www.gendercide.org
Investigates mass killings where a single gender is singled out.

German Propaganda Archives
http://www.calvin.edu/cas/gpa/
Who did you think you were kidding, Mr Hitler?

Global Ideas Bank
http://www.globalideasbank.org
Suggest and rate schemes to improve our standard of life.

Grassroots.com (US)
http://www.grassroots.com
Tracks political action and election policies across the board, aided by *TV Nation* champ Michael Moore (http://www.michaelmoore.com).

Greenpeace International
http://www.greenpeace.org
Rebels with many a good cause.

Hate Monitor
http://www.hatemonitor.org • http://www.splcenter.org
http://www.publiceye.org
Shining the public flashlight on hate groups and political forces that
threaten to undermine democracy and diversity.

Hindu Holocaust Museum
http://www.mantra.com/holocaust/
Contends that the – largely undocumented – massacre of Hindus during
Muslim rule in India was of a scale unparalleled in history.

InfoWar
http://www.infowar.com
Warfare issues from prank hacking to industrial espionage and military
propaganda.

Jane's IntelWeb
http://intelweb.janes.com
Brief updates on political disturbances, terrorism, intelligence agencies
and subterfuge worldwide. For a full directory of covert operations, see:
http://www.virtualfreesites.com/covert.html

Liberty
http://www.liberty-human-rights.org.uk
Championing human rights in England and Wales.

National Charities Information Bureau
http://www.ncib.org • http://www.charity-commission.gov.uk
Investigate before you donate.

National Forum on People's Differences
http://www.yforum.com
Toss around touchy topics such as race, religion and sexuality, with a
sincerity that is normally tabooed by political politeness.

One World
http://www.oneworld.net
Collates news from over 350 global justice organizations.

Open Secrets
http://www.opensecrets.org
Track whose money is oiling the wheels of US politics.

More keeping 'em honest at: http://www.commoncause.org

Oxfam
http://www.oxfam.org
Pitch in to fight poverty and inequality.

The Perpetual Warlog
http://www.dack.com
So you thought the War on Terror made sense?

The Progressive Review
www.prorev.com
Washington dirt dug up from all sides of the fence. For darker soil, try:
http://www.realchange.org

Project Censored
http://www.projectcensored.org
News stories that seem to fall through the cracks.

Protest.net – A Calendar of Protest Worldwide
http://protest.net
Find a nearby riot you can call your own.

Revolutionary Association of the Women of Afghanistan
http://www.rawa.org
And you think *you* have problems with men.

Spunk Press
http://www.spunk.org
http://www.infoshop.org
All the anarchy you'll ever need, organized neatly and with reassuring
authority.

Trinity Atomic Web Site
http://nuketesting.enviroweb.org/
See what went on (and what went off) fifty-odd years ago, then file into the archives of high-energy weapon testing and see who else has been sharpening the tools of world peace.

US Census Bureau
http://www.census.gov
More statistics on the US and its citizens than you'd care to know. For UK and Australian stats, see: http://www.statistics.gov.uk and http://www.abs.gov.au

Property

Australian Real Estate
http://www.propertiesaustralia.com.au
http://propertyweb.com.au
http://www.realestate.com.au
Combines listings from hundreds of Australian brokers.

FinanCenter
http://www.financenter.com
Figure out your monthly payments or what you can't afford.

HomeAdvisor (US)
http://homeadvisor.msn.com
Slick one-stop shop for finding homes and loans.

HouseWeb (UK)
http://www.houseweb.co.uk • http://www.findaproperty.com
http://www.propertylive.co.uk • http://www.propertyfinder.co.uk
Rent, buy or sell property within the UK.

ihavemoved.com (UK)
http://www.ihavemoved.com
Bulk-notify UK companies of your new address.

International Real Estate Digest
http://www.ired.com

Locate property listings, guides and property-related services world-wide.

Realtor.com (US)
http://www.realtor.com
Lists over a million US properties.

Spring Street
http://www.springstreet.com • http://www.apartments.com
Rent or buy a US apartment.

UpMyStreet
http://www.upmystreet.com
Astounding wealth of house price, health, crime, schools, tax and other statistics on UK neighbourhoods. Mighty useful if you're shifting base.

Radio and Webcasts

While almost all radio stations have a website, only a fraction pipe their transmissions online. The ever-increasing percentage that do usually broadcast (webcast) in RealAudio and/or Windows Media Format (see p.286), so grab the latest copies of their players. Both come with in-built station directories along with Web-based event guides – fine for starting out, but they're nowhere near complete. Yahoo! also runs a service that keeps tabs on notable audiovisual happenings:

RealGuide http://realguide.real.com
Windows Media Guide http://windowsmedia.com
Yahoo! Events http://broadcast.yahoo.com

Not enough? Then try one of the specialist radio directories. These list physical radio stations with websites along with full-time stations that only exist online, normally lumped together by country or genre. If they don't provide a direct link to the live feed, visit the station's site and look for a button or link that says "live" or "listen".

chapter 14 • website directory

Internet radio directories

BBC Radio http://www.bbc.co.uk/radio/
BRS Web-Radio http://www.web-radio.com
ComFM http://www.comfm.fr/live/radio/
Live Radio http://www.live-radio.net
Radio Locator http://www.radio-locator.com
RadioNow http://www.radionow.co.uk (UK)
RadioWise http://www.radiowise.com.au/stations_live.htm
Sunset Radio http://sunsetradio.com
Virtual Tuner http://www.virtualtuner.com

Apart from the traditional single-stream broadcasters, dozens of sites host multiple feeds. These might be live, on demand, on rotation, archived or once-off events. They tend to work more like inflight entertainment than radio.

Multistream webcasters

Anime Hardcore http://www.animehardcoreradio.net
Betalounge
http://www.betalounge.com
GoGaGa http://www.gogaga.com
House of Blues
http://www.hob.com

Interface http://interface.pirate-radio.co.uk
Online Classics http://www.onlineclassics.net
Radio SonicNet http://radio.sonicnet.com
Spinner http://www.spinner.com
The Womb http://www.thewomb.com
Yahoo! Radio http://radio.yahoo.com

If you fancy setting up your own station or listening to the online equivalent of pirate radio, try:

DIY stations

GiveMeTalk (Talk only) http://www.givemetalk.com
Icecast.org http://www.icecast.org
Live365 http://www.live365.com
MyPlay http://www.myplay.com
Shoutcast http://www.shoutcast.com
Spotlife http://www.spotlife.com

To promote your own station or search for a song or artist currently playing across thousands of others:
RadioSpy http://www.radiospy.com

Or to see, hear and link to buy what's playing, or played recently, on hundreds of US FM stations:
Clango http://www.clango.com
Emarker http://www.emarker.com
StarCD http://www.starcd.com

For everything else related to professional or amateur radio broadcasting:
Radio Directory http://www.radiodirectory.com

Crystal Radio
http://www.midnightscience.com
Build a simple
wireless that
needs no battery.

Phil's Old Radios
http://www
.antiqueradio.org
If you ever drifted
to sleep bathed
in the soft glow
of a crackling

Bakelite wireless, Phil's collection of vacuum-era portables may instantly flood you with childhood memories.

Pirate Radio
http://pirateradio.about.com
Stake your claim on the airwaves.

Police Scanner
http://www.policescanner.com
http://www.apbnews.com/scanner/
http://www.javaradio.com
Live emergency scanner feeds piped into RealAudio. Eavesdrop on busts in progress. More on scanners at: http://www.strongsignals.net

Reference

With the Net threatening the very foundations of the encyclopedia industry, it should come as no surprise to find most of the household names firmly entrenched online. While they're not all entirely free, they're certainly cheaper and more up-to-date than their bulky paper equivalents.

Britannica http://www.eb.com
Columbia http://www.bartleby.com/65/
Encarta http://www.encarta.com
Macquarie http://www.macnet.mq.edu.au
World Book http://www.worldbook.com

Nupedia is a new open-content encyclopedia project collated by volunteers. You're invited to contribute:
Nupedia http://www.nupedia.com

For one-point access to over a thousand dictionaries across almost every language:
Dictionary.com http://www.dictionary.com
One Look http://www.onelook.com

YourDictionary.com http://www.yourdictionary.com

To query a broad selection of prominent reference works from Oxford University, Houghton Mifflin, Penguin, Macmillan, Bloomsbury and Market House Books, consult:
Xrefer http://www.xrefer.com

Naturally, there are oodles of reference portals brimming with helpful reference tools. For instance:
Digital Librarian http://www.digital-librarian.com
Librarian's Index http://www.lii.org
LibrarySpot http://www.libraryspot.com
Open Directory http://dmoz.org/Reference/
Refdesk.com http://www.refdesk.com
Yahoo! http://dir.yahoo.com/reference/

Acronym Finder
http://www.acronymfinder.com • http://www.ucc.ie/acronyms/
Before you follow IBM, TNT and HMV in initializing your company's name, make sure it doesn't mean something blue.

All Experts
http://www.allexperts.com
http://www.askme.com
http://www.abuzz.com
Ask any question and let unpaid experts do the thinking.

>abuzz.
An Interactive Knowledge Sharing Community

Altavista Translations
http://world.altavista.com
Translate text, including webpages, in seconds. Run some text back and forth a few times (http://www.telalink.net/~carl/multibabel/) and you'll end up with something that wouldn't look out of place on a Japanese T-shirt. If you can't identify what it is in the first place, try:
http://www.dougb.com/ident.html

chapter 14 • website directory

Alternative Dictionary
http://www.notam.uio.no/~hcholm/altlang/
Bucket your foreign chums in their mother tongue.

American ASL Dictionary
http://www.handspeak.com
http://www.bconnex.net/~randys/
Learn sign language through simple animations.

Anagram Genius
http://www.anagramgenius.com
Recycle used letters.

Aphorisms Galore
http://www.aphorismsgalore.com
Sound clever by repeating someone else's lines.

Bartleby Reference
http://www.bartleby.com/reference/
Free access to several contemporary and classic reference works such as the American Heritage dictionaries, the *Columbia Encyclopedia*, *King's English*, Emily Post's *Etiquette*, the *Cambridge History of English and American Literature* and the *Anatomy of the Human Body*.

Biography
http://www.biography.com
Recounting more than 25,000 lives.

Calculators Online
http://www-sci.lib.uci.edu/~martindale/RefCalculators.html
Awesome directory of some 10,000 online tools to calculate everything from how much sump oil to put in soap to the burden of bringing up brats.

Cliché Finder
http://www.westegg.com/cliche/
Submit a word or phrase to find out how not to use it.

Dictionaraoke
http://www.dictionaraoke.org
Pocket Oxford enters the Eurovision Song Contest.

Earthstation1
http://www.earthstation1.com
The 20th century captured in sound and vision.

eHow
http://www.ehow.com
http://www.soyouwanna.com
Make yourself useful through step-by-step tutorials.

Encyclopedia Mythica
http://pantheon.org/mythica/
Hefty album of mythology, folklore and legend.

The Farmer's Almanac
http://www.almanac.com
Synchronize your sheep breeding with phases of the moon.

How to Speak to an Extraterrestrial
http://adrr.com/lingua/alien.htm
Crash course in ET101.

InfoPlease
http://www.infoplease.com
Handy, all-purpose almanac for stats and trivia.

Internet Archive
http://www.archive.org
Wormhole your way into Web history.

Ka-BOOM! A Dictionary of Comic Book Words
http://www.geocities.com/Athens/Marathon/5150/dictionary/
Become fluent in the language favoured by leading superheroes.

Comic words beginning with K are often related to explosive sounds. KA- and variations like KE- or KER- are used to intensify the basic sound effect.

Megaconverter
http://www.megaconverter.com
Calculate everything from your height in angstroms to the pellets of lead per ounce of buckshot needed to bring down an overcharging consultant.

Princeton Review
http://www.review.com • http://www.collegeboard.org
Crack the SATs.

Rap Dictionary
http://www.rapdict.org
Hip-hop to English. Parental guidance recommended.

RhymeZone
http://www.rhymezone.com
Get a hoof up in putting together a classy love poem.

Roget's Thesaurus
http://www.thesaurus.com
New format – useless as ever.

Satellite and Aerial Imaging
http://www.terraserver.com • http://terra.nasa.gov
http://www.crworld.co.uk • http://www.photolib.noaa.gov
http://www.globexplorer.com • http://www.multimap.com (UK)
See why nine out of ten Martian honeymooners prefer your planet.

Skeptic's Dictionary
http://www.skepdic.com
Punch holes in mass-media funk and pseudo-sciences such as homeopathy, astrology and iridology.

Spellweb
http://www.spellweb.com • http://bodin.org/altameter/
Compare two words or phrases and see which gets more hits in a search engine. If it demonstrates anything worthwhile, it's that the Web is strung together with a lot of bad spelling.

The Straight Dope
http://www.straightdope.com
Cecil Adams's answers to hard questions. Find out how to renounce your US citizenship, what "Kemosabe" means and the difference between a warm smell of colitas and colitis.

Strunk's Elements of Style
http://www.bartleby.com/141/
The complete classic of English usage in a nutshell, though unfortunately not the latest edition. For more on grammar and style:

Education Finder http://www.edunet.com/english/grammar/

Garbl's Writing Resources http://www.garbl.com

Symbols
http://www.symbols.com
Ever woken up with a strange sign tattooed on your buttocks? Here's where to find what it means without calling Scully and Doggett.

Text Files
http://www.textfiles.com
Chunks of the junk that orbited the pre-Web Internet. For a slightly more modern slant, see: http://www.etext.org

Urban Legends
http://www.urbanlegends.com • http://www.snopes.com
Separate the amazing-but-true from popular myths.

What Is?
http://www.whatis.com • http://www.webopedia.com
Unravel cumbersome computer and Internet jargon without having even more thrown at you.

Relationships and Friendship

Breakup Girl
http://www.breakupgirl.com
How to mend a broken heart and get on with your life. Here's how not to do it: http://www.crazy-bitch.com

Bestest of friends

Just when those emotional scars had begun to heal, along rumbles one of the biggest bandwagons of recent years – the reunion website. So scribble a success-story biog and invite all those old school pals to lunch on your yacht at:

ClassMates.com http://www.classmates.com (US, CAN)
Friends Reunited http://www.friendsreunited.co.uk (UK)
School Friends http://www.schoolfriends.com.au (AUS)

Cyberspace Inmates
http://www.cyberspace-inmates.com • http://www.jailbabes.com
Strike up an email romance with a prison inmate; maybe even one on death row.

Exso
http://www.ex-so.com
Tell the world why your ex is your ex.

Hot or Not?
http://www.hotornot.com • http://www.ratemyface.com
Submit a flattering photo and have it rated by passing chumps. So popular it has spawned a string of spoofs, such as:
http://www.amigeekornot.com • http://www.amifuglyornot.com
To sort by rating, see: http://log.waxy.org/hot/
To instantly create your own custom Am I page:
http://www.iamcal.com/ami/

Infidelity.com
http://www.infidelity.com
They're all no-good, lying, cheating slime. But at least there's help.

Love Calculator
http://www.lovecalculator.com
Enter your respective names to see if you're compatible.

Matchmaking Directories
http://www.singlesites.com
http://dmoz.org/Society/Relationships/
Come aboard – they're expecting you.

PlanetOut
http://www.planetout.com
http://www.qrd.org • http://www.datalounge.com
http://www.queertheory.com
http://www.rainbownetwork.com (UK)
Directories to all that's that way inclined.

Relationships Directory
http://www.yahoo.com/Society_and_Culture/Relationships/
Advice and links on everything from hugging to divorce.

Secret Admirer
http://www.secretadmirer.com • http://www.ecrush.com
Find out whether your most secret crushed one digs you back.

So There
http://www.sothere.com
A place to post your parting shots.

Swoon
http://www.swoon.com
Dating, mating, and relating. Courtesy of Condé Nast's *Details*, *GQ*, *Glamour* and *Mademoiselle*. For dessert, try: http://dating.about.com

Vampire Exchange
http://www.vein-europe.demon.co.uk
http://www.sanguinarius.org
Give blood as an act of love.

Weddings in the Real World
http://www.theknot.com • http://www.nearlywed.com
Prepare to jump the broom – or untie the knot:
http://www.divorcesource.com

Religion

So many answers, so little time on earth. If you haven't yet signed up with a religious sect or are unhappy with the one passed down by your folks, here's your opportunity to survey the field at your own pace. Most are open to newcomers, though certain rules and conditions may apply. For a reasonably complete and unbiased breakdown of faith dealerships, try:

BeliefNet http://www.beliefnet.com
Comparative Religion http://www.academicinfo.net/religindex.html
Religious Tolerance http://www.religioustolerance.org

But don't expect such an easy ride from those demanding proof:

Atheism http://atheism.miningco.com
Christian Burner http://www.christianburner.com
The Secular Web http://www.infidels.org

Anglicans Online
http://anglicansonline.org
Catapult gently into the Church of England worldwide.

Avatar Search
http://www.AvatarSearch.com
Search the occult Net for spiritual guidance and lottery tips.

The Bible Gateway
http://bible.gospelcom.net
Set your table with the Good Book.

The Brick Testament
http://www.thereverend.com/brick_testament/
And on the eighth day God created Lego ...

Catholic Church – God's One and Only Church
http://www.truecatholic.org
More troops armed with the truth.

Catholic Online
http://www.catholic.org
Saints, angels, shopping, discussion and a portal to the online territory occupied by Catholics.

Celebrity Atheist List
http://www.celebatheists.com
Big names you won't spot in Heaven.

Cheesy Jesus
http://www.cheesyjesus.com
http://www.ship-of-fools.com/Gadgets/
Buy gadgets to bring you closer to God.

Chick
http://chick.com
Hard-core Christian porn.

Christian Answers
http://christiananswers.net
Movies and computer games reviewed, and hard questions answered, by Christians who know what's good for you and your family.

Christians v Muslims
http://debate.org.uk • http://www.rim.org/muslim/islam.htm
http://members.aol.com/AllahIslam/
http://www.answering-islam.org
http://www.muslim-answers.org
http://www.biblicalchristianity.freeserve.co.uk
Put your faith on the line.

CrossSearch
http://www.crosssearch.com
Set sail through safe waters to find Christian groups of all denominations.

Crosswalk
http://www.crosswalk.com
Catch up with the latest on Jesus.

Demon Possession Handbook
http://diskbooks.org/hs.html
Train for a job with the Watcher's Council.

The Greatest Truth Ever Revealed
http://www.sevenseals.com
Revelations from survivors of the Waco siege.

The Hindu Universe
http://www.hindunet.org
Hindu dharma – the philosophy, culture and customs.

The Holy See
http://www.vatican.va
Official hideout of the pope and his posse.

Islamic Gateway
http://www.ummah.net • http://www.musalman.com
http://www.fatwa-online.com
Get down with Mohammed (*sallallahu `alaihi wa sallam*).

Jediism
http://www.jediism.org
You too can feel the Force. Alternatively, give in to your hate and embrace the Dark Side:
http://www.forceacademy.com/Dark/

Jesus of the Week
http://www.jesusoftheweek.com
The original Mr Nice Guy in 52 coy poses per year.

Jesus Puzzle – Was There No Historical Jesus?
http://human.st/jesuspuzzle/ • http://jesuspuzzlerings.com
http://www.jesusdance.com
Solve the riddle; buy the ring; do the dance.

Miracles Page
http://www.mcn.org/1/miracles/
Spooky signs that point towards a cosmic conspiracy.

Not Proud
http://www.notproud.com
Confess your most entertaining sins.

Peyote Way Church of God
http://www.peyoteway.org
Unless you're Native American or live in select southern US states, you
stand to be locked up for finding God through the psychedelic cactus.
Otherwise, feel free to fry your brain; just don't drive home from church.

Prophecy and Current Events
http://www.aplus-software.com/thglory/
http://www.prophezine.com
You'll never guess who's coming to dinner. Don't bother cooking,
though – he's supposed to be a real whiz with food.

Satanism 101
http://www.satanism101.com
Enter this address and go straight to Hell:
http://www.what-the-hell-is-hell.com • http://www.virtualhell.org

Ship of Fools: The Magazine of Christian Unrest
http://ship-of-fools.com
The lighter side of Christianity.

Skeptics Annotated Bible
http://www.skepticsannotatedbible.com
Contends that the Good Book is a misnomer.

Stories of the Dreaming
http://www.dreamtime.net.au
Selection of enchanting bedtime stories in text, video and audio that
explain creation from an Aboriginal perspective. Don't believe in creation? Go tell it to the jury: http://www.talkorigins.org

Totally Jewish
http://www.totallyjewish.com • http://www.maven.co.il
http://judaism.about.com • http://aish.com
Spiritual guidance and community portals for chosen people
(http://www.chosen-people.com) and curious *goyim* alike.

Universal Life Church
http://ulc.org
Become a self-ordained minister.

The Witches' Voice
http://www.witchvox.com
http://www.witchesweb.com
Expresses a burning desire to correct misinformation about witchcraft, a legally recognized religion in the US since 1985.

Zen
http://www.do-not-zzz.com
Take a five-minute course in meditation.

Science

To keep abreast of science news and developments stop by **Scitech**, which aggregates stories from the leading scientific media, and *New Scientist*'s Site of the Day:

Scitech Daily Review http://www.scitechdaily.com
Site of the Day http://www.newscientist.com/weblinks/

Or go straight to one of the many science journals:

Archaeology http://www.archaeology.org
BBC http://news.bbc.co.uk
Beyond 2000 http://www.beyond2000.com
British Medical Journal http://www.bmj.com
Bulletin of Atomic Scientists http://www.bullatomsci.org

Discover http://www.discover.com
Discovery Channel http://www.discovery.com
Earth Times http://www.earthtimes.org
Edge http://www.edge.org
Highwire Press http://highwire.stanford.edu
The Lancet http://www.thelancet.com
National Geographic http://www.nationalgeographic.com
New Scientist http://www.newscientist.com
Popular Mechanics http://www.popularmechanics.com
Popular Science http://www.popsci.com
Science à GoGo http://www.scienceagogo.com
Science Magazine http://www.sciencemag.org
Science News http://www.sciencenews.org
Scientific American http://www.scientificamerican.com
The Scientist http://www.the-scientist.com
Skeptical Inquirer http://www.csicop.org/si/
Technology Review http://www.techreview.com

Looking for a something specific or a range of sites within a strand? Try browsing or searching a directory:

About Science http://home.about.com/science/
Hypography http://www.hypography.com
Open Directory http://dmoz.org/Science/
SciSeek http://www.sciseek.com
Treasure Troves of Science http://www.treasure-troves.com
Yahoo! http://dir.yahoo.com/science/

The Braintainment Center
http://www.brain.com • http://www.mensa.org
http://www.iqtest.com • http://www.mind-gear.com
http://www.mindmedia.com
Start with a test that says you're not so bright, then prove it by buying loads of self-improvement gear. Short on brains? Try:
http://www.brains4zombies.com

Cool Robot of the Week
http://ranier.hq.nasa.gov/telerobotics_page/coolrobots.html
Clever ways to get machines to do our dirty work. For a directory of
simulators, combat comps, clubs and DIY bots, direct your agent to:
http://www.robotcafe.com

Documentation and Diagrams of the Atomic Bomb
http://serendipity.magnet.ch/more/atomic.html
Let's hope this doesn't fall into the wrong hands. Imagine the effect on
your neighbourhood:
http://www.pbs.org/wgbh/amex/bomb/sfeature/mapablast.html

History of Mathematics
http://www-groups.dcs.st-andrews.ac.uk/~history/
The life and times of various bright sparks with numbers.

HotAir – Annals of Improbable Research
http://www.improbable.com
Science gone too far. Includes the Ig Nobel awards for achievements
that cannot, or should not, be reproduced.

How Stuff Works
http://www.howstuffworks.com
Unravel the mysterious machinations behind all sorts of stuff, from
Christmas to cruise missiles.

Integrator
http://integrals.wolfram.com
Solve nasty differential equations with a single click.

Interactive Frog Dissection
http://teach.virginia.edu/go/frog/
Pin down a frog, grab your scalpel and follow the pictures.

The Lab (AUS)
http://www.abc.net.au/science/
ABC science news and program info with Q&As from Aussie pop-sci
superstar, Dr Karl Kruszelnicki.

MadSciNet: 24-Hour Exploding Laboratory
http://www.madsci.org

Collective of more than a hundred scientific smarty-pantses set up specifically to answer your dumb questions. More geniuses for hire at:
http://www.ducksbreath.com • http://www.wsu.edu/DrUniverse/
http://www.sciam.com/askexpert/ • http://www.sciencenet.org.uk

MIT Media Labs

http://www.media.mit.edu
If you've read *Being Digital* or any of Nicholas Negroponte's *Wired* columns, you'll know he has some pretty tall ideas about our electronic future. Here's where he gets them.

Museum of Dirt

http://www.planet.com/dirtweb/dirt.html
Celebrity dirt of an entirely different nature.

Netsurfer Science

http://www.netsurf.com/nss/
Subscribe to receive weekly bulletins on science and technology sites.

Nobel e-Museum

http://www.nobel.se
Read all about Nobel Prize winners.

Rocketry Online

http://www.rocketryonline.com
Take on NASA at its own game.

Scirus

http://www.scirus.com
Science-specific searching. White coats optional.

Skeptics Society

http://www.skeptic.com • http://www.csicop.org
Don't try to pull a swifty on this crowd.

USGS National Earthquake Info Center

http://gldss7.cr.usgs.gov
http://www.gps.caltech.edu/~polet/recofd.html
Stats and maps of most recent quakes worldwide.

Volcano World
http://volcano.und.nodak.edu
Monitor the latest eruptions, see photos of every major volcano in the world and virtually tour a Hawaiian smoky without choking on sulphur fumes.

Web-Elements
http://www.webelements.com
http://www.chemsoc.org/viselements/
Click on an element in the periodic table and suss it out in depth. Now cross-check its comic-book reference:
http://www.uky.edu/Projects/Chemcomics/
and recite its poem:
http://www.superdeluxe.com/elemental/

Weird Science and Mad Scientists
http://www.eskimo.com/~billb/weird.html
http://www.student.nada.kth.se/~nv91-asa/mad.html
Free energy, Tesla, anti-gravity, aura, cold fusion, parapsychology and other strange scientific projects and theories.

Why Files
http://whyfiles.news.wisc.edu
Entertaining reports on the science behind current news.

Space

If you have more than a passing interest in space, skip the popular science mags (p.454) and newswires (p.426), and go straight to the source:
NASA http://www.nasa.gov

Or try any of these specialist space ports:
About Space http://space.about.com
Amateur Astronomy Magazine http://www.amateurastronomy.com
Astronomy.com http://www.astronomy.com
Astronomy Now http://www.astronomynow.com

Explorezone http://explorezone.com
Human Spaceflight http://spaceflight.nasa.gov
Jet Propulsion Lab http://www.jpl.nasa.gov
Planetary Society http://planetary.org
Sky & Telescope Magazine http://www.skypub.com
Space.com http://www.space.com
SpaceRef http://www.spaceref.com
SpaceScience http://www.spacescience.com
Universe Today http://www.universetoday.com

Alien Bases on Earth
http://www.earth-today.com
See, in great detail, where the gods have parked their chariots.

Artemis Project
http://www.asi.org
Join a queue to go to the moon.

Astromart
http://www.astromart.com
Buy and sell your way into space.

Astronomy Picture of the Day
http://antwrp.gsfc.nasa.gov/apod/astropix.html
Enjoy a daily helping of outer space, served up by a gourmet astrochef.

Auroral Activity
http://www.sec.noaa.gov/pmap/
Instantly see the current extent and position of the auroral oval above each pole.

Auroras: Paintings in the Sky
http://www.exploratorium.edu/learning_studio/auroras/
http://www.alaskascience.com/aurora.htm
If you're ever lucky enough to see the aurora during a solar storm, you'll never take the night sky for granted again. The Exploratorium does a commendable job in explaining a polar phenomenon that very few people understand. Except, maybe, these champs:
http://www.haarp.alaska.edu

Bad Astronomy
http://www.badastronomy.com
Ditch your lifetime's supply of space misconceptions and clichés.

Clickworkers
http://clickworkers.arc.nasa.gov
Wangle a NASA job onto your CV by counting craters on Mars.

Comets & Meteor Showers
http://comets.amsmeteors.org
Be on the lookout for falling rocks.

Darksky
http://www.darksky.org
Join the campaign against wanton street lighting. You'll see why in the gallery.

Deep Cold
http://www.deepcold.com
Artistic mock-ups of chic space racers that never left the hangar.

Earth Viewer
http://www.fourmilab.ch/earthview/
View the Earth in space and time.

Heavens Above
http://www
.heavens-above.com
Correctly identify nearby satellites and space stations.

Hubblesite
http://hubble.stsci.edu
Intergalactic snapshots fresh from the Hubble telescope.

Inconstant Moon
http://www.inconstantmoon.com
Click on a date and see what's showing on the moon.

International Star Registry

http://www.starregistry.co.uk
Raise your flag in outer space.

Mars Home Page

http://mpfwww.jpl.nasa.gov
Get a bit more red dirt live from NASA's space safari before you stake out your first plot at: http://www.marsshop.com. For the latest news, see: http://www.marsnews.com

Mr Eclipse

http://www.mreclipse.com
Dabble in the occultations.

Net Telescopes

http://www.telescope.org/rti/ • http://denali.physics.uiowa.edu/
Probe deep space by sending requests to remote telescopes.

Scope Reviews

http://www.scopereviews.com
Read first, buy later – or maybe build your own:
http://www.atmjournal.com

Seti@home

http://setiathome.ssl.berkeley.edu • http://setifaq.org
Donate your processing resources to the non-lunatic end of the search for extraterrestrial intelligence by downloading a screensaver that analyses data from the Arecibo Radio Telescope. Progress reports at:
http://www.seti.org • http://planetary.org
http://seti.uws.edu.au

Solar System Simulator

http://space.jpl.nasa.gov
Shift camp around the solar system until you find the best view.

Space Calendar

http://www.jpl.nasa.gov/calendar/
Guide to upcoming anniversaries, rocket launches, meteor showers, eclipses, asteroid and planet viewings, and happenings in the inter-galactic calendar.

Space Weather
http://www.spaceweather.com
http://www.windows.ucar.edu/spaceweather/
Monitor the influence of solar activity on the Earth's magnetic field.

Sport

For live calls, scores, tables, draws, teams, injuries and corruption inquiries across major sports, try the newspaper sites (p.422), breaking news services (p.426) or sporting specialists like:

BBC Sport http://news.bbc.co.uk/sport/
CBS Sportsline http://www.sportsline.com
Fox Sports (Aus) http://www.foxsports.com.au
SkySports (UK) http://www.skysports.com
Slam Sports (Can) http://www.canoe.ca/slam/
Sport365 http://www.sport365.com
Sportal (INT) http://www.sportal.com
Sporting Life (UK) http://www.sporting-life.com
Sports.com (Euro) http://sports.com
Sports Illustrated http://sportsillustrated.cnn.com
Wide World of Sports (Aus) http://sports.ninemsn.com.au

But, if your interest even slightly borders on obsession, you'll find far more satisfaction on the pages of something more one-eyed. For clubs and fan sites, drill down through Yahoo! and the Open Directory. They won't carry everything, but what you'll find will lead you to the forces that understand you better than your partner:

Open Directory http://dmoz.org/Sports/
Yahoo! Sports http://dir.yahoo.com/recreation/sports/

Adventure Sports Directory
http://www.adventuredirectory.com

http://dmoz.org/Sports/Extreme_Sports/
For all that falls under the banner of "extreme sports", from taking your pushbike offroad to the sort of sheer recklessness that would get you cut from a will. For something more flashy, check out:
http://www.pie.com and http://expn.go.com

Australian Football League
http://www.afl.com.au
Men in tight shorts play aerial ping-pong.

The Bladder (AUS)
http://www.thebladder.com.au
Australian sport meets *The Onion*.

CricInfo – The Home of Cricket on the Internet
http://www.cricket.org
Because every ball matters.

Fishing Directories
http://www.thefishfinder.com
http://fishsearch.com
Trade tips and generally exaggerate about aquatic bloodsports.

Fitness Online
http://www.fitnessonline.com
Log your training and nutrition regime online.

Goals – Global Online Adventure Learning Site
http://www.goals.com
Chase adventurous lunatics like Mick Bird, who's circling the globe in a canoe.

NBA.com
http://www.nba.com
Pro basketball news, picks, player profiles, analyses, results, schedules and highlight videos. See also Major League Baseball:
http://www.mlb.com

chapter 14 • website directory

NFL
http://www.nfl.com • http://www.nfluth.com
Media schedules, chats, news, player profiles, stats and streaming
highlight videos from the National Football League's past and current
seasons.

Rugby League/Union
http://www.rleague.com • http://www.ozleague.com
http://www.scrum.com
Up-to-the-minute coverage of hard men trotting in and out of the blood
bin.

Sailing Index
http://www.smartguide.com • http://www.madforsailing.com
Everything seaworthy – from swapping yachts to shopping for GPS.

SkiCentral
http://www.skicentral.com • http://www.skiclub.co.uk
Indexes thousands of ski-
related sites, such as snow
reports, resort cams, snow-
board gear, accommodation
and coming events in resorts
across the world. For snow-
boarding, see:
http://www.snowboard.com
http://www.soltv.com
http://www.twsnow.com
http://www.board-it.com

SoccerNet
http://www.soccernet.com
ESPN's shrine to football in England and beyond. Not enough news? Try:

FA Premier http://www.fa-premier.com

Football365 http://www.football365.co.uk

Nationwide http://www.football.nationwide.co.uk

When Saturday Comes http://www.wsc.co.uk

For game, club and player stats, see:

Soccerbase http://www.soccerbase.com

Teamtalk http://www.teamtalk.com

Stats
http://www.stats.com
Pig in to an overflowing trough of US sport statistics.

Tennis
http://www.tennis.com
http://www.tennisforall.org
See what the Deuce is going on at *Tennis* mag's in-depth site.

World Motorsports
http://www.motorsport.com
Start here for your gasoline-induced pleasure.

World Surfing
http://www.surfline.com
Every day's like big Wednesday. For daily breaks and Aussie seaboard cams, see: http://www.coastalwatch.com

Wrestling
http://www.wrestlezone.com • http://www.wrestlingdotcom.com
Vent the frustration of helplessly watching your boofhead heroes being piledriven, suplexed and moonsplashed by spilling some virtual hard-way juice. If you'd prefer seeing them smack each other in the scone, see: http://www.secondsout.com

Telecommunications and Post

Compare Phone Charges
http://www.buy.co.uk (UK)
http://www.magsys.co.uk/telecom/ (UK)
http://www.uswitch.com (UK)
http://www.ccmi.com (US) • http://www.getconnected.com
http://lowestphone.com (US) • http://www.phonesaver.com (US)
http://www.lowermybills.com (US)
http://10-10phonerates.com (US)
Shop around for the best phone rates.

Efax
http://www.efax.com • http://www.j2.com
Free up a phone line by receiving your faxes by email.

FedEx
http://www.fedex.com
Book shipping, track parcels or compare rates with UPS
(http://www.ups.com) and TNT (http://www.tnt.com).

Free Fax Services
http://www.tpc.int
Transmit faxes via the Internet – free.

Letterpost
http://www.letterpost.com
Buy a stamp. Type a message. Have it posted.

Mail2Wap
http://www.mail2wap.com
Collect your POP3 mail on a WAP phone.

MobileWorld
http://www.mobileworld.org
http://www.unwin.co.uk/phonez.html
Assorted info on mobile phones and cellular networks.

Postcode Pages
http://www.grcdi.nl/linkspc.htm
Find a postcode in almost any country.

Reverse Phone Directory
http://www.reversephonedirectory.com
Key in a US phone number to find its owner. To find a UK location, see:
http://www.warwick.ac.uk/cgi-bin-Phones/nng/

SMS Text Messages
http://www.mtnsms.com
Send free text messages to mobile phones worldwide.

Stamps.com (US)
http://www.stamps.com • http://www.estamp.com
Buy your US stamps online.

The Telegraph Office
http://fohnix.metronet.com/~nmcewen/tel_off.html
http://www.navyrelics.com/tribute/bellsys/

Trip through the history of wired communications from Morse telegraphy to the Bell System.

UK.Telecom FAQ
http://www.gbnet.net/net/uk-telecom/
Satisfy your curiosity about the British phone network.

US Postal Services
http://www.usps.com
Look up a zip code, track express mail, sort out your vehicle registration or just get philatelic.

What Does Your Phone Number Spell?
http://www.phonespell.org
Enter your phone number to see what it spells. The reverse lookup might help you choose a number.

World Time and Dialling Codes
http://www.whitepages.com.au/wp/search/time.html
International dialling info from anywhere to anywhere, including current times and area codes.

Time

Calendarzone
http://www.calendarzone.com
Calendar links and, believe it or not, calzone recipes.

DateReminder
http://www.datereminder.co.uk
Remind yourself by email.

The Death Clock
http://www.deathclock.com
Get ready to book your final taxi.

Industorious clock
http://yugop.com/ver3/stuff/03/fla.html
Flash-powered handwritten clock. If you can stand more than a few seconds, you've obviously got too much time on your hands.

International Earth Rotation Service
http://hpiers.obspm.fr
Ever felt like your bed's spinning? The truth is even scarier.

iPing (US)
http://www.iping.com
Arrange free telephone reminders for one or many.

Time and Date
http://www.timeanddate.com
http://www.smh.com.au/media/wtc/smhwtc.html
Instantly tell the time in your choice of cities. And keep your PC clock aligned with a time synchronizer:
http://www.eecis.udel.edu/~ntp/software/index.html

Time Cave
http://www.timecave.com
Schedule an email to be
sent at a specific time in
the future.

Time Cube
http://www.timecube.com
Disprove God through the
simultaneous Four-Day
Time Cube.

World Thirteen Moon Calendar Change
http://www.tortuga.com
Know where the word "lunatic" comes from?

Transport

Buying a car

Before you're sharked into signing on a new or used vehicle, go online and check out a few road tests and price guides. You can complete the entire exercise while you're there, but it mightn't hurt to drive one first. Start here, and then search Google for enthusiast sites and forums.

Autobytel (INT) http://www.autobytel.com

Auto Channel http://www.theautochannel.com

Autohit (UK) http://www.autohit.co.uk

Autolocate (UK) http://www.autolocate.co.uk

Autotrader (UK, IE, Eur, SA) http://www.autotrader.co.uk

AutoWeb http://www.autoweb.com

BBC Top Gear (UK) http://www.topgear.beeb.com

CarClub http://www.carclub.com

Car Importing (UK) http://www.carimporting.co.uk

Carnet (Aus) http://www.car.net.au

CarPrice http://www.carprice.com

CarsDirect http://www.carsdirect.com

Carseekers (UK) http://www.carseekers.co.uk

Carstreet (IND) http://www.carstreet.com

DealerNet http://www.dealernet.com

Drivers Seat http://www.driversseat.com

Edmunds http://www.edmunds.com

Exchange & Mart (UK) http://www.ixm.co.uk

Kelly Blue Book http://www.kbb.com

Microsoft CarPoint http://carpoint.msn.com

Microsoft CarPoint (Aus) http://carpoint.ninemsn.com

Oneswoop (UK) http://www.oneswoop.com

What Car? (UK) http://www.whatcar.co.uk

Aviation

Am I Going Down?
http://www.amigoingdown.com
Enter your flight details to rate your chance of survival.

chapter 14 • website directory

Airdisaster.com
http://www.airdisaster.com • http://come.to/crashes/
http://www.aviationnewsweb.com • http://planecrashinfo.com
Way more goes wrong up in the air than you realize. Here's why you
should be terrified to fly. For first-hand tales of terror, see:
http://www.pprune.com

Airsafe
http://www.airsafe.com
Overcome your fear of plummeting.

Air Sickness Bag Virtual Museum
http://www.airsicknessbags.com
Bring up some treasured memories.

Aviation
http://aviation.about.com • http://www.airliners.net
If it takes off and lands, you'll find it here.

More Web wheels

Concept Carz
http://www.conceptcarz.com
If space for the shopping isn't too much of a priority.

Layover
http://www.layover.com
Long, wide loads of truckin' stuff
for prime movers and shakers.

Licence Plates of the World
http://worldlicenseplates.com
Ring in sick, cancel your date, unplug the phone and don't even think
about sleep until you've seen EVERY LICENCE PLATE IN THE WORLD.

NMRA Directory of Worldwide Rail Sites
http://www.ribbonrail.com/nmra/ • http://www.trainorders.com
Locophilial banquet of online railway shunts.

Radar Test
http://www.radartest.com
Outsmart the law through consumer electronics.

Train Pain
http://www.trainpain.com
Offload your beef with British railways.

Woman Motorist
http://www.womanmotorist.com
The demographic group that motor vehicle insurers prefer.

Travel

Whether you're seeking inspiration, planning an itinerary, shopping for a ticket or already mobile, there'll be a tool online worth throwing in your box. You can book flights, reserve hotels, research your destination, monitor the weather, convert currencies, learn the lingo, locate an ATM, scan local newspapers, collect your mail from abroad, find a restaurant that suits your fussy tastes and plenty more. If you'd like to find first-hand experiences or travelling companions, hit the Usenet discussion archives at **Google** (http://groups.google.com) and join the appropriate newsgroup under the **rec.travel** or **soc.culture** hierarchies. As with all newsgroups, before you post a question, skim through the FAQs first:

Air Travel Handbook
http://www.cs.cmu.edu/afs/cs/user/mkant/Public/Travel/airfare.html

Rec.Travel Library http://www.travel-library.com

You could also try consulting a volunteer "expert":

Abuzz http://www.abuzz.com/category/travel/
All Experts http://www.allexperts.com/travel/
Ask Me http://www.askme.com

Then see what the major guidebook publishers have to offer:

Fodors http://www.fodors.com
Frommers http://www.frommers.com
Insiders http://www.insiders.com
Let's Go http://www.letsgo.com
Lonely Planet http://www.lonelyplanet.com
Moon Travel http://www.moon.com
Robert Young Pelton http://www.comebackalive.com
Rough Guides http://www.roughguides.com
Routard http://www.club-internet.fr/routard/

While it might seem like commercial suicide for a publisher like the Rough Guides to give away the full text of its guides to more than 10,000 destinations, the reality is that books are still more convenient – especially on the road, when you need them most. If you'd like to order a guide or map online, you'll also find plenty of opportunities either from the above publishers, the online bookshops (p.344), or from travel bookshops such as:

Gorp http://www.gorp.com
Literate Traveller http://www.literatetraveller.com
Stanfords (UK) http://www.stanfords.co.uk

Many online travel agents also provide destination guides, which might include exclusive editorial peppered with chunks licensed from guidebooks, linked out to further material on the Web. For example:

Away.com http://away.com

The biggest problem with browsing the Web for regional information and travel tools is not in finding the sites, but wading through them. Take the following directories, for example:

About Travel http://travel.about.com
Excite Travel http://travel.excite.com

Lycos Travel http://travel.lycos.com
My Travel Guide http://www.mytravelguide.com
Open Directory http://dmoz.org/Recreation/Travel/
Traveller Online http://www.travelleronline.com
Trip Advisor (US) http://www.tripadvisor.com
Virtual Tourist http://www.vtourist.com
World Travel Guide http://www.travel-guide.com
World Travel Net http://www.world-travel-net.com
Yahoo! Directory http://www.yahoo.com/Recreation/Travel/
Yahoo! Travel http://travel.yahoo.com

These are perfect if you want to browse through regions looking for ideas, or to find a range of sites on one topic – health, for example. But if you're after something very specific you might find it more efficient to use a search engine such as Google. Keep adding search terms until you restrict the number of results to something manageable. If you'd like to coincide your vacation with a festival or event, go straight to:

What's Going On http://www.whatsgoingon.com
What's On When http://www.whatsonwhen.com

Or for entertainment, eating, and cultural events, a city guide:

Citysearch http://www.citysearch.com
Time Out http://www.timeout.co.uk
Yahoo! Local (US) http://local.yahoo.com
Zagat (Dining) http://www.zagat.com

Is **Vindigo** the future of travel guides? Download its Palm Pilot or AvantGo city guides and decide for yourself:

Vindigo http://www.vindigo.com

If you're flexible and/or willing to leave soon, you might find a **last-minute special**. These Net exclusives are normally offered directly from the airline, hotel and travel operator sites, which you'll find through **Airlines.com** (http://www.airlines.com) or Yahoo!. There are also a few Web operators that specialize in late-notice and special Internet deals on flights, hotels, events and so forth, such as:

Bargain Holidays (UK) http://www.bargainholidays.com
Best Fares http://www.bestfares.com
Lastminute.com (UK) http://www.lastminute.com
Lastminutetravel.com http://www.lastminutetravel.com
Smarter Living http://www.smarterliving.com
Travel Zoo http://www.travelzoo.com

Then there are the reverse-auction sites such as **Priceline.com**, where you bid on a destination and wait for a bite. You might strike up a good deal if you bid shrewdly and don't mind the somewhat draconian restrictions (see http://www.angelfire.com/nt/priceline/). **Hotwire** offers similar discounts on undisclosed airlines, but names the price up front. If you're super-flexible, you could try **Airhitch** or a courier:

Air Courier Assoc. http://www.aircourier.org
Airhitch http://www.airhitch.org
Hotwire http://www.hotwire.com
IAATC Air Courier http://www.courier.org
Priceline.com http://www.priceline.com

Booking a flight through one of the broad online ticketing systems isn't too hard either, but bargains are scarce. Unless you're spending someone else's money, you'll want to sidestep the full fares offered on these major services:

Expedia (UK) http://www.expedia.co.uk
Expedia (US) http://www.expedia.com
Info Hub (US) http://www.infohub.com
Travel.com.au (Aus) http://www.travel.com.au

Travelocity (INT) http://www.travelocity.com
Travel Select (INT) http://www.travelselect.co.uk
Travelshop (AUS) http://www.travelshop.com.au

Although they list hundreds of airlines and millions of fares, the general consensus is that they're usually better for research, accommodation and travel tips than cheap fares and customer service. Compare their fares with those of the airline sites and discount specialists such as:

Bargain Holidays (UK) http://www.bargainholidays.com
Cheap Flights (UK) http://www.cheapflights.com
Deckchair (UK) http://www.deckchair.com
Ebookers.com (UK, Eur) http://www.ebookers.com
Flight Centre (INT) http://www.flightcentre.com
Internet Air Fares (US) http://www.air-fare.com
1Travel.com (INT) http://www.1travel.com
Lowestfare.com (US) http://www.lowestfare.com

Or compare the prices across several agencies simultaneously using a comparision:

Farechase http://www.farechase.com
Hotwire http://www.hotwire.com
Orbitz (US) http://www.orbitz.com
QIXO http://www.qixo.com
Sidestep http://www.sidestep.com
TravelHub (US) http://www.travelhub.com

Finally, see if your travel agent can better the price. If the difference is marginal, go with the agent – at least you'll have a human contact if something goes wrong. See how the online bookers rate at:

Gomez.com http://www.gomez.com

chapter 14 • website directory

A2Btravel.com (UK)
http://www.a2btravel.com • http://www.ferrybooker.com
http://www.ukonline.co.uk/travel/
Resources for getting into, around and out of the UK – such as car-hire
comparison, airport guides, train timetables and ferry booking.

12Degrees
http://www.12degrees.com
Rope in a guidebook author to plan your adventure holiday.

Africam
http://www.africam.com
Sneak a peek at wild beasts going about their business.

Art of Travel
http://www.artoftravel.com
How to see the world on $25 a day.

ATM Locators
http://www.visa.com/atms/
http://www.mastercard.com/cardholderservices/atm/
Locate a browser willing to replenish your wallet.

Bed and Breakfast.com
http://www.bedandbreakfast.com • http://www.babs.com.au (AUS)
http://www.bedandbreakfast-directory.co.uk (UK)
http://www.innsite.com
Secure your night's sleep worldwide.

CIA World Factbook
http://www.odci.gov/cia/publications/pubs.html
Vital stats on every country. For the score on living standards:
http://www.undp.org

Concierge.com
http://www.concierge.com
Get packing with advice from *Traveler* magazine.

Danger Finder
http://www.comebackalive.com/df/
Adventure holidays that could last a lifetime.

Get a map

You can generate road and airport maps for most cities
worldwide, driving directions for North America and Europe, US
traffic reports, world maps and more at:

Expedia http://maps.expedia.com
MapBlast http://www.mapblast.com
MapQuest http://www.mapquest.com
Multimap (UK, Eur) http://www.multimap.com

To create UK or Australian street and road maps from postcodes
or addresses, see:

Streetmap (UK) http://www.streetmap.co.uk
Whereis (Aus) http://www.whereis.com.au

If you require highly detailed US topographic maps, try:

TopoZone http://www.topozone.com

For more maps, geographical and GPS resources, see:
http://geography.about.com
http://dmoz.org/Reference/Maps/

Electronic Embassy
http://www.embassy.org
Directory of foreign embassies in DC, plus Web links where available.
Search Yahoo! for representation in other cities.

Eurotrip
http://www.eurotrip.com • http://www.ricksteves.com
Look out, Europe – here you come.

Flight Arrivals and Departures
http://www.flightarrivals.com
Stay on top of takeoffs and touchdowns across North America.

Global Freeloaders
http://www.globalfreeloaders.com
Take in a globetrotting dosser in exchange for some return hospitality.

Hotel Discount
http://www.hoteldiscount.com • http://www.hotelnet.co.uk
http://www.hotelwiz.com
Book hotels around the world. For backpacker rates, try:
http://www.hostels.com

How Far Is It?
http://www.indo.com/distance/
Calculate the distance between any two cities.

IgoUgo
http://www.igougo.com
Packed full of travellers' photos and journals, this roughguides.com
partner site offers candid first-hand information.

Incredible Adventures
http://www.incredible-adventures.com
Convert your cash into adrenaline.

Infiltration
http://www.infiltration.org
Confessions of a serial trespasser.

International Home Exchange
http://www.homexchange.com • http://www.sunswap.com
http://www.homebase-hols.com
Swap hideouts with a foreigner until the heat dies down.

International Student Travel Confederation
http://www.istc.org
Save money with an authentic international student card.

Journeywoman
http://www.journeywoman.com
Reporting in from the sister-beaten track.

The Man in Seat 61
http://www.seat61.com
International rail site, courtesy of an ex-British Rail station manager.
Times and fares from London to anywhere. You'll never feel the need to
take a plane again.

My Travel Rights
http://mytravelrights.com
Disgruntled? Maybe you'll be reimbursed.

No Shitting in the Toilet
http://www.noshit.com.au
Delighting in the oddities of low-budget travel.

Roadside America
http://www
.roadsideamerica.com
Strange attractions that
loom between squished animals on US highways.

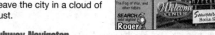

Sahara Overland
http://www
.sahara-overland.com
Leave the city in a cloud of
dust.

Subway Navigator
http://www.subwaynavigator.com
http://www.manhattanaddress.com
Estimate the journey times between city stations worldwide, or find the
right stop in NY.

TNT Live!
http://www.tntmagazine.com
Survive London and venture onward with aid from expat streetmags
TNT and *Southern Cross*.

Tourism Offices Worldwide
http://www.towd.com
Write to the local tourist office. They might send you a brochure.

Traffic and Road Conditions
http://www.accutraffic.com
Live traffic and weather updates across the US.

Travel health

Travel and Health Warnings

http://www.dfat.gov.au (Aus) • http://www.fco.gov.uk (UK)
http://travel.state.gov (US)

Don't ignore these bulletins if you're planning to visit a potential hot spot or health risk, but seek a second opinion before postponing your adventure. If you're off on business, try a professional advisory such as Kroll: http://www.krollworldwide.com

Travel Doctor

http://www.tmvc.com.au • http://www.cdc.gov/travel/
http://www.masta.org • http://www.travelhealth.co.uk
http://www.who.int

Brace yourself against the bugs eagerly awaiting your arrival. For a list of travel medicine clinics worldwide, see:
http://www.tripprep.com

And don't forget to pack *The Rough Guide to Travel Health* ...

Travelmag

http://www.travelmag.co.uk
Several intimate travel reflections monthly.

Travel Paperwork

http://www.travelpaperwork.com
Sort out the red tape – before you hit the border.

Travlang

http://www.travlang.com
Add another language to your repertoire.

Unclaimed Baggage

http://www.unclaimedbaggage.com
You lose it, they sell it.

Visit Britain
http://www.visitbritain.com • http://www.uktravel.com
Understand the Brit way of doing things.

Walkabout
http://www.walkabout.com.au
Get the lowdown on the land down under.

WebFlyer
http://www.webflyer.com
Keep tabs on frequent-flyer schemes.

World Heritage Listing
http://www.unesco.org/whc/
Plan your itinerary around international treasures.

Weather

Most news sites report the weather, but it's rarely up-to-the-minute. For that you need to go directly to your local weather bureau or a specialist weather-reporting service. For five-day forecasts, charts, storm warnings, allergy reports and satellite photos for thousands of cities worldwide, try:

Accuweather http://www.accuweather.com
CNN Weather http://www.cnn.com/WEATHER/
Intellicast http://www.intellicast.com
Weather Channel http://www.weather.com
Weather Underground http://www.wunderground.com
Yahoo! Weather http://weather.yahoo.com

For more intricate and timely detail, particularly outside the USA, drop by the local meteorological bureau:

Australia http://www.bom.gov.au
Brazil http://www.inmet.gov.br

Canada http://www.msc-smc.ec.gc.ca
China http://www.cma.gov.cn
Denmark http://www.dmi.dk
France http://www.meteo.fr
Germany http://www.dwd.de
Hong Kong http://www.info.gov.hk/hko/
India http://www.imd.ernet.in
Israel http://www.ims.gov.il
Italy http://www.meteoitalia.it
Latvia http://www.meteo.lv
Netherlands http://www.knmi.nl
New Zealand http://www.metservice.co.nz
Poland http://www.imgw.pl
Portugal http://www.meteo.pt
South Africa http://www.weathersa.co.za
Spain http://www.inm.es
Sweden http://www.smhi.se
UK http://www.metoffice.gov.uk
USA http://www.nws.noaa.gov

For other countries, amateur observations and the fanatical extremes of weather-watching, scan these specialist portals:

About Weather http://weather.about.com
Open Directory http://dmoz.org/News/Weather/
UM Weather http://cirrus.sprl.umich.edu/wxnet/
The Weather Resource http://www.nxdc.com/weather/
WMO Members http://www.wmo.ch/web-en/member.html

Climate Ark
http://www.climateark.org
Fret about coming climate change.

Ocean Weather
http://www.oceanweather.com

http://www.ssec.wisc.edu/data/sst.html
Chart swells and temperatures across the seven seas.

Snoweye
http://www.snoweye.com • http://www.snow-forecast.com
Spy on thousands of ski resorts worldwide through strategically hidden cameras, or simply have the forecasts beamed directly to your WAP phone.

WeatherPlanner
http://www.weatherplanner.com
Plan your washing around a long-term forecast.

Wild Weather
http://www.wildweather.com
http://australiasevereweather.com
http://www.storm-track.org • http://www.nssl.noaa.gov
Set your course into the eye of the storm.

World Climate
http://www.worldclimate.com • http://www.weatherbase.com
Off to Irkutzk next August? Here's what weather to expect.

World Meteorological Organization
http://www.wmo.ch
UN division that monitors global climate.

Weird

Absurd.org
http://www.absurd.org
Please do not adjust your set.

Aetherius Society
http://www.aetherius.org
Continue the legacy of the late Sir Dr George King, Primary Terrestrial Mental Channel of the Interplanetary Council.

Aliens and Soul Abduction
http://www.cia.com.au/brough/
Fact: spooky space dudes are stealing our souls. The Bible wouldn't lie: http://aliensinthebible.com

Bizarre
http://www.bizarremag.com
Updates from the print monthly that takes the investigation of strange phenomena more seriously than itself.

Christian Guide to Small Arms
http://www.frii.com/~gosplow/cgsa.html
"He that hath no sword, let him sell his garment, and buy one" – Luke 22:36. It's not just your right, it's your duty!

Circlemakers
http://www.circlemakers.org
Create crop circles to amuse New Agers and the press.

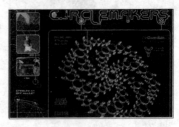

A Citizen from Hell
http://www.amightywind.com/hell/citizenhell.htm
If Hell sounds this bad, you don't want to go there.

Clonaid
http://www.clonaid.com
Thanks to the Raelians, we now know all life on earth was created in extraterrestrial laboratories. Here's where you can buy genuine cloned human livestock for the kitchen table. Ready as soon as the lab's finished.

Condiment Packet Museum
http://www.clearfour.com/condiment/
A beautiful, saucy collection of the little sachets that were designed to stop white shirts staying white.

The Darwin Awards
http://www.darwinawards.com
Each year the Darwin Award goes to the person who drops off the census register in the most spectacular fashion. Here's where to read about the runners-up and, er, winners.

Derek's Big Website of Wal-Mart Purchase Receipts
http://lightning.prohosting.com/~receipts/
An interactive collection where you can discuss everything from other people's shopping to Wal-Mart's product abbreviation policy. Trust us – it's better than it sounds.

Derm Cinema
http://www.skinema.com
Know your celebrity skin conditions. But would you recognize them under a gas mask?
http://www.geocities.com/TimesSquare/Alley/8207/

Dr MegaVolt
http://www.drmegavolt.com
The Doc sure sparked right up when they switched on the power, but could he cut it in the big league?
http://www3.bc.sympatico.ca/lightningsurvivor/

English Rose Press
http://www.englishrosepress.com
Diana sends her love from Heaven.

Flatulence Filter
http://flatulence-filter.com
Because life wasn't meant to be a gas.

Freaks, Geeks & Weirdness on the Web
http://www.rosemarywest.com/guide/
http://www.the-strange.com
http://www.student.nada.kth.se/~nv91-asa/
Make that three big sacks of assorted nuts, please.

Furniture Porn
http://www.furnitureporn.com
See well-upholstered chairs getting wood.

Future Horizons
http://www.futurehorizons.net
Snap off more than your fair share through solid-state circuitry.

Gallery of the Absurd
http://captainpackrat.com/Misc/galleryoftheabsurd.htm
Strange ways to sell strange stuff.

God Channel
http://www.godchannel.com
Relay requests to God via His official Internet channel.

Great Joy In Great Tribulation
http://www.dccsa.com/greatjoy/
Biblical proof that Prince Chuck is the Antichrist and key dates leading
to the end of the world. For more enlightenment – including how to
debug the pyramids – see:
http://members.aol.com/larrypahl/lpahl.htm

I Can Eat Glass Project
http://hcs.harvard.edu/~igp/glass.html
Deter excess foreign suitors and carpet dealers with the only words you
know in their language.

Illuminati News
http://www.illuminati-news.com
Storm into secret societies and thump your fist on the table.

International Ghost Hunters Society
http://www.ghostweb.com • http://www.ghostresearch.org
They never give up the ghost. Nab your own with:
http://www.maui.net/~emf/TriFieldNat.html

Itz Fun Tew Be Dat Kandie Kid
http://www.angelfire.com/ma/talulaQ/kandie.html
Mamas, don't let your babies grow up to be ravers.

Japanese Rabbit Balancing
http://shorterlink.com/?W2VGS5
Oolong sure can make a donkey of himself.

A Mathematical Survey of the English Language
http://www.geocities.com/garywaterbury/
Plot your future through simple arithmetic. Why didn't it occur to you before?

Mind Control Forum
http://mindcontrolforum.com
http://www.mindcontrolmanual.com
http://www.psychops.com • http://www.raven1.net
Unpick Big Brother's evil scheme and then put it to work on the dance-floor.

News of the Weird
http://www.thisistrue.com • http://www.weirdlist.com
Dotty clippings from the world press.

Nibiruan Council
http://www.nibiruancouncil.com
Stock your bar to welcome the heroic Starseeds, Walkins and Lightworkers from the Battlestar Nibiru, who will finally usher in the fifth dimensional reality.

Nobody Here
http://www.nobodyhere.com
Sometimes things with the least purpose are the most enthralling.

Non-Escalating Verbal Self-Defence
http://www.taxi1010.com
Fight insults by acting insane.

Planetary Activation Organization
http://www.paoweb.com
Prevent inter-dimensional dark forces from dominating our galaxy by ganging up with the Galactic Federation of Light.

Reincarnation.org
http://www.reincarnation-org.com
Stash your loot with this crowd, then come back to collect it in your next life.

Rense
http://www.rense.com
Fishy newsbreaks from talk-radio truth ferret, Jeff Rense. For more real life X-File blather, tune into: http://www.artbell.com

Reptoids
http://www.reptoids.com
Was that an alien or merely the subterranean descendant of a dinosaur?

Rocket Guy
http://www.rocketguy.com
Brian's about to launch himself into space. Bye-bye, Brian.

The Sacred Geometry Stories of Jesus Christ
http://www.jesus8880.com
How to decode the big J's mathematical word puzzle.

Sensoterapia
http://www.sensoterapia.com.co
Master the sex secret you'll never see revealed in this month's *Cleo*.

Sulabh International Museum of Toilets
http://www.sulabhtoiletmuseum.org
Follow the evolution of the ablution at the world's leading exhibition of
bathroom businessware. No need to take it sitting down:
http://www.restrooms.org

Things My Girlfriend and I Have Argued About
http://homepage.ntlworld.com/mil.millington/things.html
Add this page to that list.

Time Travel Devices
http://home.inreach.com/dov/tt.htm
Step back to a time that common sense forgot.

Toe Amputation Project
http://www.bme.freeq.com/spc/toecutter.htm
No big deal. He still has a couple left.

Toilet-train Your Cat
http://www.karawynn.net/mishacat/ • http://susandennis.com
How to point pusskins at the porcelain. And, for more tom(cat)foolery,
try: http://www.yogakitty.com

Xenophobic Persecution in the UK
http://www.five.org.uk
If you're below British standards, MI5 will punish you by TV.

ZetaTalk
http://www.zetatalk.com
Nancy's guests today are those elusive aliens that frolic in the autumn
mist at the bottom of her garden.

Part three

Contexts

A brief history
Glossary

15

A brief history of the Internet

The Internet may be a recent media phenomenon but as a concept it's actually older than most of its users. It was born in the 1960s – a long time before anyone coined the buzzwords "Information Superhighway". Of course, there's no question that the Net deserves its current level of attention. It really is a quantum leap in global communications, though – right now – it's still more of a prototype than a finished product. While Bill Gates and Al Gore rhapsodize about such household services as video-on-demand, most Netizens would be happy with a system fast enough to view static photos without waiting an age. Still, it's getting there.

The online bomb shelter

The concept of the Net might not have been hatched in Microsoft's cabinet war rooms, but it did play a role in a previous contest for world domination. It was 1957, at the height of the Cold War. The Soviets had just launched the first Sputnik, thus beating the USA into space. The race was on. In response the US Department of Defense formed the **Advanced Research Projects Agency (ARPA)** to bump up its technological prowess. Twelve years later, this spawned **ARPAnet** – a project to develop a military research network or, specifically, the world's first decentralized computer network.

In those days, no one had PCs. The computer world was based on mainframe computers and dumb terminals. These usually involved a gigantic, fragile box in a climate-controlled room, which acted as a hub, with a mass of cables spoking out to keyboard/monitor ensembles. The concept of independent intelligent processors pooling resources through a network was brave new territory that would require the development of new hardware, software and connectivity methods.

The driving force behind decentralization, ironically, was the bomb-proofing factor. Nuke a mainframe and the system goes down. But bombing a network would, at worst, remove only a few nodes. The remainder could route around it unharmed. Or so the theory went.

Wiring the world

Over the next decade, **research agencies** and **universities** flocked to join the network. US institutions such as UCLA,

MIT, Stanford and Harvard led the way and, in 1973, the network crossed the Atlantic to include University College London and Norway's Royal Radar Establishment.

The 1970s also saw the introduction of **electronic mail**, **FTP**, **Telnet** and what would become the **Usenet newsgroups**. The early 1980s brought **TCP/IP**, the **Domain Name System**, **Network News Transfer Protocol** and the European networks **EUnet** (European UNIX Network), **MiniTel** (the widely adopted French consumer network) and **JANET** (Joint Academic Network), as well as the Japanese **UNIX** Network. **ARPA** evolved to handle the research traffic, while a second network, **MILnet**, took over US military intelligence.

An important development took place in 1986, when the US National Science Foundation established **NSFnet** by linking five university super-computers at a backbone speed of 56Kbps. This opened the gateway for external universities to tap into superior processing power and share resources. In the three years between 1984 and 1988, the number of host computers on the **Internet** (as it was now being called) grew from about 1000 to over 60,000. NSFnet, meanwhile, increased its capacity to T1 (1544Kbps). Over the next few years, more and more countries joined the network, spanning the globe from Australia and New Zealand to Iceland, Israel, Brazil, India and Argentina.

It was at this time, too, that **Internet Relay Chat** (IRC) burst onto the scene by providing an alternative to CNN's incessant, but censored, Gulf War coverage. By this stage, the Net had grown far beyond its original charter. Although ARPA had succeeded in creating the basis for decentralized computing, whether it was actually a military success was debatable. It might have been bombproof, but it also opened new doors to espionage. It was never particularly secure, and it is suspected that Soviet agents routinely hacked in to forage for research data. In

1990, ARPAnet folded and NSFnet took over administering the Net.

Coming in from the cold

Global electronic communication was far too useful and versatile to stay confined to academics. Big business was starting to notice. The Cold War looked as if it was over and world economies were regaining confidence after the 1987 stock market savaging. In most places, market trading moved from the pits and blackboards onto computer screens. The financial sector expected fingertip real-time data and that desire was spreading. The world was ready for a people's network. And, since the Net was already in place, funded by taxpayers, there was really no excuse not to open it to the public.

In 1991, the NSF lifted its restrictions on enterprise. During the Net's early years, its "**Acceptable Use Policy**" specifically prohibited using the network for profit. Changing that policy opened the floodgates to commerce, with the greater public close behind.

However, before anyone could connect to the Net, someone had to sell them a connection. The **Commercial Internet eXchange** (**CIX**), a network of major commercial access providers, formed to create a commercial backbone and divert traffic from the NSFnet. Before long, dozens of budding ISPs began rigging up points of presence in their bedrooms. Meanwhile, NSFnet upgraded its backbone to T3 (44,736Kbps).

By this time, the Net had established itself as a viable medium for transferring data, but with one major problem. You had to know where to look. That process involved knowing a lot more about computers and the UNIX computing language than most punters would relish. The next few years saw an explosion in navigation protocols, such as WAIS, Gopher, Veronica and, most importantly, the now-dominant **World Wide Web**.

The gold rush begins

In 1989, Tim Berners-Lee of **CERN**, the Swiss particle physics institute, proposed the basis of the World Wide Web, initially as a means of sharing physics research. His goal was a seamless network in which data from any source could be accessed in a simple, consistent way with one program, on any type of computer. The Web did this, encompassing all existing infosystems such as FTP, Gopher and Usenet, without alteration. It remains an unqualified success.

As the number of Internet hosts exceeded one million, the **Internet Society** was formed to brainstorm protocols and attempt to coordinate and direct the Net's escalating expansion. **Mosaic** – the first graphical **Web browser** – was released, and declared to be the "killer application of the 1990s". It made navigating the Internet as simple as pointing and clicking, and took away the need to know UNIX. The Web's traffic increased by 25-fold in the year up to June 1994, and domain names for **commercial organizations** (.com) began to outnumber those of educational institutions (.edu).

As the Web grew, so too did the global village. The media began to notice, slowly realizing that the Internet was something that went way beyond propeller-heads and students. Almost every country in the world had joined the Net. Even the White House was online.

Of course, as word of a captive market got around, entrepreneurial brains went into overdrive. Canter & Seigel, an Arizona law firm, notoriously "**spammed**" Usenet with **advertisements** for the US green card lottery. Although the Net was tentatively open for business, crossposting advertisements to every newsgroup was decidedly bad form. Such was the ensuing wrath that C&S had no chance of filtering out genuine responses from the server-breaking level of hate mail they received. A precedent

was thus established for **how not to do business on the Net**.
Pizza Hut, by contrast, showed how to do it subtly by setting up
a trial service on the Web. Although it generated wads of positive publicity, it too was doomed by impracticalities.
Nevertheless, the ball had begun to roll.

The homesteaders

As individuals arrived to stake out Web territory, businesses followed. Most had no idea what to do once they got their brand
online. Too many arrived with a bang, only to peter out in a per-
petuity of "under construction" signs. Soon business cards not only
sported email addresses, but Web addresses as well. And, rather than
send a CV and stiff letter, job aspirants could now send a brief
email accompanied with a "see my webpage" for further details.

The Internet moved out of the realm of luxury into an elite
necessity, verging toward a commodity. Some early business sites
gathered such a following that by 1995 they were able to charge
high rates for advertising banners. A few, including Web **portals**
such as **InfoSeek** and **Yahoo!**, made it to the Stock Exchange
boards, while others, like **GNN**, attracted buyers.

But it wasn't all success. Copyright lawyers arrived in droves.
Well-meaning devotees, cheeky opportunists and info-terrorists
alike felt the iron fists of Lego, McDonald's, MTV, the Louvre,
Fox, Sony, the Church of Scientology and others clamp down
on their "unofficial websites" or newsgroups. It wasn't always a
case of corporate right but of might, as small players couldn't
foot the expenses to test **new legal boundaries**. The honeymoon was officially over.

Point of no return

By the beginning of 1995, the Net was well and truly within the
public realm. It was impossible to escape. The media became

bored with extolling its virtues, so it turned to **sensationalism**. The Net reached the status of an Oprah Winfrey issue. New tales of hacking, porn, bombmaking, terrorist handbooks, homebreaking and sexual harassment began to tarnish the Internet's iconic position as the great international equalizer. But that didn't stop businesses, schools, banks, government bodies, politicians and consumers from swarming online, nor the major **Online Services** – such as CompuServe, America Online and Prodigy, which had been developing in parallel since the late 1980s – from adding Internet access as a sideline to their existing private networks.

As 1995 progressed, **Mosaic**, the previous year's killer application, lost its footing to a superior browser, **Netscape**. Not such big news, you might imagine, but after a half-year of rigorous beta-testing, Netscape went public with the third-largest-ever NASDAQ IPO share value – around $2.4bn.

Meantime, Microsoft, which had formerly disregarded the Internet, released **Windows 95**, a PC operating platform incorporating access to the controversial **Microsoft Network**. Although **IBM** had done a similar thing six months earlier with **OS/2 Warp** and its **IBM Global Network**, Microsoft's was an altogether different scheme. It offered full Net access, but its real product was its own separate network, which many people feared might supersede the Net, giving Microsoft an unholy reign over information distribution. But that never happened. Within months, Microsoft – smarting from bad press and finding the Net a larger animal even than itself – about-turned and declared a full commitment to furthering the Internet.

Browser wars

As Microsoft advanced, Netscape continued pushing the envelope, driving the Web into new territory with each beta release. New enhancements arrived at such a rate that competitors began to drop out as quickly as they appeared. This was the era of "This page looks best if viewed with Netscape". Of course, it wasn't just Netscape, since much of the new activity stemmed from the innovative products of third-party developers such as **MacroMedia** (**Shockwave**), **Progressive Networks** (**RealAudio**), **Apple** (**QuickTime**) and **Sun** (**Java**). The Web began to spring to life with animations, music, 3D worlds and all sorts of new tricks.

While Netscape's market dominance gave developers the confidence to accept it as the de facto standard, treating it as a kind of Internet operating system into which to "plug" their products, Microsoft (an old hand at taking possession of cleared territory) began to launch a whole series of free Net tools. These included **Internet Explorer**, a browser with enhancements of its own including **ActiveX**, a Web-centric programming environment more powerful than the much-lauded **Java** but without the same platform independence, and clearly geared toward advancing Microsoft's software dominance. Not only was Internet Explorer suddenly the only other browser in the race, unlike Netscape it was genuinely free. And many were not only rating it as the better product, but also crediting Microsoft with a broader vision of the Net's direction.

By mid-1997, every Online Service and almost every major ISP had signed deals with Microsoft to distribute its browser. Even intervention by the US Department of Justice over Microsoft's (logical but monopolistic) bundling of Internet Explorer as an integral part of Windows 98 couldn't impede its progress. Netscape looked bruised. While it continued shipping minor upgrades, it no longer led either in market share or innovation. In desperation, it handed over the project of completely reworking the code to the general programming public at **Mozilla.org**. When AOL bought Netscape in early 1999, little doubt remained: Netscape had given up the fight.

Found on the Internet

Skipping back to late 1995, the backlash against Internet freedom had moved into full flight. The expression "**found on the Internet**" became the news tag of the minute, depicting the Net as the source of everything evil from bomb recipes to child pornography. While editors and commentators, often with little direct experience of the Net, urged that "children" be protected, the Net's own media and opinion shakers pushed the **freedom of speech** barrow. It became apparent that this uncensored, uncontrollable new medium could shake the very foundations of democracy.

At first politicians didn't take much notice. Few could even grasp the concept of what the Net was about, let alone figure out a way to regulate its activities. The first, and easiest, target was **porn**, resulting in raids on hundreds of **private bulletin boards** worldwide and a few much-publicized convictions for the possession of child porn. BBSs were sitting ducks, being mostly self-contained and run by someone who could take the rap. Net activists, however, feared that the primary objective was to send a ripple of fear through a Net community that believed it was bigger than the law, and to soften the public to the notion that the Internet, as it stood, posed a threat to national wellbeing.

In December 1995, at the request of German authorities, **CompuServe** cut its newsfeed to exclude the bulk of newsgroups carrying sexual material. But the groups cut weren't just pornographers: some were dedicated to gay and abortion issues. This brought to light the difficulty in drawing the lines of obscenity and the problems with publishing across foreign boundaries. Next came the **US Communications Decency Act**, a proposed legislation to forbid the online publication of "obscene" material. It was poorly conceived, however, and, following opposition from a very broad range of groups (including such mainstream bodies as the American Libraries Association), was overturned, the decision later being upheld in the Supreme Court.

Outside the US, meanwhile, more authorities reacted. In **France**, three ISP chiefs were temporarily jailed for supplying obscene newsgroups, while in **Australia** police prosecuted several users for downloading child porn. NSW courts introduced legislation banning obscene material with such loose wording that the Internet itself could be deemed illegal – if the law is ever tested. In **Britain**, the police tried a "voluntary" approach in mid-1996, identifying newsgroups that carried pornography beyond the pale and requesting that providers remove them from their feed. Most complied, but there was unease within the Internet industry that this was the wrong approach – the same groups would migrate elsewhere and the root of the problem would remain.

But the debate was, and is, about far more than porn, despite the huffing and puffing. For **Net fundamentalists**, the issue is about holding ground against any compromises in liberty and retaining the global village as a political force – one that is potentially capable of bringing down governments and large corporations. Indeed, they argue that these battles over publishing freedom have shown governments to be out of touch with both technology and the social undercurrent, and that in the long run the balance of power will shift towards the people, towards a new democracy.

Wiretapping

Another slow-news-day story of the mid-1990s depicted **hackers** ruling networks, stealing money and creating havoc. Great reading, but the reality was less alarming. Although the US Department of Defense reported hundreds of thousands of network breakins, they claimed it was more annoying than damaging, while in the commercial world little went astray except the odd credit card file. (Bear in mind that every time you hand your credit card to a shop assistant they get the same information.) In fact, by and large, for an online population greater than the combined size of New York, Moscow, London, Calcutta and Tokyo, there were surprisingly few noteworthy crimes. Yet the perception remained that the Net was too unsafe for the exchange of sensitive information such as payment details.

Libertarians raged at the US Government's refusal to lift export bans on crack-proof **encryption algorithms**. But cryptography, the science of message coding, has traditionally been classified as a weapon and thus export of encryption falls under the Arms Control acts. Encryption requires a secret key to open the contents of a message and often another public key to code the message. These keys can be generated for regular use by individuals or, in the case of Web transactions, simply for one session upon agreement between the server and client. Several governments proposed to employ official authorities to keep a register of all secret keys and surrender them upon warrant – an unpopular proposal, to put it mildly, among a Net community who regard invasion of privacy as an issue equal in importance to censorship, and government monitors as instruments of repression.

However, authorities were so used to being able to tap phones, intercept mail and install listening devices to aid investigations, they didn't relish giving up that freedom either. Government officials made a lot of noise about needing to monitor data to protect national security, though their true motives probably involve monitoring internal insurgence and catching tax cheats – stuff they're not really supposed to do but we put up with anyway because if we're law-abiding it's mostly in our best interests.

The implications of such obstinacy went far beyond personal privacy. Business awaited browsers that could talk to commerce servers using totally snooper-proof encryption. Strong encryption technology had already been built into browsers, but was illegal to export them from the US. At any rate, **the law was finally relaxed in mid-2000**.

The entertainment arrives

While politicians, big business, bankers, telcos and online action groups such as **CommerceNet** and the **Electronic Frontier Foundation** fretted the future of privacy and its impact on digital commerce, the online world partied on regardless. If 1996 was the year of the Web, then 1997 was the year the **games** began. Netizens had been swapping chess moves, playing dress-up and struggling with the odd network game over the Net for years, but it took id Software's **Quake** to lure the gaming masses online. Not to miss out, Online Services and ISPs took steps to prioritize game traffic, while hard-core corporate data moved further back on the shelves.

Music took off, too. **Bands** and **DJs** routinely streamed concerts over the Net, while celebrities such as Michael Jackson, Joe Dolce and Paul McCartney bared their souls in public chat rooms. Webpages came alive with the sound of music, from cheesy synthesized backgrounds to live radio feeds. Many online music stores like **CDNow** reported profits, while **Amazon** became a major force in bookselling.

And then there was the Net as a prime news medium. As **Pathfinder** touched down on Mars, back on Earth millions logged into NASA sites to scour the Martian landscape for traces of life. China marched into Hong Kong, Tiger Woods rewrote golfing history, Australia regained the Ashes and Mike Tyson fell from grace – all live on the Net. In response to this breaking of news on websites and newsgroups, an increasing number of **print newspapers** began delivering online versions before their hard copies hit the stands. In 1997, if you weren't on the Net, you weren't in the media.

The casualties

Not everyone had reason to party in 1997. **Cybercafés** – touted the height of cool in 1995 – tended to flop as quickly as they appeared, as did many small **Internet Service Providers** (if they weren't swallowed by larger fish). From over thirty **browsers** in early 1996, less than a year later only two real players – Netscape and Microsoft – remained in the game. The also-ran software houses that initially thrived on the Net's avenue for distribution and promotion faded from view as the two browser giants ruthlessly crammed more features into their plug-and-play Web desktops. Microsoft and scores of other software developers declared that their future products would be able to update themselves online, either automatically or by clicking in the right place. So much for the software dealer.

Meanwhile, **Web TV** arrived delivering webpages and email onto home TV screens. It offered a cheap, simple alternative to PCs, but found its way to a smaller niche market than its fanfare predicted.

The whole **Web design industry** was due for a shakeout. Web cowboys who'd charged through the teeth for cornering the homepage design scam– yet lacked the programming skills to code, the artistic merit to design or the spelling standards to edit – were left exposed by the emerging professionalism. **New media** had come of age. The top Web chimps reworked their CVs and pitched in with online design houses. Major ad agencies formed new media departments, and splashed Web addresses over everything from milk cartons to toothpaste tubes.

Bizarrely, though, 1997's best-known Web design team, **Higher Source**, will be remembered not for HTML handiwork but for publishing their cult's agenda to commit suicide in conjunction with the passing of the Hale-Bopp comet. This was the Internet as major news story. Within hours of the mass suicide, several sites appeared spoofing both its corporate pages as well as its cult, **Heaven's Gate**. Days later, there were enough to spawn four new Yahoo! subdirectories.

Back in the real world of business and money, major companies have played surprisingly by the book, observing **Netiquette** – the Net's informal code of conduct. The marriage has been awkward but generally happy. Even the absurd court cases between blockbuster sites such as **Microsoft Sidewalk v TicketMaster** and **Amazon v Barnes and Noble** (over the "biggest bookstore in the world" claim) did little to convince Netizens that they were witnessing anything more than carefully orchestrated publicity stunts. Indeed, many felt launching a website without some kind of legal suit was a waste of free publicity. It seemed like just a bit of fun. And as big money flowed in, **bandwidths** increased, content improved, ma and pa popped aboard and the online experience richened.

Alas, the same couldn't be said for the new-school entrepreneurs. Low advertising costs saw **Usenet newsgroups and email intrays** choked with crossposted get-rich schemes, network marketing plans and porno adverts. Further, unprecedented **banks of email** broke servers at AOL, MSN and scores of smaller providers. Netcom was temporarily forced to bar all mail originating from **Hotmail**, the most popular free Web email service and thus a safe haven for fly-by-night operators, due to the level of spam originating from its domain. At the same time, in July 1997, a misplaced digger ripped up a vital US backbone artery and darkened large parts of the Net – something many had presumed impossible – and reduced the worldwide network to a crawl. The Net was nuclear-proof, maybe, but certainly not invulnerable.

The world's biggest playground

By the end of 1997, the Net's population had skyrocketed to well over a hundred million. The media increasingly relied on it for research and, in the process, began to understand it. It could no longer be written off as geek-land when it was thrust this far into mainstream consciousness. Notable among the most recent arrivals were the so-called "**silver surfers**", predominantly retirees. Indeed, the Net was looking not only useful but essential, and those without it had good reason to feel left behind.

This new maturity arrived on the back of email, with the Web hot on its heels. As toner sales plummeted, surveys indicated that email had not only overtaken the fax but possibly even the telephone as the business communication tool of choice. However, at the same time, it could also lay claim to being the greatest time-waster ever introduced into an office – with staff spending large chunks of the day reading circulars, forwarding curios and flirting with their online pals.

The speed that email offered, and the ease with which entire address books could be carbon-copied, altered the six degrees of separation. Something with universal appeal – like the infernal **dancing baby animation** that did the rounds in 1999 – could be disseminated to millions within a matter of hours, potentially reaching everyone on the Net within days. And, as most journalists were hooked in by this stage, whatever circulated on the Net often found its way into other media formats. Not surprisingly, the fastest-moving chain emails were often hoaxes. One such prank, an address of sensible old-timer advice supposedly delivered by Kurt Vonnegut to MIT graduates (but actually taken from Mary Schmick's *Chicago Tribune* column), saturated the Net within a week. The director of *Romeo+Juliet*, Baz Luhrmann, was so taken he put it to music resulting in the cult hit "Sunscreen", which even more incredibly was re-spoofed into a XXXX beer advert. All within six months.

On a more annoying note, almost everyone received **virus hoaxes** that warned not to open email with certain subject headings. Millions took them seriously, earnestly forwarding them to their entire address books. An email campaign kicked off by Howard Stern propelled "Hank, the ugly drunken dwarf" to the top of *People*'s 100 Most Beautiful People poll as voted on the Net. Meanwhile, the Chinese community rallied to push Michelle Kwan into second place. But the biggest coup of all was **Matt Drudge**'s email leaking Bill Clinton's inappropriate affair with Monica Lewinsky, which sent the old-world media into the biggest feeding frenzy since the OJ trial. Although it might not have brought down the most powerful man in the world, it showed how in 1998, almost anyone, anywhere, could be heard.

The show must go on

In May 1998, the blossoming media romance with hackers as urban folk heroes turned sour when a consortium of good-fairy hackers, known as the **L0pht**, assured a US Senate Government Affairs Committee that they, or someone less benevolent, could render the Net entirely unusable within half an hour. It wasn't meant as a threat, but a call to arms against the apathy of those who'd designed, sold and administered the systems. The Pentagon had already been penetrated (by a young Israeli hacker), and though most reported attacks amounted to little more than vandalism, with an increasing number of essential services tapped in, the probability of major disaster loomed.

Undeterred, Net commerce continued to break into new territories. **Music**, in particular, looked right at home with the arrival of DIY CD compilation shops and several major artists such as Massive Attack, Willie Nelson and the Beach Boys airing their new releases on the Net in MP3 before unleashing them on CD. However, these exclusive previews weren't always intentional. For instance, Swervedriver's beleaguered "99th Dream" found its way onto Net bootleg almost a year before its official release.

By now, celebrity chat appearances hardly raised an eyebrow. Even major powerbrokers like Clinton and Yeltsin had appeared before an online inquisition. To top it off, in April 1998, Koko, a 300lb gorilla, fronted up to confess to some 20,000 chatsters that she'd rather be playing with Smokey, her pet kitten.

The red-light district

Despite the bottomless reserves of free Web space, personal vanity pages and Web diaries took a downturn in 1998. The novelty was passing, a sign perhaps that the Web was growing up. This didn't, however, prevent live Web cameras, better known as **webcams**, from enjoying a popularity resurgence. But this time around they weren't so much being pointed at lizards, fish, ski slopes or intersections, but at whoever connected them to the Net – a fad which resulted in numerous bizarre excursions in exhibitionism from some very ordinary folk. Leading the fray was the entirely unremarkable **Jennifer Ringley**, who became a Web household name simply for letting the world see her move about her college room – clothed and (very occasionally) otherwise. She might have only been famous for being famous, but it was fame enough to land her a syndicated newspaper column about showing off and, of course, a tidy packet from the thousands of subscribers who paid real money to access Jennicam.

But this was the tame end of the Net's trade in voyeurism. These were boom times for pornographers. Research suggested that as much as ninety percent of network traffic was consumed by porn images. That's not to suggest that anywhere near ninety percent of users were involved, only that the images consume so much bandwidth. The story in Usenet was even more dire, with more than eighty percent of the non-binary traffic hogged by spam and spam cancel messages. Meanwhile, the three top Web search aids, **HotBot**, **AltaVista** and **Yahoo!**, served click-through banners on suggestive keywords. However you felt about pornography from a moral standpoint, it had definitely become a nuisance.

The bottleneck

As 1998 progressed, **cable Internet access** became increasingly available – and even affordable in the USA. New subscribers could suddenly jump from download speeds of, at best, 56Kbps to as high as 10Mbps. Meanwhile several telcos, such as PacBell and GTE, began rolling out **ADSL**, another broadband technology capable of megabit access, this time over plain copper telephone wires. However, even at these speeds, users still had to deal with the same old bottleneck; namely, the Internet's backbone, which had been struggling to cope with even the low-speed dial-up traffic.

The power to **upgrade the backbone** – or (more correctly) backbones – lies in the hands of those who own the major cables and thus effectively control the Internet. It's always seemed inevitable that the global telecommunication superpowers would starve the smaller players out of the market. And the emergence of Internet telephony has forced telcos to look further down the track at the broader scenario where whoever controls the Internet not only controls data but voice traffic as well. They recognize that their core business could be eroded by satellite and cable companies. To survive, telcos need to compete on the same level, provide an alternative or join forces with their rivals. At the moment all three seem viable options.

The dust clears, but the fog remains

As we packed up shop for the millennium, fretting over double-digit date blunders, the Internet settled into a **consolidation phase**. For the most part, what was hot got hotter while the remainder atrophied. Broadband cable, ADSL and satellite access forged ahead, particularly in the US and Australia. Meanwhile, in the UK, British Telecom stooped to an eleventh-hour exploit on its unpopular metered local call system, weaselling deals with local ISPs to enable free access by divvying up its phone bill booty. Surprisingly, instead of torching 10 Downing Street for allowing the situation to exist in the first place, browbeaten Brits snapped it up, propelling free-access pioneer **Freeserve** to the top of the ISP pops within months. BT refused to budge on unmetered local calls but, in response to increasingly vocal dissent, finally launched fixed-rate modem access in 2001, with unmetered ADSL following soon after.

Interest in **online commerce** surged with explosive growth in stock trading, auctions, travel booking and mail order computers. Big-budget empire builders such as AOL, Amazon, Cisco, Disney, Excite, Microsoft and Real Networks hit overdrive, announcing intertwined strategic mergers, and continued swallowing and stomping on smaller talent. Most notably AOL, with little more than a dip into petty cash, wolfed down Netscape – not, as many assumed, for its revolutionary browser, but for the sizable user-base still buzzing its browser's default homepage. This, however, wasn't the Netscape of the mid-1990s, but a defeated relic that had lost its way, ceased innovating and appeared unable to ship products. Its legacy had been passed over to **Microsoft**, which remained in court squabbling over Internet Explorer, Windows 98 and its success in cornering all but some five percent of the operating system market share. Apart from whatever voyeuristic pleasure could be gained from king-hitting computing's tallest poppy, the Department of Justice's case grew increasingly meaningless against the broader backdrop. The computer-wielding public weren't too worried about lack of choice, but lack of quality. Even Apple's allegedly foolproof **iMac** fell way short of a sturdy carriage to traverse the

Net, play games and make life generally more push-button-friendly.

By this stage the Internet was ready to become a public utility, but both the computing and access provision industries remained rooted within a hobbyist mindset. As PC dealers shamelessly crammed their systems with interfering utilities, ISPs continued to supply inadequate bandwidth, unreliable software and irresponsible advice. Yet no alternative existed, and governments appeared incapable of intelligent input. As the twentieth century bit the dust, you didn't have to be a geek to get on the Net, but it sure didn't hurt to know your stuff.

The American dream

Doomsday was not televised live as daylight broke across the year 2000. Planes didn't crash, Washington wasn't nuked and ATMs did not randomly eject crisp dollar bills. Instead, attention turned to the ever-inflating Internet stock bubble. The new tech stocks were driving the biggest speculative frenzy since Tulipmania. Every grandmother and her cabbie wanted in on the **dotcom** action. **Cisco Systems**, a network hardware supplier and hardly a household name, celebrated its tenth birthday by briefly becoming the world's biggest company (in terms of market cap). To add further insult to the old world order, AOL, foster home to twenty million chirpy AOLers, offered its hand to the **TIME–Warner** cross-media conglomerate. Meanwhile **Bill Gates**, the billionaire icon of the new American dream, continued defiantly delivering his own brand of truth, justice and the Microsoft way to the desktops of nineteen out of twenty computers. What could possibly go wrong?

Too much gold for one gringo

Enter US **District Judge Thomas Penfield Jackson**, who

declared that Microsoft had maintained its monopoly by anti-competitive means, and that it should sever both physical and corporate ties between its Internet software and Windows. This ruling, he assured, would result in higher-quality products due to increased competition, which raised the question why software standards weren't directly on trial instead. Microsoft had made few friends outside the fans of Ayn Rand, particularly within the Mac-monopolized media, so any public spanking was welcomed. Yet, in reality, it was an unsatisfying outcome for all concerned. Not least for investors, whose tech share portfolios crumbled. And so that was it for the speculative dotcom start ups. As the house of Gates fell, so too did the bricks around it. By the time **Boo.com** folded in May 2000, "dotcom" was already a dirty word.

With an appeal pending in the Supreme Court, Microsoft brazenly released **ME**, yet another version of Windows with Internet Explorer inside, and furthermore announced that its future applications would be delivered on demand across the Net. What little sympathy remained for Bill and his merry cast of outlaws was almost completely eroded.

Nobody can stop the music

As wave after wave of email-borne viruses sneezed from Outlook address books, it seemed clear that most office workers lacked basic computer training. Overlooked in the endless blather of mass media hysteria was the simple truth that **Melissa**, **Happy 99**, **I Love You** and similar Internet worms could only be propagated by the grossly incompetent. It also seemed certain that it would happen again.

But viruses weren't the only source of mischief. A 15-year-old Canadian, going by the cute name of "Mafiaboy", unleashed a bevy of **Denial of Service** attacks, temporarily knocking out several high-profile websites such as Yahoo!, Amazon and eTrade. Despite his relatively low level of technical expertise he was able to outwit the FBI for almost three months. Even then it was only his chat-room confession that triggered the arrest.

With pirate **MP3 music tracks** hogging the bulk of college network bandwidth, legal action inevitably followed. **Napster** faced the music against stadium rockers Metallica, and the Recording Industry Association of America sued **MP3.com** over its ingenious Beam-It service. While the holders of copyright won in the courts of law, back in the real world it was business as usual – with the added extra that the publicity drew millions of new music lovers into the trading loop. As mounting legal pressure pummelled Napster into the commercial reality of blocking copyrighted material from its servers, traders merely migrated to decentralized networks such as **WinMX** and **Gnutella**.

Dumb money

As the **new economy** lay gutted on the screens of the NAS-DAQ and beyond, many predicted a global meltdown in 2001. Yet, despite ninety percent falls in dotcom blue-chips like Cisco, Amazon and Yahoo!, the broader economy remained surprisingly intact. So too did Microsoft, with the DC Court of Appeals overruling Judge Jackson's remedy to split the company. The appropriate sentence for its browser war crimes remains to be decided by the new-look Bush Department of Justice.

Hard cash failures ushered in hard cold facts, and one of those was no secret to those who'd been online since the BBS days. The Net's popularity had been largely driven by the lure of something for nothing. Few wanted to pay when so much was free. Few wanted to click on banner ads. And even fewer could profit from advertising in someone's diary. As we waved good-bye to the dumber dotcoms, we also bid farewell to a romantic delusion called **cyberspace**. The Internet was no longer an exotic frontier but a ubiquitous utility like the telephone.

And it certainly was everywhere. Suddenly it seemed mandatory to cast anything online that could be cast online, from inane Coke vending machines to inane reality TV experiments like *Big Brother*. So, of course, it seemed logical that celebrity bomber Timothy McVeigh should exit the jeering hordes live via RealVideo. When a federal judge refused the Entertainment Network's request to webcast the execution in April 2001, it was the surest sign we'd entered a brave new era – one where common sense still stood a chance.

Still rocking in the free world

When outright war was declared on a small army of Islamic revolutionaries in September 2001, interest plummeted in the plight of those suffering in the aftermath of the new media revolution. According to the papers, the Internet was henceforth last year's news. Full-colour IT lift-outs become mono spreads as sponsors cut staff and budgets to match.

But a quick trip to any backpacker ghetto would quickly dispel notions of a Net fallen from grace. Strings of cybercafés bid freshly tattooed teens to book tickets, Instant Message and Hotmail their oldies for cash. Meanwhile, back home, their chums were sampling the pleasures – and frustrations – of high-speed access via **ADSL**, **cable** and **WiFi**.

As broadband exploded, so too did **P2P** (peer to peer) **file sharing**. What began as a trickle of MP3s was now a torrent of music, movies and warez gushing across the FastTrack (Kazaa, Morpheus & Grokster) and eDonkey networks, seemingly impervious to legal intervention. Labels were already hurting, claimed the International Federation of the Phonographic Industry, pointing to a global drop in CD sales of five percent for the year 2000. Considering the economic downturn, these figures didn't seem all that bad, but as millions of new tracks hit the networks daily no one doubted their reason to worry.

So many sites, so little time

With storage freebies in freefall, independent webmasters became more concerned with staying afloat than trying to be clever. Unfortunately, popularity alone didn't guarantee survival in dot-pessimistic 2002. More likely, it meant higher hosting costs, and these were rarely offset by pathetic returns on click-thru banner ads and occasional subscriptions. Even spam magnet **Hotmail**, the original free stooge, began busking for cash to help fund its massive server farms.

Web-only entities were always going to struggle in an environment more suited to propagating real-world information. Astute organizations now recognized the Web as a media expense rather than a revenue raiser, and had gradually learned to make it work in their favour.

And so too had the clickees, who were now finding their way courtesy of **Google** rather than stumbling through long lists of links. Despite talk of doom, gloom and dot-bust, the Internet was beginning to live up to its claims, and those who'd learned to use it had every reason to feel smug.

A brighter tomorrow

Now that the **people's network** has the globe in an irreversible stranglehold, you might assume the wired revolution is as good as over. Perhaps it is, but for those in the dark the reality can be less comforting. A passable knowledge of the Internet in 1997 was enough to land you a job. Today it's becoming a prerequisite in many fields – a case of get online or get left behind. But the most worrisome aspect is not the difficulty in getting online, but the time involved in keeping up-to-date, and its stress on our physical, mental and social wellbeing.

Still, like it or not, the Net is the closest thing yet to an all-encompassing snapshot of the human race. Never before have our words and actions been so immediately accountable in front of such a far-reaching audience. If we're scammed, we can instantly warn others. If we believe there's a government cover-up, we can expose it through the Net. If we want to be heard, no matter what it is we have to say, we can tell it to the Net. And, in the same way, if we need to know more, or we need to find numbers, we can turn to it for help.

The problem with the kind of rapid improvement that we've seen over the last few years is that our expectations grow to meet it. But the Net, even at the age of thirty-something, is still only in its infancy. So be patient – enjoy it for what it is today, and complain, but not too much. One day you'll look back and get all nostalgic about the times you logged into the world through old copper telephone wires. It's amazing it works at all.

16

Glossary

A

ActiveX Microsoft concept that allows a program to run inside a webpage.

Add/Remove Programs Correct place to uninstall programs from Windows. Found in the Control Panel.

ADSL (**A**synchronous **D**igital **S**ubscriber **L**ine). Broadband over the phone line.

Anonymous FTP server Remote computer, with a publicly accessible file archive, that accepts "anonymous" as the log-in name and an email address as the password.

Antivirus scanner Program that detects, and sometimes removes, computer viruses.

AOL (**A**merica **On**line). Last surviving Online Service. Loved by all.

Applet A small program.

Archive File that bundles a set of other files together under a single name for transfer or backup. Often compressed to reduce size, or encrypted for privacy.

Attachment File included with email or other form of message.

B

Backbone Set of paths that carry long-haul Net traffic.

Bandwidth Size of the data pipeline. Increase bandwidth and more data can flow at once.

Binary file Any file that contains more than plain text, such as a program or image.

BinHex Method of encoding, used on Macs.

Bookmarks Netscape file used to store Web addresses.

Bounced mail Email returned to sender.

Bps (**B**its **p**er **s**econd). Basic measure of data transfer.

Broadband High-speed Internet access.

Browser Web viewing program such as Internet Explorer.

Buffer Temporary data storage.

Bug Logical, physical or programming error in software or hardware that causes a recurring malfunction.

C

Cache Temporary storage space.

Client Program that accesses information across a network, such as a Web browser or newsreader.

COM port See Serial port

Context menu See Mouse menu

Crack Break a program's security, integrity or registration system, or fake a user ID.

Crash When a program or operating system fails to respond or causes other programs to malfunction.

Cyber In IRC, may be short for "cybersex", that is, the online equivalent of phone sex.

Cyberspace Coined by science-fiction writer William Gibson, to describe the virtual world that exists within the marriage of computers, telecommunication networks and digital media.

D

Default The standard settings.

Dialog box Window that appears on the screen to ask or tell you something.

Dial-up connection Temporary network connection between two computers via a telephone line.

Digital signing Encrypted data appended to a message to identify the sender.

DNS **D**omain **N**ame **S**ystem. The system that locates the numerical IP address corresponding to a host name.

Domain Part of the DNS name that specifies details about the host, such as its location and whether it is part of a commercial (**.com**), government (**.gov**) or educational (**.edu**) entity.

Download To copy files from a remote computer to your own.

Driver Small program that acts like a translator between a device and programs that use that device.

DSL (**D**igital **S**ubscriber **L**ine). Encompasses all forms including ADSL. Sometimes called xDSL.

E

Email Electronic mail carried on the Net.

Email address The unique private Internet address to which email is sent. Takes the form **user@host**

F

FAQ (**F**requently **A**sked **Q**uestions). Document that answers the most commonly asked questions on a particular topic.

File Anything stored on a computer, such as a program, image or document.

File compression Reducing a file's size for transfer or storage.

File extension Set of characters added to the end of a filename (after a full stop) intended to identify the file as a member of a category (file type). For example, the extension .TXT identifies a text file.

Finger A program that can return stored data on UNIX users or other information such as weather updates. Often disabled for security reasons.

Firewall Network security system used to restrict external and internal traffic.

Firmware Software routines stored in the read-only memory of a hardware device.

Frag Network gaming term meaning "to destroy or fragment". Came from DOOM.

FTP **F**ile **T**ransfer **P**rotocol. Standard method of moving files across the Internet.

G

GIF (**G**raphic **I**mage **F**ile format). Compressed graphics format prefered for use in small Web images such as buttons and icons.

Google Popular Web search engine located at
http://www.google.com

Gopher Defunct menu-based system for retrieving Internet archives, usually organized by subject.

H

Hacker Someone who gets off on breaking through computer security and limitations. A cracker is a criminal hacker.

Header Pre-data part of a packet, containing source and destination addresses, error checking, and other fields. Also the first part of an email or news posting which contains, among other things, the sender's details and time sent.

Home page Either the first page loaded by your browser at startup, or the main Web document for a particular group, organization or person.

Host Computer that offers some sort of services to networked users.

HTML (**H**yper**T**ext **M**arkup **L**anguage.) The language used to create Web documents.

HyperText links The "clickable" links or "hot spots" that interconnect pages on the Web.

I

ICQ Popular Instant messaging program. http://www.icq.com

Image map A Web image that contains multiple links. Which link you take depends on where you click.

IMAP (**I**nternet **M**essage **A**ccess **P**rotocol). Standard email access protocol that's superior to POP3 in that you can selectively retrieve messages or parts thereof as well as manage folders on the server.

Infinite loop See loop.

Install To place a program's working files onto a computer so that it's ready to be set up and used. Normally done by clicking on a setup file (often called setup.exe).

Instant Messaging Point-to-point chat such as ICQ.

Internet Co-operatively run global collection of computer networks with a common addressing scheme.

Internet connection sharing (ICS) Allows a networked computer to access the Internet through another's connection. A feature of Windows 98 SE and later.

Internet Explorer Microsoft's Web browser bundled with the operating system since Windows 98. Download from: http://www.microsoft.com/ie/

Internet Favorites Internet Explorer folder for filing Web addresses.

Internet Shortcut Microsoft's terminology for a Web address or URL.

IP (**I**nternet **P**rotocol). The most important protocol upon which the Internet is based. Defines how packets of data get from source to destination.

IP address Every computer connected to the Internet has an IP address (written in dotted numerical notation), which corresponds to its domain name. Domain Name Servers convert one to the other.

IRC (**I**nternet **R**elay **C**hat). Internet system where you can send text, or audio, to others in real time, like an online version of CB radio.

ISDN (**I**ntegrated **S**ervices **D**igital **N**etwork). International standard for digital communications over telephone lines. Allows data transmission at 64 or 128 Kbps.

ISP (**I**nternet **S**ervice **P**rovider). Company that sells access to the Internet.

J

Java Platform-independent programming language designed by Sun Microsystems. **http://www.sun.com**

JPEG/JPG Graphic file format preferred online because its high compression reduces file size, and thus the time it takes to transfer.

K

Kbps (**K**ilo**b**its **p**er **s**econd). Standard measure of data transfer speed.

Kill file Newsreader file into which you can enter keywords and email addresses to stop unwanted articles.

L

LAN (**L**ocal **A**rea **N**etwork). Computer network that spans a relatively small area such as an office.

Latency Length of time it takes data to reach its destination.

Leased line Dedicated telecommunications link between two points.

Link In hypertext, as in a webpage, a link is a reference to another document. When you click on a link in a browser, that document will be retrieved and displayed, played or downloaded depending on its nature.

Linux Freely distributed implementation of the UNIX operating system.

Log on/Log in Connect to a computer network.

Loop See Infinite loop.

M

MIME (**M**ultipurpose **I**nternet **M**ail **E**xtensions). Standard for the transfer of binary email attachments.

Mirror Replica FTP or website set up to share traffic.

Modem (**Mo**dulator/**Dem**odulator). Device that allows a computer to communicate with another over a standard telephone line, by converting the digital data into analogue signals and vice versa.

Mouse menu Useful custom menu that pops up when you right-click (by default) on screen items such as icons, Web links and taskbars.

Mouse wheel Rolling wheel positioned between the right and left mouse buttons on suitably equipped mice. Invaluable for scrolling pages and selecting weapons in first-person shooters.

MP3 A compressed music format.

MPEG/MPG A compressed video file format.

Multithreaded Able to process multiple requests at once.

N

Name server Host that translates domain names into IP addresses.

The Net The Internet.

Netscape Web browser – and the company that produces it, now owned by AOL.

Newbie Newcomer to the Net, discussion or area.

Newsgroups Usenet message areas, or discussion groups, organized by subject hierarchies.

NNTP (**N**etwork **N**ews **T**ransfer **P**rotocol). Standard for the exchange of Usenet articles across the Internet.

Node Any device connected to a network.

O

Online 1. The state of being connected to a network, typically the Internet. 2. Describes a resource that is located on the Internet.

Outlook Microsoft's business email program incorporated into MS Office. Includes scheduling and contact tools, but no Usenet reader.

Outlook Express Leaner version of the above that's bundled free with Internet Explorer, and Windows 98 and later. Smarter choice for home use.

P

Packet Unit of data. In data transfer, information is broken into packets, which then travel independently through the Net. An Internet packet contains the source and destination addresses, an identifier, and the data segment.

Packet loss Failure to transfer units of data between network nodes. A high percentage makes transfer slow or impossible.

Patch Temporary or interim add-on to fix or upgrade software.

Ping Echo-like trace that tests if a host is available.

Platform Computer operating system, such as Mac OS, Windows or Linux.

Plug-in Program that fits into another.

POP3 (**P**ost **O**ffice **P**rotocol). Email protocol that allows you to pick up your mail from anywhere on the Net, even if you're connected through someone else's account.

POPs (**P**oints **of P**resence). An ISP's range of local dial-in points.

Port number The numerical address of a process running on a computer attached to the Internet.

Portal Website that specializes in leading you to others.

Post To send a public message to a Usenet newsgroup.

Protocol Agreed way for two network devices to talk to each other.

Proxy server Sits between a client, such as a Web browser, and a real server. Most often used to improve performance by delivering stored pages like browser cache and to filter out undesirable material.

Q

QuickTime Apple's proprietary multimedia standard. Commonly used to preview movies online. Download the Windows player from **http://www.quicktime.com**

R

README file A last-minute document, included with program setup files, that gives installation instructions and other messages from the developers. Sometimes useful when things go wrong.

RealAudio A standard for streaming compressed audio over the Internet. See: **http://www.real.com**

Registry Windows database for system and software configuration settings. Edit (at your own risk) by typing **Regedit** at the Run command in the Start menu.

Robot Program that automates Net tasks such as collating search engine databases or automatically responding in IRC. Also called a Bot.

S

Search engine Database of webpage extracts that can be queried to find reference to something on the Net. Example: Google (**http://www.google.com**)

Serial port An old-school socket that allows data transfer one bit at a time.

Server Computer that makes services available on a network.

Shareware Software with a free trial period, sometimes with reduced features.

Signature file 1. Personal footer that can be attached automatically to email and Usenet postings. 2. Database used by virus scanners to keep track of strains. Update regularly.

Spam (n & v). Junk email or Usenet postings.

Streaming Delivered in real time instead of waiting for the whole file to arrive, eg RealAudio.

Stuffit Common Macintosh file compression format and program.

Surf Skip from page to page around the Web by following links.

T

TCP/IP (**T**ransmission **C**ontrol **P**rotocol/**I**nternet **P**rotocol). The protocols that drive the Internet.

Telnet Internet protocol that allows you to log on to a remote computer and act as a dumb terminal.

Temporary Internet Files Special system folder used by Internet Explorer to store webpages, contents for quick recall when backtracking. Wise to empty contents regularly through Internet Properties, General tab.

Trojan (horse) Program that hides its true (usually sinister) intention.

Troll Prank newsgroup posting intended to invoke an irate response.

U

Update To bring a program, program version, operating system or data file (such as a virus scanner signature) up to date by installing a patch, revision or complete new version.

Upgrade A newer, and presumably improved version of a hardware or software system, or the process of installing it.

Upload Send files to a remote computer.

UNIX Operating system used by most ISPs and colleges. So long as you stick to graphic interfaces, you'll never notice it.

URL (**U**niform **R**esource **L**ocator). Formal name for a Web address.

USB (**U**niversal **S**erial **B**us). High-speed serial bus standard that allows for the connection of up to 127 devices and offers advanced plug-and-play features. Gradually replacing the serial, parallel, keyboard and mouse ports.

Usenet User's Network. A collection of networks and computer systems that exchange messages, organized by subject into newsgroups.

Utility program A small program which extends, supplements or enhances the functionality of the operating system.

UUencode Method of encoding binary files into text so that they can be attached to mail or posted to Usenet. They must be UUdecoded to convert them back. Most mail and news programs do it automatically. Alternative to MIME.

chapter 16

V

Vaporware Rumoured or announced, but nonexistent, software or hardware. Often used as a competitive marketing ploy.

Version number Unique code used to distinguish between product releases.

W

Warez Slang for software, usually pirated.

The Web The World Wide Web or WWW. Graphic and text documents published on the Internet that are interconnected through clickable "HyperText" links. A webpage is a single document. A website is a collection of related documents.

Web authoring Designing and publishing webpages using HTML.

Webmaster Person who maintains a website.

World Wide Web See Web, above.

WYSIWYG (**W**hat **Y**ou **S**ee **I**s **W**hat **Y**ou **G**et). What you type is the way it comes out.

Y

Yahoo! The Web's most popular Web portal:
http://www.yahoo.com

Z

Zip PC file compression format that creates files with the extension .zip, usually using the WinZip program (http://www.winzip.com). Frequently used to reduce file size for transfer or storage on floppy disks.

Still confused?

Then try:

PC Webopedia http://www.webopedia.com
What Is? http://www.whatis.com
Netlingo http://www.netlingo.com

index

index

index

Feedback

This guide has already helped more than 3 million people online since 1995, many of whom have written back with suggestions. We're grateful for this feedback – it makes the job of keeping the book up-to-date and useful so much easier.

You're now holding the eighth edition. That means it's been written eight times – each time undergoing a major overhaul. That's how much the Internet changes each year. Sites disappear, addresses change and things that are hot suddenly go cold. So don't be too alarmed if the sands have shifted slightly since this was written. Nonetheless, if you find errors I'd like to know.

Being such a popular book means it's spawned many imitators, which you'll no doubt see in the shelves beside it. Please compare this guide to those and, if you feel they do a better job, then write to us and tell us where we've gone wrong.

If you feel we've cheated you out of your money, you can get even by giving this book a scathing review at one of the online bookstores (p.344).

Angus Kennedy
angus@easynet.co.uk

around the world

Alaska ★ Algarve ★ Amsterdam ★ Andalucía ★ Antigua & Barbuda ★
Argentina ★ Auckland Restaurants ★ Australia ★ Austria ★ Bahamas ★
Bali & Lombok ★ Bangkok ★ Barbados ★ Barcelona ★ Beijing ★ Belgium &
Luxembourg ★ Belize ★ Berlin ★ Big Island of Hawaii ★ Bolivia ★ Boston
★ Brazil ★ Britain ★ Brittany & Normandy ★ Bruges & Ghent ★ Brussels ★
Budapest ★ Bulgaria ★ California ★ Cambodia ★ Canada ★ Cape Town ★
The Caribbean ★ Central America ★ Chile ★ China ★ Copenhagen ★
Corsica ★ Costa Brava ★ Costa Rica ★ Crete ★ Croatia ★ Cuba ★ Cyprus ★
Czech & Slovak Republics ★ Devon & Cornwall ★ Dodecanese & East
Aegean ★ Dominican Republic ★ The Dordogne & the Lot ★ Dublin ★
Ecuador ★ Edinburgh ★ Egypt ★ England ★ Europe ★ First-time Asia ★
First-time Europe ★ Florence ★ Florida ★ France ★ French Hotels &
Restaurants ★ Gay & Lesbian Australia ★ Germany ★ Goa ★ Greece ★
Greek Islands ★ Guatemala ★ Hawaii ★ Holland ★ Hong Kong & Macau ★
Honolulu ★ Hungary ★ Ibiza & Formentera ★ Iceland ★ India ★ Indonesia
★ Ionian Islands ★ Ireland ★ Israel & the Palestinian Territories ★ Italy ★
Jamaica ★ Japan ★ Jerusalem ★ Jordan ★ Kenya ★ The Lake District ★
Languedoc & Roussillon ★ Laos ★ Las Vegas ★ Lisbon ★ London ★

in twenty years

London Mini Guide ★ London Restaurants ★ Los Angeles ★ Madeira ★
Madrid ★ Malaysia, Singapore & Brunei ★ Mallorca ★ Malta & Gozo ★ Maui
★ Maya World ★ Melbourne ★ Menorca ★ Mexico ★ Miami & the Florida
Keys ★ Montréal ★ Morocco ★ Moscow ★ Nepal ★ New England ★ New
Orleans ★ New York City ★ New York Mini Guide ★ New York Restaurants
★ New Zealand ★ Norway ★ Pacific Northwest ★ Paris ★ Paris Mini Guide
★ Peru ★ Poland ★ Portugal ★ Prague ★ Provence & the Côte d'Azur ★
Pyrenees ★ The Rocky Mountains ★ Romania ★ Rome ★ San Francisco ★
San Francisco Restaurants ★ Sardinia ★ Scandinavia ★ Scotland ★
Scottish Highlands & Islands ★ Seattle ★ Sicily ★ Singapore ★ South Africa,
Lesotho & Swaziland ★ South India ★ Southeast Asia ★ Southwest USA ★
Spain ★ St Lucia ★ St Petersburg ★ Sweden ★ Switzerland ★ Sydney ★
Syria ★ Tanzania ★ Tenerife and La Gomera ★ Thailand ★ Thailand's
Beaches & Islands ★ Tokyo ★ Toronto ★ Travel Health ★ Trinidad &
Tobago ★ Tunisia ★ Turkey ★ Tuscany & Umbria ★ USA ★ Vancouver ★
Venice & the Veneto ★ Vienna ★ Vietnam ★ Wales ★ Washington DC ★
West Africa ★ Women Travel ★ Yosemite ★ Zanzibar ★ Zimbabwe

also look out for our maps, phrasebooks, music guides and reference books

Rough Guide restaurants series

Dining out?

Annually updated
£7.99–£12.99/US$12.95–US$19.95.

Informed, independent advice
on the major gaming platforms

Punchy reviews
of the top games in every genre

Hints, tips and cheats
to crack each game

Directories
of the best Web sites and gaming resources